Interdisciplinary perspectives on modern history

Editors
Robert Fogel and Stephan Thernstrom

Making the second ghetto

Blacks picket City Hall and protest the continued violence at the Trumbull Park Homes, 1955. (Photograph © *Chicago Sun-Times*, 1955; reprinted with permission.)

Making the second ghetto

Race and housing in Chicago, 1940–1960

ARNOLD R. HIRSCH

Department of History and School of Urban and Regional Studies
University of New Orleans

CAMBRIDGE UNIVERSITY PRESS

Cambridge
London   New York   New Rochelle
Melbourne   Sydney

Published by the Press Syndicate of the University of Cambridge
The Pitt Building, Trumpington Street, Cambridge CB2 1RP
32 East 57th Street, New York, NY 10022, USA
296 Beaconsfield Parade, Middle Park, Melbourne 3206, Australia

First published 1983

Printed in the United States of America

Library of Congress Cataloging in Publication Data
Hirsch, Arnold R. (Arnold Richard), 1949–
Making the second ghetto.
(Interdisciplinary perspectives on modern history)
Includes index.
1. Afro-Americans – Housing – Illinois – Chicago –
History. 2. Chicago (Ill.) – Race relations – History.
3. Chicago (Ill.) – Housing policy – History.
4. Discrimination in housing – Illinois – Chicago – History.
I. Title. II. Series.
HD7288.72.U52C454   1983   363.5'9   82–22022
ISBN 0 521 24569 9

Portions of chapters 2, 3, and 7 have appeared in Melvin G. Holli and
Peter d'A. Jones, eds., *The Ethnic Frontier* (Grand Rapids:
William B. Eerdmans Publishing Co., 1977).

To Rosanne

Contents

Tables and maps

Tables

Maps

Preface

Martin Luther King, Jr., remains the tragic embodiment of the Civil Rights Era. The moving eloquence of his speech at the March on Washington in 1963 captured the optimism and idealism of the assault on Jim Crow, which had accelerated so rapidly since the end of World War II. But his assassination still sears the American memory with terrible failure. His greatest triumphs came in the South; de jure segregation was an obvious, if not always easy, target to shoot at. The immediate aftermath of his premature death, however, was punctuated by a wave of race riots in Northern cities that left Americans groping for explanations and reminded them, painfully, of the great social and economic problems left untouched by Jim Crow's demise.

The riots focused attention upon the massive ghettos of the urban North and made them the subject of intense scrutiny. A series of monographs detailed the origins and dynamics of ghetto life in New York, Chicago, Detroit, Cleveland, and other cities. Though in large part inspired by the racial crusades and violence of the 1960s, these ground-breaking studies dealt with those events by indirection and implication. They provided the foundation for the study of race relations and black history in urban America; but because they halted their analyses before the coming of the Depression, little attention has been given to developments in the post–World War II city.

The present work also had its beginnings in the afterglow of the fires that illuminated the inner city. As a student of race relations in Gilbert Osofsky's 1970 seminar at the University of Illinois at Chicago, I was particularly interested in contrasting Chicago's 1919 interracial war with the apparently peaceful interlude following World War II. Actual investigation, of course, has a way of undermining assumptions: The peace I had presumed did not exist. True, no single explosion matched the 1919 riot, but a persistent undercurrent of violence lurked beneath the headlines, just beyond the recall of popular memory. I spent the rest of that year exploring the "hidden" violence of the 1940s and 1950s.

As the riots of the 1960s receded into the past and the grim fascination with violence cooled, it became increasingly clear that interracial confrontation – although certainly meriting study in its own right – was just an occasional and spectacular manifestation of a deeper struggle. All the riots that I unearthed in the immediate postwar period had a common impulse: Each resulted from the shifting of racial residential boundaries in modern Chicago. More than a simple legacy of the past, the contemporary ghetto appeared a dynamic institution that was continually being renewed, reinforced, and reshaped.

Racial violence, consequently, no longer occupied center stage in my research. I now looked upon rioting as merely a single part in a broader historical process, a contributory agent in the emergence of what I call the "second ghetto." Resistance to desegregation, from both the public and the private sector, prevented any fundamental alteration in Chicago's established residential patterns despite the city's rapid increase in black population and the appearance of the civil rights movement after World War II. My focus thus shifted from violence to the larger process of ghetto maintenance.

From the beginning, limits had to be imposed to make the study manageable. This is a book about the *making* of the second ghetto, not the ghetto itself. Earlier works on the era of the Great Migration usually dealt with both the creation of black urban enclaves and the quality of life within them. I found the task of detailing the course of ghetto reinforcement, and the forces behind it, sufficiently complex and lengthy by itself. Black institutions, politics, organizations, and ideology deserve far more attention than I could give them here. In the following pages they are discussed only as they relate to the questions of housing and residential concentration. This book is, consequently, more a work in race relations and urban history than it is a study in black history.

As such, primary attention is devoted to whites. That is where the power was. This is not to say that blacks have simply "reacted" to the actions of others and do not "act" in their own behalf. But what we are looking at here is the construction of the ball park within which the urban game is played. And there is no question that the architects, in this instance, were whites.

If united by color, the "whites" were not without their differences. Indeed, those forces confining Chicago's black population did not always work in unison, and, at times, their struggles over homes, "turf," and property brought them into conflict with each other. Private business reacted to the economic and social realities of the postwar city by experimenting with redevelopment and renewal. These activities, as well as the augmented black presence, drove "ethnic" whites in the vast residential midsection of the city to battle determinedly for the preservation of their homes and neighborhoods. And both business and neighborhood interests ultimately sought political and governmental solutions to their problems. The result was an era of ghetto maintenance and expansion that was designed, in large part, to meet the needs of the contending white factions. Out of the chaos emerged the second ghetto, an entity now distinguished by government support and sanction.

A final word needs to be said about the "ethnics." To say that some fought racial succession and valued stable, centrally located urban neighborhoods is not to claim that all did. Although the numbers are impossible to determine, it seems certain that the vast majority of the descendants of both the "old" and "new" immigrations became assimilated and mobile, joined the post–World War II trek to the suburbs, and never bothered to look back. But a link needs to be reestablished between broad trends in social analysis and "events" – the stuff of more "traditional" history. If the inner-city "ethnics" who were concerned about communal stability and neighborhood solidarity were statistically insignificant compared with their more assimilated counterparts (and this is only a supposition), their impact on postwar public policy in Chicago was considerable. They were instrumental in lending their weight to the walls supporting the second ghetto and were of prime significance in shaping the city's public housing program.

There is a danger, of course, in linking the appearance of residential segregation to "ethnic" characteristics. Racial segregation is a national phenomenon, affecting Northern cities, Southern cities, those that received large numbers of immigrants, and those that welcomed few. But the universality of segregation should not imply an identical process in every case. It is a form of historical reductionism and a logical fallacy to assume that like results must always flow from identical forces or motivations. There are variants of racism in the United States and a textured complexity to the problems of race and ethnicity that escape unnoticed if – after noting the basic black–white dichotomy in American society – one probes no deeper. In raising such issues, *Making the Second Ghetto* makes no pretense of offering definitive conclusions. It will, I hope, generate some discussion.

Chronologically, the limits of this study are defined by the war and postwar decades. By 1960, even though the ghetto continued to grow, the tools that shaped and conditioned its expansion were already in existence. Significant redevelopment and renewal legislation had been placed on the books, on both local and national levels, and a massive public housing program, explicitly designed to maintain the prevailing pattern of segregation, was well under way. Furthermore, the postwar wave of white-initiated violence, carefully kept hidden from public view, had run its course during the 1950s and – save for its lingering influence on public policy – disappeared.

Finally, there are geographical limits. Case studies are usually justified on the basis that they are, in some fashion, representative of broad phenomena and are thus a proper foundation for generalization. My work on Chicago, however, began simply as a labor of love and convenience. I am a native Chicagoan whose family was caught up in the great movements described in these pages, and one of modest enough means to equate bus fare and a transfer with "travel money." It was only after I was deeply engaged in my research that I learned that Chicago's experience was, indeed, of national significance.

It was not that Chicago represented a rigid pattern of urban and ghetto renewal that was mechanistically replicated in city after city. Chicago was, however, a persistent pioneer in developing concepts and devices that were later incorporated into the federal legislation defining the national renewal effort. The tools that were developed to control and mitigate the consequences of racial succession in Chicago were thus made available to the country at large. Other cities were not compelled to use them in such a way as to provoke charges of "Negro removal" or claims that the program was anti-poor and merely subsidized those who needed aid least. But many did just that, using devices precisely tailored to achieve those ends. The legal framework for the national urban renewal effort was forged in the heat generated by the racial struggles waged on Chicago's South Side. The nation now lives with that legacy.

The debts incurred in writing this book are of such magnitude as to preclude adequate recognition. My greatest intellectual debt is to the late Gilbert Osofsky, who was an inspiration as both mentor and friend. This work is poorer for not having the benefit of his inimitable red scrawl. I can only hope that it begins to measure up to his standards. It is my greatest regret that he cannot read it. Two others, Robert V. Remini and Melvin G. Holli, helped see the dissertation on which this book is based through to completion and I am grateful for their assistance. They were there when I needed them most. Others who read all or part of the manuscript and offered valuable suggestions were Michael Perman, Leo Schelbert, Peter Coleman, Peter d'A. Jones, Perry Duis, Glen Holt, Ira Katznelson, Joseph

Logsdon, David Katzman, Leon Despres, and Bud Hirsch (my brother, the English professor). Fellow graduate students who offered the proper blend of friendship, advice, and support were Paul Barrett, Dominic Pacyga, Stephen Hansen, Norman Eder, Deborah White, Louise Kerr, Jacqueline Peterson, Blanche Hersh, Rita Rhodes, and Michael Ralston. I am grateful to them all. This work would not have been completed without the generous assistance of the staffs of several libraries, especially those at the University of Illinois at Chicago, the University of Chicago, the University of New Orleans, and the Municipal Reference Library in Chicago's City Hall. Archie Motley and the Chicago Historical Society deserve special thanks. I am also indebted to Frank Smith of Cambridge University Press for his encouragement and expertise; to Ann Ivins, whose meticulous copyediting was indispensable; and, of course, to Stephan Thernstrom. A University of Illinois Research Fellowship and a summer grant from the University of New Orleans College of Liberal Arts provided valuable financial support.

Finally, there is my family. The appearance of this work will, I hope, reward, if not fully justify, the faith and inexhaustible patience of my mother, Mollie Bernover, and my step-father, Manuel Bernover. This book could not have been written without their generous and loving support. My two sons – Adam, who was born as the dissertation was being written, and Jordan, who was born as the manuscript was being revised – both maintained and challenged my equilibrium and made my labors worthwhile. And then there is my wife, Rosanne. Catalyst, supporter, helper, driver, she held it all together in good times and bad. This one is for her.

Arnold R. Hirsch

New Orleans, Louisiana
November 1982

1   *The second ghetto and the dynamics of neighborhood change*

> I have walked the South Side Streets (Thirty-first to Sixty-ninth)
> from State to Cottage Grove in the last 35 days searching for a flat.
>
> Anonymous to the *Chicago Defender*,
> November 28, 1942

> Something is happening to lives and spirits that will never show
> up in the great housing shortage of the late '40s. Something is
> happening to the children which might not show up in our social
> records until 1970.
>
> *Chicago Sun-Times*, undated clipping, Chicago
> Urban League Papers, Manuscript Collection,
> The Library, University of Illinois at Chicago

The race riot that devastated Chicago following the drowning of
Eugene Williams on Sunday, July 27, 1919, was notable for its numerous brutal confrontations between white and black civilians. White
hoodlums sped through the narrow sliver of land that was the Black
Belt, firing their weapons as they rode, wreaking havoc and killing
at least one person.[1] Nor was that all. Aside from the many assaults
and casualties taken in the Stock Yards district immediately west of
the Black Belt, serious clashes occurred in the Loop and around the
Angelus building, a rooming house that remained the abode of white
workers in the predominantly black area around Wabash Avenue
and 35th Street. Blacks retaliated by attacking whites unfortunate
enough to be caught on their "turf."[2] By the time the riot ended, 38
persons – 23 blacks and 15 whites – lay dead and 537 were injured.[3]

In early April 1968, following the assassination of Dr. Martin Luther King, Jr., Chicago was again the scene of serious violence.
Although labeled a "race riot," the events of 1968 differed sharply
from those of 1919. Instead of an interracial war carried on by black
and white citizens, the "King riot," largely an expression of outrage
by the city's black community, was characterized by the destruction
of property. The deaths that did occur during the riots (there were

1

nine) resulted primarily from confrontations between black civilians and the police or National Guard.[4]

There were other significant differences as well. The worst rioting in 1968 occurred on the West Side. Merely a minor black enclave in 1919, by the time of Dr. King's assassination Chicago's West Side housed more than twice the number of blacks resident in the entire city during the earlier riot. A vast ghetto of relatively recent origin, the West Side thus established itself as a scene of racial tension to rival the older, and larger, South Side Black Belt. Moreover, the Loop, where blacks were viciously hunted in 1919, was now subjected to roving groups of black youths who had walked out of nearby inner-city high schools. This time, however, harassment of pedestrians and petty vandalism replaced the deadly violence of the earlier era. Confrontations such as the one around the Angelus building were impossible in the more rigidly segregated city of the 1960s, and white injuries, reportedly few in number, generally occurred as motorists were unluckily trapped in riot areas. There were no armed forays into "enemy" territory. In sum, clashes between black and white Chicagoans (other than the police) were infrequent, fortuitous, and not lethal. The prevailing image of the 1968 disorder was evoked not by mass murder but by the flames that enveloped stores along a 2-mile stretch of Madison Street and those that engulfed similar structures along Western, Kedzie, and Pulaski avenues.[5]

The close relationship between the growth of the modern black metropolis and the changing pattern of racial disorder is clear. After an era of tremendous ghetto expansion and increasing racial isolation, "communal" riots on the scale of those that shook the nation in 1919 became impossible. The thought of white mobs attacking the black ghettos of the 1960s boggles the imagination. Additionally, the large concentration of blacks in the inner city rendered exceedingly unlikely the stalking and killing of individual blacks on downtown streets. The burning and looting of primarily white-owned property in massive black ghettos was the most visible manifestation of racial tension permitted in the modern city. Able to quarantine black neighborhoods, police were much less able to control actions taken within them. The eruption of the "commodity" riots of the 1960s heralded the existence, in Chicago at least, of that city's "second ghetto."[6]

 The reasons for making a distinction between the "first ghetto" of the World War I era and the "second ghetto" of the post–World War II period are quantitative, temporal, and qualitative. As Morris Janowitz noted in his analysis of racial disorders in the twentieth century, the "commodity" riots of the 1960s took place in black communities that had grown enormously in both size and population.[7] Ten times as many blacks lived in Chicago in 1966 as in 1920. Representing but 4% of the city's population in the latter year, blacks accounted for nearly 30% of all Chicagoans by the mid-1960s. The evolution of the West Side black colony, from enclave to ghetto, was a post–World War II development. And the South Side Black Belt's expansion between 1945 and 1960 was so pronounced that its major business artery shifted a full 2 miles to the south, from 47th Street to 63rd.[8]

There is a chronological justification for referring to Chicago's "second ghetto" as well. The period of rapid growth following World War II was the second such period in the city's history. The first, coinciding with the Great Migration of southern blacks, encompassed the years between 1890 and 1930. Before 1900, the earliest identifiable black colony existed west of State Street and south of Harrison; an 1874 fire destroyed much of this section and resulted in the settlement's reestablishment between 22nd and 31st streets. By the turn of the century, this nucleus had merged with other colonies to form the South Side Black Belt. Where, according to Thomas Philpott's meticulously researched *The Slum and the Ghetto*, "no large, solidly Negro concentration existed" in Chicago until the 1890s, by 1900 the black population suffered an "extraordinary" degree of segregation and their residential confinement was "nearly complete." Almost 3 miles long, but barely a quarter mile wide, Chicago's South Side ghetto – neatly circumscribed on all sides by railroad tracks – had come into being.[9]

By 1920 the Black Belt extended roughly to 55th Street, between Wentworth and Cottage Grove avenues. Approximately 85% of the city's nearly 110,000 blacks lived in this area. A second colony existed on the West Side between Austin, Washington Boulevard, California Avenue, and Morgan Street. More than 8,000 blacks, including some "scattered residents as far south as Twelfth Street," lived here. Other minor black enclaves included the area around Ogden Park in Englewood, Morgan Park on the far South Side, separate settlements in Woodlawn and Hyde Park, and a growing community on the near North Side. Between 1910 and 1920 three additional colonies appeared in Lilydale (around 91st and State streets), near the South Chicago steel mills, and immediately east of Oakwood Cemetery between 67th and 71st streets.[10]

Ten years later it was possible to speak of an almost "solidly" black area from 22nd to 63rd streets, between Wentworth and Cottage Grove. Whole neighborhoods were now black where, according to Philpott, "only some buildings and some streets and blocks had been black earlier." By 1930 even such gross measuring devices as census tracts documented a rigidly segregated ghetto. In 1920 there were no tracts that were even 90% black; the next census revealed that two-thirds of all black Chicagoans lived in such areas and 19% lived in "exclusively" (97.5% or more) black tracts. The West Side colony grew as well. Although it expanded only two blocks southward to Madison Street, it went from only 45% black to nearly all black in the same period; and a new colony appeared in an area previously occupied by Jews near Maxwell Street. By the time of the Depression, Black Chicago encompassed five times the territory it had occupied in 1900. Its borders were sharp and clear, it had reached maturity, and all future growth would spring from this base.[11]

The Depression, however, marked a relaxation in the pace of racial transition, in the growth of Chicago's Black Belt. Black migration to the Windy City decreased dramatically, thus relieving the pressure placed on increasingly crowded Black Belt borders. The period of the 1930s, consequently, was an era of territorial consolidation for Chicago's blacks. Over three-quarters of them lived in areas that were more than 90% black by 1940, and almost half lived in areas that were more than 98% black. On the eve of World War II, Chicago's black population was, according to sociologist David Wallace, "very close to being as concentrated as it could get."[12]

This meant that the 1930s and early 1940s produced only slight territorial additions to the Black Belt (such as the opening of the Washington Park Subdivision). Such stability provoked few black–white clashes, and a similar calm prevailed in the border areas surrounding the other enclaves. The colony in Englewood saw whites replace the few scattered blacks on its periphery, whereas its core around Ogden Park became increasingly black. The Morgan Park community grew in both numbers and area, but its population became virtually all black, and its expansion was accomplished through new construction on vacant land rather than the "invasion" of white territory. The Lilydale enclave followed the same pattern. The South Chicago and Oakwood settlements likewise grew in numbers but actually decreased in size as they became more solidly black.[13] By 1940, St. Clair Drake and Horace R. Cayton were able to assert that the Black Belt "had virtually ceased to expand."[14]

The two decades between 1940 and 1960, and especially the fifteen years following the conclusion of World War II witnessed the renewal of massive black migration to Chicago and the overflowing of black population from established areas of residence grown too small, too old, and too decayed to hold old settlers and newcomers alike. It was during the 1940s and 1950s that the Black Belt's boundaries, drawn during the Great Migration, were shattered. To the east, the Cottage Grove Avenue barrier – which had been buttressed by the activity of local improvement associations after the 1919 riot – fell as blacks entered the communities of Oakland, Kenwood, Hyde Park, and Woodlawn in large numbers. To the south and southwest, Park Manor and Englewood also witnessed the crumbling of what were, by 1945, traditional borders. On the West Side, the exodus of Jews from North Lawndale created a vacuum that was quickly filled by a housing-starved black population. The first new black settlement since the 1920s, the North Lawndale colony was the largest of several new black communities created in the post–World War II period.[15]

Every statistical measure confirmed that racial barriers that had been "successfully defended for a generation," in Allan Spear's words, were being overrun after World War II. The number of technically "mixed" census tracts increased from 135 to 204 between 1940 and 1950. The proportion of "non-Negroes" living in exclusively "non-Negro" tracts declined from 91.2% in 1940 to 84.1% in 1950, reversing a twenty-year trend. Moreover, of the city's 935 census tracts, only 160 were without a single nonwhite resident in 1950; there were 350 such tracts just ten years earlier. Such startling figures prompted the Chicago Commission on Human Relations to hail them as signifying a reversal of the city's march toward complete segregation. Their conclusion, however, was hastily drawn.[16]

The census figures for 1950 revealed not a city undergoing desegregation but one in the process of redefining racial borders after a period of relative stability. Black isolation was, in fact, increasing even as the Black Belt grew. Nearly 53% of the city's blacks lived in exclusively black census tracts in 1950 compared with only 49.7% in 1940; more people moved into the Black Belt than were permitted to leave it. As overcrowded areas became more overcrowded, the pressure of sheer numbers forced some blacks into previously all-white areas. Thus, whereas blacks were becoming more isolated from the white population generally, a large number of whites found themselves living in technically "mixed" areas. Segregation was not ending. It had merely become time to work out a new geographical accommodation between the races.[17]

If, however, the territorial arrangement forged by the end of the 1920s needed revision, the postwar era provided, theoretically at least, an opportunity for dismantling, instead of expanding, the

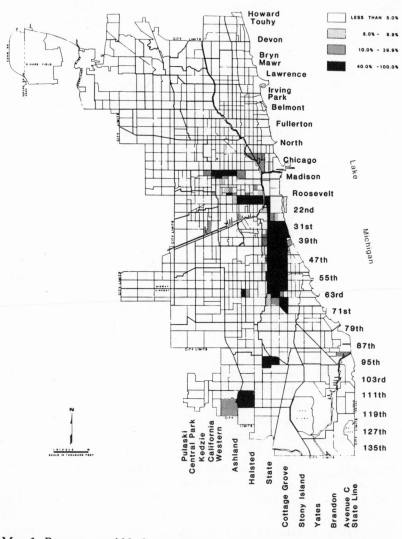

Map 1. Percentage of black population, in census tracts, city of Chicago, 1940. (*Source:* U. S. Bureau of the Census, *Population and Housing Characteristics*, 1960.)

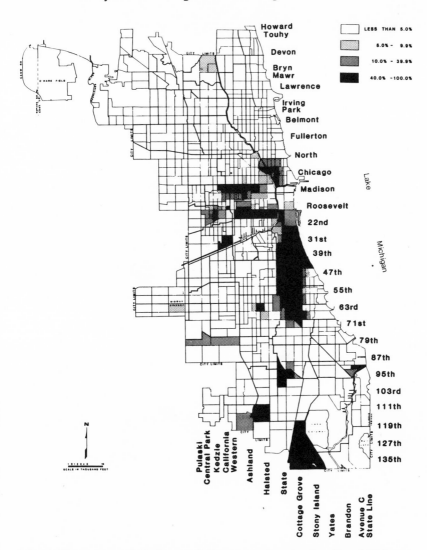

Map 2. Percentage of black population, in census tracts, city of Chicago, 1950. (*Source:* U. S. Bureau of the Census, *Population and Housing Characteristics*, 1960.)

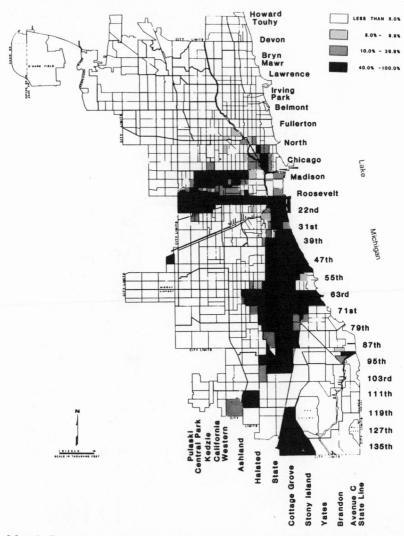

Map 3. Percentage of black population, in census tracts, city of Chicago, 1960. (*Source:* U. S. Bureau of the Census, *Population and Housing Characteristics,* 1960.)

ghetto. That such a possibility existed has been obscured by the dreadful air of inevitability that permeated the ghetto studies produced in the 1960s and that sped analysis from the Stock Yards to Watts.[18] Such telescopic vision blurred what occurred in between, placed an unfair measure of responsibility on those living in the World War I period for what later transpired, and provided absolution through neglect for those who came later. Indeed, the real tragedy surrounding the emergence of the modern ghetto is not that it has been inherited but that it has been periodically renewed and strengthened. Fresh decisions, not the mere acquiescence to old ones, reinforced and shaped the contemporary black metropolis.

Certainly close observers of the housing situation in the years following World War II saw nothing inevitable about the continued expansion of preexisting ghetto areas. Robert C. Weaver, a member of the Mayor's Committee on Race Relations and later the first secretary of the Department of Housing and Urban Development, emphasized the malleability of the future in *The Negro Ghetto*, the most significant contemporary survey of the problem. Viewing the increased involvement of government on all levels in urban affairs, he expressed with some trepidation the notion that postwar redevelopment could be either a "threat or an opportunity." "Provision of more space for minorities is the most immediate need," Weaver wrote, "and it will be accelerated by a sound national housing program which insists upon widespread participation by all elements in the population." "But it is extremely important," he warned, "that we avoid the creation of additional ghettos."[19] Weaver's sense of uncertainty and opportunity were genuine. The 1960s fires, which illuminated the past as well as the present (and thus facilitated the use of hindsight), should not be permitted to obscure the fact that paths other than the one eventually taken were available. Moreover, by stressing the role to be played by government intervention in urban affairs, Weaver pinpointed the qualitative distinction that separated the second ghetto from the first.

The most distinguishing feature of post–World War II ghetto expansion is that it was carried out with government sanction and support. As black migration northward increased in the first quarter of the twentieth century and racial lines began to harden, it was apparent that white hostility was of paramount importance in shaping the pattern of black settlement. Sometimes violent, sometimes through the peaceful cooperation of local real estate boards, white animosity succeeded, informally and privately, in restricting black areas of residence.[20] Direct government support for segregation, before the New Deal, consisted primarily of the judicial enforcement of privately drawn restrictive covenants.

After World War II, however, government urban redevelopment and renewal policies, as well as a massive public housing program, had a direct and enormous impact on the evolution of the ghetto. In Chicago such programs reshaped, enlarged, and transformed the South Side Black Belt. Decaying neighborhoods were torn down, their inhabitants were shunted off to other quarters, and the land upon which they stood was used for middle-class housing and institutional expansion. High-rise public housing projects, created, in large part, to rehouse fugitives from "renewed" areas, literally lined State Street for miles as a new, vertical ghetto supplemented the old. To the east, Hyde Park became first a new area of black settlement and later, after implementation of an urban renewal program designed specifically to meet the challenge of racial succession, an obstacle around which most blacks had to move en route to accommodations farther south. The peculiar characteristics of Chicago's racial geography – the Black Belt's concrete northern end, the white thorn in its flank, and its newly occupied southern and western provinces – were all, in some measure, acquired through government action after World War II.

Increased government concern with housing was apparent, of course, before the postwar period. Beginning in the 1930s, and continuing thereafter, the operation of national agencies such as the Home Owners Loan Corporation (HOLC) and the Federal Housing Administration (FHA) reflected prevailing segregationist attitudes. Indirectly at least, they furthered the racial segmentation of metropolitan America and inner-city decay by supporting the flight of the white, middle-class population to the suburbs (which, despite government support, remained closed to blacks). A contemporary survey revealed, for example, that of 374 FHA-guaranteed mortgages in metropolitan Chicago, only 3 were in the central city.[21] More direct and immediate, however, were the federal government's attempts to clear slums and provide public housing to the urban poor. Although these programs were limited in scope and halting in practice, they pointed the way to the future. The ghetto was to be reinforced with taxpayers' dollars and shored up with the power of the state.

The first signs that this was happening in Chicago came with the construction of the Ida B. Wells housing project in the late 1930s. Covering 47 acres and costing nearly $9 million, the Ida B. Wells Homes provided shelter for 1,662 black families. Like similar proj-

Black construction workers labor at the Ida B. Wells Homes, 1940. (Photograph courtesy of the Chicago Housing Authority.)

ects in Cleveland, this black development was located in the ghetto, between 37th and 39th streets, South Parkway (now Martin Luther King Drive), and Cottage Grove. Opposition to the project came only from realtors and others outside the black community. Never once raising the issue of segregation, the Chicago *Defender* claimed that nearly "all of our political leaders, our ministers, social workers and civic organizations have united their resources to combat the opposition." The completion of the project, the black press asserted, was a "brilliant climax to Mayor Kelly's fight to see to it that the people of Chicago are properly housed." The reasons for such enthusiasm were apparent. Conditions within the Black Belt were so appalling that decent housing, wherever it was located, was desperately desired by the community, leaders and masses alike. The huge Wells development was a gift horse (albeit a Trojan one) not to be scrupulously examined. And, in some ways, the project did represent a gain for "the race." Black contractors, technicians, engineers, draftsmen, architects, and skilled and unskilled laborers were all employed in the construction process. Nonwhite plumbers, lathers, steam fitters, and structural-steel workers were granted temporary

South Side blacks march in dedication day ceremonies for the Ida B. Wells
Homes, 1941. (Photograph courtesy of the Chicago Housing Authority.)

union cards so that they, too, could labor at the Wells Homes. Such
"firsts," the promise of decent, safe, and sanitary dwellings, and the
prospect that slum areas would be redeemed were more than enough
to assure the undivided support of Black Chicago.[22]

This pattern of federal action, which became firmly established
with the wartime emergency, soon generated bitter denunciations,
however. As early as 1943 black Chicagoans were calling for the
dismissal of the National Housing Agency's John Blandford for his
"deference to the principle of residential segregation." There was
truth to the charge. Federal respect for restrictive covenants and the
delegation of site selection responsibilities to local interests vitiated
all efforts to house black war workers. By 1944, despite the documented presence of 500 "emergency" cases and 10,000 other eligible
in-migrants, the NHA had contributed but 93 units to the black
housing supply. Blandford, the *Defender* charged, lacked even the
"backbone of a jellyfish."[23]

Proposed solutions to the problem emphasized this growing black
concern and awareness of the potential impact of government action. One possibility was temporary housing; yet the mere mention

of such quarters sparked stinging rebuttals from blacks who suspected the units would be placed in their areas and who, like Chicago Housing Authority (CHA) chairman Robert R. Taylor and onetime alderman Earl Dickerson, rejected "any palliative that preserved [the] ghetto." Well-meaning whites hesitated before suggesting these emergency measures in 1944, knowing that their counsel "place[d] us under suspicion by Negroes, because they place segregation above all other problems." Similarly, proposals to rebuild the ghetto with high-rise apartment buildings "so that the same area can take care of a greater number of people" led Robert Weaver to denounce them as "inconsistent" with the American creed. Moreover, Weaver felt, once the "existing Negro population became accommodated" to such an arrangement, "bars to its future expansion would become more inflexible than they are now."[24]

However, the Depression-era and wartime government building programs were not particularly large, and their significance lay elsewhere. By the end of the war the Chicago Housing Authority operated 7,644 permanent low-income housing units, including the nearly 4,000 that segregated blacks in the Ida B. Wells, Robert H. Brooks, and Altgeld Gardens projects. But this was merely a fraction of the nearly 40,000 such units in existence by 1976 (contained in 1,273 separate buildings and housing roughly 5% of the city's population).[25] The significance of these early government efforts lay in their demonstration of the difficulty in breaking established racial patterns. The building of ghettos was a cumulative process. The existence of the first ghetto made the rise of the second much easier, if it did not, in fact, produce overwhelming forces assuring its appearance. Ultimately, the dismantling of the ghetto in postwar Chicago under the hammerblows of a massive, nondiscriminatory government building program proved an insurmountable challenge. Local and federal authorities sustained, rather than attacked, the status quo.

At times the ties between the first and second ghettos were close and direct. Charles S. Duke, an architect and consulting engineer on the Wells Homes, as well as one of the select black group that had originally sponsored the project, was also the author of *The Housing Situation and the Colored People of Chicago, with Suggested Remedies and Brief References to Housing Projects Generally*. Published in April 1919, shortly before the riot of that year, Duke's treatise condemned "all attempts at racial segregation" but called for new construction and "decent living conditions" within existing black communities as a means of relieving both their distress and the pressure they placed on adjacent white neighborhoods. Duke was concerned not only with housing but also with the economic benefits such activity would bring to black realtors and businessmen; it was an attempt – in the context of the racial hatreds of that era – to deal constructively with the fact of segregation and real black needs. His approach was emulated by the governor's riot commission, which investigated the ensuing holocaust. The commission's report, *The Negro in Chicago*, denounced *forcible* segregation while proposing, in Thomas Philpott's words, a "dual solution" to the city's racial and housing difficulties; it recommended "not open housing but better *Negro* housing" as the solution to racial tension. For a decade after the riot, reformers, philanthropists, and entrepreneurs tried to provide more and decent housing for blacks and working-class whites while observing both the color line and the bottom line. The construction of the Garden Homes, the Marshall Field Garden Apartments, and the Michigan Boulevard Garden Apartments (Rosenwald Gardens), however, was testimony only to their good intentions, the strength of the "business creed," and their futility – except for their success in leaving the prevailing pattern of segregation intact. If the private sector's "dual solutions" proved abortive in the twenties, though, they were substantially resurrected and brought to fruition in the modern era through the exercise of public power. One need only look, in 1980, at the unbroken wall of high-rise public housing along State Street, stretching all the way from Cermak Road (22nd Street) to 55th, to realize that the riot commission's recommendations were followed in spirit, if not in detail, more than a generation after they were made.[26]

Similarly, forces at work on the national level stretched back to the age of Progressive reform. Former settlement house resident, NAACP leader, and Chicagoan Harold Ickes headed the housing division of the Public Works Administration (PWA). Perhaps wishing to make the novel federal presence in urban America as unobtrusive as possible, it was Ickes who promulgated the "neighborhood composition rule," which prevented government projects from altering the racial composition of their host neighborhoods. Progressive willingness to work within the constraints of the color line, so evident at the beginning of the century, thus left its mark on the early federal programs as well. Not only were the "black" projects located in ghetto areas, but Chicago's Lathrop and Trumbull Park Homes, located in white areas, excluded blacks; and the Jane Addams Homes, which adhered to a racial quota in keeping with previous black presence on the site, was alone in its mixed clientele in the prewar era.[27] Federal policy later changed, of course, but these precedents were difficult to overcome and they became sources of controversy in the postwar period.

Other links between the first and second ghettos were less visible but equally important. The emergence of Chicago's "black metropolis" gave rise to institutional, economic, and political forces that had their roots, and therefore a stake, in the ghetto. The white hostility that isolated blacks spatially necessitated the creation of an "institutional ghetto," a city within a city, to serve them. It also produced a leadership class eager, or at least willing (as suggested by Duke's approach to housing), to pursue separate development rather than total assimilation – which is to say it created interests that could only view the ghetto's destruction with grave misgivings.[28]

In the late 1940s and 1950s, given the growing significance of government action, the conservative nature of black politics and politicians was of particular importance. Throughout the period, Chicago's black leadership was fragmented by the issues of redevelopment and renewal, and those who joined the opposition received little help in the political arena from William L. Dawson's black "sub-machine." Constrained by their accommodation to Chicago's brand of ethnic and machine-style politics, and their subordination to the dominant, white-controlled Cook County Democratic Organization, the professional black politicians lacked the desire or ability to fight those forces shaping the postwar ghetto. They would, according to political scientist Milton Rakove, "rather gild the ghetto than break it up." Such action, Rakove asserted, "insure[d] their tenures of office, indebt[ed] their constituencies to them, and enable[d] them to advance themselves within the Democratic machine in the city." The ghetto was a self-sustaining organism, which, politically at least, could not effectively challenge the forces that preserved and enlarged it.[29]

It was the sheer presence of the first ghetto and the white reaction to it, though, that did the most to produce the second. In creating it, white Chicago conceived a "Frankenstein's monster," which threatened to "run amok" after World War II. The establishment of racial borders, their traditional acceptance, and the conditions spawned by unyielding segregation created an entity that whites feared and loathed. Those who made it were soon threatened by it, and, desperately, they both employed old techniques and devised new ones in the attempt to control it. Others elected to flee to the suburbs, thus compounding the difficulties of those left behind. In any event, the very process of racial succession, dormant for nearly a generation, inspired both the dread and the action that called forth the second ghetto.

As with any migration, a combination of "push" and "pull" factors produced the movement of blacks across Chicago's racial frontier. The resurgence of large-scale black migration to the city during the war and postwar eras was the most conspicuous force pushing blacks into heretofore white areas. Also of great importance was a housing shortage, which, for blacks, antedated the war and grew increasingly severe throughout the 1940s. The horrendous conditions produced by confining a rapidly growing black population in an already overcrowded, aged, and deteriorating housing supply drove many to seek shelter outside their traditional communities. As long as the housing shortage persisted, though, the situation remained relatively stable. There were simply no vacancies in which to move. The renewal of housing construction on the city's outskirts and in the burgeoning suburbs in the years following World War II, however, indirectly pulled blacks into neighborhoods previously closed to them. As whites in the central city began the trek to Chicago's fringes, vacancies began to appear around the Black Belt. The availability of this housing, and the blacks' ability to pay for it, rendered unstable the old geographical accommodation. The Supreme Court's ruling on restrictive covenants in 1948 simply delivered the final blow to a device that was already growing unequal to the task of preserving the racial homogeneity of white neighborhoods beleaguered by mounting economic and social pressures. Additionally, as migration out of the Black Belt progressed, the conditions that produced it – the desperate need for more black housing, the suburban exodus of middle-class whites, and the increased ability of blacks to compete economically with those who remained – made certain that the growth of Chicago's black community would be a conflict-ridden process.

Chicago's black population grew significantly during the twentieth century. Although the percentage increase was greatest during the initial period of ghetto formation, the largest increase in absolute numbers came during the 1940s and 1950s. Analysts of the 1919 riot never fail to cite the growth of Chicago's black population: more than 148% between 1910 and 1920. Yet, it was the addition of 65,355 new black Chicagoans to a relatively small existing black population that accounted for the large percentage increase. Between 1940 and 1950 Chicago's black population swelled by 214,534; between 1950 and 1960 it grew by 320,372. Although the percentage growth during these two decades cannot compare with that associated with the

Table 1. *The black population of Chicago, 1890–1960*

Year	Black population	Increase	Percentage increase	Percentage of total population
1890	14,271	—	—	1.3
1900	30,150	15,879	111.3	1.9
1910	44,103	13,953	46.3	2.0
1920	109,458	65,355	148.2	4.1
1930	233,903	124,445	113.7	6.9
1940	277,731	43,828	18.7	8.2
1950	492,265	214,534	77.2	13.6
1960	812,637	320,372	65.1	22.9

Source: U.S. Census Reports, 1890–1960.

Great Migration, the absolute numbers of new black residents represented a movement of unprecedented scale.[30] In 1920 Chicago's black population totaled 109,458; between 1940 and 1960 it grew from 277,731 to 812,637 (Table 1).

Most of this increase was due to renewed migration from the South. St. Clair Drake and Horace R. Cayton estimated that 60,000 black migrants seeking jobs in Chicago's labor-hungry war industries entered the city between 1940 and 1944.[31] The migration continued, on an increasingly large scale, and the Chicago Community Inventory estimated an average annual increase in the nonwhite population of 27,000 between 1940 and 1950 and 38,100 between 1950 and 1956. The new in-migration was calculated at 21,000 per year in both periods.[32] When combined with white out-migration, this fresh upsurge in black population took on an even greater significance. Where blacks represented only 4.1% of the city's total population in 1920 and but 8.2% in 1940, they accounted for 13.6% of the city's total in 1950 and 22.9% in 1960. Clearly, this was a population movement that dwarfed the earlier Great Migration.

If Chicago offered the migrants work, however, the city was much less able to provide them with shelter. Aggravating the situation was the shortage of black housing that existed before the wartime migration began. After a building boom in the 1920s, which saw more than 287,000 dwelling units constructed, the Depression brought the housing industry in Chicago to a standstill. From the peak year of 1926, when 42,932 units were built, new construction sank to a low of 137 units in 1933. Throughout the 1930s, only 15,500 homes and apartments, slightly more than 5% of the total built in the 1920s, were constructed. As for the city's less well-to-do inhabitants, the Metropolitan Housing and Planning Council (MHPC) reported in 1937 that there had been "virtually no new building" for the bottom half of Chicago's population for the "last generation."[33]

Not only was there little construction during the 1930s, but the city began a demolition program in 1934 that destroyed 21,000 substandard housing units; about one-third of the demolition occurred in black areas. Even the steps taken to relieve the poor housing condition of the black population were hardly unmitigated blessings. The construction of the Ida B. Wells public housing project destroyed nearly as many apartments as it supplied. When the project finally opened in 1941, 17,544 applications were received for its 1,662 units.[34]

There was, consequently, a severe housing shortage for Chicago's black community well before the Japanese attack on Pearl Harbor. Administrators of Chicago's relief effort noted that the lack of facilities compelled black welfare recipients to pay two to three times the rent paid by white families on public assistance. The housing shortage was such, a Chicago Urban League executive stated, that it produced the "peculiar phenomena of increasing rents during a depression period." Other tendencies that became painfully evident in the postwar era were apparent earlier to the discerning observer. Overcrowding, for example, was already a serious Black Belt problem. A special 1934 census found that the average black household contained 6.8 persons compared to the 4.7 persons found in the average white household; 66% of the white families studied had fewer than one person per room, whereas only 25.8% of the black families examined met that standard. "Kitchenette" apartments proliferated as real estate speculators and absentee landlords exploited the situation by cutting up large apartments into numerous small ones. These units frequently lacked plumbing and often a solitary bathroom served all the families on a floor. A Chicago Urban League investigation of the Armour Square neighborhood found many homes lacking the most "ordinary conveniences," such as water and toilets, and the widespread use of kerosene lamps. The infant mortality rate for the area was 16% higher than that for the city as a whole, the tuberculosis rate was twice as high, and the general mortality rate was 5% higher. This was the state of black housing in Chicago as World War II and a new wave of black migration began.[35]

Little new construction was undertaken, of course, with the onset of hostilities. Men and material were diverted to the production of the necessities of war. The Chicago Housing Authority did construct

Basement at 3106 Wentworth where ten families occupied cardboard cubicles in 1947. The "apartments" had no windows or toilets and shared a single broken stairway and stove. (Metropolitan Housing and Planning Council Papers, Manuscript Collection, University of Illinois at Chicago, The Library; photograph by Mildred Mead.)

several projects such as Lawndale and Altgeld Gardens, and the Cabrini, Brooks, and Bridgeport homes, but these were neither sufficient to meet the incoming flood of war workers, nor a solution to the city's preexisting housing problems. The domestic crisis precipitated by the war effort saw the entire city – not just its black community – struggle under the burden of a severe housing shortage. The 1940 vacancy rate for Chicago was only 3.9%. The Metropolitan Housing and Planning Council believed a 5% rate to be the "danger line" below which a genuine shortage existed. By mid-1941, however, the vacancy rate dropped to 1.5% and plummeted even further, to 0.9%, by April 1942. Conditions deteriorated so rapidly that less than a year after Pearl Harbor the MHPC suggested that homeowners rent out vacant rooms to war workers wherever feasible. They also proposed the "commandeering of empty houses, conversion to add more units, [and]...even compulsory billeting."[36]

In the context of the general wartime shortage, the coincidence of plentiful jobs and scarce housing simply produced added frustration within Chicago's Black Belt. For some, lack of money was no longer a serious obstacle to the purchase or rental of new living quarters – but there was no shelter available. The heads of black families, columnist Frayser T. Lane wrote in July 1943, "have sufficient income with which to pay rent but are unable to find suitable places in which to live." A private construction firm building 65 apartments received 12,000 applications from Black Belt residents even though they required an $850 down payment. Fifty-two homes being constructed for blacks in the South Side West Chesterfield neighborhood were literally sold before their blueprints were completed. Even the oldest buildings found many willing to pay for their shelter. The Pythian Temple at 37th Place and State Street stood vacant since the Depression; as a haven for squatters it was condemned as uninhabitable. Yet, with the war, the government bought it and began renovations. In a single day more than 200 people sought information on how to obtain apartments there. Soon the building had a waiting list, which, its operators felt, would "take years" to accommodate.[37]

Moreover, if Chicago's black community was virtually unable to locate new housing, it had to fight tenaciously simply to hold on to its current dilapidated stock. The most notable incident, and one that poignantly illustrates the desperation of the age, involved the Mecca building at 34th and State streets. Built to house visitors to the 1893 World's Columbian Exposition, the Mecca building was obtained by the Illinois Institute of Technology in 1941 with the under-

Squatters occupy a condemned building at 2818 S. LaSalle lacking heat, light, and all other utilities, 1948. (Metropolitan Housing and Planning Council Papers, Manuscript Collection, University of Illinois at Chicago, The Library; photograph by E. Rhodes.)

standing that it was to be demolished. Eviction of the Mecca's tenants, however, necessitated turning 1,000 to 1,500 people into the streets. Only the feeling that "rioting would be inevitable if this demolition were carried out" saved the building. The Mecca subsequently became the subject of heated legislative debate in the General Assembly of Illinois, and later a shelter of last resort for homeless squatters who moved into the structure after the original tenants had departed. It took more than a decade before the Illinois Institute of Technology could clear the land it desired for campus expansion.[38]

As the war entered its final stages, fearful speculation focused on postwar prospects. The *Defender* shuddered at the thought of a "million Negroes...homeless after the war." "In the past we have had occasion to protest holdup rents for ramshackle hovels," the *Defender* wrote. "Today, however, there are no broken down hovels to be had at any price."[39]

There was good reason for concern. As the war ended and the postwar era began, the shortage, for both blacks and whites, grew worse. There were two crises embedded within the desperate housing situation. The first was the long-standing problem of slums. The Chicago Plan Commission documented the existence of 23 square miles of "blight," containing more than 242,000 units, within city boundaries. Another 100,000 substandard units, it was estimated, were scattered outside the designated "blighted" areas. Based on data collected before the tremendous wartime migration, additional aging, overcrowding, and overuse of the city's static housing supply rendered the situation even more grim after the war.[40]

The second problem involved returning veterans. Even before the war had ended, the War Housing Center in Chicago noted that veterans were rapidly surpassing war workers as the group most in need of accommodations. Rental units were "disappearing from the market" as veterans claimed units owned by their families. The winding down of the war also produced an increase in evictions as property owners turned out current occupants in favor of returning family members; fully 25% of all evictions in the summer of 1945 involved such cases. By 1947 more than 175,000 veterans had registered their families with the War Housing Center in the attempt to locate new housing; 140,000 of these (80%) lived doubled-up with others and, when added to the estimated 70,000 families that were living doubled-up even before the war, represented a social problem of catastrophic proportions.[41] To meet this crisis, the city developed an Emergency Veterans Temporary Housing Program, which called for a total of 6,100 units. Of these, only 3,400 were ever constructed.

Old military barracks, Quonset huts, and government trailers were converted into temporary "apartments" and filled as soon as they became available. By the end of 1947 the Chicago Commission on Human Relations noted the dearth of real progress; it reported that at least 200,000 new units were needed to meet the city's needs.[42]

The city, however, proved incapable of responding quickly to what was called the "most critical housing shortage since the Chicago fire." Construction continued to lag for a variety of reasons. Only 33,034 new units, an average of only 6,600 per year, were built in Chicago from 1945 through 1949. Even the persistent application of emergency wartime measures, such as the renovation of vacant, condemned, or commercial properties, failed to help.[43]

The most dismal situation, of course, existed in black residential areas. Of 441 "social problems" cases handled by the Chicago Urban League between January 1947 and September 1948, 259 (59%) dealt with housing. Of the 1,686 individuals involved in the total case load, 1,178 (70%) needed shelter. Within the main South Side Black Belt, it was estimated that 375,000 blacks resided in an area equipped to house no more than 110,000. The overcrowding evident before the war was intensified; where previous reports placed fewer than a dozen people in the more crowded rooms, reputable observers now counted fifteen.[44]

The extent of the tragedy, however, was revealed not by cold statistics but by the desperate measures taken by those who sought relief. A variety of "con games" were developed to take advantage of the insatiable demand for housing and the vulnerability of inner-city residents. The more gullible were taken by crude operators such as the man who held "office hours" in his home between 7:00 and 9:00 in the evening and a woman who solicited customers in taverns and beauty shops. Both offered "apartment finding" services at substantial prices. Others bought tax delinquent lots from the city at auction and, misrepresenting them as unencumbered, resold them to unsuspecting buyers. Some went so far as to offer Chicago Housing Authority apartments for sale. Even the more sophisticated and "street-wise" Chicagoans, their resistance broken by an enervating mixture of desperation and hope, proved susceptible to the more polished enterprises. "Vampire" rental agencies opened offices, charged finder's fees, and sometimes collected rent in advance for nonexistent dwellings. One developer actually collected more than $500,000 from 470 blacks for homes that he had no intention of building. The most sophisticated operations were obviously well capitalized as they ran large advertisements in the black press, celebrating the "opening" of new buildings for blacks "east of Cottage Grove" and in other previously all-white areas. Although numerous indictments were returned and court proceedings instituted against the worst of these racketeers, the *Defender* still found it necessary in 1951 to establish a Housing Referral Bureau "to protect prospective home investors from the greedy clutches of unscrupulous speculators." The unprecedented degree to which the housing situation was exploited by the "fast-buck" artists was the best indication of the severity of the shortage.[45]

The persistent victimization of desperate home-seekers was also testimony to the deplorable living conditions that existed. Data collected during 1949 and 1950 reveal that, although the city, as a whole, still staggered under the burden of a housing shortage, there were signs that conditions were beginning to ease for whites, whereas they continued to grow worse for blacks. It was apparent at midcentury that thousands of Chicagoans were still compelled to share accommodations with relatives and friends. The 1950 census uncovered 79,300 married couples without their own households; 64,860 "subfamilies" (groups related to and living with the enumerated primary family) and 32,334 "secondary families" (groups unrelated to but living with the enumerated primary family) were also discovered. It is certain that a substantial number of these people would have lived elsewhere if given the opportunity. Opportunities, though, remained few. The vacancy rate for Chicago stayed at a paltry 0.8%.[46]

By 1950, however, there were also indications that the worst had passed for the city's whites. Whereas the white population actually decreased by 0.1% between 1940 and 1950, the number of dwelling units occupied by whites *increased* by 9.4% during that decade. The number of overcrowded units occupied by whites (defined as those units containing more than 1.51 persons per room) also declined; where 5% of Chicago's whites lived in overcrowded homes in 1940, 4% did so in 1950. The process of "undoubling" the white population had begun.[47]

The same could not be said for Chicago's blacks. Chicago's nonwhite population increased by 80.5% between 1940 and 1950, but the number of dwelling units they occupied increased by only 72.3%. Not unexpectedly, the percentage of nonwhites living in overcrowded accommodations rose from 19% in 1940 to 24% in 1950.[48] In absolute numbers, overcrowded nonwhite households increased by 14,942, whereas overcrowded white households *decreased* by 1,241. Significantly, this more than doubled the number of existing overcrowded nonwhite households. Much of the black population also continued to be squeezed into the ever-increasing number of "kitchenette" apartments. The Chicago Community Inventory estimated that there were at least 80,000 such "conversions" between 1940 and 1950. The white population was becoming less cramped even as blacks became more so.[49]

Such intense overcrowding and the proliferation of "kitchenette" apartments were instrumental in driving people to seek new homes elsewhere. First of all, the division of large apartments meant that only a lucky few would have their own bathrooms. The number of dwelling units lacking private bath facilities went from 85,492 in 1940 to 130,200 in 1950 – an *increase* of 36,248 units (52.3%).[50] Sanitary living was also rendered difficult by the amount of garbage produced in homes that housed many more people than they were designed to hold. Building inspections and garbage collection, the Metropolitan Housing and Planning Council noted in 1944, fell "far below the minimum mandatory to healthful sanitation."[51] The demand for housing and the subsequent lack of incentive for landlords to make repairs aggravated an already intolerable situation.

One result, aside from the omnipresent threat of disease, was a plague of rats. Rat attacks on sleeping children were frequent occurrences and it was not uncommon to hear reports of children being maimed or even killed. In 1940 the MHPC succeeded in getting the city to sponsor a massive anti-rat campaign. More than 100 men were taken off relief rolls and given the work of spreading poison in alleys and streets; an estimated 1.5 million rats were killed the first year as 29 tons of the rodents were collected from city thoroughfares.[52] The coming of the war, however, crippled this effort. The employment boom took able-bodied men off the relief rolls and Axis control of the Mediterranean closed the only reliable source of the poison then being used. Rats continued to flourish in Chicago, and by the summer of 1953 the city's rat-control officer estimated that there were as many rats as humans in the city. Tenants unable to cope with the problem were reduced to taking pride in its enormity. Responding to a friend's claim that she had rats "big enough to ride on," another woman commented that her rats came "in teams." "Sometimes," she added boastfully, they "have enough for a ball game."[53]

The threat of fire was another "constant and agonizing worry to thousands of Southside Negroes," especially those confined to the ubiquitous kitchenettes, according to the *Defender*. Divided by partitions that were often themselves flammable, the "rabbit warrens" that filled large old buildings made escape difficult, if not impossible,

A family waits its turn to look into the converted stable where six people perished in a flash fire, October 3, 1950. (Metropolitan Housing and Planning Council Papers, Manuscript Collection, University of Illinois at Chicago, The Library; photograph by Mildred Mead.)

in time of emergency. Buildings packed with families and their furnishings, which often served as so much kindling, were also rendered vulnerable by their frequent lack of heat and cooking facilities. Gas stoves, routinely kept in closets, served as 24-hour-a-day kitchens and heaters in cold weather. One alderman consequently labeled the entire Black Belt a "gigantic fire trap." Between November 1946 and November 1947 at least 751 fires occurred betwen 26th and 59th streets and Halsted and the lake. The conflagrations, which left "unnumbered thousands" homeless, amounted in the *Defender*'s estimation, to "another Chicago Fire except that it has been on a three-month installment basis." Even more alarming, more than 180 "slum dwellers" died in fires between 1947 and 1953; and at least 63 of the victims were less than ten years old.[54]

Nor were all the fires accidental.[55] One landlord, determined to evict his tenants to allow conversion of his building into kitchenettes, set fire to the structure after the tenants refused to vacate. The four children of James Hickman were killed in the blaze. Hickman later fatally shot the landlord in revenge and was eventually sentenced to two years probation for his act.[56] Survivors suffered in other ways as well. With no place to go, the Metropolitan Housing and Planning Council reported, "they moved their smoke-weighted and water-soaked possessions back into rooms with charred walls, without roofs, and without plumbing."[57] The need to escape such conditions was clear. The only question was: Where could one go?

As long as the housing shortage existed for both blacks and whites, the desire to escape deplorable living conditions could not be satisfied. By 1950, however, the first signs that the housing market was displaying some flexibility were apparent. What began as a trickle in the late 1940s became a flood in the mid-1950s as a new construction boom developed to meet the area's housing needs. Of prime significance were the character and location of the new dwellings. Most were built for the middle or upper-middle class on the fringes of the city or in outlying areas. The well-known "suburban exodus" that ensued, so often the focus of attention when social movements of the 1950s are discussed, had deep ramifications for the central city. As the more well-to-do whites were selectively drained from Chicago's core, vacancies began to appear around the Black Belt. The desperate need for new housing and the blacks' improved economic condition combined to render old borders unstable. The underside of the process of suburbanization was the redefinition of the city's geographical racial accommodation.

Between 1945 and 1949 Chicago and its suburbs produced 137,388 new residential units. New construction accelerated rapidly thereafter. More than 260,000 new units were built in the Chicago area between 1950 and 1954, and another 290,000 were added between 1955 and 1959. In the first fifteen years following the end of World War II, 688,222 new homes were erected in the Chicago metropolitan area.[58]

The most salient features of this new construction were that most of the units were single-family homes and that the overwhelming majority were located either in the suburbs or on the city's farthest reaches. Between 1945 and 1959 more than 77% of the new units were located in the suburbs. Moreover, 76% of the units were single-family dwellings. Most of the construction within Chicago was located on outlying vacant land that had remained undeveloped before the war. Socially and economically, the neighborhoods being built on the far Northwest, Southwest, and South sides resembled suburbs far more than they did the inner city. Within the "central" city (North Avenue to 47th Street between Western Avenue and the lake), the only new construction undertaken was that associated with government programs, public housing, or private institutional redevelopment plans.[59]

The redistribution of the region's population followed hard upon the building boom. Between 1940 and 1960 the population of the Chicago Standard Metropolitan Statistical Area (SMSA) grew from 4,569,643 to 6,220,913. But the city's share fell from 74% (3,396,208) in the former year to 57% (3,550,404) by the latter; and the city itself had been losing population since 1950. Moreover, the type and location of the new construction ensured that the redistribution of Chicago's population would be very selective. Single-family homes were placed in outlying areas by private developers who simply did not "build for Negroes." Indeed, the Illinois Inter-Racial Commission in its 1951 report stated only that "recent residential construction has somewhat alleviated housing problems of whites in the upper or middle income bracket." The poor and the nonwhite were not mentioned. The result was that the white suburban population increased by 1,440,606, whereas the number of black suburbanites grew by only 52,729. Where blacks represented 6.6% of the SMSA's people and 2.1% of all suburbanites in 1940, they accounted for 14.3% of the SMSA but still only 2.9% of the suburban group in 1960. More ominously, 401,816 whites fled Chicago proper during that span, more than 270,000 leaving between 1950 and 1956 alone.[60]

The desertion of the city by middle- and upper-class whites had serious residual effects on those left behind. As vacancies began to appear around established black communities in the late 1940s and 1950s, black "pioneers," eager to escape ghetto conditions and both willing and able to compete economically for the inner-city housing becoming available, moved into previously all-white neighborhoods. Officials estimated that 15 dwelling units changed from white to black occupancy for every 100 units built in the suburbs. Based on the rate of construction, this meant that nearly 4,000 dwelling units underwent racial transition in each year between 1945 and 1949. This rate of succession increased to 7,100 units per year between 1950 and 1954 and grew to 7,800 units per year between 1955 and 1959.[61]

There is no doubt that many blacks were ready to take advantage of the new housing opportunities as they appeared. Both during and after the war, sustained economic gains permitted an increasing number of blacks to better their situation. Adjusting for inflation, an income of $5,000 in 1950 was roughly equivalent to earning $6,000 in 1960. In 1950, 10,200 (8.9%) of Chicago's nonwhite families earned $5,000 per year. Ten years later, 63,100 (34.1%) of the city's nonwhite families earned $6,000 or more. By the mid-1950s, the National Housing Inventory found 45,000 black families in Chicago in the market for middle- or upper-income housing.[62]

The augmented financial resources of at least some blacks were crucial to the destabilization of old racial borders. The high degree of residential segregation in Chicago produced a dual housing market: one for whites, another for blacks. The restricted black housing supply and the overwhelming demand for new homes combined to inflate the cost of black housing. Rents in black areas ranged from 15% to 50% higher than that paid by whites for similar accommodations, the Illinois Inter-Racial Commission wrote in 1944. The difference was especially great, they added, in areas just beginning the process of racial succession.[63] By 1960, even after a decade of new construction, the rents paid by blacks were still 10% to 25% higher than those paid by whites for equivalent shelter. Not only were rents higher, but the cost of purchasing housing was greater for blacks. Despite this fact, however, the limits on the black rental market forced many into homeownership – even at the cost of over-extending family finances.[64] As whites living around the Black Belt were attracted elsewhere, blacks moved in, for the prices property owners could get for their accommodations were much higher if rented or sold to blacks. The "willingness" and ability to pay higher prices thus destabilized a large portion of Chicago's racial frontier.[65]

The forces promoting a durable and unchanging racial border – the dual housing market, the cost of black housing, restrictive covenants – were, at first, buttressed by the housing shortage. Once new construction began, however, those same forces became an overwhelmingly powerful engine for change. With an increase in housing alternatives for whites, the economic forces of the racial housing market all worked *for*, rather than against, racial succession. The one remaining element upholding the old accommodation – restrictive covenants – proved unequal to the task of maintaining neighborhood stability.

Despite the rhetorical and legal attacks mounted against restrictive covenants in the 1940s, it was clear that the housing shortage was most instrumental in sustaining old racial barriers. The problematical judicial enforcement of restrictive covenants and their fundamental weakness in the face of countervailing economic forces were revealed as early as 1940 in the *Hansberry* case, which resulted in the black occupation of the Washington Park Subdivision. When blacks first bought property in that "white island" next to the Black Belt, suits were brought to prevent the blacks from occupying their homes. The Supreme Court eventually ruled in favor of the blacks, but even before that ruling other white property owners opened their buildings to blacks and extracted high rentals for accommodations that were unable to attract white tenants. Rather than suffer financial losses, they elected to violate existing covenants and fill their vacant units with blacks. Organizing themselves into the Small Property Owners Associated, Inc., these white property holders noted the "great financial detriment, mental anguish, and impracticability" of enforcing restrictive covenants. For their own reasons, they stood with the blacks in seeking the judicial overthrow of "vainly impotent racial rental restrictions."[66]

Throughout the 1940s, restrictive covenants in Chicago served as little more than a fairly coarse sieve, unable to stop the flow of black population when put to the test. Five years before the Supreme Court finally rendered all restrictive covenants unenforceable (*Shelley* v. *Kraemer*, 1948), Judge Samuel Heller regularly refused to uphold them in Chicago's Municipal Court. Heller, consequently, became something of a hero in the black press for his "many" decisions in which he refused to evict blacks occupying property bound by restrictive covenants. Other local covenant cases were simply withdrawn, and some that were won were never enforced as plaintiffs viewed the black occupation of their structures or neighborhood as an irreversible fait accompli.[67]

After the war, restrictive covenant cases began to appear with increasing frequency in local courts. The determined attempt to invoke them did not mean, however, that they were being vigorously enforced. Indeed, it meant only that they were being broken with mounting regularity. By 1946 the *Defender* was already referring to "rapidly tumbling restrictive covenants" and concluding that the system was "falling apart at the seams." A year later the *Defender* feared not that restrictive covenants would be used to prevent black movement but that successful court proceedings might compel the eviction of hundreds of blacks already occupying covenant-bound property. There was little need to worry. Evidence of actual evictions carried out through the enforcement of covenants was rare, and the *Defender* wrote in late April 1948 that the eviction of four families from an apartment building on 60th Street was "the first resulting from a court order upholding restrictive covenants in Chicago." This forced removal, it should be noted, took place less than two weeks before the *Shelley* v. *Kraemer* decision was handed down. Insofar as that ruling had a direct impact on Chicago, it was not to dissolve an "iron ring" of restrictive covenants but to dispel the legal clouds that shrouded property already in black possession.[68]

The cold fact of racial succession was greatly complicated by the very nature of the process. As the expanding Black Belt approached white residential areas, those neighborhoods entered what realtors called a "stagnant" period. Whites no longer bought homes in the community and blacks had yet to make their first appearance. Rents and purchase prices were lowered in the futile attempt to attract white residents, lending agencies refused to grant mortgages to whites in such "threatened" areas, and, of course, they demurred in providing financing to the first blacks to "break" a block. With the future of the area uncertain and income restricted, landlords and homeowners often cut back on the maintenance of their properties. Deterioration thus frequently set in before blacks moved into the community. Vacancies began to appear and the economic pressures of the dual housing market pushed white property owners to rent or sell to blacks. It was at this point that the real estate speculator entered the neighborhood.[69]

The speculator filled the vacuum created by the reluctant lending agencies and realtors. Whites in transition areas sold their properties to them for several reasons. First, the white seller often did not want to deal directly with blacks or thought he could "save face" in the community by selling to another white. Second, and probably more important, the speculators had more cash to offer than did the typical black buyer. Fleeing to a new home, the seller required cash for a down payment of his own and was aided by the speculator's desire to complete the transaction quickly.[70] Blacks dealt with speculators because they had difficulty in securing their own financing. A survey of 241 white savings and loan associations found that only one made an initial mortgage to a black family in an all-white area. An examination of 141 commercial banks and 229 life insurance companies revealed that they refused to make "even a token number of conventional mortgages ... for the typical Negro home buyer."[71] The result was that blacks turned to the speculators as the middlemen who facilitated the transition of property from white to black hands. The speculators provided the property, money, and, needless to say, the terms through which the black demand for housing could be met.

The speculators, of course, played their seemingly essential role because of the huge profits that were available to the brokers who bridged the white and black housing markets.[72] Exploiting the fears held by whites, promising cash and a quick sale, the speculator bought cheaply from transition-area customers. Providing financing and new housing to a literally captive market, they sold dearly to blacks and made profits on both transactions.

The device most frequently used in the sale of property to blacks was the installment land contract. An attorney who studied such dealings estimated that 85% of the property sold to blacks in transition areas was sold on contract. The Chicago Commission on Human Relations corroborated those figures. In a CHR study of one square block in the Englewood area, investigators found that 24 of the 29 parcels of property that underwent a change in ownership between 1953 and 1961 were purchased by installment contracts.[73]

When selling on contract, the speculator offered the home to a black purchaser for a relatively low down payment – often several hundred dollars would suffice. For bringing the home within the reach of a black purchaser, however, the speculator extracted a considerable price. In the Commission on Human Relations study, the percentage increase in the cost of the home from the speculator's purchase price to that of the black consumer ranged from a minimum of 35% to 115%; the average increase was 73%. Also of crucial importance was the fact that the speculator retained title to the property. If purchasers failed to keep current on the installment payments, they were subject to eviction. The tenant had no equity in his home until the terms of the contract were fulfilled. Accordingly, at least one speculator retrieved more than 150% of his original investment in less than a year simply by evicting those who missed installments and collecting successive down payments. In any event, with the speculators' small cash investment and the high monthly payments made by blacks unable to obtain conventional financing, most contract sellers were able to have their entire cash equity returned in two years; payments collected after that were sheer profit.[74]

For blacks, purchasing property under land contract was a way of life. In researching Englewood, representatives of the Commission on Human Relations found that many of the black contract purchasers believed that "the installment contract was the only means by which Negro families...could acquire property."[75] If the low down payment permitted the move into new and better quarters, however, the total cost of the home and the high monthly payments created fresh problems. Testifying before the United States Commission on Civil Rights, Frederick D. Pollard, acting executive director of the CHR, told the commissioners that any black who bought on such terms was "going to have to abuse his property in some way to meet this financial burden." Overcrowding, poor maintenance, and illegal conversion were all means through which black contract purchasers tried to save or earn the money to meet their obligations. On Chicago's West Side, Pollard specifically concluded, the "most deteriorating structures" were "almost certainly" those bought on contract from speculators.[76]

In transition areas where apartment buildings, rather than single- or two-family homes, were prevalent, the process of transition was different, but the opportunity for profit and the results were the same. In one area on the near North Side, a real estate operator purchased a large building, which was built in the 1880s. After converting the structure into more than 100 one-room units, he opened it to black tenants. The building was quickly filled with blacks who were willing to pay more than the previous white occupants. Almost overnight the neighborhood acquired nearly 300 new black residents.[77] Throughout the city, large converted kitchenette buildings proved lucrative investments and there was considerable incentive to purchase, convert, and pack such structures with paying black families. Older middle-class areas with many apartment buildings, such as Hyde Park, felt this sort of pressure most sharply. Those large units not reduced to kitchenettes became paying enterprises through the high rents extracted from middle-class blacks and the money saved by reducing operating costs and upkeep. No matter how it was done, there was considerable money to be made in the racial transition of white neighborhoods.[78]

The conditions produced by this process often resembled those created by contract buying. Those existing in the kitchenettes are well known. But even the middle-class areas began to deteriorate under the pressure of too many people and too little maintenance. One black woman complained bitterly that landlords were "fast making slums" out of middle-class areas and that "we have been urged to take roomers to pay the fantastic rentals." She appealed to the Urban League to "take a stand and publicize what is being done to Negro people who are capable of paying reasonable rents, but cannot have the privilege of maintaining a home...in decent apartments without additional roomers."[79] The pressures of the marketplace, however, were too great. In all the census tracts undergoing racial transition, the population increased faster than the number of dwelling units, and the increases in units that did occur were usually the result of conversions rather than new construction. Overcrowding increased as succession progressed.[80]

Theoretically, of course, there was a housing code, building inspectors, and court procedures to assure that no one had to live in overcrowded, unsanitary, or dilapidated buildings. Throughout the 1940s and 1950s, however, the system never posed a serious threat to those who systematically exploited the housing situation. During the war, for example, the city had only a handful of inspectors – eight in 1941, only four for much of 1943. New York, in comparison, had 232.[81] After the war, the building inspection staff was augmented, but other problems remained to thwart the effective enforcement of the housing code. Responsibility for inspection was fragmented, the city's bureaucracy handled the necessary paperwork sloppily (files on the "hottest" cases were frequently and inexplicably misplaced), and many of those serving as inspectors acquired their jobs because of their political, rather than their professional, abilities.[82] Moreover, a Metropolitan Housing and Planning Council study of the city's worst housing code violators revealed that it was more profitable for slum operators to go to court *even if they lost* than it was to repair their properties. The council discovered that the city's twenty-six worse violators were fined an average of only $32.06 for each suit brought against them; for every $100 in fines requested by the city attorneys, the courts actually fined the defendants $3.12. Nor were these twenty-six operators merely an insignificant number of property owners; they owned 868 buildings during the time of the study (1950–62). With many buildings housing dozens, if not hundreds, of individuals, the scope of their operations accounted for the miserable living conditions endured by uncounted thousands.[83]

The process of racial succession was thus a time of desperation and fear for many whites. It began with the speculators who were better known as "block busters" or "panic peddlers." Some of the more unscrupulous were not above harassing vulnerable homeowners by telephone in the middle of the night or hiring blacks to conspicuously and noisily walk and drive through border areas. But the panic that often ensued was not the sole product of these real estate mavericks. In her study of Chicago realtors, Rose Helper found varying degrees of "respectability" among them. Some of the more proper firms refused to sell property to blacks until 50% or more of the area had "gone." Others utilized successively lower percentages, and some proved willing to do business if only a handful of blacks occupied a previously all-white block. The result was that even though each of the "respectable" realtors adamantly refused to "break" an area, they had a great financial stake in the successful operation of the "panic peddler." Once the "disreputable" dealer had done his job, the more "respectable" flocked to do business in transition neighborhoods where their own particular "black threshold" had been inevitably met. In operation, this produced a "gold rush" effect and reluctant residents were literally besieged by hordes of soliciting realtors. Working virtually, if not covertly, in tandem, the panic peddler and the "respectable" broker earned the greatest profits from the greatest degree of white desperation.[84]

In areas where apartment buildings were being converted to kitchenettes and black tenancy, there was, if anything, a sense of helplessness greater even than the fear and desperation. In these neighborhoods white tenants were often evicted in favor of higher paying blacks. In one Oakland apartment, for example, the space that was rented to one white family at $25 per month was able to house three black families at $100 per month. For the working- and lower-middle class whites caught in this economic squeeze, there was nowhere to go. The cost of the new accommodations being built on the urban fringe was beyond their means and, lacking the mobility of those who left the inner city by choice, the prospect of being ousted from reasonably priced, centrally located housing inspired dread. Indeed, a contemporary South Side study of attitudes toward racial succession found that among lower status whites it was the fear that they would be dispossessed that inspired the most antiblack sentiment. The vigorous rejection of even (perhaps especially) middle-class blacks by these vulnerable whites stemmed not only from imagined "status" differences that were impervious to the bleaching power of money but also from the fear that they could not compete against such opponents in the "life and death" struggle for housing.[85]

Finally, as racial succession progressed, the conditions produced by real estate speculation and exploitation began to yield visible proof to those who believed that black "invasion" meant slum creation. "The buildings into which the negroes are being moved," Lea Taylor, head resident of the Chicago Commons settlement, wrote in 1945, "are producing such congestion...that it...is impossible for them to live decently. The inference [in the neighborhoods] is that that is the way negroes like to live." Even in areas of single-family homes, the effects of contract buying, Frederick Pollard observed, led whites to "accept uncritically the idea that communities deteriorate when Negroes move in."[86] For whites perceiving themselves as the victims of black territorial expansion, the entire process of racial transition, from beginning to end, guaranteed strong responses.

There were two primary white reactions to racial succession that were of long-range importance for the city as a whole. The first was one with which the city was familiar: violence. Although Chicago avoided the massive racial explosions that plagued other cities during the war, there were indications as early as 1943–4 that territorial clashes between the races were manifesting themselves in a deadly manner that had not been seen in twenty years. The second major response was less direct. The war years also saw the first attempts in Chicago to expand and harness governmental powers under the guise of "urban planning" in order to reshape the local environment and control the process of succession. It was a response that became increasingly important in the postwar era. Ultimately, the most significant result was the impact the first response had upon the second. Violence took on a new importance as it not only targeted blacks but was aimed at influencing white policy makers as well.[87]

The first signs that territorial conflict was capable of sparking lethal violence came in the heavily Italian neighborhood near the Chicago Commons settlement house on the near North Side. The Grand Avenue border, which separated a nearby black community from the Italians, was first breached in 1943 and broken with increasing regularity in succeeding years. At first, vacant and dilapidated structures were taken for black tenants. Later, real estate firms took over buildings occupied by Italians and began evicting them in favor of blacks who paid "exorbitant rates" for their new quarters. At the time of the first such move-in there was talk of "murder and arson." By the mid-1940s they became realities.[88]

Although there was nothing that could be called a "riot," arson became a real problem. Buildings housing black newcomers and even those that had been inspected by blacks but were as yet unoccupied were attacked. Black desperation for living space, however, overrode fear. As soon as a structure damaged by fire was made habitable, blacks were repeatedly moved back in. "I think they must have taken the apartments sight unseen," Lea Taylor wrote as one group of blacks moved into a charred hulk, "as it would take some real courage to move into a building in which all the first floor windows were broken out by firemen, and which has to have a police guard." Black determination, though, was met with equally determined resistance, and the police detail became a 24-hour-a-day necessity. Finally, in October 1947, fire swept through a large kitchenette building that had only recently been converted to black ten-

Building at 940 W. Ohio where ten blacks died in an arson-related blaze in
October 1947. Rear portion of the building (at left) remains boarded up
while the rest was still occupied when the photograph was taken in 1949.
(Metropolitan Housing and Planning Council Papers, Manuscript Collection, University of Illinois at Chicago, The Library.)

ancy. Ten of the building's residents perished in the conflagration.[89]
The depth of the bitterness exhibited here reappeared elsewhere in
the city in ensuing years.

Two other neighborhoods eschewed violence and sought more
respectable means of controlling their environment. In Englewood,
on the city's South Side, the Southtown Planning Association (SPA)
was created in 1939 to manufacture "ingenious ways of preventing
Negroes from moving into the area." The Southtown Land and
Building Corporation was created by the association in 1943 to buy
property from blacks who bought into the community. The corporation was also used to obtain structures for demolition and rehabilitation if those alternatives were deemed necessary to keep property
out of black hands.[90]

The SPA's most original activity, though, came through its involvement in the passage of the Illinois Redevelopment Act of 1941

and its plans to "redevelop" the black community around Ogden Park. The association's plans called for the demolition of the area's black settlement, the construction of new middle-class housing, and the virtual colonization of Englewood's refugees in the all-black suburb of Robbins, Illinois. In 1945 the SPA's Fred Henderson helped Robbins set up planning, zoning, and other legislation needed to get the village to qualify for aid under the redevelopment act passed four years before. Although nothing ever came of these grandiose designs, the bureaucratic groundwork laid by Henderson was used later by Hyde Park and the University of Chicago.[91]

The other neighborhood that sought legal solutions to racial succession was the Oakland-Kenwood area on the South Side. Here, the Oakland-Kenwood Property Owners' Association (OKPOA), under the leadership of Phillip Toomin, instinctively followed the lead of the 1919 Riot Commission and sought rehabilitation and new construction in black areas as a means of relieving pressure on their community.[92] After the war, it became clear to Toomin, as it had to the SPA, that restrictive covenants were ineffective and that some other means would have to be found to control the neighborhood. Toomin and the OKPOA embarked on two paths. First, they began negotiating with the Chicago Commission on Human Relations, the Chicago Urban League, and the National Association for the Advancement of Colored People to find some workable alternative to the rapid transition and deterioration of the community. The latter groups were interested in pressing "conservation agreements," which would bind owners to the proper maintenance of their property. The OKPOA agreed to an experimental program, but it was clear from the negotiations that its intention was not the removal of racial restrictions on the area but the "de-conversion" of buildings already occupied by blacks. Despite the fact that the OKPOA, as part of the program, ceased prosecuting its pending covenant cases, its actions did not constitute a radical shift in its antiblack policy.[93]

Even as those negotiations were going on, Toomin began developing a second alternative. As did their compatriots in Englewood, the OKPOA investigated the redevelopment tool as a means of "preserving" their community. Indeed, one reason they sought a test area for the "conservation agreements" was to stabilize a particular segment of their community for which they were devising redevelopment plans. By the time preliminary outlines of the project were drawn, OKPOA's leadership was speaking in planner's jargon and muting racial issues. There was talk of age, obsolescence, neglect, and uneconomic uses, but little mention was made of the changing color of the area's population. The organization that in previous years had symbolized white intransigence and the restrictive covenant was able to pursue old aims in new, less obvious ways.[94]

As in Englewood, events overtook the planners in Oakland-Kenwood. But these early attempts to harness public powers pointed the way toward the future. There was little doubt that Chicago's geographical racial accommodation was being drastically revised in the 1940s and 1950s. Those caught up in the changes responded with the best tools at their command. It was the ultimate combination of these responses – violent and legal, crude and sophisticated, successful and unsuccessful – that produced Chicago's second ghetto.

2　An era of hidden violence

Daylight saving time and warm summer evenings are almost universally popular in Chicago. But a change in heart for some of us came in about 1947. We began to dread the long summer evenings. Rain and cool evenings were something to pray for. Anything that would keep people off the streets.

The Reverend Daniel M. Cantwell, "Riot Spirit in Chicago," *Commonweal* (September 14, 1951), p. 375

These Commissions on Human Relations seek to quarantine the most explosive Human Relations elements and situations so that they will not and cannot infect the rest of the city.

Thomas Wright, executive director of the Chicago Commission on Human Relations, quoted in Sister Claire Marie, O.S.F., "A Study of the Department of Civil Rights of the Chicago Commission on Human Relations From 1943 to 1954" (M.A. thesis, Loyola University, Chicago, 1956), p. 41

The late 1940s and 1950s have been viewed as a relatively quiescent period insofar as the outbreak of racial violence is concerned. Circumscribed chronologically by the riots of 1943 and the massive explosions of the 1960s, this era is characterized as the peaceful interlude between recurring large-scale disorders. So visible and alarming were the peaks of twentieth-century racial violence that the absence of disorders, which killed dozens and engulfed whole cities, was interpreted as the presence of peace.

Yet, for Chicago, the decade following the conclusion of World War II was anything but a peaceful interlude. True, many of the old sources of racial conflict, which had produced the disastrous 1919 conflagration, were no longer at issue. Flush times after the war and the growth of unionization eliminated the bitter labor strife that had helped provoke the earlier outburst. Similarly, the blacks' desertion of the Republican party made political disputes between blacks and their traditional enemies a matter for intraparty, rather than interracial, confrontation. The black militancy so apparent in the "New Negro" philosophy popular during World War I was also missing after World War II. Where such militancy had earlier exacerbated racial tensions and contributed to the eruption of violence, it was now subdued, awaiting revival in the 1960s.[1]

Only the housing issue remained to disrupt the peace of the city. In 1919 territorial clashes between whites and blacks had merged with economic, political, and ideological conflicts to produce the archetypal "communal" riot. By 1945 the struggle for living space, alone, continued in aggravated form. Consequently, in the years immediately following World War II, Chicago endured a pattern of chronic urban guerrilla warfare that was related less to ideological currents than to the ebb and flow of populations.

The first signs of trouble were evident even before the war had ended. As refugees from the disastrously overcrowded Black Belt sought new homes in previously restricted areas of the city, the number of violent incidents aimed at driving out black "invaders" increased dramatically. The late 1940s became an era analogous to that of 1917–21, when one racially motivated bombing or arson occurred every twenty days.[2] Moreover, large housing riots – the mobbing of black homes by hundreds, if not thousands, of whites – broke out, thus revealing a form of resistance rarely seen outside the context of a large citywide disorder.[3]

Once black residency had been established and increasing numbers of newcomers had consolidated a "beachhead" in a previously all-white area, the pattern of violence shifted. The 1950s witnessed the eruption of battles over the use of community facilities and the virtual cessation of large-scale housing riots. Where there were few instances of interracial friction at the city's parks and beaches in the 1940s, such conflict dominated the succeeding decade. The issue was no longer the racial homogeneity of a given area but rather the prerogatives attendant upon neighborhood control. Fought over the issues of homes and "turf," a series of smaller disorders replaced the lone, all-encompassing riot of the World War I era.

The sheer fury of the 1919 riot far surpassed its midcentury counterparts, but the later riots, despite their undeserved obscurity, often involved thousands of participants and continued for days. One disorder, that at the Trumbull Park Homes on the city's far South Side, dragged on for years as community residents raged against the Chicago Housing Authority (CHA) and fought unwanted black "intruders." The shroud that currently envelops these incidents is hardly due to their insignificance. A conscious city policy to keep them from public view accounts for their continued lack of exposure.

The agency responsible for the hush-hush press policy regarding racial violence was the Chicago Commission on Human Relations (CHR). Created in the panic that followed in the wake of the 1943 Detroit riot, the CHR, for the best of reasons, minimized inflammatory reports of racial confrontations. Most Chicagoans thus remained ignorant of the day-to-day violence that was both disfiguring and reshaping the face of the city. It was not until the suburban Cicero riot of 1951 that the intrusion of television destroyed the practical significance of newspaper silence. By that time, however, the worst of the rioting had ended and the few later incidents that were exposed stood as isolated testimony to the perversity of particular neighborhoods rather than the final battles in a long and bitter struggle.

The race riot that erupted in Detroit on June 20, 1943, transmitted shock waves throughout the nation. A series of earlier racial outbursts had already stung Mobile, Alabama, Beaumont, Texas, and Los Angeles, but it was the Detroit riot that transformed the latent dread of interracial conflict into openly expressed fear.[4]

The most frightening prospect was that Detroit represented only the start, and not the culmination, of America's racial problems. *Newsweek* articulated this haunting fear when it asserted that the Detroit outbreaks were merely "a symptom of racial tension festering all over the country." Cities that had previously refused to admit the possibility of racial violence for fear of provoking it now dwelt morbidly on its prospect. The "potential" for disaster suddenly became apparent in innumerable towns and there was talk of a "succession of Detroits," which, if not ruinous for the war effort, would certainly mean "the loss of the peace."[5]

The depth of the panic generated by the specter of racial violence in 1943 was best revealed by the creation of a new urban institution. At least thirty-one cities created municipal interracial commissions between the summers of 1943 and 1944. Unofficial citizens' committees, often working with the cooperation and approval of city fathers, also took root in more than fifty urban centers during that same period. By the fall of 1945 more than 200 such agencies were in existence. It was the specific intent of these bodies to deal concretely with the improvement of race relations on the local level. Representing every region in the nation, they all had as their first goal the prevention of riots similar to the one that crippled Detroit. Nor was this all. The institutionalization and professionalization of the "sci-

ence" of race relations continued with the concomitant establishment of eleven state interracial agencies all directed toward the same
end.[6]

Of all the cities, however, Chicago felt the reverberations of the
Detroit disorder with the most acute sensitivity. Even before the
Detroit fires were extinguished, the Army's Sixth Service Command
requested the shipment of 12,000 tear gas and smoke grenades and
10,000 12-gauge shotgun shells to Fort Sheridan, Illinois, "for use in
the event of disorders in Chicago." Mayor Edward J. Kelly responded
almost as quickly in a July 2 Civil Defense radio broadcast: "Recent
acts of intolerance and race discrimination in different parts of our
own country away from our peaceful city are equal to the destruction of American life and property by enemy bombs." Kelly later
added, "You can tell the country that we are not going to have what
happened in Detroit."[7]

The mayor's immediate actions to forestall a race riot in Chicago
consisted of a barrage of calming pronouncements and the implementation of emergency police procedures. "The vast majority of
our Negroes and our white people are law abiding citizens," Kelly
affirmed, "and we are going to remove every cause of friction between the great peaceful elements of the two...As to law violators
and criminals, that is another story. They are going to be dealt with
– in all races – with the full strength of our law enforcement facilities."[8]

Even as Kelly was speaking, those charged with enforcing the law
were given special instructions. Police on Chicago's South Side,
with the aid of community leaders, implemented a program of "unexpressed, expedient segregation." Although the police felt they
could not actually restrict the public's movements, they took a "realistic view of conditions" and decided to "encourage" members of
both races to "avoid known areas of conflict." Black officers, moreover, were routinely assigned to handle "Negro trouble" and those
incidents that displayed "provocative racial qualities."[9]

Citizen reaction to the Detroit riot forced officials to move in another direction as well. The day after news of the Detroit riot became
known, a dozen black community and political leaders were called
into the officers of the *Defender* to study local conditions and seek
ways to prevent violence. This meeting was symbolic of the massive
outpouring of public concern and apprehension emanating from
both whites and blacks. Though University of Chicago sociologist
Louis Wirth felt such gatherings were unproductive, "largely preachy,"
and merely "expressive of goodwill," enough pressure was brought
to bear on authorities to produce an Emergency Citizens' Confer-

ence at City Hall. It was the intent of the various civic organizations that called for the conference to ask Mayor Kelly and Governor Dwight Green to form a commission "similar to the one appointed by Gov. [Frank] Lowden [after the 1919 riot]." The rationale for this action was candidly supplied by a black politician: "During the last war we made a study *after* the riot. . . . [T]his time let's make the study before."[10]

The desire to forestall disorder and the subsequent Emergency Citizens' Conference led to the rapid creation of a number of agencies that placed Chicago and the state of Illinois in the vanguard of the national riot prevention movement. A private citizens' group, Chicago's Council Against Discrimination (CAD), was quickly established as a result of the conference, but it was clearly supplementary to the official action taken. Hints of what was to come were found in the Chicago Urban League's call for an "inter-racial commission to safeguard the peace of the community and remove the causes of inter-racial clashes." The result was the creation of an "action rather than a merely academic" agency. The Mayor's Committee on Race Relations (MCRR), established less than a month after the Detroit violence, was charged with the responsibility of not only locating but also alleviating sources of racial friction.[11]

The MCRR was funded by the mayor's contingency fund and operated out of the mayor's office until 1947 when it was made an official department of the city government (its name was changed to the Chicago Commission on Human Relations and it will hereafter be referred to as the CHR). Chicago thus became the first city in the nation to "establish a human relations committee supported by public funds." For the first time there was "an official acceptance of public responsibility for the social health of the city." Governor Green did not lag far behind. By the end of July 1943 the Illinois Inter-Racial Commission (later renamed the Illinois Commission on Human Relations) was created and similarly handed the delicate task of ensuring racial peace.[12]

Officials approached their riot prevention task earnestly for two very good reasons. The first was that the resumption of black migration from the South in conjunction with the wartime emergency was more than vaguely reminiscent of the events preceding Chicago's dreadful 1919 violence. The executive director of the CHR commented later that "the wary needed only to look back to 1919 . . . to recognize the danger signals." The arrival of roughly 60,000 blacks between 1940 and 1944 exacerbated the "already troublesome problems of inadequate housing, congestion, inferior recreational facilities, and overcrowded schools," St. Clair Drake and Horace R. Cayton noted in *Black Metropolis*. "Half-forgotten memories of the Great Migration and of the Race Riot and its aftermath were revived among both Negroes and whites," they wrote. "The Negro was once more becoming a 'problem' and racial conflict seemed to loom in the offing."[13]

Sporadic flashes of interracial warfare taking place *within* Chicago were just as frightening as those occurring beyond its borders. The second reason why Chicagoans responded so rapidly to the news of the Detroit riot was rooted firmly in the city's present rather than its past. Racial tensions in Chicago had been escalating throughout the spring and summer of 1943 and there was legitimate concern for the safety of the city. Louis Wirth analyzed Chicago's racial situation in the wake of the Detroit riot at the request of the Office of War Information (OWI). "Given the proper provocation," he wrote, the situation could develop "to a point comparable to Detroit." CHR officials agreed. "The heat of . . . [Detroit's] fire was felt in Chicago," they noted, "as a good look at our own city showed the brush here was dangerously dry also, and the sources of friction were many."[14]

Such fears were well founded. Virtually every section of the city labored under the burden of localized and generalized racial tensions. The most dangerous situation existed on the near North Side in the Sicilian Little Hell District. Blacks had been moving into the area and interracial skirmishing had already broken out. A group of white toughs known as the Black Hand Gang was particularly hostile to black youths entering their "turf."[15]

Most alarming, though, was the confrontation that had developed over the occupation of the newly constructed Frances Cabrini Homes. Planned in the months before the war as a slum clearance project, 80% of the projected 586 units were to be given to the poor and inadequately housed Italian population, with the remaining 20% allotted to blacks. The site had been cleared but construction had not yet begun when the Japanese attacked Pearl Harbor. The onset of hostilities led the federal government to change the development from one housing the local poor to one that gave top priority to migrant war workers. Consequently, the Italians, who represented 380 of the 538 families dispossessed by the planned project, were not able to return to the area. Bitterness turned to hatred as blacks proved the primary beneficiaries of the project's change in status. The *Defender* hailed the rapid integration of the area and proclaimed, overoptimistically, that Little Hell was becoming a "Seventh Heaven" for blacks. "With its numerous murders, high delinquency rates and

Construction goes on at the Frances Cabrini Homes, 1942. (Photograph courtesy of the Chicago Housing Authority.)

shabby housing units," the *Defender* euphorically and prematurely declared, " 'Little Hell' has died."[16]

The resentment felt by the remaining local residents toward the newcomers created the potential for violence. An uneasy accommodation permitted blacks to use only one of the area's two parks and that for only "a few hours [per day]." At the time of the Detroit riot, 140 apartments in the completed project stood empty as eloquent testimony to the depth of local opposition, which refused to allow blacks to occupy more than the originally agreed upon 20% of the units. A small riot did, finally, erupt between nearly 300 blacks and whites in April 1943 when gunshots were fired into an apartment occupied by blacks. Although tension had been declining in the weeks preceding the Detroit riot, the situation, Wirth noted in a letter to the OWI, was still explosive.[17]

Conditions on the South Side were only slightly less disturbing. Whites in the Roseland community were also gathering to protest the construction of living quarters for blacks in the spring of 1943.

Move-in day at the Frances Cabrini Homes, 1942. (Photograph courtesy of the Chicago Housing Authority.)

The ire of local residents, first aroused by a privately developed and financed project for blacks in Princeton Park (95th and Wentworth), was intensified when the Chicago Housing Authority announced plans for a project at 130th and Langley. Construction of these two developments, along with the existing black settlements in Morgan Park and Lilydale, left the white Roseland community hemmed in by three separate black districts. Though the potential for violence clearly existed, the white protests in this area remained merely verbal.[18]

Localized interracial tensions in Chicago were supplemented by more generalized feelings of racial hostility. This was especially true of the residents of the city's Black Belt. Even before the war, Chicago's blacks were commenting bitterly on the possibility of again marching off to defend the white man's democracy. Sentiments that would later be popularized by the *Pittsburgh Courier*'s "Double-V Campaign" (Victory for Democracy – At Home and Abroad) were common in Chicago months before Pearl Harbor. A sign in a tailor shop on east 35th Street proclaimed in the autumn of 1941 that "We

Can't Fight Over There for Something We Don't Have Over Here." Such feelings, the *Defender* concluded, were "the unexpressed thought of almost every Negro who is called upon to serve in the army."[19]

When the war did come, such attitudes were most often translated into a loyalty that was sincerely, but not blindly, offered. "IN THIS CRITICAL HOUR OF OUR NATION'S HISTORY THE HEART OF THE AMERICAN NEGRO PEOPLE BEATS AS ONE WITH THE HEART OF THE OTHER CITIZENS OF THIS LAND," the *Defender* editorialized. "However," the editors added, "in pledging our allegiance to the flag and what it symbolizes, we are not unmindful of the broken promises of the past. We ask that America give the Negro citizen the full measure of the democracy he is called upon to defend."[20] Other blacks would not go as far as the *Defender*. Some felt a fleeting, vicarious pride in the successful assault launched by another "colored" race.[21] Still others, more extreme and relatively few in number, joined various "cults" that were openly pro-Japanese. The prosecution of individuals belonging to these groups for draft resistance was viewed as racially inspired and caused "a great deal of grumbling" in certain sections of the black community.[22]

A more serious chink in the "Armor of Democracy" related to the role permitted blacks in defense industries. In the early days of the war, the continued acceptance of "White Only" job orders from defense contractors by the Illinois State Employment Service was especially galling.[23] Nearly two years later, black dissatisfaction with the "employment situation" remained a sore point. The potential for violence was not lost on anxious whites. Several of Chicago's economic power brokers and influential citizens were urged to take "constructive" steps in this area, "which might tend to alleviate the situation and...avoid what may develop into serious results."[24]

The domestic strains induced by total war provided additional sources of friction. In Chicago, one of the most likely areas of overt conflict involved white merchants in the black community. Louis Wirth learned that "there is wholesale ceiling price violation and antagonism against...white merchants to a point where windows might be broken and riots take place." Aggravating the situation were long-standing grievances against these same businessmen. Particularly annoying were claims that they failed to employ sufficient black clerks and that they competed with black merchants. Other irritants brought about by wartime conditions included rising prices, meat and poultry shortages, and overcrowding on public transportation. This latter problem was most troublesome on the "El" platform at 43rd Street where "great crowds congregate[d] and jostle[d] one another." Shortages in the civilian labor force also made difficult the conduct of the most ordinary transactions. Long queues formed at banks, post offices, and stores, and "where a mixture of the races [was] involved," one commentator noted, "it became very easy to attribute frustrations to the other race" and "carry a chip on one's shoulder."[25]

The wave of racial violence that seemed to grow as the war progressed also stirred black Chicagoans. The black press tried, at first, to minimize racial tensions resulting from the coverage of such incidents. The *Chicago Bee* refuted a false wire service story that a black army lieutenant had been brutally beaten by Georgia police and warned against the blind acceptance of every lurid tale.[26] As rioting swept the South and then found its way into the urban North, however, both the *Bee* and the *Defender* were compelled to give those events "considerable play."[27] Appalling news of the ever-increasing tide of violence made headlines throughout the summer of 1943 and, after the Harlem riot, where 6 people were killed and more than 300 injured following the rumored murder of a black by police, both major black newspapers took special pains to see that their coverage was not provocative. The *Defender* refused to publish any photographs of the Harlem riot though "at least a dozen" were available. The *Bee* went even further. Its first edition after the Harlem riot carried no specific mention of that disorder and editorialized against the "careless" use of the term "race riot." That phrase was a "misnomer when applied to most of the situations in which Negroes are involved" and, according to the *Bee*, served only to "incite to violence the thoughtless and irresponsible elements of both races."[28]

Despite such attempts to defuse interracial tension, knowledge of the bitter social warfare was both general and disquieting. Even before the Detroit riot, special steps were taken to ensure the peace of Chicago's streets. In the summer of 1942 the Black Belt was declared "off limits" to white sailors. A "verbal" order, perhaps prompted by the still tender memories of the difficulties surrounding the "black and tan cabarets" of the World War I era, forbade entry into the area bounded by 37th, 70th, Cottage Grove, and State streets. The Shore Patrol stationed guards outside the famous Rhumboogie Club and both the owners of the Rhumboogie and the Club DeLisa were ordered not to admit white navy men. Not satisfactorily assured that a riot was still unlikely, blacks took their own precautions. The black market in weapons and ammunition was booming on Chicago's South Side by the summer of 1943. "Although revolver shells are selling in the Negro district for twelve cents instead of two cents, their usual price," the OWI was told, "there are plenty of customers for them." "Occasionally one can see a colored man carrying a rifle or a shot gun wrapped up in a newspaper or a gunny sack," Louis Wirth noted. But he believed it was nothing to be alarmed about, "merely a sign that if trouble does start, the Negroes do not want to be unprepared."[29]

"Trouble" appeared to arrive in spring of 1943 when police shot and killed Elmo Vasser, a sixteen-year-old black. "Angry crowds" gathered for the boy's funeral and extra police were "instructed to stand by." Although no violence occurred, the aroused Morgan Park community demanded and received a grand jury investigation. Just days before Detroit erupted, the grand jury made its report and refused to indict. Once news of the Detroit riot reached Chicago, however, Police Commissioner James P. Allman ordered charges placed against the two officers involved in the shooting. The boy's body was exhumed in an attempt to gather further evidence and, apparently, to mollify Chicago's seething black community. Such was the atmosphere in Chicago during the bloody summer of 1943. Harboring anxieties born of past and present conditions, the city was burdened with a terrible fear. When Detroit exploded, Chicago jumped.[30]

The Chicago Commission on Human Relations worked feverishly to forestall a riot in its first summer of existence. A total of eight private meetings and two public hearings were held during those warm months, and, whether due to its efforts, the general reaction against the horror of the Detroit riots, or sheer luck, the summer passed peacefully and the panic inspired by the thought of domestic warfare receded. Indeed, the apparent return of interracial peace was so reassuring that it threatened the CHR's existence. After a relatively quiet year and a half, interest in the CHR began to wane and the commission's full-time executive director resigned.[31]

Edwin R. Embree, president of the Julius Rosenwald Foundation and the commission's chairman, hired Thomas H. Wright as the new executive director in an attempt to revive the dormant agency. A former philosophy teacher who had been educated for the ministry, Wright knew that, even though rioting had been avoided, Chicago had not begun to solve the economic and social problems that were almost certain to cause trouble in the future. Wright, therefore, set two tasks for himself. The first was to strengthen the commission. The second involved the development of a plan of action that would effectively maintain the city's peace.[32]

In pursuit of his first goal, Wright solicited the support of organized labor, the Catholic archdiocese, the Protestant church federation, and "nearly every city-wide group." His next step was to ask the city council to triple the commission's operating budget. With Mayor Kelly's support, he succeeded in more than doubling it. The money was quickly used to hire a staff of six "experts" and several office clerks; previously the commission had enjoyed the services of only two full-time workers and a stenographer.[33] The executive director turned next to the formation and implementation of commission policy.

The omnipresent shadow of 1919 provided a spur to action and a guide. Wright's response to the stimulus furnished by the specter of 1919 was the creation of a sophisticated machine dedicated to the prevention or, at worst, control of interracial violence. One wall in the CHR office was adorned with a large "tension map" of Chicago. Commission staff members identified attacks on individuals or property, demonstrations dispersed by police, and housing project sites by sticking colored pins into the map. An index card file contained a brief description of each reported incident. Word of potentially dangerous situations was received through a network of individuals ("listening posts") scattered throughout the city who kept a wary eye on their own neighborhoods for the CHR. Wright had gathered the names of people interested in the commission's work and asked their cooperation in collecting information and reporting rumors. Not merely passive receivers of information, these allies, white and black, frequently rode through their respective areas in streetcars, listening to conversations in the attempt to glean useful bits of knowledge. Consequently, Wright and the CHR staff often knew of impending trouble before the police did. First established in 1945, the "listening posts" proved so effective that their numbers were greatly augmented in succeeding years.[34]

The most important feature of the commission's operation involved its close relationship with the city's news media. The roots of the CHR's press policy, more than any other aspect of its program, were directly traceable to Chicago's 1919 experience. During that riot, the commission believed, "the press reflected and enhanced the misunderstanding and hysteria that gripped the city." The widespread dissemination of unsubstantiated rumors by the city's newspapers multiplied police difficulties and undoubtedly contributed to the violence. In light of that record, the commission "encouraged the press to give factual, unsensational reports when trouble occurs . . . so that crowds will not go into the area and enlarge the problem of the police."[35]

Chicago's newspapers were not averse to taking the suggestion. Robert Kennedy, chief editorial writer for the *Sun-Times*, revealed the reasons behind the media's receptivity in an address to the Fourth Chicago Conference on Civic Unity. Newsmen were now "extremely conscious of the impact on the community of news that hurts rather than helps relations between groups," Kennedy declared. Making specific reference to the findings of Governor Lowden's commission, published in *The Negro in Chicago*, he described, apologetically, the role played by the press in 1919 and vowed that Chicago's newspapers would not make the same mistake again. The *Sun-Times* editor was not alone. Editors and staff members of each of the city's major papers informed interested observers that "they remember 1919 and the Detroit riots and are willing to go along with the policy of suppression." Although "suppression" might seem a strong term for the CHR's call for "factual" reporting, it was, apparently, taken that way by newsmen and proved to be an accurate characterization of the practical results of that policy. There was a unanimity born of fear as the city's sordid past and uncertain future were contemplated.[36]

The city's interracial truce was shattered where it had always only tenuously existed: at the edge of the Black Belt. The earliest disorders, beginning in May 1944, were individualized hit-and-run attacks on homes occupied by blacks in previously all-white areas. Reminiscent of those territorial assaults that accompanied the first Great Migration to the urban North, they heralded the emergence of housing as the city's most explosive racial issue.[37] Of the 485 racial "incidents" reported to the CHR between 1945 and 1950, 357 (73.6%) were directly related to housing or residential property. Areas immediately adjacent to the old South Side Black Belt suffered the most violence. Nearly two out of every three episodes (64.5%) occurred in such neighborhoods and fully 85.1% of all incidents took place on the fringes of black residential concentrations.[38] "The pattern of terrorism is easily discernible," the CAD concluded. "It is at the seams of the black ghetto in all directions." The area enduring the most attacks was that west of Wentworth between 26th and 43rd streets; Englewood ranked second.[39] Also notable was the seasonality of the violence. There were no "long, hot summers" during these early postwar years but rather a yearly cycle of violence that had two peaks: one in spring and another in autumn, during the traditional moving seasons. Both the CHR and the Illinois Inter-Racial Commission subsequently concluded that housing was the "chief" cause of racial friction.[40]

This first phase of the city's postwar violence was such, however, that the press was not directly confronted with the problem of implementing CHR policy. The lesser incidents involving vandalism or the stoning of homes hardly appeared "newsworthy" and the more serious attacks – arson and bombings – were not the sort of activities that brought huge crowds into the street. The white press thus easily overlooked such occurrences. The escalation of the violence brought no greater coverage. From May 1944 through July 1946, forty-six black residences were assaulted (nine were attacked twice and one home was targeted on five separate occasions) in the most serious wave of racial disorder since the World War I era. Beginning in January 1945 there was at least one attack every month (save for March 1946), and twenty-nine of the onslaughts were arson-bombings. At least three persons were killed in the incidents. Yet, despite this upsurge in deadly violence, the major dailies provided "scant coverage" and the "white community [was] unaware of the situation."[41]

Beginning in late 1946, however, a brief period of large-scale housing riots tested the connection between the press and the CHR.[42] The working relationship proved strong and news of these explosive disorders was effectively suppressed. The extent of the violence, as well as the degree to which it was kept hidden from public view, is best illustrated by way of contrast. The most widely publicized racial disorder of these years occurred not within the city proper but at its western edge in the working-class suburb of Cicero. Allen Day Grimshaw, a serious observer of American racial violence, wrote in 1959 that the Cicero uprising was, in fact, "the major disturbance in a Northern city since the war."[43] There, in the summer of 1951, a mob of 2,000 to 5,000 angry whites assaulted a large apartment building that housed a single black family in one of its twenty units. The burning and looting of the building's contents lasted several nights until order was finally restored by the presence of some 450 National Guardsmen and 200 Cicero and Cook County sheriff's police.[44]

The reaction to this incident was immediate, worldwide outrage. Governor Thomas E. Dewey of New York, visiting Singapore, was "shocked" to find the Cicero riot front-page news in Southeast Asia; the *Singapore Straits Times* even ran photographs of the mob to augment its coverage. News of the riot was also carried in the *Pakistan Observer* and apparently reached Africa as well. A resident of Accra wrote to the mayor of Cicero protesting the mob's "savagery" and asking for an "apology to the civilized world."[45]

At home, the Chicago press provided extensive coverage of the riot, complete with editorials denouncing the violence and letters to the editor protesting racial barbarism. Buried among those letters, though, was one of a slightly different tone written by Homer Jack, a Unitarian minister and co-founder of the Congress of Racial Equality (CORE). The Cicero disorder "contained perhaps more vandalism than recent racial disturbances in Chicago," Jack wrote, "but fortunately there was no persistent attack on the police...or violence towards Negroes" as had been the case in the city.[46] Jack was referring to two recent Chicago riots, one at the Chicago Housing Authority's Fernwood Park Homes and another in the South Side Englewood community. In each case the issue was the same: the introduction of black residents into previously all-white communities. Yet, though he was minimizing the level of violence seen in Cicero as compared to these other disorders, it was only through his role as a social activist that Jack was aware of them at all. The Chicago press had virtually ignored these earlier riots and, as a contemporary observer noted, "the man in the street...[was] wholly unaware that a cruel kind of warfare...[was] going on in the no-man's land around Chicago's Black Belt."[47]

The Fernwood riot surpassed the Cicero incident in ferocity, scope, and the counterforce called forth to suppress it. Erupting over the placement of black veterans in a temporary CHA project, the community surrounding the project rioted for three successive nights in mid-August 1947. During the first two evenings of disorder, crowds ranging from 1,500 to 5,000 persons battled police who frustrated their attempts to enter the project. Unable to penetrate defense lines, mobs broke off their engagements with the police and assaulted cars carrying blacks through the area. Whereas a mere building was attacked in Cicero (there was not a black within miles of the apartment when the rioting started), the Fernwood mob eagerly sought and found human victims. Police unfortunate enough to get in the mob's way were struck by bricks and rocks. Blacks were hauled off streetcars and beaten in a fashion reminiscent of 1919. Roaming gangs covered an ever-widening South Side area throughout the disorder. Attacks were reported as far north as 98th Street and as far south as 111th; assaults on vehicles along 103rd Street occurred between Michigan Avenue and Vincennes, a distance of nearly 2 miles. The CHR printed an "incomplete" list that included 35 blacks who were known injured by white gangs, and the *Defender* reported that at least 100 cars driven by blacks were attacked. Eventually more than 1,000 police were dispatched to the area (the Cicero disturbance was quelled with the presence of only 650 peace officers), and more than 700 remained in the vicinity a full two weeks after the riot had "ended." Heavy police details were compelled to patrol nearly 8 square miles of the city's South Side (from 95th to 130th and from Michigan to Vincennes), whereas, in comparison, only a single square mile had to be quarantined in Cicero. Massive black retaliation was only narrowly avoided, and the Metropolitan Housing and Planning Council felt that the violence at Fernwood represented "about as bad a situation as any seen since the riots of 1919."[48]

The Englewood riot was also more devastating than Cicero's. The presence of blacks at an informal union meeting in a house at 5643 S. Peoria precipitated the rumor that the home was being "sold to niggers." The neighborhood, situated between the Black Belt to the east and a small black enclave to the southwest, had been tense for more than a week. The sale of a local home to a black family in early November 1949 had been met by the community's frantic effort to repurchase the house. When a woman spied blacks in Aaron Bindman's living room on November 8, the block organization that had been created to meet the first emergency was mobilized to face a new "crisis." Crowds gathered outside the home, and community representatives met with Bindman, himself a newcomer to the area, to brief him on the conduct expected of a friend and neighbor. Bindman's status as a labor organizer, a Jew, and, as the community eventually learned, a Communist greatly complicated the situation. After two days of bruiting rumors about a Jewish-Communist plot to destroy the neighborhood, the crowd, which had congregated nightly outside the home, turned to violence.[49]

Estimates of the Englewood crowds varied from several hundred at the riot's inception to as many as 10,000 at its peak. As at Fernwood, they were not satisfied with mere property destruction. The house at 5643 S. Peoria, an early target of the mob, sustained only minor damage because police let the mob get no nearer than a literal stone's throw away. But "strangers" who entered the area to observe the white protestors and innocent passers-by were victimized by roving gangs. Denounced as Jews, Communists, and – apparently worst of all – University of Chicago meddlers, whites unfamiliar to local residents were brutally beaten. From November 10 through November 12, 1949, such whites and a few blacks who inopportunely entered the district were assaulted. The uprising, as one contemporary noted, was "fantastic in its ramifications." "It involve[d] prejudice against Negroes, Jews, University of Chicago students, outsiders, everybody and everything."[50] That a false rumor that blacks were about to move into the area was enough to trigger the riot also indicated the depth of the tension current in many white areas bordering the Black Belt.

These Chicago riots were only two of many such incidents. The Fernwood riot was the second disorder to erupt at a veteran's housing project. The Airport Homes at 60th and Karlov on the Southwest Side suffered a riot comparable to Cicero's in December 1946. There, a mob of between 1,500 and 3,000 persons engaged police in battle and destroyed property in an attempt to prevent blacks from moving into the emergency shelters erected in their neighborhood. Together with the Fernwood disorder, the difficulties at the Airport Homes illustrated the reaction provoked by a new agency of social change: the Chicago Housing Authority. With the advent of public housing, the matters of site selection and tenant selection became grave racial issues. Now even communities situated considerable distances from areas of black concentration found their homogeneity threatened. The last large housing riot of the period, that which struck the housing authority's Trumbull Park Homes in 1953, demonstrated clearly that the CHA could easily bridge the gap between any neighborhood and the Black Belt. At that project, after an initial outburst protesting the accommodation of blacks, whites in the South Deering community engaged in a war of attrition against the CHA. The use of explosives, the harassment of black tenants, and large demonstrations continued for a decade as whites restricted both the numbers of blacks permitted in the project and their access to community facilities.[51]

Similarly, the block-by-block expansion of the ghetto was not Englewood's concern alone. To the south of the Black Belt, the Park Manor neighborhood suffered a series of disorders throughout the period. Located squarely in the traditional path of black territorial expansion, Park Manor was one of the first areas to react against racial shifts in the private housing market. Arson and vandalism were frequent occurrences from 1945 to 1950.[52] The first large mob incident took place on July 1-2, 1946, as 2,000 to 3,000 people gathered to protest the presence of a black doctor in his newly purchased home. The crowd set the garage on fire and bombarded the house with rocks, breaking several windows. The doctor left his home after the first night of disorder and, by July 3, decided not to return.[53] Immediately following this incident, the CHR conducted a survey of attitudes in the area bounded by 71st, 73rd, South Parkway, and St. Lawrence avenues.[54] The commission found "a pretty solid and uniform point of view against Negroes moving in regardless of their economic and cultural status." Subsequent CHR efforts

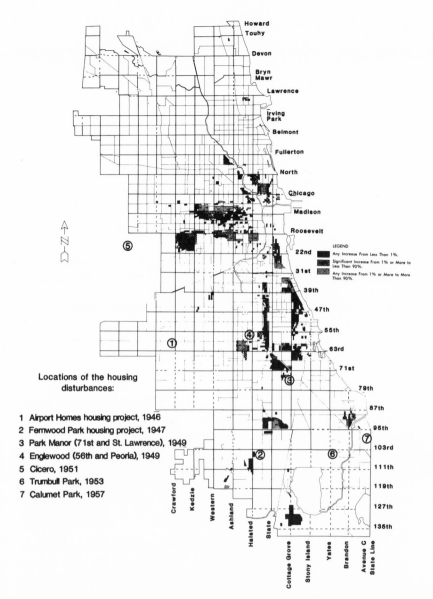

Map 4. City of Chicago, areas of black residence in which black households comprised a significantly greater percentage of all households, 1950 over 1939, and locations of housing disturbances, 1946–57. The percentage increases considered significant were determined in accordance with the 1939 black percentage concentration. For example, increases that were deemed significant include: (1) an increase from no black households in 1939 to 1% or more black households in 1950, (2) an increase from 25% in 1939 to 35% or more in 1950, and (3) an increase from between 1% and 90% in 1939 to 90% or more in 1950. (*Source*: Metropolitan Housing and Planning Council, *Areas of Negro Residence in Chicago, 1950* [Chicago: Metropolitan Housing and Planning Council, 1952].)

in the neighborhood "had to be limited to work with the police department, since no local group of citizens or civic organizations was available to work within the community." The usually successful Thomas Wright, in this instance, was unable to find a single individual willing to cooperate with the CHR.[55]

The respite gained through mob action was short-lived. For years, the "no-man's land" of light industry between 63rd and 67th streets acted as a physical and psychological buffer between the Black Belt to the north and Park Manor to the south. The railroad lines atop high embankments seemed to reinforce the geographical barriers separating the black metropolis from the white.[56] By the late 1940s, however, a virtual guerrilla war raged between 67th and 71st streets as increasing numbers of blacks moved into the area.[57] During 1947, blacks occupied four pieces of property in this section and each acquisition produced hostile crowd demonstrations. More blacks entered the community the succeeding year, and violent incidents were reported in February, May, and June. Arson, vandalism, and even a random shotgun blast were used in the unsuccessful attempt to drive the "invaders" out. Police protection, as between 1917 and 1921, proved ineffective, and the repeated suspension of officers for "inattention to duty" neither saved black property nor improved the department's arrest record. Blacks in one home that had been attacked on seven different occasions finally armed themselves and drove off later assailants with gunfire. By August 1948, thirty-five additional pieces of property had changed hands, and the CHR reported that black families were entering the area at the rate of three to four per week. They also noted that the incidence of violence had "risen sharply." With the newcomers firmly entrenched in the area, though, white resistance was reduced to hit-and-run attacks on residences occupied by blacks or those thought to be in the process of transition.[58]

The worst of the Park Manor violence erupted when the 71st Street border was trespassed. On July 25, 1949, a crowd of at least 2,000 descended upon the two-flat bought by Roscoe Johnson at 7153 St. Lawrence. Although police prevented the crowd from entering the building, they failed to disperse it and permitted white protestors to remain across the street. "We barricaded the doors with furniture and put a mattress behind it," Mrs. Ethel Johnson recalled. "We crawled around on our hands and knees when the missiles started coming in through the windows.... Then they started to throw gasoline-soaked rags stuck in pop bottles. They also threw flares and torches. As fast as they came in either the fireman or the policeman would step in to put them out. They were in and out of the house all the time. . . . The crowds didn't leave . . . until daybreak." The next day a CHR official reported that "all of the front windows with the exception of a few basement windows had been broken, and the brick front of the house was scarred and pitted by the numerous bricks thrown against it." On succeeding nights the police cordoned off the area extending two blocks on either side of St. Lawrence between 71st and 73rd streets.[59]

This incident may have served as a turning point for the community. Until late 1949, black admission to Park Manor was financed by individual owners or black investment sources. Soon thereafter, the First Federal Savings and Loan Association and the Chicago City Bank decided the neighborhood was "gone" and became "major lenders" for blacks entering Park Manor. This change of policy on the part of large lending institutions accelerated the process of succession. "It has become easier to move out of Park Manor than it has to stay," one white resident decided. "We cannot get mortgages in the area and all day real estate men call us up and want to know if we would like to sell, and of course it is always to Negroes."[60] By late 1953, Urban League field representatives reported that the area from 67th to 80th street (between State and Cottage Grove) was 70% to 80% black, with most of the white population concentrated on the community's southern periphery below 75th Street. Most of the remaining whites resisted the league's efforts to organize block clubs, as they "said their property was for sale or that they were moving." Having lost the war, most survivors preferred an orderly retreat.[61]

The diehard white resistance, under the leadership of Joseph Beauharnais, coalesced in the White Circle League. Created in the wake of the July 1949 riot, the league's primary purpose was to "keep white neighborhoods free from negroes." Beauharnais and his cohorts entertained pretensions of getting 1 million Chicago whites to join their ranks, but their main area of concentration was always Park Manor, their point of origin. By the summer of 1950, liberal observers commented on the existence of a "well-knit organization in this area with the ability to put people quickly on the street to form crowds." It was, they noted, "locally generated pressure," with no evidence of outside participation. There were a few final Park Manor flare-ups in 1949 and 1950, but the violent struggle for the community came to a rapid conclusion after the lending institutions assured the transition of the area. The later outbursts lacked both the strength and the significance of those occurring when the future of the community was in doubt.[62]

The housing riots at Airport Homes, Fernwood Homes, Park Manor, and Englewood presented the CHR and the press with the problem of reporting large-scale racial incidents in an "unsensational" manner. The lines of cooperation in such emergency situations were quickly drawn during the first major disorder. When violence broke out at the Airport Homes, Thomas Wright, having secured Mayor Kelly's permission, asked the city's editors to avoid the use of "inflammatory pictures and interpretations." Each of the newspapers, Wright reported, "immediately agreed" to cooperate. Several short stories on the incident appeared, with the *Tribune* providing the most extensive coverage; the *Daily News* ignored the incident entirely. The CHR concluded that "the newspaper handling of racial matters was lifted to a new level through the emergency at Airport Homes."[63]

Although the Airport Homes rioting was, as the *Defender* phrased it, Chicago's "worst instance of race inspired violence in nearly 30 years," it was not nearly as serious as most of the later episodes. Its crowds were probably the smallest of all the major riots, and, like Cicero, they concerned themselves primarily with property destruction. Yet, of all the disorders, the Airport Homes incident received the most extensive coverage. As the rioting became more serious, and officials became more alarmed, the CHR and the press exerted tighter control over the flow of information and the reports of interracial conflict grew scantier as the violence escalated.

The coverage afforded the Fernwood Homes disturbances exemplified the treatment given serious disorders. During the first night of rioting, Thomas Wright and Homer Jack met with city editors and carefully delineated the three stages of reporting that they felt should be used. The first stage, to be implemented while the disorder was in progress, consisted of "circumspect and nonsensational coverage of the event" and the total omission of photographs. The second and third phases of riot coverage included "emphasizing the constructive action taken by police," the reproduction of public statements issued by "responsible civic organizations," and editorials denouncing the outbreak of violence. "In every case the newspaper representatives showed understanding and [a] sense of responsibility," Wright noted, "and agreed to cooperate fully." The result was, by the CHR's own admission, the appearance of "very limited" reports in the *Times* and *Tribune*. The *Tribune*, moreover, simply referred to the incident as a "demonstration" and gave no hint that serious violence was taking place. The *Daily News* and the *Sun*, showing excessive restraint, made no reference to the riot at all while it was in progress; a few short and oblique stories appeared well after the disturbance had ended.[64]

The later incidents in Park Manor and Englewood received essentially the same coverage. Although stories concerning these disturbances were more numerous, they were still abbreviated and, more important, extremely difficult to locate in the dailies' interior pages.[65] Moreover, it was in connection with these disruptions that the first complaints were heard concerning the CHR's influence with the press. Several local labor leaders criticized the CHR's "hush-hush" policy as "an attempt to cover up for white mobsters." The *Defender* also voiced objections. "As soon as a mob forms, we are called by some official and asked to keep the facts out of the newspaper," its editors declared. "Lawless elements are encouraged by a say-nothing, do-nothing policy," they concluded.[66]

Yet, despite its protestations, the *Defender*, as well as the white press, cooperated with the CHR. Publisher John Sengstacke met personally with Thomas Wright and Mayor Martin Kennelly during the Fernwood riots and submitted, prior to publication, a list of those injured. Sengstacke also prepared a calming statement to his readers that appeared in the *Defender* as Kennelly's own. If the black press chafed under CHR policy, its disputations were still those of the loyal opposition.[67]

Dissatisfaction with the press's handling of racial disorders culminated in the creation of the Committee to End Mob Violence. Conceived in the aftermath of the Peoria Street incident, Chicago Urban League Executive Secretary Sidney Williams was the driving force behind the CEMV. "For too many years we Negro citizens have been plagued by the 'hush-hush' policy of our daily newspapers – a policy which was sponsored by a few of the 'responsible' human relations organizations," Williams wrote Homer Jack. It was a "shameful failure," rather than a sign of efficiency, that "no Chicago newspaper has carried an adequate account of the many serious incidents of the past few years." Perhaps worst of all, as Williams accurately noted, the practice had proved a "colossal failure." The riots continued unabated and the "conspiracy of silence" simply permitted the city administration to "continue in its ineptitude." The necessary result, Williams believed, was a black initiative to publicize the situation and thus mobilize public opinion on the side of law and order.[68]

Williams was not alone in his feelings. Concerned whites such as Alderman Robert Merriam, Louis Wirth, and community organizer Saul Alinsky attended CEMV meetings and worked with the black leadership to produce a "Statement of Principles," which focused considerable attention on the proper press treatment of interracial discord. Largely following suggestions made by Louis Wirth, the "Statement of Principles" criticized the coverage given earlier riots. The CEMV pointed out, for example, the futility of "editorializing without previous...news reporting." "Unless people have an adequate background of news," the conference noted a bit sarcastically, "they cannnot understand or respond to editorials."[69]

In defense of his agency, Thomas Wright dredged up the now stale memories of 1919 and the Detroit riot of 1943.[70] Such arguments still attracted powerful adherents. The Chicago chapter of the American Civil Liberties Union was not at all disturbed that the "press was asked, and voluntarily agreed, to be extremely cautious in handling...news" of racial disturbances. Had riotous disorders been "played up" by the press, its officials asserted, "thousands of people would likely have jammed the area [in turmoil] and greatly enhanced the possibility of a full-fledged race riot." The ACLU had "only praise for the intelligent way in which they responded" in emergency situations.[71] Unable to make the distinction between informing the public and "sensationalizing" inflammatory events, the CHR's policy of "circumspection" remained in effect until the Cicero riot of 1951.

When Cicero exploded, the Chicago press hesitated before granting it massive exposure. The riot occurred July 10-12, 1951, and, for the first two days, the Chicago dailies remained silent. It was not until the afternoon of July 12 that the *Daily News* responded with page-one headlines, photographs, and two full pages of articles. The *Tribune* and the *Sun-Times* waited until the morning of July 13 before giving the disorder the same extensive treatment.[72] The city's editors apparently had intended to treat this riot as it had the others, but several novel factors rendered a continued silence impossible. First, when Cicero's fifty-man police force lost control of the situation and Chicago's police, fearful of additional disorders in the city, refused to divert their own forces to lend aid, the suburb had no choice but to appeal for the National Guard. Chicago, in contrast, had been able to dispatch more than 1,000 of its own police to calm far more serious disorders without asking for outside help. Thus the city had been able to avoid publicity arising from the presence of bayonet-armed troops. Also of critical importance, the Cicero riot was the first racial disturbance covered by local television. Most Chicagoans viewed the uprising in Cicero from the comfort of their living rooms before they read about it in the papers.[73] Whereas the people on the North Side of Chicago had no knowledge of events in Fernwood, Park Manor, or Englewood, the intrusion of the electronic media exposed a serious, but decidedly second-rate, disturbance for the world to see.

The press silence of the late 1940s relegated Chicago's housing riots to a carefully hidden niche in a largely forgotten past. Only one incident, that at the Trumbull Park Homes, qualified as a "housing" riot in the post-Cicero era. Such disturbances, linked to a phase of the geographical redistribution of races in the city, passed from the scene just as they were exposed to public view. The Cicero eruption was both the world debut and the dramatic climax to the era of large-scale housing disorders. Even the number of individual hit-and-run attacks dropped precipitously in the early 1950s. By mid-1952 knowledgeable commentators were referring to the "almost spectacular decline" in such incidents.[74] As the flow of black population into previously restricted areas increased, the CHR recorded a decrease in the number of black families requesting police protection. It was apparent that once the pattern of resistance in a given area was broken, and the first few black families were safely entrenched, subsequent move-ins were quickly and peacefully conducted.[75] Although housing assaults did not end (the Oak Park home of Dr. Percy Julian, Chicagoan of the Year for 1949, suffered both bomb and arson attacks in 1950 and 1951), their relative infrequency made them much less a problem than they had been in the immediate aftermath of World War II.[76]

The violence was not ending, however. Just as the postwar pattern of disorder shifted from individual to collective onslaughts, now a third phase of Chicago's interracial conflict emerged. With the growing black population consolidating its position in recently acquired territory, new disputes arose over the perquisites of neighborhood control. Battles over the use of schools, playgrounds, parks, and beaches became the dominant mode of interracial conflict in the 1950s.[77] Although these incidents occurred less often than did the housing riots of the 1940s, they involved interpersonal confrontations and necessarily included attacks on people rather than property.[78]

Interracial violence at parks and beaches was rare between 1940 and 1950. With Chicago's 1919 experience and Detroit's horrible 1943 example before them, many in the mid-1940s "believed that we would experience racial clashes at those points where the races come together in large numbers, such as public parks, bathing beaches, sports events, dance halls, bowling alleys, street car transfer points, etc." Having survived the summer of 1943 unscathed, these observers indulged in a little civic gloating and boasted that "Chicago can well be proud of the fact that no such clashes occurred here."[79] This unexpected calm continued for most of the decade. Three "minor incidents" ruffled the parks' tranquility "for the first time in three years" in 1946, but "quick and decisive actions" on the part of officials rapidly restored order. Such disturbances again "dwindled to a minimum," and in 1951 the CHR could find "only one significant incident of this sort."[80]

The one exception to this placid picture reveals the pattern of disorder subsequently followed by much of the South Side during the 1950s. Situated wholly within the white community of East Chesterfield, Tuley Park bordered the relatively well-to-do black enclave of West Chesterfield.[81] Racial tension had been high in the area since 1944 when the Chicago Housing Authority located 250 low-income units in the black section.[82] After the war, developments in Park Manor (barely 2 miles to the north) and the increased black demand for the use of local facilities multiplied the sources of friction. Finally, on September 27, 1946, a crowd of 100 to 150 whites used sticks and bricks to drive a black football team out of the park.[83]

The sequence of events was apparent: Black entry to the area, in significant numbers, led to clashes over the use of public conveniences. When isolated or few in number, blacks often chose not to enter "hostile" territory, or when they did, their presence was not deemed threatening. The change in residential patterns, however, clearly antedated the confrontation over local facilities, and it was also obvious that blacks had to be present in substantial strength before a challenge could be mounted.[84] From the black perspective, the question was simply one of fair play. Did they or did they not have the right to use the park nearest their homes? From the whites' vantage point, the issue was one of community control. Given their view of such racial issues as "all or nothing" propositions, "integration" was a meaningless concept to them. Black access to community facilities simply meant that they would soon "take over" the neighborhood and drive the whites out. Consequently, the forceful reassertion of Tuley Park as "white property" in 1946 went undisputed for four additional years. Fresh attempts to open the park for black use in 1950 were met by a fresh outburst of violence. Individuals of both races were assaulted in aggressive and retaliatory attacks, and black access to the park could only be secured under police guard.[85]

Black bids for the unrestricted use of parks, schools, stores, churches, and commercial recreational facilities invariably followed the entry

into previously all-white areas. Students in the transition neighborhoods surrounding Englewood and Calumet High Schools went on
"hate strikes" in 1945 to protest the shifting racial balances in their
schools.[86] Stores in Englewood also resisted black patronage in an
attempt to placate their white clientele.[87] Establishments such as the
White City Roller Rink at 63rd and South Parkway, the Trianon
Ballroom on Cottage Grove near 62nd, and the Metropole Theater in
Bridgeport, especially vulnerable to the organized challenges of civil
rights groups, similarly resisted the black "intrusion." The outcomes
of these confrontations were mixed. Blacks gained entry to the White
City Roller Rink, re-segregated the Trianon (only a "sprinkling" of
whites patronized it after blacks gained access to it), and were sent
flying back "across Wentworth" from the Metropole Theater.[88]

Always, however, the worst violence occurred when the use of
public parks and beaches was contested. The city's Southeast Side
was particularly hard hit by disturbances at public recreational facilities in the 1950s and early 1960s. Repeated troubles occurred at
Rainbow Beach, Bessemer Park, and Calumet Park.[89] There had long
been a small black enclave near the steel mills of South Chicago and
its families had made occasional use of the area's public facilities
before the mid-1950s. Friction increased, however, as the Black Belt
edged nearer. After a black soldier raped and killed a white girl in
Calumet Park in 1955, tension neared the breaking point. For a short
time local blacks considered Calumet Park and the Bessemer Park
swimming pools "out of bounds," and mothers sent their children
to the 63rd Street Beach for a safe swim. When blacks again attempted to use these parks in the late 1950s and early 1960s, trouble
developed. Changing residential patterns merged with the growing
civil-rights movement to produce a "wade-in" at Rainbow Beach on
July 5, 1961. A crowd of 1,000 whites mobbed and stoned the bathers
and thus assured themselves of an entire summer of similar demonstrations.[90] Crowds including as many as 2,000 persons harassed
blacks as they entered and left Bessemer Park.[91] The most serious
rioting, however, erupted at Calumet Park during the summer of
1957.[92]

On July 28, 1957, a crowd of 6,000 to 7,000 whites attacked 100
black picnickers who occupied a portion of the park that had previously been "reserved" for whites. Though blacks had used the
park in the past, they were customarily restricted to certain portions
of it. More than 500 police were needed to calm the area after two
days of disturbances. On the first day alone at least forty-seven
persons were injured and sixty to seventy cars stoned. Rioters spilled

out of the park, attacked police officers attempting arrests, and, eventually, placed the entire area between the nearby Trumbull Park Homes and Calumet Park in turmoil. Police squadrons had to form a "flying wedge" to break through the crowd to rescue blacks besieged in the park.[93]

News coverage of this event was far more extensive than that granted the earlier housing riots. The CHR, in fact, used the press's response to this incident to clear itself of censorship charges made years before. The commission subsequently gathered all published references to the episode and circulated them in mimeographed form to show the extent of the coverage. Respected local sources, such as the *New World* (the organ of the Archdiocese of Chicago) and the *Daily Calumet*, supplemented the metropolitan dailies and replaced their earlier silence with denunciations.[94] Southeast Side whites were "very much hurt by the adverse criticism" of the press. Singled out for exposure, in much the same way as those in Cicero were, local whites were perceived by outsiders as atavistic freaks whose bigotry was surpassed only by their brutality.[95]

A sympathetic white lawyer noted the melancholy choices available to Southeast Side residents. Referring to three neighborhoods that were overwhelmed by black territorial expansion and one that was not, he told residents that their area could "become another Englewood, Chatham, Woodlawn, or hypocritical Hyde Park. Or it can become a hated but happy community."[96] Defensive whites subsequently sought an "honorable" solution through which they could retain control of their community. The East Side Civic League was formed in the aftermath of the Calumet Park riot to prevent through "nonviolent means" the moving of "Negroes into the far southeast side of Chicago." "Their aim," a liberal infiltrator informed the American Friends Service Committee, "is to become a respected and respectable organization."[97] The league's leadership took options on all vacant land in the area and sought to impress "the political leadership in Chicago" with their potential power. Within their community, they hoped to provide individuals with a strong sense of neighborhood identification and thus prevent the sale of homes to "undesirables." Should these measures fail, however, it was clear that at least some residents would be willing to accept the hate attendant upon their "happiness." When an observer asked for an explanation of the league's nebulous determination to "apply pressure when and if necessary," he was quietly told of two situations: A house had been burned down and a homeowner who entertained black guests had been beaten and forced to move.[98]

More than a string of isolated incidents, the violence that gripped Chicago in the postwar years was an ordeal by fire as the spatial accommodation of the races underwent adjustment. The housing riots, which were kept from the public eye, and the battles over public facilities, which often were not, were integral parts of a single process. The redefinition of racial borders necessarily entailed the struggle for public facilities, "turf," as well as homes. The focusing of attention on a few isolated instances of violence obscured the larger chain of events and permitted the city the luxury of condemning the wicked while assuming that racial conflict was a local, rather than metropolitan, problem. But the sheer force of numbers was compelling the alteration of heretofore rigid racial boundaries. It proved to be a painful procedure.

3   Friends, neighbors, and rioters

This crowd...is all from the mill and most of them live in the vicinity and they are mixed nationalities but they are not the kind that would belong to any organization. Just hard workers and hard drinkers and with out very much education.

> Operative L. G., Confidential Report, June 15,
> 1954, American Civil Liberties Union – Illinois
> Division Papers, the Department of Special
> Collections, University of Chicago Library

Though this violence has been the work of a few, it has been silently approved, when not sanctioned and abetted by the multitudes...And the multitudes...include too many churchmen, too many aldermen, too many community leaders.

> The Reverend Daniel M. Cantwell, "Race
> Relations and Housing," address to the
> National Association of Housing Officials,
> Regional Conference, April 21, 1948,
> Daniel M. Cantwell Papers, Chicago Historical
> Society

The race war that flared so dramatically in Chicago during the "Red Summer" of 1919 was a "struggle for living space" in the broadest sense.[1] It was symbolic of the determination of Chicago's whites to fix the political, economic, and territorial position of the city's enlarged black population. Following hard upon a bitter and racially divisive mayoral campaign, the riot swept through the stockyards and its surrounding neighborhood even as ethnic gangs swarmed and attacked black homes scattered outside what had already become prescribed racial borders. As such, it was a "communal" riot par excellence, to borrow Morris Janowitz's phrase; "an interracial clash, an ecologically based struggle at the boundaries of the expanding black neighborhoods," the Chicago riot served as a model for Janowitz's typology.[2]

But the "communal" riots linked to the initial era of ghetto formation did not disappear as quickly or completely as supposed. Indeed, the assaults upon blacks who encroached upon white "turf" by ethnic gangs were a distinguishing feature of the 1919 disorder but hardly restricted to such large-scale outbursts. The opportunity afforded by the riot to attack black homes simply intensified the wave of such onslaughts, which began in 1917 and continued for another two years after the riot had ended. Similarly, despite the shift to "commodity" style rioting, which Janowitz detected beginning in World War II, the housing battles persisted throughout the 1940s and 1950s. The ethnic crowds that were found restricting black residential mobility early in the twentieth century by Philpott, Osofsky, and Kusmer in Chicago, New York, and Cleveland, respectively, were matched, in Chicago at least, by similarly composed but even larger mobs in the post–World War II period.[3]

These more recent outbreaks were, moreover, "communal" riots in another sense as well. Not only were they a form of "ecological warfare" that represented a "direct struggle between the residents of white and Negro areas," but the participants in these riots were a cross section of their respective communities.[4] Active mob members, almost inevitably residents of the areas involved, were demographically, ethnically, and economically representative of their neighborhoods. Local by nature, these housing riots saw individual communities, one by one, call forth their own "defenders" as the tide of racial succession lapped at their borders.

Still, if prominent features of 1919-style rioting were apparent in the 1950s, the failure of such incidents to provoke widespread bloodshed remains an obvious difference in the two periods. Janowitz speculated that technologically advanced and more efficient police contained these incidents and prevented larger outbursts after World War II. A close examination of the Chicago disturbances, however, reveals that police performance was inconsistent at best and that the extent and duration of rioting was keyed to the achievement of the rioters' goals. It was the self-motivated and disciplined behavior of the mob, more than the forces of social control, that dictated the nature and scope of the violence.[5]

The first step in any analysis of crowd behavior is the identification of the rioters. Arrest lists compiled for five of Chicago's worst postwar riots demonstrate clearly that the participants in "contested area" riots were, with few exceptions, residents of the territory involved.[6] Of the total of 319 persons arrested for whom addresses were found, 78.7% lived within 1 mile of their respective riot areas and 87.5% lived within 1½ miles; only 22 of the arrestees lived more than 3 miles

Table 2. Residential proximity of arrestees to riot areas by number and percentage

Distance	Fernwood[a] Park	Park[b] Manor	Englewood[c]	Trumbull[d] Park	Calumet[e] Park	Total
0–4 blocks[f]	89 (78.8)	9 (50.0)	10 (34.5)	76 (70.4)	35 (68.6)	219 (68.7)
5–8 blocks	13 (11.5)	3 (16.6)	3 (10.3)	5 (4.6)	8 (15.7)	32 (10.0)
9–12 blocks	4 (3.5)	2 (11.1)	9 (31.0)	12 (11.1)	1 (2.0)	28 (8.8)
13–16 blocks	0 (0.0)	1 (5.5)	4 (13.8)	3 (2.8)	1 (2.0)	9 (2.8)
17–24 blocks	2 (1.8)	3 (16.6)	2 (6.9)	2 (1.9)	0 (0.0)	9 (2.8)
25–32 blocks	2 (1.8)	0 (0.0)	1 (3.4)	3 (2.8)	1 (2.0)	7 (2.2)
Over 32 blocks	3 (2.7)	0 (0.0)	0 (0.0)	7 (6.5)	5 (9.8)	15 (4.7)
Total	113 (100.1)	18 (99.8)	29 (99.9)	108 (100.1)	51 (100.1)	319 (100.0)

[a] Though this riot started at the site of the Fernwood Park Homes, it became a more generalized conflict in which blacks throughout the community were attacked. It was therefore deemed more appropriate to measure the distance between the addresses of the arrestees and the main riot area rather than the distance between those addresses and the project proper. The riot area, defined by the placement of police barricades intended to quarantine the violence, stretched from 95th to 130th and from Michigan Avenue to Vincennes and the city limits.

[b] All addresses were measured from the intersection of 71st and St. Lawrence; the house under attack was located at 7153 St. Lawrence.

[c] This riot was generalized throughout the community. The police, however, did not establish a clearly defined riot area as had been the case at Fernwood. Thus, the intersection of 56th and Peoria, the riot's point of origin, was taken as the base from which to measure between the arrestees' addresses and the scene of the riot. This procedure would, obviously, *overestimate* the distance between the arrestees' homes and the locale of disorder. Those arrested during the first two nights of rioting here were not included as it was impossible to separate rioters from victims on the arrest lists.

[d] The project site was the base from which the rioters' addresses were measured.

[e] This riot began at Calumet Park (95th to 102nd on the lakefront) but spread throughout the area and eventually included disorders at the nearby Trumbull Park Homes. As the Chicago Commission on Human Relations reported numerous related incidents occurring between the park and the CHA project, the area from 95th to 109th and from Lake Michigan and the Indiana state line to Bensley was considered the riot area. All addresses were measured from that base.

[f] Eight blocks are equal to 1 mile.

away. Most notable in this regard was the Fernwood riot, where only 7 of the 113 arrestees lived more than 3 miles away from the officially designated riot area. Moreover, of the 22 "outsiders," 10 came from the Trumbull Park Homes disorders – the only incident covered by television, given national publicity, and of several months' duration. But even during this disturbance, 7 of every 10 rioters arrested lived either within the project or less than a mere four blocks away; 86.1% of those arrested lived within twelve blocks of the project. Despite the television coverage and widespread publicity, the participants in the Trumbull Park Homes uprising conformed to the pattern established by the earlier and lesser-known incidents – a pattern that saw nearly 90% of all rioters living within twelve blocks of their riot scenes (Table 2).

The seeming exceptions to these findings, upon closer examination, proved to be no exceptions at all. The Peoria Street incident in Englewood provides the most illuminating case. At first glance it appears that the rioters in this episode came from all over the city. Nearly a quarter of the 66 arrestees lived more than 4 miles away from the house whose rumored sale precipitated the riot (Table 3). A look at the conduct of the police during the riot, however, reveals that for the first two nights of the disorder police officers sympathetic to the mob arrested victims as well as attackers. It was only on the third night, after the Commission on Human Relations complained about police actions, that the authorities cracked down on the rioters rather than on their prey.[7] A comparison of arrests made the third night with those made the previous evenings discloses the distribution anticipated if local residents were, indeed, the rioters. Three out of four arrested on the third night lived within twelve blocks of the riot scene, and all sixteen of those living more than 4 miles away were arrested during the first two nights and probably were victims.[8]

A similar situation prevailed during the Cicero riot. After that disturbance, local residents scanned the names of those arrested during the disorder and proclaimed with righteous indignation that outsiders dominated the mob. What they failed to note, however, was that no arrests were made during the first two days of rioting and that none was made on the third day until "late night" when the National Guard arrived. This meant, commented Edward H. Meyerding of the American Civil Liberties Union, "that no arrests were made during the entire period when the destruction of the building [occupied by blacks] was being accomplished." The ACLU had its own observers who were "native to that section," and it was

Table 3. *Residential proximity of arrestees to riot area at 56th and Peoria (Englewood) by time of arrest*

Distance	All three nights	First two nights	Third night
0–4 blocks	19	9	10
5–8 blocks	6	3	3
9–12 blocks	9	0	9
13–16 blocks	5	1	4
17–24 blocks	8	6	2
25–32 blocks	3	2	1
Over 32 blocks	16	16	0
Total	66	37	29

their view that "the riot was begun and carried out in the first two days almost exclusively by persons from the immediate vicinity." "It was not until the third night, after the riot had hit the front pages of the newspapers," Meyerding concluded, "that outsiders came in." It was this development that fostered the growth of the "myth about 'outsiders' " and permitted the people of Cicero to "salve their consciences...instead of facing up to the immorality of their community."[9]

The one virulently racist organization active during these years that could, perhaps, have instigated some violence was notable only for its weakness. Significantly, the White Circle League was founded in Park Manor *after* that area's worst riot. Moreover, both the American Civil Liberties Union and the Chicago Commission on Human Relations kept a wary eye on the league's activities, and neither was particularly frightened by what it saw. So evident was the organization's weakness that the ACLU heaped insult upon injury by attempting to restrain legal action taken against the league. "It is often better tactics," the ACLU declared, "to move carefully and quietly and not build the other man's organization by giving him publicity." The league was a nuisance to be ignored, not a dangerous enemy to be confronted.[10]

The central fact that emerges from this analysis is the prominence of local defenders in each of the rioting communities. Although there were widely shared assumptions regarding the undesirability of racial change, the various neighborhoods responded to it independently, reacting only as it actually touched them. The housing battles, the struggles over "turf," were local by nature. Black residence in a particular home or use of a certain park were not issues around which a city of millions could be mobilized. They did, however, have great impact on those who perceived themselves to be immediately threatened. That a wave of such disorders occurred testified only to the magnitude of the changes sweeping the city. The typical Chicago housing riot was thus a "communal" riot in the most literal sense of the term. Each community rose up in its own "defense" and proceeded to fight for its self-defined interests.

The truly communal nature of these scattered uprisings is further revealed by the representative character of the mobs involved. Although arrest lists supply valuable information regarding the most visibly active participants, they tend to emphasize the role played by young males – that social segment from which the "soldiers" in any battle are traditionally drawn. Eyewitness accounts of these housing riots, however, bring into clear relief not only the supportive roles played by older males but also the truly instrumental part played by women. The division of labor that, more or less, naturally appeared during these disturbances simply placed the young males in the greatest danger of arrest. The relative absence of women, children, and older men from such lists cannot be interpreted as evidence of their nonparticipation.[11] Indeed, the typical housing riot was a complex communal endeavor launched by a demographic cross section of the area involved. The violent ones who were most often arrested were the community's representatives, not, as was believed by those denouncing the criminality of "hoodlums," its abberrations.

The most destructive mobs, those attacking persons as well as property, had the youngest arrestees. The average age of 44 persons arrested during the 1957 Calumet Park riot was 22.6 years and the average age of those arrested on the third night of the Peoria Street disturbance was only 20 years.[12] The Fernwood riot, however, though as violent as any of the others, had rioters who averaged a mature 27.8 years of age. More important, fully 34.3% of the 108 arrested rioters for whom information is available were 30 or more years of age. Lending additional weight to the adult-role argument is the fact that 16.6% of the Fernwood rioters were over 40 and that eight of those (8.3%) were at least 50 years old.

The more typical housing mobs, those that confined themselves largely to harassment and property destruction, had an age distribution similar to that of the Fernwood crowd. The average age of those arrested in the 1949 Park Manor disturbances was 27.1 years. Even if one assumes that the four unidentified "juveniles" arrested there were each only 16 years old, the average age of the Park Manor rioters is still 25 years. Over a fifth (22.2%) were at least 40 and a third (33.3%) were more than 30. The same apparently holds true for the Trumbull Park Homes incident. Although the incomplete data suggest caution (ages were found for only 29 of 109 rioters), these arrestees had an average age of 33.3 years. Moreover, nearly half of the rioters in South Deering (48.3%) were over 30 years of age and more than a quarter of them (27.6%) were over 40.

Eyewitness accounts of these disorders provide further proof that they were not merely the productions of uncontrollable youths. The people in Park Manor, for example, displayed their ingenuity as police developed techniques for keeping the streets and walks clear in front of the homes of unwanted black neighbors. Families threw open their front porches and yards, sometimes provided refreshments, and furnished legal sanctuary for their friends who, in a grim parody of a community sing, hurled racial epithets along with an occasional rock or bottle at the neighborhood's "intruders." In one 1950 Park Manor disorder, CHR observers reported that "about 150 people had gathered on the porches and in the yards" of five homes within shouting distance of a new black resident. From there, "shouting and heckling... became organized" and cries of "bring out Bushman," "get the rope," and "string him up" could be heard. Songs such as "Old Black Joe" and "Carry Me Back to Old Virginny" were sung in derision.[13]

The Cicero riot was a communal endeavor of a similar sort. One observer reported that "boys and girls" aged 12 to their "late teens" gathered rocks and broke bricks for the older boys to throw. "There was a great deal of camaraderie and spirit of fun throughout this whole group," the observer wrote, "and it was apparent that all were having a good time." Included within that group were adults who encouraged their children's actions and whose approval took the form of "urging and initiating the aggression."[14]

The same set of circumstances prevailed in other riots as well. The crowds at the Airport Homes and 71st and St. Lawrence were also composed of "men and women, boys and girls of all ages." At 56th and Peoria "many babes in arms, children just able to walk at [their] mother's sides, sub-teenagers, plus middle aged and older people" were seen in the mob. The older men, moreover, were observed providing the missiles thrown by young boys. Trumbull Park rioters fleeing the police routinely sought refuge, as did their counterparts in Park Manor, in the homes of neighbors. CHA officials considered it noteworthy when such refuge was refused.[15]

The broad community participation characteristic of most of these incidents, however, is best demonstrated by the roles played by women. It was a woman who first alerted the Englewood community to the presence of blacks in the home at 56th and Peoria, and adult women, no less than youngsters, were seen arming Cicero's brick throwers.[16] Women were certainly present, if not prominent, in the yards and porches of Park Manor. In the Airport Homes and the Trumbull Park disorders, though, women demonstrated that they not only supported but at times supplanted men as the most violent antiblack protestors.

At the Airport Homes the CHA tried to move in black veterans during daylight hours when most of the community's men were at work. The task of protesting that development consequently fell to the area's women and older men. Both groups kept up a "constant shouting" as officials tried to escort blacks into the project. One eyewitness felt the crowd was composed of "mostly women" who "booed and hissed...civic leaders, talked with newspaper photographers, and made numerous threats" before the fighting broke out. When the violence did erupt, it was found that "a great many women were in the front ranks of the mob" and that it was they who "began to fight with policemen, kicking and scratching and slapping at them." The police made no arrests but were compelled, the *Tribune* noted with a trace of condescension, to "spank unruly housewives" with their clubs. It proved a dangerous task as one lieutenant was struck on the head by a missile "while preventing a woman from taking away his...club." Thus, although no feminine names graced any police blotters, their protest was duly registered. The next day several appeared at the project, pushing their baby carriages and "carrying sticks and bricks."[17]

Women were equally involved in the Trumbull Park Homes disorders. There, as at the Airport Homes, women carried on alone in the front lines when the community's men were away at work. The women freed neighbors arrested by the police and battled the latter hand-to-hand. One police sergeant had to be hospitalized after being kicked in the groin by a female rioter. The most notable incident, however, came in October 1953 when the CHA again attempted a midweek daylight move-in of new black tenants. The Commission on Human Relations reported that several local women

A policeman seizes a woman protestor at the Airport Homes, 1946. (Photograph courtesy of the *Chicago Tribune*.)

literally hurled themselves, first at a truck loaded with the newcomers' furniture, and later at a new car driven by the head of one Negro family. A gray-haired woman of about 65 fell prostrate in front of the car. . . When the halted car began to inch ahead, the woman clung to its front bumper. Police seized her, and carried her, kicking and fighting, to a curb.

The men of South Deering were not unmoved by that display. At a later fund-raising dinner, the lawyer for the local improvement association paid homage to the three mothers arrested that day and "in tribute to them sang 'Mother Machree.' " It was an accolade that could have been given to the community's women as a group. For the first time, police were forced to arrest women as well as men in significant numbers. Nearly 1 out of every 5 persons (21 out of 109) held by police in connection with these disturbances was female. So startling was this last development that trained observers were moved to comment that the South Deering opposition was "unique" because it was "frequently" led by "older women."[18]

These communal uprisings and their participants were more than demographically representative of their respective areas. They were also expressions of the general feelings of the city's white "ethnics." As native whites and the more mobile descendants of the "old" immigration moved to the city's periphery or its suburbs, the children and grandchildren of predominantly Catholic Irish and southern and eastern European immigrants were left to face a rapidly growing and territorially starved black population. Unable, or simply not wanting, to leave their old neighborhoods, they were reacting against their unwilling transformation into "buffers" between fleeing whites and inner-city blacks. This growing confrontation between "ethnic and black metropolis" is especially evident in the riots occurring during or after 1949; before then, the housing shortage was unrelieved and even those possessing the means and desire to leave the city were left no alternative to racial succession save the physical "defense" of their homes.[19] Consequently, one of the earliest housing riots included substantial representation from the "old" as well as the "new" immigration. Once new housing construction permitted the possibility of flight, however, those who wished to avail themselves of it did so and thus not only left behind those who could not similarly leave but also, in some cases, the very vacancies into which blacks could move.

The impressionistic evidence rendered by knowledgeable observers is notable for the numbing regularity with which the role of the Irish and the "new" immigrant groups in these housing riots is emphasized. The ACLU recorded, for example, that the area around 56th and Peoria was "traditionally Irish." Indeed, the Englewood riot took place in Visitation parish, a neighborhood largely built by Irish stockyard workers whose "Celtic trust in the Most High" was evidenced by the construction of Visitation Church on the southeast corner of 55th and Peoria, only one block away from the riot's point of origin.[20]

If the Irish were singled out in Englewood, the Czechs and Poles were much in evidence in Cicero and Trumbull Park. Our Lady of the Mount parish included the riot area in Cicero and was the "center of Czech social and cultural traditions in the community." One Czech informant in the area said that the "in-group feeling" there was so intense that only twenty-five years before parishioners had held a protest meeting when the first German Catholic family attended services. Early Protestant residents who were not of Czech or Polish descent met with similar suspicion.[21] Other observers pointed to the pride with which "Czech housewives" maintained their homes and the value placed on property by the "Czech people." This combination of factors led a worker for the Catholic Interracial Council to conclude that "property values and Bohemian characteristics are the essential elements of anti-Negro sentiment in Cicero."[22]

In Trumbull Park there was virtual unanimity on the decidedly "ethnic" character of the rioters. Winston Kennedy, manager of the Trumbull Park Housing Project, felt that the "togetherness" of the South Deering community was due to its isolation from other areas, the fact that most of the community's workers toiled in the local steel mills, and that a "majority" of its residents came from southern and eastern European backgrounds.[23] Kennedy was not alone in this perception. When the ACLU sought to infiltrate the area to get inside information as to who was behind the recurring violence, they placed a young Polish-speaking male in one of the steel mills and had him regularly make the rounds of area taverns with his co-workers.[24] The local whites and the police, the two groups in closest touch with the day-to-day events in South Deering, further confirmed the CHA and ACLU views. The former claimed that Poles and Italians were the mainstays of the antiblack resistance, whereas the latter complained of harassment by "damned Polacks."[25]

Most significant, perhaps, was the blacks' awareness of the sources of the most active and violent opposition to their movement. In each of the major riots occurring in the 1950s, black commentators noted repeatedly, and sometimes disparagingly, the ethnic origins of anti-black rioters. Walter White, executive secretary of the NAACP, compared the Cicero crowd to southern lynch mobs and felt that he had never encountered as much "implacable hatred as I found in Cicero." "Some of those with whom I talked," he added, had "such thick Bohemian, German, Polish, or Greek accents that it was not always easy to know what they were saying." "It was appalling," he concluded, "to see and listen to those who were but recently the targets of hate and deprivations, who, beneficiaries of American opportunity, were as virulent as any Mississippian in their willingness to deny a place to live to a member of a race which had preceded them to America by many generations."[26]

Complementary conclusions were drawn by blacks regarding the Trumbull Park Homes disorders, the Calumet Park riot, and lesser 1950s disturbances as well. St. Clair Drake reported on the "vicious and poisonous" propaganda circulating in the neighborhood press serving the Calumet Park area. These local newspapers "boast[ed] that it was Southern and Eastern Europeans who really built this country while Negroes were 'swinging in trees,' 'eating each other.' " This and an examination of the names of the arrested rioters led him to believe they were "immigrants and the children of immigrants."[27] The *Defender* had much the same to say about the Trumbull Park violence and some minor West Side incidents. Crowds screaming in "thick foreign-accent[s]" were denounced, as was the "strange paradox" that saw "foreigners, some of them not yet naturalized, who can scarcely speak English," denying freedom and justice to others even as the immigrants themselves were seeking them. "Evidently the free courses in Americanism which are offered to prospective citizens have failed of their mark," the *Defender* editorialized. "Or perhaps," it concluded even more ominously, "they are taught by people who inject the venom of race prejudice into the bloodstream of the newcomer."[28]

The growing sense of frustration and bitterness felt toward these racially aggressive immigrants was epitomized by Chandler Owen, onetime Socialist and advocate of working-class solidarity, and A. L. Foster of the Urban League. Owen literally urged the adoption of a vigorous deportation campaign as a means of bringing the Trumbull Park violence to an end. Even this Draconian measure, however, was not enough for A. L. Foster. Foster understood that many of the rioters were "first generation Americans who do not fully appreciate the concept of democracy." But this, according to Foster, was no excuse for the "defiance of law and order." If the police failed to protect citizens and their property by "persuasive methods," Foster decreed, they "have no choice but to use their night sticks, tear gas and, in the final analysis, their guns."[29]

Such impressionistic conclusions proved accurate. The names on the arrest lists for the Fernwood riot of 1947, the Park Manor and Englewood riots of 1949, and the Trumbull Park Homes and Calumet Park disorders of the mid-1950s reveal that both concerned observers and the victims of the housing riots had a clear idea who the perpetrators of violence were.[30] Only one of the five mobs studied failed to have a majority of its members drawn from Irish and "new" immigrant stock.[31] As expected, the earliest riot, that at Fernwood, had only 30.4% of its rioters with such surnames. After the Park Manor upheaval, however, the remaining three incidents displayed a mob composition in which approximately 60% or more of those arrested appear to have been of Irish or "new" immigrant ancestry. Descendants of the "old" immigration represented 41.4% of the more than 300 persons for whom ethnicity was determined but only 26.0% of 200 rioters arrested during or after 1949.[32] In contrast, those of Irish or "new" immigrant origins represented 54.0% of all rioters and 67.2% of those arrested in the four later riots (Tables 4–6).

None of the riots was characterized by the exclusive confrontation of a single nationality group defending its ethnically homogeneous territory against a black "invader." Only the riot at 56th and Peoria, where 51.2% of those arrested were apparently Irish, had even a bare majority of its participants drawn from a single group. In each of the other riots a liberal mixture of white "ethnics" seemed content to live in proximity to each other but not in proximity to blacks. Aside from persons with Anglo-sounding surnames, those of Irish and Slavic origin dominated the Calumet Park mob, representing 18.4% and 14.5% of the known rioters. An additional 24.5% of the rioters were either Polish or Italian. At Trumbull Park no group could claim more than 25.5% of the rioters as its own; yet the Irish, Slavs, Italians, and Poles represented at least 67.8% of that incident's known arrestees. Whatever the degree of white interethnic hostility (and it did exist – South Deering's Poles were often heard to complain about the "dago" president of the local improvement association), it was subordinated to an overriding concern. The *Defender* was probably characterizing most housing mobs when it said of one crowd that "although there was no unity in the language backgrounds [of the individuals in the shouting mob], they had a common. . . hatred for Negroes."[33]

The components of these ethnic crowds, moreover, did not appear in random fashion. Linked geographically by their proximity to the omnipresent house, apartment, or park that was about to "change" racially, they were nearly as ethnically representative as they were demographically representative of the communities involved. The Irish predominated in Englewood, with the Germans the next most populous foreign-born group. Together these two nationalities supplied 73.8% of those taken into custody there. Slavs, Poles, and Italians were the most numerous foreign-born groups in the Calu-

Table 4. *Ethnicity of arrestees by percentage and riot*

Ethnicity	Fernwood Park 1947 (N = 113)[a]	Park Manor 1949 (N = 18)	Englewood 1949 (N = 29)	Trumbull Park 1953–4 (N = 109)	Calumet Park 1957 (N = 51)	Total (N = 320)
Anglo	22.4	35.3	16.6	13.6	22.4	19.6
Irish	7.7	25.5	51.2	19.6	18.4	18.2
Slav	4.4	0.0	6.0	25.5	14.5	13.0
Italian	6.5	25.5	0.0	12.0	7.9	9.0
Polish	5.3	0.0	0.0	10.7	16.4	8.2
Southeastern Europe[b]	6.2	0.0	1.2	6.9	4.6	5.5
Dutch	26.3	0.0	0.0	0.0	0.0	9.4
German	14.7	9.8	22.6	5.7	3.3	10.3
Scandinavian	5.6	0.0	0.0	0.3	0.0	2.1
Jewish	0.0	0.0	0.0	0.0	1.3	0.2
Spanish (surnamed)	0.0	3.9	2.4	4.7	10.5	3.7
Other	0.8	0.0	0.0	0.9	0.7	0.7
Total	99.9	100.0	100.0	99.9	100.0	99.9

Note: The percentages were produced by averaging the findings of the three independent surveys of the arrest lists.
[a] *N* represents the number of those arrested.
[b] Persons of uncertain nationality but with obviously southern or eastern European names were included in this category.

Table 5. *"Old" versus "new" immigration by percentage and riot*

	Fernwood Park 1947 (N = 113)[a]	Park Manor 1949 (N = 18)	Englewood 1949 (N = 29)	Trumbull Park 1953–4 (N = 109)	Calumet Park 1957 (N = 51)	Total (N = 320)
Anglo + "old" immigration	69.0	45.1	39.3	19.6	25.7	41.5
Irish + "new" immigration	30.4	51.0	58.3	74.8	61.8	54.0
Spanish (surnamed)	0.0	3.9	2.4	4.7	10.5	3.7
Other	0.6	0.0	0.0	0.9	1.9	0.8
Total	100.0	100.0	100.0	100.0	99.9	100.0

Note: The percentages were produced by averaging the findings of the three independent surveys of the arrest lists.

Table 6. *Ethnicity of arrestees by percentage and time of riot*

	All riots 1947–57 (N = 320)	Four riots after 1947 (N = 207)	Two riots after 1950 (N = 160)
Anglo	19.6	18.0	16.4
Irish	18.2	24.1	19.2
"Old" immigration	21.8	7.9	5.1
"New" immigration	35.7	43.0	51.4
Spanish (surnamed)	3.7	5.8	6.6
Other	1.0	1.2	1.3
Total	100.0	100.0	100.0

Note: The percentages were produced by averaging the findings of the three independent surveys of the arrest lists.

met Park area in 1960; in 1957, those three groups or their descendants provided 47.5% of that community's rioters. The same was true of Trumbull Park. Slavs were both the most numerous and the most arrested foreign-born group in the area; Italians and Poles were not far behind in either category. Most significant of all, perhaps, was the fact that the Roseland community, which supplied most of the Fernwood rioters, was founded by Dutch farmers who were followed into the area by Swedish, German, Italian, and Polish settlers. The Fernwood riot furnished all the Dutch and virtually all the Swedes arrested for racial rioting in Chicago; more than one-third of all the Germans arrested also came from this single disturbance. When the Poles and Italians are added to the other founding groups, fully 58.4% of Roseland's rioters are accounted for.[34]

Another common denominator among riot participants, aside from their geographical affinity, stemmed from the fact that most appeared to be working-class Catholics. Hard data on the occupational levels of individual rioters are scanty, but the information is internally consistent and coincides with general economic descriptions of the neighborhoods involved. An exploratory study obtained by the Catholic Interracial Council surveyed 100 arrests made during the Trumbull Park Homes disturbances but was able to identify only 34 of the rioters by occupation: 7 "laborers," 7 steel mill workers or laborers, 4 carpenters, 3 unemployed, and 1 steel inspector, ironworker, crane operator, machinist, pipe fitter, railroad worker, salesman, mail carrier, stock boy, army private, grocer, filling station employee, and typist. The rioters, who were thus overwhelmingly of working-class origins, came from an area that had 70.2% of its labor force characterized as "laborers, operatives, craftsmen, or kindred workers."[35]

The Calumet Park rioters were largely drawn from the same industrial area that provided many of the Trumbull Park arrestees. Of the 33 Calumet Park rioters identified by occupation (through press accounts), there were 7 laborers, 3 truck drivers, 2 United States marines, 2 clerks, and 1 ironworker, hooker [sic], weighmaster, postal employee, lather, shipping clerk, machinist, student, bricklayer, butcher, mover, steelworker, exterminator, switchman, electrician, technician, pressman, factory worker, and 1 unemployed. Researchers for the Chicago Urban League who attended court proceedings for the Calumet Park rioters further identified those who appeared as "working class people."[36]

If the evidence concerning the occupational status of the rioters is consistent though scanty, that regarding their religion is both consistent and abundant. In virtually every case (the Fernwood riot is again the lone exception), the central role played by Catholics is apparent. Writing in 1949, the Catholic Interracial Council noted that the antiblack housing mobs in Park Manor, Englewood, and other South Side areas included "many...Catholics." At both Airport Homes and Park Manor the Commission on Human Relations brought Catholic clergy to the riot scene in the hope that "the presence of a priest...would tend to calm and restrain the people." In the latter case, moreover, members of the local Catholic hierarchy were persuaded to devote their sermons and parish visits to preserving order as "many Catholics appeared to be participating in the anti-racial disturbances."[37]

Frequently, however, the feelings of parishioners would be such that the local clergy could not effectively oppose them, and, sometimes, they were not disposed to do so. In Englewood, rumors that a home had been sold to blacks preceded the riot at 56th and Peoria by a week. The resulting tension spawned a community gathering in the Visitation parish hall during which a group of block organizations was formed to "keep up the neighborhood." The group was created with the permission of Monsignor Daniel Byrnes whose promise to buy up property "before permitting Negroes to move in" was known throughout the neighborhood. It was this network of block organizations that facilitated the spread of the rumor and mobilized the crowds that touched off the November 1949 riot. "Even though many of the people engaging in the violence were members of the church," a community worker wrote, "the pastor did nothing about it." Members of the Catholic Interracial Council subsequently deplored the "use of parish halls for anti-racial meetings" and wondered if "the Mayor, a Catholic, [could] see the Cardinal about doing something about Monsignor Byrnes."[38]

In both Cicero and Trumbull Park the local Catholic clergy, although not in the vanguard of antiblack protest as in Englewood, did little to ease or fight racial tension. In Cicero, the area around the disputed building was "heavily Catholic," and competent observers identified young members of the crowd as Catholic by the high school sweaters and the religious medals they wore. Cicero's "shame," one writer concluded, belongs "partly to the Catholic schools and churches of the area." In Trumbull Park, the South Deering Improvement Association, which was heavily implicated in the antiblack violence, apparently had more influence on the church than vice versa. The SDIA had "a majority of Catholics among its leadership and members" and its adherents were found "in most of the parish organizations." SDIA members still served as ushers at St. Kevin's two years after the violence began and one was head of the parish's Big Brothers. It was alleged that this latter member was responsible for "getting some of the little brothers in the streets with crow bars to damage cars owned by Negroes." It was nearly another year before SDIA members were "quietly" removed from important parish positions.[39]

The church, and especially the Catholic Interracial Council, were greatly concerned over the prominence and notoriety Catholics earned through their violent actions. The radical press, of course, quickly condemned church involvement in racial disorders. Catholic clergymen, *The Worker* declared, "lent their church in Englewood as a base of racist operations" to the mob at 56th and Peoria and were part of the "alarming rise of fascist activity in this city." But more respectable, and hence more troubling, criticisms were also heard. Homer Jack, a Unitarian minister and co-founder of CORE, similarly attacked Englewood's Catholics and Monsignor Byrnes for sanctioning block organizations designed to keep blacks out of the area and for not "lift[ing] a finger to stop the violence against the Negroes and other people."[40]

Charges leveled in connection with the Trumbull Park Homes disturbances finally prompted stinging rebuttals from concerned Catholics. Lloyd Davis, speaking for the CIC, responded with a litany of Catholic actions intended to alleviate conditions in South Deering.

Foremost among these activities was the distribution of 25,000 pieces of literature "aimed at Catholics" at "local steel plants in the area and through Catholic organizations."[41] He also expressed "deep disappointment" over the South Deering Methodist Church's self-serving declaration that the "bulk" of Trumbull Park's problems was due to the area's Catholics. Davis took exception to "the rather ruthless attack...made upon the Roman Catholic Church" and felt that such endeavors "will not help us to solve the problem."[42]

Even more discouraging, though, was the apparent desertion of liberal "friends" several months after the violence at Trumbull Park began. "I am greatly disturbed," Lloyd Davis wrote, "by what appears to be a failure on the part of some CAD leadership to admit that Catholics have done anything positive in regard to this recent disturbance." The Council Against Discrimination newsletter failed to carry CIC statements or that of any other Catholic organization "along with statements of the Protestant and Jewish Faiths." This seemingly anti-Catholic attitude "has been also noted at several public meetings sponsored by the Council Against Discrimination," Davis added, "and is proving to be most distressing." The defensiveness and acute sensitivity to the charge that racial disorders were a "Catholic problem" were characteristic responses. Liberal Catholic organizations such as the CIC were forced to be defensive because of the patently obvious roles played by Catholics in Chicago's racial disorders. Their sensitivity was further reflected in the steps taken to prevent further occurrences.[43]

After each of the major riots of the 1950s, the CIC implicitly recognized the validity of many of the charges made against their coreligionists by organizing local chapters of the CIC in knee-jerk fashion in riot-torn areas. A lay organization, the CIC was formed in 1945 "to educate and mold public opinion, particularly the opinion of Catholics in matters calling for the application of the Catholic principles of interracial justice."[44] As a citywide organization, it subsequently felt the need to establish local chapters in both Cicero and Calumet Park immediately following their disorders.[45] In response to the Trumbull Park problems, the CIC proposed the establishment of a committee on Catholic Nationality Organizations, which would provide the CIC with an "entree" to the different nationality groups in tension areas.[46] If it was possible to take umbrage at the claim that the riots were exclusively a "Catholic problem," the CIC was still compelled to confront the fact that it was, at the very least, a problem involving many Catholics.

Despite the independent nature of these uprisings, the behavior of the crowds displayed remarkable similarity. First, the spontaneity of the violence was evident in the vast majority of cases. The city's first two postwar riots, those at the temporary veterans' quarters at the Airport Homes and Fernwood Park, erupted without benefit of prior planning despite earlier organized protests against the CHA's nondiscriminatory policies. At the Airport Homes, crowds gathered in front of the apartments on the day they were scheduled to be occupied. Their protests were merely verbal until a truck carrying furniture and two black veterans tried to enter the project. At that point, attention shifted immediately to the blacks and their truck, with the latter being brought under attack. Debris found on the ground and clumps of dirt – hardly the arsenal of a mob that antici-pated violence – served as weapons. The attack on the black vet-erans was solely the result of their untimely appearance in an exceptionally tense situation. It was neither a well-orchestrated nor a previously organized onslaught.[47]

At the Fernwood Park Homes there was no single, clearly defined precipitating incident as there was at the Airport Homes. Augmented police forces and a minor car accident, which diverted attention from the project, permitted the handful of blacks assigned to the apartments to enter peacefully. Violence came only on the following night and appeared, according to official reports, as if by spontane-ous generation from a protesting crowd gathered outside the proj-ect. Several CHR supporters looked upon the mysterious origins of the disturbance with suspicious eyes and charged that there was "a conspiracy involved to deprive Negroes of [their] rights." An inves-tigative report on the riot commissioned by the American Jewish Congress, however, noted that these charges came from those who became "highly emotional in condemning the Fernwood commu-nity" and concluded, after a sober second look, that "nothing ever materialized to substantiate those suspicions of organized planning behind the violence."[48]

Several other riots were even more clearly spontaneous in origin. The Park Manor disorder at 71st and St. Lawrence began after it became evident that the black man moving furniture into a newly purchased home was not a laborer but the new owner. Here, there was no time for planning; people simply filled the streets as "word" passed through the neighborhood. The ensuing rock-throwing at-tack on the home caught even the usually alert Commission on Human Relations by surprise. Through its "listening posts" in the community and associations with local black organizations, the com-mission had always had advance warning when blacks were about to move into an all-white area. This time no one had been fore-warned. The move-in, which had been conducted without advance publicity and as unobtrusively as possible, was followed almost immediately by rioting.[49]

Similarly, the disorders at 56th and Peoria and in Calumet Park flowed from events so patently fortuitous that any attempts to ascribe them to prescient conspirators would appear ludicrous. In the former case a rumor that a house was being "shown" to blacks sparked the violence. Growing out of the mere appearance of blacks in a local home (they were attending a union meeting), the rumor called forth large crowds, which registered a destructive protest against the presence of blacks, Jews, University of Chicago students, communists, and "outsiders" in general.[50] In Calumet Park, the attacks on blacks were precipitated by their use of a portion of the park that had previously been "reserved" for whites. It was an event to which white residents could react but not one that they themselves could have planned.[51]

Only the Trumbull Park Homes rioting, which evolved into a war of attrition intended to harass and drive out black tenants, displayed a considerable degree of organization and planning. It was reported that the South Deering Improvement Association paid for explosives and distributed them to the "kids" of the area through stores operated by association members. The local youths detonated the home-made bombs to terrorize blacks "when they [received] the orders from these store keepers."[52] But even here the origin of the disturbances was spontaneous. The belated discovery that a black woman had "passed" for white in applying for a Trumbull Park apartment prompted the first rock- and bottle-throwing mobs. Only later, after the situation had become a test of wills between the community and the CHA, did the local residents, aided by the South Deering Improvement Association, plan, coordinate, and organize their violent activities.[53]

The only crowd organization evident in the vast majority of cases was, consequently, of an ad hoc nature. Victims of the Englewood mob were convinced of the "highly organized" character of the aggressors because the mob "spotted 'outsiders' immediately." However, an experienced CHR observer felt the crowd was "completely disorganized." There was "no plan," he felt, "no prior collaboration except in small groups of 5 or 8."[54] Other witnesses similarly concluded that the 71st Street group operated "without apparent organization." A report filed on the Cicero crowd at work characterized most housing mobs:

> A group of youths...will follow one youth who is the biggest, has the loudest voice, and is the most daring. That, of course, will give rise to some kind of organization, such as a plan to go through an alley-way in order to skirt the police line, or something similar. There was that kind of planning but that is somewhat different from some of the allegations that have been made.[55]

This was the sort of organization and leadership, the report surmised, that "invariably comes from these mob situations."[56] The evidence that prompted the Englewood victims to charge "conspiracy" was proof only of the mob's purposefulness, not of its prior organization.

Indeed, the absence of actual planning in nearly every case did not mean that the actions of those engaged in the violence were chaotic or uncontrolled. In terms of target selection, the housing riots were models of limited, purposeful violence. The crowd at the Airport Homes, for example, displayed considerable discrimination as the units occupied by blacks, the trucks moving their furniture, and cars belonging to blacks and city officials were attacked. The extreme selectivity of the West Lawn residents was shown when they overturned and looted one official's car even though it was parked several blocks away – no other property nearby was damaged. The police also came under attack, but this was due to their efforts to protect the blacks and their subsequent placement between the crowd and the objects of its anger.[57] The police became a target of the Fernwood crowd under similar conditions, and, in this later riot, assaults on nearby black motorists were initially conceived as a tactic to get the police away from the project. An eyewitness to the episode described the scene:

> One of the agitators in the mob yelled that if they could stop traffic, the cops would have to straighten it out, at which time the crowd could break through the weakened police lines and rush the project. So the traffic was impeded. Then a boy shouted "Nigger, Nigger." A stone flew, a safety-glass window crunched. And there started a bloody game of "bash their dirty brains in" which continued unchecked for almost 20 minutes. Every Negro driver was attacked.[58]

The Park Manor and Cicero rioters were no less discriminating in their choice of targets. The main objective of the July 1949 Park Manor mob was the first home bought by blacks in the area south of 71st Street – a street that had been considered a tentative boundary in a changing community. Secondary targets included those homes owned by blacks in the already changing area north of 71st Street. In

Whites overturn a car belonging to a black at the Airport Homes, 1946. (Photograph courtesy of the *Chicago Tribune*.)

Cicero, the crowd's sole target was the building in which the suburb's new black tenants were to move, a building that the landlord, after a dispute with her tenants, had threatened to open to blacks.[59]

Most notable, perhaps, was the generally limited nature of the violence involved. In Park Manor, as at the Airport Homes, the violence was never random, and despite the presence of the southern border of the Black Belt only five blocks away, there was no assault upon black individuals or forays into the district by white gangs.[60] In Cicero the crowd was content to merely "pull down" the building that threatened the homogeneity of the community. Indeed, the control of the typical housing mob was such that it asserted itself even when the opportunity for greater violence was present. In a Bridgeport incident, crowds gathered outside a home rumored sold to blacks and attacked it while less than a quarter block away blacks strolled by en route to a White Sox ball game at Comiskey Park. Black transients posed no threat to the residents,

Broken windows and trees mark the building assaulted by a Cicero mob, 1951. Authorities flooded the lot in the foreground after the initial rioting to control later crowds. (© *Chicago Sun-Times*, 1951. Photograph reprinted with permission.)

though, and were ignored; it was their permanent presence in the area, albeit only rumored, that sparked, but also limited, the mob's action.[61]

Before the post-1950 confrontations over the use of community facilities, the Fernwood and Peoria Street disturbances were the most serious in terms of human casualties. The feature that distinguished these neighborhoods from those whose defense took the form of property destruction was the absence of any alternative to violent resistance to avoid racial succession. Each of these communities was being surrounded by black enclaves; and each had a history of hostile and violent reactions against their transformation into white islands in a black sea. The threat they perceived was deemed far more serious than the presence of a few isolated blacks, as was the case in the militantly all-white communities surrounding the

Airport Homes, Trumbull Park, and the ill-fated building in Cicero. The level of violence increased in Fernwood and Englewood because the desperation and fear of the residents were proportionately greater and also because the very situation evoking their anxiety provided ample targets at which to lash out.[62]

The mobs perpetrating the worst violence, additionally, were methodical, if not meticulous, in their actions. In Calumet Park, as dusk fell on the scene that saw whites attacking cars occupied by blacks, white handkerchiefs appeared on the antennas of cars driven by whites so that, in the diminishing visibility, the rioters would suffer no problems in selecting their targets. As this disorder spread into Trumbull Park, such handkerchiefs also materialized on the doors of project units so that they might be distinguished from the apartments housing the unwanted black tenants.[63]

This sort of calculation was also present in the Peoria Street incident, the one riot considered most "irrational" by contemporaries. Precipitated by the rumor that a house was being sold to blacks, the Englewood residents blamed "outsiders" for their problems and attacked an array of "subversives." Strangers in the area were asked by roaming gangs to produce identification. Only *after* their status as an "outsider" was officially ascertained were they attacked. Jews were targeted by the mob and proved especially vulnerable as they lacked a ready answer to the often asked question: "What parish are you from?"[64] Significantly, once the riot shifted from an antiblack to an anti-Semitic and antiradical demonstration, blacks were not attacked. In all, only four blacks were set upon by the mob and three escaped without injury. Unable to attribute any purpose to the mob, the CHR accepted sheer luck as the explanatory variable. It was only through "great good fortune that the influence and highly emotional temper of the mobs of young men who flooded out into Halsted Street, chasing people whom they thought of as 'strangers' in the area, did not turn toward attacking Negroes on the streetcars or in automobiles passing through the area."[65] The ACLU also noted that not all Jews were attacked. Only those who did not "belong" in the area were victimized. The Jewish merchants on Halsted, the ACLU reported, were left alone. As for the mob's success in selecting its targets, it was further reported that "many of the persons attacked" were undoubtedly students from the University of Chicago who were "attracted by the occasion."[66] The rationality of the rioters' initial assumptions may be questioned, but the actions that flowed from them were both logical and coherent.

Ultimately, the best evidence of the control under which even the most violent mobs operated was the actual cessation of rioting on the part of the participants themselves when they felt sought-after goals had been achieved. Although ineffectual police work accompanied and, perhaps, permitted many disorders, the increased exertion of the "forces of social control" seldom brought an end to disturbance. Police work during these riots was heavily criticized, and in at least two cases the political context of events played a role equal to, if not more instrumental than, that of the police in ending a disorder.

Complaints regarding police inefficiency followed virtually every racial outburst. White veterans living in the Airport Homes protested the "continued failure of police to maintain law and order," and the *Daily News* characterized the police as "extremely patient" during this incident.[67] Human relations officials were also unanimously critical of police in their handling of the incident at 71st and St. Lawrence. Waitstill Sharp of the Council Against Discrimination decried police policies on mob dispersal and the deployment of forces as "totally ineffective." CHR representatives also protested to Mayor Martin Kennelly that "despite the fact that there were at least 2,000 people riotously endangering the peace of the city for upwards of six hours, only one arrest had been made."[68]

The thought that one of these episodes might escalate into a citywide conflagration plagued the CHR, but its pleas for improved police efficiency had little effect. The outburst at 56th and Peoria, which displayed the sympathy many officers had for the mob, developed as it did because police refused to disperse protesting crowds. Mayor Kennelly should have been "deeply disturbed by the continuing manifestations of police incompetence in handling riotous mobs," the *Daily News* declared. The attitude and conduct of some officers "seemed almost provocative," the editorial went on, and it was only "good luck" that prevented this last incident from becoming a "1919 disaster." Stringent criticism of police handling of this incident by the CHR's Thomas Wright led to a personal clash between the executive director and Police Commissioner John C. Prendergast. Mayor Kennelly and the commissioner, always cool to the advice of human relations officials, subsequently broke off contact with them at the height of the rioting. Rain and cold weather finally did as much to curb the Englewood violence as did the police.[69]

During earlier disorders, especially that at Fernwood, the police not only failed to confine the violence but actually contributed to its spread. If the city avoided a repetition of 1919, it was done *despite*, and not because of, the police. At Fernwood the primary police task was the protection of the housing project. When the rioters began attacking automobiles driven by blacks, the police reinforcements on hand were insufficient to guard both the project and the motorists. To meet this emergency, police rerouted traffic from Halsted, a main thoroughfare, to a narrow side street only one block away. Traffic became hopelessly snarled, black motorists remained within easy reach of the mob, and the police did little to protect them from the attacks that followed. This single incident and the police practice on succeeding nights of merely pushing mobs away from the project without dispersing them resulted in numerous attacks on cars driven by blacks over a 2-mile length of 103rd Street.[70]

The possibility of black retaliatory violence subsequently became real *because* of the way the police handled the initial outburst. Rumors persisted that police had deliberately "set up" black drivers, and the stream of damaged autos and bloodied passengers that found sanctuary in the Black Belt so aroused the community that an attempt was made to organize an avenging expeditionary force. Retaliation was avoided only through the efforts of the CHR and Archibald Carey, Jr., a black alderman who convinced an angry and growing crowd of the futility of such action. Recalling the role played by his father in an earlier era, Carey later wrote, "I have been in '47 what Papa was in '19."[71]

If the police did little to contain the Fernwood riot, they can be given only slightly more credit for ending it. The Fernwood rioters knew well the success violent protest had enjoyed during the troubles at the Airport Homes less than a year before. Mob gatherings had frightened away the first black who was supposed to move in and had done the same to all but two families in the second group assigned. Later, these two brave families felt compelled to leave when gunshots ripped through their apartments. At the time of the Fernwood rioting, the Airport project was, through successful intimidation, all white.[72] A delegation from the afflicted Roseland community conferred with Mayor Martin Kennelly with an eye toward the same end and left with the impression that the unwanted blacks would be removed if the whites kept "quiet." CHR observers in the neighborhood reported that "such was the 'talk' in the community" and felt that this, in conjunction with increased police activity, produced the "sudden calm" that descended on the area after days of bitter fighting.[73]

City authorities recognized police deficiencies and launched a series of reforms to improve their performance. Plans for a general reorganization of the police department were announced in the wake of the Fernwood riot; and in April 1948 a Human Relations section was created to deal specifically with racial problems. A circular order requiring district stations to forward all reports of racial incidents to the Human Relations section was issued and a permanent record of such incidents was started. By sharing incoming information with the CHR, police were able to keep a finger on the "pulse" of the city.[74]

More important than these institutional modifications were the tactical changes compelled by continued police inefficiency. The first alteration involved the mode of police reinforcement in riot-torn areas. Prior to January 1949 a district commander who needed assistance simply called upon the commanders of adjacent districts to send additional officers. As the CHR commented, "it would take a commander of rare indifference to the problems of his own primary area of responsibility not to answer such a request by sending those men whom he would miss the least." Consequently, the dangerous and sensitive task of riot control was "handed to men who were the least competent in their regular assignments." A series of discussion groups that included the mayor, CHR representatives, and police officials produced an order that provided for the regular rotation of assignments and ended the routine detailing of officers "below the average of police competence" to racial disorders.[75]

New plans for the "quick mobilization" of police were also implemented less than a year after the Fernwood riot. The first practice run of Plan Five (the disaster plan) brought 27 squad cars to a designated location in less than fifteen minutes. In 1949, to assure an even more rapid assembly of police at the scene of civil disorder, an Emergency Regiment was established. Consisting of four battalions of 660 men each and a total of 98 vehicles, this special police unit could reach any point in the city on "short notice." Heavy "racial details" were also instituted in tension areas on a regular basis. Their presence became so pronounced that residents of those areas could tell from the level of police strength whether more blacks were moving into the neighborhood.[76]

The Peoria Street riot precipitated a final tactical modification: the adoption of an immediate "dispersal policy." The CHR had long argued that "crowds gathered to express...antagonism against a person or his property because of his race" should be quickly broken up. The riot at 56th and Peoria, erupting after several days of unrestrained demonstrations, seemed to prove the commission's argument. Within days of the quelling of that disorder, and with criticism of the police reaching a climax, the mayor directed police officials to implement such a policy.[77]

These institutional and tactical reforms, however, were not sufficient in themselves to ensure the effective control of racial disturbances. True, the police now had the intelligence to deploy officers with foresight, the skill to dispatch them quickly, and plans to use them effectively. But the most glaring weakness in law enforcement, the point at which all the reforms broke down, was neither institutional nor tactical. The failure was individual.

The bias of individual officers was most evident in the Englewood disorder, though it was apparent in lesser degree in virtually every case. Reform measures were designed to remedy this problem as well as the others, but the courses in human relations offered to lieutenants and captains failed to reach those most in need of them. Nor could a few hours of classroom training alter beliefs and patterns of behavior that were a lifetime in the making.[78]

The enduring violence of Trumbull Park, the first major uprising to occur within the city after most police reforms were instituted, revealed the continued failure of the police to effectively control or end racial disorders. After the initial outburst subsided and police established an around-the-clock guard and a special headquarters within the project itself, "surprise" was no longer a factor in poor performance. The mobilization of adequate manpower was also well handled; when the situation warranted, the police were able to dispatch as many as 1,200 officers to the housing project. The police presence in South Deering became so formidable, in fact, that anti-black forces in the area tried to have the guard weakened by claiming that the investment of men and money to "protect a few black families" rendered the rest of the city unsafe. Yet, despite these measures, many of the old complaints about the police were heard.[79]

The black families of Trumbull Park were the most vociferous in the denunciation of poor police work. Donald Howard, head of the first black family to enter the project, felt the police were largely "ineffective" and "seemed more intent upon protecting white families from contact with us than in protecting my family from . . . white mobsters."[80] Other black tenants agreed. "The overriding concern expressed by all of the families as to police action," the executive secretary of the Chicago Housing Authority explained, "is with their inaction in the face of overt violence and lawlessness and their refusal to effectively disperse mobs before they reach major proportions."[81] White liberals and the black community at large became so distressed at the chronic violence and the apparent inability of the police to cope with it that they contemplated appealing to Governor William Stratton to send the militia.[82]

It was evident to all, as the *Sun-Times* editorialized, that the police were "sympathetic" to the mob. Several observers noted a "gulf between top police officials" who were concerned with impartial law enforcement and the "morale and actions of individual policemen."[83] But even this fissure does not fully explain the situation. The highest police officials in the area, despite their desire to preserve order, were also unmistakably sympathetic to the whites. The chief of the Park District Police openly commiserated with the antiblack protestors when addressing the SDIA. "It is unfortunate the colored people chose to come out here," he began, "but there is nothing we can do about it." "I know how you feel about this," he concluded; "I had to move three times myself."[84]

Rioting whites read well the signals given them by unenthusiastic patrolmen and officials. Whatever deterrent effect the large numbers of police might have had was, therefore, seriously undermined. The beating of a black and vandalism by whites under the steady but unconcerned gaze of the police placed antiblack protestors "in great spirits" and made it appear to them that "some one has...put the fix in." Even when police were compelled to make arrests, local whites knew they had little to fear. Youthful bomb throwers were occasionally apprehended, one commentator observed, but only *after* their explosives were detonated. Moreover, the charges filed against them were usually minor.[85] Although the presence of massive numbers of police had to inhibit the outbreak of violence somewhat, the authorities were neither determined nor effective in suppressing riotous behavior.

The ebb and flow of violence at the Trumbull Park Homes was, as at Fernwood, closely keyed to political developments. After nearly a year of intermittent destructive protests over the presence of blacks in the project, several clashes took place during the summer of 1954 as black groups from outside the community tried to use the athletic facilities within Trumbull Park. Though white residents had failed to have the black families removed from the area, they had been successful in denying free access to public facilities to all blacks – including those from the project. After a serious incident between local residents and blacks who had been using one of the park's baseball fields, community representatives met with city political leaders claiming a "deal" had been made. The number of black families in the nearly 500-unit project would be limited to twenty, the leaders said, if only the violence would cease. When publicized, city fathers denied making any such "deal," but the next week black demonstrators played ball unmolested in the same park where they had been mobbed a week before. The SDIA had passed the "word" around area taverns that the blacks were to be given the "silent treatment" and that all whites were to "stay away" from the park when the blacks arrived. However much a "deal" might be denied, the SDIA acted on the assumption that one existed and prevented – where the police could not – the recurrence of violence.[86]

The typical Chicago housing riot thus emerges as one in which the participants were an "ethnic" amalgam of working-class Catholics. Not motivated simply by a blind, consuming, and uncontrollable racial hatred, their racial animosities were very often channeled, if not harnessed, toward political goals. The police were frequently ineffective in controlling these disorders and the modernization of the department was not sufficient in itself to remedy the situation. Indeed, as late as the Calumet Park riot in 1957, complaints were still heard that the "failure of police to localize and suppress mobs as they are forming" would make possible the outbreak of "city-wide racial violence."[87] Yet, despite police inadequacies, citywide violence did not occur. Ultimately, this must be attributed to the inherently limited goals of the mobs themselves. Their destructiveness was constricted by their localized character and the specific nature of the grievances that called them into being. As long as retaliatory violence could be avoided, there was much less chance of a 1919-style riot than most people assumed. Rioting was undertaken for particular reasons and not as a generalized expression of racial hostility. Those reasons, and not the external forces of social control, were primarily responsible for the development, intensity, and duration of disorder.

4 The Loop versus the slums: downtown strikes back

Whether the ancient protection of English common law of the rights of private property against incursions by the State shall be wholly abandoned is a question which probably will have to be left to history since we seem to be well on our way.

> L. D. McKendry, vice-president, Chicago Title and Trust Company, to Holman D. Pettibone, November 11, 1948, Holman D. Pettibone Papers, Chicago Historical Society

The inability to move, combined with the struggle of operating in a choking environment, has made the institutions perhaps more than all others the champions of the cause of redevelopment.

> Anonymous handwritten note, n.d., Metropolitan Housing and Planning Council Papers, Manuscript Collection, The Library, University of Illinois at Chicago

The expansion of the ghetto and the deterioration of the central city alarmed corporate property holders, but their response differed from that of individual homeowners or renters. Downtown businesses and institutions located in slum or transition areas turned not to violence or suburban flight but rather to the use of political and legal power. Locked in a desperate struggle for survival, the city's large institutions used their combined economic resources and political influence to produce a redevelopment and urban renewal program designed to guarantee their continued prosperity. Their response to the changing condition of the city was not a fundamentally different form of behavior; it was simply a different mode of reaction within a white consensus. If the white ethnic working class felt driven to the streets to protect its self-defined interests, Chicago's business and institutional interests resorted no less forcefully to the political arena.

Entering the postwar era without the legislative tools necessary to reconstruct its decaying neighborhoods, the city moved swiftly to remedy this weakness. A series of enactments, from the Blighted Areas Redevelopment Act of 1947 to the Urban Community Conser-

100

vation Act of 1953, expanded the municipality's power and enabled
it to begin its "renewal." Powerful, but severely threatened, private
interests devised and implemented the legislation in each case. Unable to save themselves, they harnessed greatly augmented public
powers to ensure their own survival.

The large Loop interests dominated the first phase of the city's
rebuilding program. Even before World War II had ended, downtown businesses – especially the State Street department stores under
the leadership of Marshall Field and Company – devised plans for
the revitalization of Chicago's central districts. Although humanistic
concern for the quality of life in such areas was often expressed,
simple economics governed the Loop's devotion to its hinterland.
Chicago's business elite clearly envisaged a postwar building boom
on the city's periphery, the flight of the middle class, and the insulation of State Street from its "normal market." They subsequently
tried to counter the forces promoting decentralization through the
"complete rehabilitation of the center of the city." "The real purpose
of redevelopment," one knowledgeable observer later noted, was
"to reattract solvent population and investment to the dying areas of
the city."[1]

There were other economic concerns as well. Not only did the
burgeoning suburbs attract much of the Loop's clientele, but the
subsequent decay of the inner city placed severe financial burdens
on the city and, especially, its large businesses. Slums meant increased costs for police and fire protection and decreased revenues
resulting from tax delinquencies. Should the physical deterioration
of the central districts continue, immobile businesses and institutions would have to pay increased taxes to offset the city's rising
costs and shrinking income. It was necessary to "restore deteriorated areas to profitable uses" so that "the speeding up of decentralization with further loss of jobs, business, families and tax revenues"
could be halted.[2]

The key figures coordinating the efforts of these large interests
were Milton C. Mumford, an assistant vice-president of Marshall
Field and Company, and Holman D. Pettibone, president of the
Chicago Title and Trust Company. More than any others, they were
the architects of Chicago's postwar plans. Both were almost stereo-
typically small town, Midwestern, and Protestant in origin. Pettibone's
grandfather established himself in the real estate business in Rock-
ford, Illinois, around 1850, and although Pettibone's father was born
there, the family later moved to Albion, Nebraska, where Pettibone
was born in 1889. He came to Chicago in 1911 to attend Kent Law

School and took a "temporary" job at the Chicago Title and Trust Company for $10 a week to help support himself. Despite earning his law degree in 1914, Pettibone stayed on in the title business, learning it from company president Harrison B. Riley. In true Horatio Alger fashion, Pettibone worked his way up to the presidency at Chicago Title and Trust and eventually established a residence in the posh northern suburb of Winnetka. Similarly, Mumford was born in Marissa, Illinois, in 1913, graduated from the University of Illinois in 1935, and began working his way up the corporate ladder at Marshall Field and Company where he was hired as a correspondence clerk the year he left school. By 1946 he was an assistant vice-president and, like Pettibone, he soon trekked to the suburbs, making a home in Evanston.[3]

These notables were aided by the Metropolitan Housing and Planning Council, a private reform group with numerous downtown connections. The MHPC was led by president Ferd Kramer, head of one of the city's largest realty firms and a past president of the Chicago Real Estate Board. Kramer was also a member of the board of Michael Reese Hospital and, during the war, served as deputy defense housing coordinator for the city. MHPC policy was established by a board of forty governors, comprised, according to Martin Meyerson and Edward C. Banfield, of mostly "prosperous lawyers, architects, bankers, and industrialists."[4] The council maintained close ties to the city's economic elite and was anxious to remain both respectable and acceptable to "people of wealth, power, and social standing." When vacancies appeared on the board of governors in the years immediately following the war, Kramer – always eager to enhance the group's stature and connections – recruited vice-presidents from International Harvester and Marshall Field and Company, as well as the president of the Illinois Institute of Technology, to fill the gaps. Preferring to exercise influence quietly, behind the scenes, Kramer worked "indefatigably," according to MHPC executive director Dorothy Rubel, to bring prominent business leaders who had "considerable power in political circles" into the council. Together, Pettibone, Mumford, and the MHPC devised a redevelopment formula based on private profit and public power and saw their program accepted by both Mayor Martin H. Kennelly and the state legislature. Redevelopment in Illinois followed the path cut for it by its corporate pioneers. More important, the nation followed as well. The Chicago plan embodied the concepts later enacted in the federal Housing Act of 1949.[5]

At war's end, three obstacles prevented the redevelopment of blighted areas by private enterprise. Milton Mumford felt that the two biggest problems were those of land assembly and land cost. Holman Pettibone agreed. These were, he believed, "threshold difficulties," which prevented the implementation of any plan, no matter how well conceived. Given the prevailing assumption that any redevelopment project should be large enough to dominate its immediate environment, the acquisition of sufficient property proved an unacceptable risk to private investors. Inner-city land was prohibitively expensive; and, lacking the power of eminent domain, a developer had no guarantee that he could obtain every parcel on a prospective site. To these obstacles, developer and MHPC board member Philip Klutznick added a third. The final problem, Klutznick believed, was the rehousing of displaced persons. No redevelopment site could be cleared until the current residents were relocated. Given the housing shortage, he declared, "it would be inhuman and immoral to undertake a slum clearance and redevelopment program without a clearly defined method for the handling of displaced families." These seemingly insurmountable tasks were, in Holman Pettibone's words, "placed upon the public."[6]

The Metropolitan Housing and Planning Council began to "think seriously" about Chicago's postwar redevelopment as early as June 1942. There was a planning vacuum as the agencies that should have been concerned with such problems – such as the Chicago Plan Commission (CPC) and the Association of Commerce – were either apathetic or incapable of taking action. The Plan Commission, MHPC board members felt, was a "creature of the aldermen" and thus "limited by their pressures." As for the Association of Commerce, it had simply "indicated indifference to its own best interests." The MHPC decided to assert itself by "taking the lead in post war planning for Chicago." Its leaders thought the council could "become an extremely powerful organization... if it seizes the opportunity and draws up plans with sufficient boldness and vision."[7]

The MHPC established a redevelopment subcommittee, which produced an "experimental" study and plan for an aging section of the near West Side. It was the council's explicit intention to test the feasibility of private redevelopment of blighted areas and to "formulate a long run plan" for the revitalization of the city. Its leadership considered the development and support of necessary legislation axiomatic.[8]

In struggling with the problems of land assembly and cost, private subsidies were considered too small to produce the desired "chain reaction" of necessary developments. The subcommittee also rejected tax concessions because they, too, were too small to be effective and because the very idea of tax incentives was "offensive to some people." The most compelling reason for their dismissal, however, was that the city would have to provide them. The MHPC had clearly set its sights on state and federal funds to ease the city's financial plight. "We must find something," the subcommittee chairman wrote, "which will permit the job to be done in big enough bites, fast enough, with the use of [outside] funds..., and which contains the chain reaction principle."[9]

The council's final report proposed the acquisition of land by a public agency for private redevelopment. Public funds would then be used to "write down" the land from its acquisition cost to its "real use value." In other words, the public agency would obtain the land (through purchase or condemnation), clear the land at its own expense, and make it available to private redevelopers at a fraction of its original cost. The MHPC report styled this procedure as a "one-time subsidy" to contrast it with the continuing subsidy provided for public housing in the form of a tax exemption. The planners believed that the subsidy would eventually be recovered through the increased tax revenues produced by a profitable project. Theirs was an innovative solution, the MHPC realized, that required a "large program of education and influence" before it gained acceptance. An October 1946 luncheon was selected as the proper forum in which to unveil the MHPC's formula, and Henry Heald, president of the Illinois Institute of Technology, was chosen to advance the council's plan as the "only practical method of getting a real redevelopment program going."[10]

Heald described the city's dilemma before an audience of 100 civic leaders and representatives of the press:

> All around us we see increasing evidence of the decline in the heart of the city – tax delinquencies, slums, absentee ownership. And with them we see the increases in municipal costs – fire, police, juvenile delinquency, health; we see the continual flight away from the city by those who can afford it, the escape to greener pastures.

As the spokesman for a major South Side institution, Heald knew that "we really had only two choices – to run away from the blight or to stand and fight." Rallying behind the slogan Stand and Fight, Heald outlined the four-point "program of action" devised by the MHPC. The first three points incorporated the findings of the council's West Side study. The fourth point called for "assistance to displaced families in finding other housing." Having announced their redevelopment formula, it remained, the MHPC believed, to "put it over with the city's business leaders," Democratic Mayor Martin H. Kennelly, and Republican Governor Dwight Green.[11]

How much did the council have to "sell" the city's largest businessmen? To some degree, the latter apparently "sold" the former. Loop interests were involved with the MHPC and its postwar plans as early as 1943. It was then that Ferd Kramer requested economic support from several "State Street groups...who...[had] a financial interest in the future plans and objectives of the...Council." Kramer "found keen interest among this group" and was confident that "some contributions" could be secured from individual stores. Perhaps sensing future difficulties should they be identified as backers of the MHPC, Kramer noted that "such contributors might not wish to have their names publicized."[12]

Far more important than financial connections were interlocking leadership positions. It was Milton C. Mumford of Marshall Field and Company, for example, who chaired the MHPC subcommittee that created the postwar housing program. Mumford was also the author of the MHPC memorandum that outlined the proposals later publicized by Heald. Dorothy Rubel even claimed that these influential businessmen "became sold" on the council's program "through working on our committees." Actually, the latter had their own reasons for working with the MHPC. Well aware that their plans would encounter "difficulty if not...defeat" if the effort was seen as a priority of the "big business interests," Mumford went to great lengths to avoid that possibility. "That was the reason," he later wrote Holman Pettibone, "that you and I went all around the barn with such groups as [the] Metropolitan Housing [and Planning] Council, the South Side Planning Board, the Civic Federation, the City Club, some committees of the Chicago Association of Commerce and Industry, etc., etc." Rather than having to be "sold" on the program, Mumford and Pettibone had been devising their own redevelopment plans since before the war's end, and it was they who personally secured the support of Mayor Kennelly and Governor Green.[13]

Holman Pettibone met with Hughston McBain, president of Marshall Field and Company, and W. S. Street, a Field vice-president who was assuming the leadership of the State Street Council, in early April 1945. They expressed mutual concern over the blighted areas "near the central business district," and McBain noted that his company had "a very vital interest in trying to remedy conditions in this nearby area." He also proposed that a "small number of firms" try to develop a specific project. Pettibone offered his own services and the financial resources of the Chicago Title and Trust Company. McBain pledged similar financial assistance and the time of Milton Mumford.[14] It was a powerful combination.

The two firms shared the cost of bringing planner Miles Colean to Chicago to inspect virtually the same West Side area covered by the MHPC's experimental program. They also shared the expenses of a survey by the Real Estate Research Corporation for the "analysis of Loop employment pools in terms of their constituting a market for close-in, high density, private residential development." The corporation's report included an assessment of the "Negro Housing Market," which provided surprising results. The "severely limited" housing opportunities for "upper income Negroes," and their "willingness to spend a higher proportion of their incomes" on rent than was "customary" among whites, led to the conclusion that "a well-planned Negro project, carefully managed and well-located in respect to the Negro community, will enjoy greater earning stability . . . than a relatively large project for white occupancy." McBain and Pettibone consequently paid for two Colean reports. The first proposed an all-white project for Loop workers on the West Side, and the second contemplated an all-black project on the near South Side. Both would remove slums, "anchor" the Loop, and provide new infusions of money into the central city.[15]

Even as these studies were in progress, Hughston McBain and Pettibone were meeting with Mayor Edward J. Kelly to discuss long-range redevelopment plans. As early as March 1946, more than six months before Henry Heald announced the MHPC's four-point program, the presidents of Marshall Field and Company and the Chicago Title and Trust Company broached the subject of the city's absorbing the cost of assembling and clearing land for private redevelopers who would then purchase the property at a price "less than the cost of acquisition."[16] By July 1946 Pettibone opened discussions with Republican Governor Dwight Green on the same matter. He outlined a series of measures that clearly anticipated those suggested at the MHPC's October luncheon. "The Governor expressed himself very favorably impressed with the idea of a 'one-time' subsidy," Pettibone noted. Given this promising start, he retained an attorney to "draft two or more bills for introduction at the next regular session of the [General] Assembly." The October unveiling of these redevelopment concepts was merely the public debut of ideas that had gestated in Loop boardrooms. In suggesting the luncheon, Mumford declared that "we simply felt it was time to get this idea out in the open, get it discussed publicly . . . and begin to build the base of public understanding and support" needed for its adoption.[17]

A major step toward the passage of the redevelopment program was achieved with the departure of the scandal-ridden administration of Ed Kelly in 1947. Shaken by charges of corruption, Chicago's Democrats selected Martin Kennelly as the party's standard-bearer that year precisely because of his "clean," nonmachine image and his weak ties to the regular party structure. A self-made success in private business, Kennelly was a firm believer in the free-enterprise system and was ideologically at ease with other executives; he was by temperament receptive to the "business creed" and its brand of reform. He also became politically indebted to the Field-owned *Sun-Times* during his successful mayoral campaign. When he entered office, Kennelly thus inherited both a housing crisis and a virtually completed redevelopment program. Previously, Kelly had simply referred the Pettibone-McBain proposals to the executive secretary of the Chicago Housing Authority, Elizabeth Wood. There they rested. Now, within days of the 1947 mayoralty, outlines of proposed state legislation were on Holman Pettibone's desk. Action came quickly.[18]

Even before Kennelly's inauguration, Milton Mumford contacted others, including Newton Farr, a past president of the Chicago Real Estate Board, and solicited their aid in presenting "constructive suggestions" to the new mayor on how best to provide housing for the city. Kennelly had noted in his campaign that private enterprise should do the "major part" of rebuilding the city, but he also realized that government help was imperative. Farr, who knew that Mumford represented "State Street and a group of institutions who are willing to provide equity money for housing," was more than willing to offer guidance to Kennelly. After "clearing" the composition of his delegation of local businessmen with the Chicago Association of Commerce, he asked that they "advise the Mayor that we shall be prepared to see him...[to] review legislation necessary to carry out a constructive program."[19]

Less than two months after Kennelly took office, these men secured the passage of the Redevelopment and Relocation acts of 1947. During that period, Pettibone and Mumford served as negotiators and counselors to both the mayor and Governor Green in an effort to get bipartisan support. As Newton Farr and his delegation met with Kennelly, Pettibone was in Springfield conferring with the governor. He met little resistance; as a "highly regarded" Republican, both "downstate and in Washington," Pettibone proved persuasive. Green proclaimed the outlines of proposed legislation "satisfactory" and stated his willingness to "make them the chief ingredients of his housing-slum clearance program."[20] Kennelly moved forward as well. In one of his first official acts, he appointed a Housing Action Committee, which consisted largely of persons already involved in redevelopment planning. He selected Holman Pettibone to chair the committee and placed Milton Mumford and James C. Downs, Jr., president of the Real Estate Research Corporation, in subordinate leadership positions. Three members of the MHPC's board of governors were also placed on the committee. Charged with the task of developing a housing program for the city, they simply used their positions within the new city administration to complete the work they had already begun.[21]

The Housing Action Committee, in fact, became little more than a vehicle for Pettibone and Mumford as they continued their "shuttle diplomacy" between Chicago and Springfield. Time was of the essence. The committee was not constituted until the end of April and the General Assembly of Illinois was scheduled to adjourn on July 1. "Unless this legislation is presented to the Assembly within the next week or ten days," Pettibone told Kennelly on May 2, "it is not likely to receive any serious attention." He further told the mayor that the governor was eager to cooperate if an agreeable program could be devised. To that end, Pettibone had already scheduled a meeting with Green to define what was "acceptable" to the state's Republican leadership. Kennelly was thus placed in the position of authorizing Pettibone to bypass his own committee and negotiate personally with the governor to produce satisfactory legislation.[22]

Pettibone and Mumford met with the governor in the Union League Club in Chicago. Green detailed the fundamentals of an acceptable program and suggested a follow-up meeting with his political advisers in Springfield. Mumford and Pettibone dutifully reported back to Kennelly, obtained his approval for the basic features of the program, and prepared for the Springfield meeting with the state's Republican leadership.[23]

Henry Heald of IIT joined Pettibone and Mumford in their meeting with Green, his Senate Policy Committee, and Temple McFayden, chairman of the Illinois State Housing Board.[24] They told the group that the housing and slum clearance issues were of such importance that "no administration or political party can successfully ignore them." Wielding the carrot as well as the stick, they then declared that the time had come for the Republican party to "assume leadership" with a program that made it possible for private enterprise to do the job. "This is the only way to combat the pressure for a large-scale public housing program," they emphasized, and the only way to attract private capital before the "moneys available for this type of investment...will...be committed elsewhere." In sum, they concluded, the clearance and redevelopment of slums was a public purpose that justified both the use of eminent domain and the "temporary" investment of public funds. Convinced, the Republicans agreed to present the bills the following week, and the governor pledged $30 million in state aid to launch the program.[25]

The major objection downstate Republicans had to the package concerned its use of state funds to support public housing. Rural legislators had no special love for Chicago, blacks, or a program they considered "socialistic." Governor Green had raised this point in his very first discussion with Pettibone and again in his Union League meeting with the latter and Mumford. "There is in the Assembly," Green noted in the earlier encounter, "very strong opposition to any state participation in public housing projects." Once more, however, Pettibone and Mumford overcame the obstacles.[26]

Two issues had to be faced. First, there was controversy over the use of state funds for public housing. Second, there was a dispute over which public agency should acquire land for private redevelopment.[27] In the first instance, Mumford and Pettibone insisted that public housing had to be a part of the overall program. Their persistence was rewarded. At the Springfield meeting, the emissaries from Chicago warned that the failure to provide public housing imperiled the entire program. If redevelopment sites could not be cleared of their current residents, the rest of the legislation was useless. Mumford and Pettibone felt that "the greater bulk" of uprooted families could be accommodated "without additional public housing units." They foresaw, however, "a hard core of low-income families who probably...could not be taken care of except through the provision of...low rent units." "Even a relatively few such families can block an entire project," they admonished. The production of public housing, "reserved for families displaced by a redevelopment project, and used over and over again as 'decanting' units for such purpose," was, therefore, "essential." Should private redevelopment fail to materialize for want of relocation housing, they added ominously, "this will only cause further claims that private enterprise cannot do the job, and that the only answer is a complete public housing program."[28] Given the choice of a little public housing or a lot, the downstaters chose the former.

The Chicagoans, however, had to compromise on the second issue. Henry Heald's 1946 address had contemplated the use of the Chicago Housing Authority, which already had the power to invoke eminent domain and resell property thus acquired, as the public agency best suited to clear land for redevelopment.[29] However, downstate assemblymen who were "very hostile" to public housing refused to grant state funds to the CHA. Pettibone later recalled:

> It was made clear that there would be no legislation unless land acquisitions for redevelopment. . . were handled by an agency which had no right to erect and operate housing. The legislators wanted to take no chances on any agency which had a choice of selling for private development or holding for building and operating housing as a continuing drain on the public purse.[30]

The result was Governor Green's insistence that state appropriations be funneled through Land Clearance commissions created by the various municipalities. He placed this demand before Mumford and Pettibone at the Union League Club meeting, and subsequently Kennelly approved it as one of the program's "fundamental" features before the final Springfield negotiations.[31] Such commissions had only one purpose: to purchase, condemn, clear and resell slum properties to private developers. They had no power to build or operate their own housing. Pettibone and Mumford acquiesced in this compromise, although they disavowed responsibility for it. "While Pettibone and I thoroughly. . . concur in the wisdom of a land clearance commission for this purpose," Mumford informed McBain, "it has been the Governor's decision and not ours that that method must be used."[32]

There were also more subtle reasons for the creation of the Chicago Land Clearance Commission. Superficially, Republican insistence on a bill that could not be interpreted as a "public housing program" seemed "reasonable," although, according to Mumford, it was a potentially explosive problem. Segments of the black community and white sympathizers were dismayed by the circumvention of the CHA and viewed the term "land clearance commission" as a red flag. The crucial point was that the Chicago Housing Authority, which operated *publicly* owned housing, had a nondiscriminatory tenant selection policy. Under the 1947 legislation, however, redevelopment projects would be *privately* owned and thus exempt from CHA restrictions.[33] The CHA supporters had good reason for their suspicions. Ira Bach, who became the executive director of the Chicago Land Clearance Commission (CLCC), later recalled that a crucial factor in his agency's creation was the fear inspired by the CHA and its executive secretary, Elizabeth Wood. She spoke about "racial mixes and building in white neighborhoods," Bach remembered, and was "a little too far out to satisfy Pettibone, Mumford, and the others involved."[34]

The explosive potential of the race issue and indications that

Kennelly's program was not his own were manifested in the reactions that followed the governor's press release announcing the proposed legislation. Tremendous pressure was immediately placed on the mayor by "the extreme liberals, the negroes, [and] the public housers" who felt the program "by-passed" the CHA. Mumford worried that Kennelly "may find that this question is so hot politically that he may...repudiate the program." Mumford ruefully informed McBain: "I can only conclude that when he gave his acquiescence to the Governors' basic requirement of a land clearance commission he did not really know what was involved."[35]

Mumford and Pettibone worked assiduously to mute the race problem. They reassured Kennelly and hoped, in fact, to "keep the basic state legislation entirely free of any reference to racial distinctions or restrictions." They also sought shelter in the separate but equal doctrine. "It has been our view that there should be a project for colored on the near south side, and that it should be worked out either first or contemporaneously with another project for white persons," Pettibone told Kennelly in a letter that conjured up images of the Riot Commission's "dual solution." In any event, they advised handling the problem administratively and hoped that each race would be accommodated.[36]

The resolution of another potential problem similarly illustrated the lengths to which the bills' authors went to avoid racial confrontations. A provision in the original proposal stated that sites for relocation housing should be in "reasonable proximity" to the designated project area. This clause "seemed offensive to some colored groups," whereas others feared its proposed abolition. Mumford and Pettibone knew that the former were afraid of being kept in an overcrowded ghetto and that the latter were fearful of being "built out" of their neighborhoods by white developers. Unable to see a way out of this dilemma, the authors arranged a conference with black leaders in the Illinois General Assembly and gave them the option to strike the offending passage or substitute "very general permissive language...which will leave the decision up to the local authority." Pettibone and Mumford had no great stake in the eventual decision and wanted only to prevent divisive racial issues from threatening the entire program. Eventually, the restriction linking relocation housing to project sites was dropped from the legislation.[37]

Chicago's political leaders finally acceded to the Mumford-Pettibone package by the first week in June, but only after some members of the city council had tried to obtain discretionary power to use the CHA instead of a land clearance commission. Pettibone and Mumford, however, won the council's approval for legislation that ignored the CHA and thus assured the cooperation of Chicago Democrats and downstate Republicans in the General Assembly. Several other minor problems that revolved around the city's attempt to obtain the "greatest local autonomy which can be secured" were also worked out in conference with city council leaders.[38]

The passage of the Redevelopment and Relocation acts in June 1947 was hailed as an event of the greatest significance. "This legislation marks a milestone in the approach to a long term, sound program for rebuilding slum and blighted areas in the larger cities of the country," Holman Pettibone wrote Governor Green. "It is a pioneering combination of public authority and public funds with private initiative and private capital. This is the most important legislative approach yet presented in the country for a long range, major program for...redevelopment."[39] The MHPC also felt the legislation was "an innovation" that "thrust Chicago into the foreground of American cities as a laboratory for the determination of the ability of urban centers to rejuvenate themselves."[40] Even the passage of time failed to take the glow away from the achievement. Looking back in 1952, Pettibone asserted that the 1947 Illinois legislation was more significant than the federal Housing Act of 1949. The Illinois-Chicago program was the model for the nation, he claimed, and "was in no way dependent on Federal legislation."[41]

Pettibone and the MHPC had reason to gloat. Not only had they created a workable redevelopment formula (one later adopted by Congress), but they had adapted the "business creed" to modern urban realities. The profit motive would govern redevelopment, and the process itself would remain in private hands. Augmented government powers and support were necessary to aid the private sector, to enable it to accomplish that which it could not do by itself. But the priorities, goals, and implementation of the program were left to the traditional forces of privatism.

The Blighted Areas Redevelopment Act and its companion measure, the Relocation Act, presented the legislative framework within which redevelopment in Chicago began. By declaring that slum clearance was, indeed, a "public purpose," the legislature had vastly extended the use of eminent domain. The Land Clearance commissions, which gained this power, could clear acquired property and make improvements "essential to the preparation of sites for use in accordance with a redevelopment plan." Once this was accomplished, the commissions were directed to convey that property to private redevelopers. They could not build any housing themselves, and they could only operate existing housing on their acquisition sites pending their demolition. At most, 15% of the land held by a Land Clearance Commission could be turned over to local housing authorities for projects intended to house low-income displaced families.[42]

The authors of the final bill made only one reference to race in their effort to remove it as a possible source of friction. Racially restrictive covenants had become a *cause célèbre* among liberal groups in the 1940s. The Supreme Court made them unenforceable less than a year after the passage of the Illinois Redevelopment Act. Mumford and Pettibone knew that the issue raised strong emotions and probably saw that restrictive covenants were of questionable legal value. They consequently made certain that the Redevelopment Act contained a clause prohibiting covenants that restricted the occupancy of redevelopment projects on the basis of "race, creed, or color." Their failure to include such a prohibition, they knew, would surely produce a disturbing public controversy.[43]

The passage of the Relocation Act vindicated the efforts of Mumford and Pettibone to see it through. True, Republicans had allocated state funds for public housing "only upon a finding of the State Housing Board that such use was necessary . . . to rehouse displaced families," but the authors of the bill had staged a political coup to get the approval of *any* state expenditures for that purpose. They also succeeded in persuading the General Assembly of Illinois to grant the Chicago City Council the right of approval over the sites selected for relocation projects, a move that guaranteed that the program would not disrupt the racial status quo. In sum, the Pettibone-Mumford package, as it was laid out on the governor's table in May 1947, was passed virtually intact.[44]

The applause in Chicago was not unanimous. An anonymous CHA staff member ripped apart the legislation's "basically incorrect approach." Among the more serious problems, the critic charged, was the role assigned public housing. The new laws gave only minor attention to the "all-important problem of housing for 'disaster' cases – veterans and displaced families in the low-income and middle-income groups." Moreover, the level of funding granted relocation housing was "not nearly enough." The critique also claimed that the program could not be quickly carried out, that there was no control over rents in new projects, and, most important of all, that it would do nothing to relieve the city's disastrous housing shortage. In fact, the redevelopment envisaged by the law would reduce the number of dwelling units in an acquisition area and thus not only fail to improve housing conditions for blacks but add to their problems as well.[45]

Rather than detailing fatal flaws in the plan, the critic merely documented the disparity between his assumptions of what the city's housing program should contain and those that guided the program's framers. It was an honest mistake. The preamble to the Redevelopment Act stressed the human toll exacted by living under blighted conditions. Such areas "contribute to the development and cause an increase in the spread of disease, crime, infant mortality and juvenile delinquency, and constitute a menace to the health, safety, morals and welfare of the residents," the law declared. The main thrust of the argument for slum clearance thus emphasized the plight of the inner-city resident. Since the authors of the law had not outlined their objective to break down the "insulation" that separated State Street from its "natural market," the unwary reader could only assume that the eradication of slums should result in the improvement of the quality of life for those housed in them.[46]

From Pettibone's and Mumford's perspective, the blemishes detected in their program were virtues. The complaint that the law ignored "disaster" cases and inadequately funded public housing proceeded on the mistaken assumption that such housing was intended for all who needed and desired it. The Republican-controlled legislature agreed to permit 15% of the land cleared for new projects to be used for public housing only to remove those low-income families whose presence on an acquisition site stalled redevelopment plans. They agreed reluctantly even to that provision only because a private survey had found that 15% of the families in an inner-city sample area would be unable to relocate themselves if evicted from their present homes.[47] The explicit proviso that such public housing could be built only for those displaced by redevelopment reemphasized the point. Similarly, the objection that rentals in new construction would be uncontrolled was irrelevant to the program's intent. The promoters wanted to reattract "solvent" population to the central city, not to provide new housing for those who could not afford it. Finally, the rebuttal that the plan would not relieve the city's housing shortage was also true but beside the point. The bill's architects had never contemplated such a goal. The critic did not understand the forces at work in Springfield.

Kennelly's Housing Action Committee had waited for the state to take action on its program before issuing its final report in July. Its recommendations included endorsement of the state legislation, submission of two $15 million bond issues (one for public housing and one for the acquisition of slum property), and the creation of a not-for-profit corporation to provide middle-income housing. The committee also recommended the appointment of a Housing and Redevelopment Coordinator to oversee the city's reconstruction. Kennelly named Milton C. Mumford to fill that position.[48]

Mumford moved quickly to assure the successful implementation of the program. Two immediate problems involved the untested constitutionality of the redevelopment formula and the composition of the Chicago Land Clearance Commission. Mumford realized that his plans rested on new legislation, "which extend[ed] the concept of a public purpose a good ways beyond past court decisions." He laid out the strategy that eventually saw the legislation upheld. Mumford's influence with Kennelly was even more apparent in the naming of the Chicago Land Clearance Commission. He detailed the criteria for appointment in a lengthy memorandum to Kennelly and went so far as to suggest that one "carefully selected" black – that is, one who would not push racial issues – be placed on the agency "in view of the special effect of slum redevelopment" on black neighborhoods.[49]

His management of the campaign for the bond issues turned Mumford into a political, as well as a housing, adviser to the mayor. Mumford desired a short, intensive campaign, beginning no more than six weeks before the November 4 election. Wishing to avoid the agitation of the issue following the state's passage of his legislation, Mumford tried "desperately . . . to get the subject off the front pages." He also persuaded Kennelly to delay naming his appointments for the Land Clearance Commission so that they might have the most beneficial effect on the November referendums. A new state law, which permitted the bond issues to be placed on the ballot shortly before the election, worked to Mumford's advantage; on his advice, they were not submitted for city council approval until September 10. Finally, to initiate the campaign, Mumford arranged for Kennelly to speak before a sympathetic Chicago Association of Commerce luncheon on September 25. Kennelly dutifully appeared and made his first vigorous public defense of the bond issues.[50] The referendums passed easily. The city could finally begin its rebuilding program.

Redevelopment began in Chicago with the New York Life Insurance Company's near South Side Lake Meadows project. It was situated on one of two sites recommended in the Miles Colean studies commissioned by Marshall Field and Company and the Chicago Title and Trust Company. The project was not, however, the sole production of "downtown" interests. Local institutions such as Michael Reese Hospital and the Illinois Institute of Technology were influential not only in attracting private capital to their immediate environs but also in selecting tenants as well. Initially conceived by Pettibone, Mumford, and Colean as a "Negro project," Lake Meadows, at the urging of local institutions that were more sensitive to the racial situation, became an experiment in integrated living. However, the racial issues, which had been skillfully ignored earlier, had to be confronted and resolved before Lake Meadows was assured of completion.

Whereas the Loop was cut off from its customers by a ring of "slums," Michael Reese Hospital and IIT existed in their midst. The institute was the first to respond as it embarked on an ambitious expansion program in 1940. With a sizable investment in its existing physical plant, its growth from a 7-acre campus to one of 110 acres was undertaken as an act of self-preservation. Removal of surrounding slums and concomitant development was viewed as the only way to attract and maintain students and faculty. Nearby property was purchased as it came on the market, and lacking the benefit of legal or financial aids, the university "virtually bled itself white" in doing so. Ferd Kramer later credited IIT with being the "keystone" to "reclaiming" the near South Side as it was "the first institution . . . to take responsibility for rejuvenating its environment."[51]

Michael Reese Hospital did not lag far behind. By the mid-1940s it too faced a crucial decision. Could the hospital, its directors asked themselves, "continue its natural growth physically and scientifically in the midst of slums, or should it abandon its existing buildings, pull up stakes, and construct a new hospital on a more favorable site?" They decided to do neither. They could neither desert their existing physical plant nor find suitable, inexpensive sites in centrally located areas. Besides, they had no assurance that a new neighborhood would not undergo the same transition "in the course of one or two generations." Having no choice but to stay, the directors decided to take "aggressive" measures to rid themselves of surrounding decayed areas.[52]

In 1945 the hospital created its own planning staff under Reginald Isaacs, who devised a blueprint for both short-run and long-term goals. Isaacs called for the acquisition of surrounding properties and the construction of buildings for which funds were already available. By late 1946, in a manner that anticipated the Redevelopment Act of the following year, the hospital worked in collaboration with the Chicago Housing Authority, which assembled land and then sold it at auction. The Michael Reese planners, however, were "acutely aware of the principle that a healthy island could not exist long in a sea of blight." Thus Isaacs's group joined with the planners at IIT to form the nucleus of the South Side Planning Board (SSPB), which was created in 1946.[53]

Representing interests that were "practically anchored to the area," the SSPB brought together other private and public groups to create a redevelopment plan for the whole near South Side.[54] The result of this collaborative effort was *An Opportunity for Private and Public Investment in Rebuilding Chicago* under the joint authorship of the Illinois Institute of Technology, Michael Reese Hospital, the SSPB, the Metropolitan Housing and Planning Council, Pace Associates, Architects, and the Chicago Housing Authority.[55] Released within days of the passage of the Redevelopment Act, the report was "specifically designed to point out to investors and the general public the attractive possibilities of large-scale urban development in the central South Side.[56] MHPC president Ferd Kramer felt that there was "little question that this report had much influence" in attracting the New York Life Insurance Company. The publication revealed an institutional commitment to the area, which proved an attraction for potential investors. Indeed, Miles Colean believed that the rebuilding efforts already undertaken by IIT and others provided "substantial anchors" that would protect the area from future deterioration and encourage "redevelopment of the whole area."[57]

However influential the endeavors of all these local institutions, Holman Pettibone and Milton Mumford remained the key movers behind Chicago's reconstruction; their personal negotiations brought about the New York Life Insurance Company's investment in the redevelopment of the South Side. As early as July 1947 they met with officers of the Metropolitan Life Insurance Company in an attempt to interest them in a Chicago project. Pettibone and Mumford also contacted several other large insurance companies before the negotiations with New York Life, which began in February 1948, were successfully completed.[58] A series of personal meetings between Holman Pettibone and Otto L. Nelson, a New York Life vice-president, culminated in the company's financial commitment to the city. Mayor Kennelly announced the offer of the New York Life Insurance Company to rebuild a decayed section of Chicago's South Side in late July 1948.[59] With the necessary legislative tools in existence and the funding for the city's initial project assured, Mumford resigned his post as housing coordinator. "The results originally envisioned can be achieved," Mumford informed the mayor, "dependent only upon the vigorous action of the administrative agencies and particularly of the elected officials of the city."[60]

A new Illinois Institute of Technology dormitory looms behind the lone survivor on a nearby block. The view is westward from the 3100 block on Wabash in the 1950s. (Courtesy of the Hyde Park Historical Society; photograph by Mildred Mead.)

If the Lake Meadows project was dependent on the city, those deeply involved in redevelopment felt that the city was no less dependent on the New York Life Insurance Company. In seeking a legislative formula for slum clearance, they always insisted upon the "chain reaction" principle – the idea that the public's investment was merely "seed" money for a series of subsequent efforts by private developers. With the New York Life Insurance Company's offer, Lake Meadows became Chicago's grand experiment. If it failed, most observers doubted whether the city would ever again be able to attract private capital for investment. Mumford clearly warned Kennelly in his letter of resignation that future successes depended "in large measure" on the profitable completion of this project.[61]

Even before the New York Life Insurance Company made its offer, it placed demands on the city that demonstrated the tension be-

tween private and public interests. "It is vital," Holman Pettibone
wrote after meeting with Otto Nelson, that the company "have the
East boundary of the development adjacent to the railroad in order
that the buildings may be planned to command a view of the lake."[62]
Mumford was "concerned" that this site definition "included areas
in which there were a number of good buildings." Pettibone dismissed such considerations. He felt that opposition was inevitable
in any site selection and that the overwhelming necessity was to
"take areas in which the operating result[s] are likely to be satisfactory." If a profitable housing development demanded a view of the
lake, sacrifices would have to be made.[63]

Once committed, a virtual tug-of-war ensued as both the city and
New York Life tried to gain advantage. The investor demanded that
the city protect the "integrity of the Site Plan" by preventing the
"adverse use of immediately adjacent land." Other issues, such as
the closing of Cottage Grove Avenue at 33rd Place, the securing of a
school and park, and the enactment of "appropriate rezoning with
the approval of the Plan," were so "fundamental" to a profitable
enterprise that "no compromise seem[ed] possible on these points."
Otto Nelson, characterized as a "determined West Pointer" by Ira
Bach, director of the Chicago Land Clearance Commission, went so
far as to tell Kennelly that he "could save an awful lot of trouble in
the future" if the city would settle these matters before they became
"major issues." The city, however, moved slowly.[64] The Board of
Education, for example, complained that they lacked the money
necessary to build all the schools needed in the city and that the one
for Lake Meadows would have to wait until a construction schedule
"of sufficient units to justify" the expenditure was produced. Nelson claimed that he needed the school to attract tenants and issued
barely veiled threats to drop the whole plan should he not be ap-
peased. Eventually, the city gave New York Life what it wanted in
virtually every case.[65]

The most important service provided by the city was relocation. In
his campaign address before the Chicago Association of Commerce,
Kennelly forcefully asserted that persons currently residing on redevelopment sites "must have a place to live." Ferd Kramer agreed;
there was "no chance of redevelopment," he asserted, "if there is no
place for the people displaced to go."[66] The pain of dislocation was
also acknowledged from the outset. The chairman of the MHPC's
redevelopment committee, for one, knew that "severe problems"
would confront site residents. The authorities and institutions involved, he advised, must take every step "within reason" to mini-

mize these difficulties and "to sympathetically provide for their diminution."[67]

Yet, despite the knowledge that relocation was both necessary and difficult, neither the framers of the redevelopment legislation nor the New York Life Insurance Company assumed any responsibility to see that it was "sympathetically" carried out. The city itself and the MHPC showed more concern, but the nature of the program prevented that concern from dominating. They all perceived relocation simply as a means to an end. They assigned top priority to the clearing of the developer's land, not to the rehousing of its previous occupants.[68]

This emphasis was evident in the provisions for relocation contained in *An Opportunity for Private and Public Investment in Rebuilding Chicago*. This report expressed concern for the "human" element in relocation, but it offered no practical solution. Using the dated 1940 Census as the basis for its estimates, the study contemplated the relocation of 25,900 families. Of these, it was determined that 6,530 would be eligible for public housing if CHA entry requirements were "modified" to accommodate them. Of the rest, 8,460, under "optimum conditions," were to relocate themselves in the private housing market and 4,600 "families" consisting of single individuals or childless couples were exiled to "rented rooms and small furnished apartments." The remaining 5,000 were to occupy "transitional" housing, which, though not defined in the published report, was characterized in rough drafts as publicly supplied relocation units.[69]

The relocation scheme that found its way into the final study received considerable "in house" criticism before its publication. "In the body of the report," Reginald Isaacs and Martin Meyerson of Michael Reese Hospital's planning staff accurately noted, "there is no mention that the bulk of the families are Negro and . . . there does not seem to be adequate recognition that rehousing Negro families in Chicago is not a simple . . . matter." Unless previously restricted areas were opened to blacks, they concluded, the private housing market would not be able to "siphon off" the displaced population. Black critics were more pointed in their remarks. Referring to the 4,600 families that were to find accommodations in the "nooks and crannies of the City's housing supply," one such critic replied that local residents "were already living in coal-bins, out-houses, and other cubbyholes of squalor." "The theoretical disposal of the childless couples by the 'waving of a wand' is a most inhumane treatment of human beings," he declared, "and has little or no element of realism."[70] The critics also raised other issues. They questioned the reliability of the data and, especially, the extensive reliance on public housing that had yet to be built. "Surely much more material on relocation will be incorporated [in the final report]," Meyerson and Isaacs implored, "for so far this is not a program." "Who is to do what and how in the relocation process? Who is to provide for the transitional housing?" These questions were never answered.[71]

This lack of concern was still evident after the actual process of relocation began on the Lake Meadows project. For more than a year, the Chicago Land Clearance Commission kept no records of its relocation efforts. When the federal Housing Act of 1949 made funds available for the Chicago project, approval of the city's application was contingent upon the satisfactory relocation of displaced persons in "decent, safe, and sanitary" dwellings. When the CLCC could not certify that its earlier relocatees had found such units, the Housing and Home Finance Agency (HHFA) censured CLCC practices. Repeated attempts on the part of federal authorities to get the city to produce a proper relocation plan only produced delaying tactics. Chicago's leaders viewed the demands of the Washington officials, like the people whose presence blocked construction, as obstacles to be overcome. Ira Bach epitomized this point of view when he complained that he "was much perturbed" by "the unreasonable requirements...being imposed by Washington."[72]

The preliminary relocation plan submitted by Bach in early 1951 only continued the myopic approach taken in *An Opportunity*. Both Bach and the earlier study placed great emphasis on Chicago's expanding housing supply and the ability of displaced families to relocate themselves in the private housing market. Implicitly, but necessarily, the reliance on such housing to absorb thousands of blacks meant the acceleration of racial succession in other areas. Bach's presentation simply assumed the transition of previously all-white areas as a source of black relocation. The CLCC also had a further stake in the "changing" of white neighborhoods. Given the existence of the dual housing market for whites and blacks, the illegal conversion of large apartments into many smaller units generally accompanied black entry into a neighborhood. Bach attempted to use the increased number of dwellings thus created to prove that an expanding black housing supply could accommodate the Lake Meadows relocatees.[73]

More than a projection, this portion of Bach's "plan" accurately reflected the relocation process in operation. A Chicago Urban League report on the impact of urban renewal charged that the city was "forcing new slums to develop in place of those it clears" as blacks were compelled to "double-up in areas of transition."[74] A more detailed study of the displacement accompanying the Lake Meadows project found that the relocatees were not the "pioneers" who opened white areas to blacks; instead, they flooded into areas beginning transition and thus helped speed the process. This pattern was especially true of those displaced families who were able to purchase new homes. Of the nearly 1,000 traceable New York Life site families (out of 3,500), it was found that nearly one in four bought new accommodations. Of these, 21% moved *outside* areas that were 10% or more black occupied. At least eighty-five properties bought by black relocatees were situated east of Cottage Grove Avenue – the dividing line that separated the Black Belt from the Hyde Park-Kenwood area.[75] Moreover, the impact of these purchases was probably greater than their number suggests. The Metropolitan Housing and Planning Council found that "a number" of the property owners occupying the Lake Meadows site operated furnished apartments or took in lodgers and that such "set-ups...have moved intact into transitional neighborhoods." "They represent," the MHPC declared, "a direct transplantation of 'a cut of the slums' from the clearance area to a new location, subtenants and all."[76]

Increased access to private housing units was only one of the two major means of relocation. The second, which was equally important to Bach's plan as well as that found in *An Opportunity*, was public housing. Foreseen by Mumford and Pettibone as essential to redevelopment, Chicago's public housing program had its original mission subverted until it became merely an appendage to the redevelopment program. The primary purpose of public housing, the CHA's executive secretary wrote in 1950, had "always been to provide adequate dwellings to low income families for whom private enterprise could not provide other than sub-standard quarters." Shortly thereafter, however, Ferd Kramer claimed that public housing was also "the critical key to freeing land for redevelopment by private enterprise."[77] The Lake Meadows project, though, did more than simply add to the CHA's duties; it initiated a function that soon demanded all the CHA's resources.

The alteration of the CHA's mission was evident in the legislation that provided funds for its relocation projects. Mumford and Pettibone convinced the Republican-controlled General Assembly to support public housing only because it was necessary to private redevelopment. Mayor Kennelly presented his housing program and attendant bond issues to the public on that same basis and thus secured the support of such traditional enemies of public housing as the *Chicago Tribune*, the Citizens' Association of Chicago, and the Civic Federation.[78]

The shift in purpose was even more apparent, however, in actual CHA operations. The housing authority's unfinished Dearborn Homes at 27th and State was designated as a relocation project for those living on the New York Life site. Located on densely crowded slum property, the CHA was placed in the bizarre position of having to relocate residents displaced by the relocation housing project before the land could be cleared.[79] This task "superseded all other housing emergencies" for the CHA and compelled it to violate its own rules in the attempt to quickly vacate the area. Admission standards were "temporarily amended" and income limits were raised to permit otherwise ineligible site residents to enter other projects – despite the fact that the CHA did not have enough units to house those eligible under the old guidelines. Later, the altered income limits were extended to "off-site" families so that they might be induced to apply for public housing and thus create nonproject vacancies for those who still failed to qualify for public housing.[80] The CHA also engaged in "checkerboarding" – the movement of relocatees from one temporary home to another "as though they were checkers or chessmen" – when a single family remained in a building scheduled for demolition.[81] Finally, the CHA violated its long-standing policy that permitted project managers some measure of power in selecting their own tenants. It created a centralized relocation office to receive reports of all CHA vacancies, and by February 1950 the project manager of the Dearborn Homes was "taking families from relocation areas exclusively and had nothing to say about who would be admitted."[82]

So clearly was the CHA's new task simply one of clearing land for private redevelopment that it not only ignored its earlier function but contributed to the creation of conditions it originally intended to remedy. In relocating the residents of the Dearborn Homes site, the MHPC noted that in "many cases" it had been "necessary to break up the family in order to place them in any kind of home." Such practices continued with the clearance of the Lake Meadows site. A family consisting of a grandmother, mother, and four children, unable to relocate themselves, followed a CLCC suggestion that the grandmother leave the family to permit the others to qualify for Aid to Dependent Children and public housing. Two months after the grandmother left, her daughter and the children were placed on ADC and in the Dearborn Homes.[83]

Panorama of the Dearborn Homes site reveals both new construction and the extent of clearance on previously densely populated inner-city land, 1949. (Photograph courtesy of the Chicago Housing Authority.)

By early 1951 the redevelopment committee of the MHPC noted that the Land Clearance Commission was able to "fill all available CHA units as they are completed."[84] Although this situation eased as the CHA constructed more projects throughout the decade, between 1950 and 1954 more than half of all public housing units constructed (2,363 apartments out of 4,636) were allocated directly to families displaced by government building programs. Dorothy Rubel noted that relocation had so manifestly become public housing's top priority that "the original requisite of it being provided for deserving low income people...[has] been lost over the years." Other observers, by 1956, were able only to speculate that public housing "might be necessary even if there were no renewal problems." Public housing had become the cornerstone of private redevelopment and, in turn, was dominated by it.[85]

The Lake Meadows episode also made clear that private redevelopment was, in large part, creating the demand for public housing – or at least that part of the demand that attracted powerful political support. And the urgency was so great that expediency became the main criterion when relocation sites were being debated. Those who might have been given pause by the city council's choice of public housing sites capitulated to the need to see the units built quickly. With grave consequences for the future, once the council established the pattern of selecting ghetto sites for rehousing fugitives fleeing the wrecker's ball, it proved impossible to break.

The race issue, muted as the legislation enabling redevelopment sped through the General Assembly, was brought into the open after it became apparent that Project No. 1 would entail the massive redistribution of black population. First to respond was the black community and especially those living on the redevelopment site. As Mumford feared, individual property owners complained that their holdings were not slums. Those whose homes were taken primarily for the view they offered of the lake informed the city council that the project "ignores actual slum areas completely and plans the demolition of a well-kept Negro area where the bulk of property is resident owned, its taxes paid, and its maintenance above par." But the most deep-seated, widespread, and powerful opposition expressed the fear that blacks would be displaced from their traditional areas and left homeless in a city that was reluctant to house them.[86] Emotions ran high and the local opposition held an apocalyptic view of the future. Handbills warned blacks not to be "Duped again by Lyers [sic] and Land-Grabbers who seek to herd you like INDIANS and JEWS to Reservations or Consentration [sic] Camps in the Bad Land." "The master plan," it was claimed, sought the removal of blacks "from 12th to 63rd." Milton Mumford realized that such feelings were the results of "a very real, and to some extent, natural fear that the redevelopment program is a mechanism to build the Negro out of the South Side." "Actually," Mumford stated, "this fear is unfounded and no such process will take place."[87]

No one, of course, knew better than Mumford that there was no plan to rid the near South Side of its black population. Yet the blacks' fears were not simply the products of paranoia. The Lake Meadows project was always conceived as a middle-class development, and if there were no qualms about accepting blacks, it was clear that the site residents hardly qualified. Their suspicions were eventually confirmed as the new project's rentals were 300% to 600% above the 1940 average. Even allowing for unnaturally low 1940 rent levels, inflation, and the developer's announced intention to "keep the rentals as low as is consistent with a financially sound and

Danger--   Danger--   Danger--

NEGROES OF CHICAGO

Tenants-- Property Owners.. And Business Men..

This is the Zero-Hour for Negroes

Dont be Duped again by Lyers and Land-Grabbers who seek to herd you like INDIANS or JEWS to Reservations or Consentration Camps in the Bad Land.

Wake up and fight, or suffer the fate of Indians or Jews.

The Handwriting is on the Wall, The Alarm is Sounding, Join in the Struggle to Save your homes. Let them Build Houses on Vacant Lots--- Don't let the Planers tear down the homes of the POOR-- To build for the RICH.

No Negro Home on the S. S. is Safe.

The master plan goes from 12th to 63rd

Mass Meeting - Lobby of City Hall

Friday March 18th - 9:30 a. m.

Warning! Beware of Information Seekers spying for the Planers

Attend P. K. L. Council Meeting Thursday Evening 8 p. m. We will tell you all about it, Be on time.

3121 Cottage Grove Ave.

The Park Lake Council, The Champions, The South Side Property Owners Assn., The Neighborhood Civic Improvement Club, Tenants and Home Owners, Englewood Citizens Protective Assn., Property Owners Assn., 43rd Civic Block Orgn. Youth Champions, R. A. Crulley Block Club, Juanna Snowden Council, Mothers and Housewives, Southside Housing Comm. and 50 other Organizations.

Handbill protesting the New York Life Insurance Company's construction of the Lake Meadows development. (Chicago Urban League Papers, Manuscript Collection, University of Illinois at Chicago, The Library.)

attractive project," it was clear that the new housing was not intended for the locale's old occupants.[88]

Class was not the only criterion separating the development's prospective tenants from the area's original ones. Race was, to a certain extent, also a factor. Local institutions, especially Michael Reese Hospital, eagerly sought the return of white population to the area. As early as 1946 the South Side Planning Board informed the committee preparing *An Opportunity* that "the same people within the area were not necessarily to be the group planned for" and that, ideally, the neighborhood was "to be at least 50-50" in its racial composition. Although Pettibone, Mumford, and the New York Life Insurance Company originally planned the development as an all-black project, they were not adamant on the point. Thus New York Life proposed that "first preference for initial occupancy" of the new apartments be given to those displaced by the construction and that a "second preference" be extended to "other Negro families."[89] Mumford approved the careful phrasing of the tenant selection policy, which permitted the freedom of taking white tenants "at some future time." By the summer of 1954, the company was pressing the city to construct a school within the project so that it might "attract white tenants," and by 1956 whites were being offered free rent in completed apartments if they would sign a lease for one not yet finished.[90]

The blacks' search for some assurance that they would be able to return to the neighborhood after their homes were demolished led, in late 1948 and early 1949, to the fight over the Carey Ordinance. The proposed law provided that all housing built on land conveyed to private interests by the CHA or the CLCC "shall be made available for ownership, use, or occupancy without discrimination or segregation on account of race, creed, color, national origin, or ancestry." Alderman Archibald Carey acknowledged that blacks "always feared" that slum clearance was really "Negro clearance" and that they would oppose it "every step of the way" without a guarantee that the program would be nondiscriminatory. The community viewed Carey's proposal as that guarantee.[91]

Introduction of the ordinance confirmed Milton Mumford's earlier prediction that "some of the fanatics in the picture will undoubtedly try to insist on a policy of non-discrimination." The error in this view, according to the pragmatic Mumford, was that it would "virtually kill the slum clearance program" without doing anything of a "positive nature." Declaring that private investors would be deterred by such constraints, he warned that "you cannot accomplish or demonstrate non-discriminatory housing in units which never get built."[92] Although expediency was the main argument, opponents also claimed that the projects would be privately owned and operated and that the ordinance was unnecessary, given the Redevelopment Act's ban on restrictive covenants. The city's major newspapers, the Metropolitan Housing and Planning Council, the Citizens' Association, and other protectors of the redevelopment program all joined the opposition. The Field-owned *Daily News* even injected scare tactics into the campaign by editorializing that the ordinance would compel "an admixture of white and colored people in every apartment building that might be constructed under the Illinois-Chicago plan."[93]

The measure's proponents took the high ground of principle. "It is inconceivable to me," Carey wrote, "that Chicago would invite in any wealthy investors from Hitler's Germany to impose Hitler's standards upon Chicago just because they would be willing to finance parks, schools, superhighways, or anything else that would be otherwise desirable."[94] The Chicago Council Against Discrimination similarly fought the contention that the Carey Ordinance offered a choice between "moral principles and shelter."[95] They were not persuasive. Developer and MHPC board member Philip Klutznick, who was also a significant figure in the Anti-Defamation League, lamented the fact that the matter was "simply a question as to whether or not the moral issue overrides the practical housing fact." He finally decided to "stay as far away from this issue as I can." Hyde Park's alderman, Robert Merriam, also hedged. He, however, was finally driven into the proponents' camp by the testimony of an opposition witness who stated his refusal to invest in any house "if some law tells me to take one white and one nigger."[96]

Bitterly contested, the fight over the ordinance provoked extreme reactions before the measure was finally defeated. The opposition, fearing the demise of the entire program, was not above distorting New York's experience under a similar law in city council hearings or attempting to discredit the ordinance's supporters.[97] Ultimately, however, the most telling actions were taken by Mumford and Kennelly. Mumford released an influential letter detailing his views to the mayor. Carey could only express his "surprise and disappointment" at the fact that Mumford, who was not in the city during the hearings on the issue, "sent out nine pages of opposition to the ordinance without permitting the opportunity of cross-questioning."[98] More surprising, and perhaps an indication of the seriousness of the situation, Kennelly broke his self-imposed custom of "refraining from influencing the legislative action of aldermen" by taking the council floor to denounce the measure immediately before it was brought to a vote. The ordinance was defeated 31 to 13.[99]

There was also a deeper significance to the battle over the Carey Ordinance. Introduced by a black *Republican* alderman, the whole controversy revealed the inability, or at least the great reluctance, of William L. Dawson's black "sub-machine" to press racial issues in the political arena. Dawson was not always so reticent about battling for racial causes. As a fledgling Republican in 1928 he took on the incumbent white alderman in his district's primary, demanding that blacks be represented by one of their own. Though he lost that year, he finally won the coveted council seat in 1933. Defeated for reelection as a Republican in 1939, Dawson and the city's growing Democratic machine found each other in a state of mutual need. Democratic mayor Ed Kelly, successor to the assassinated Anton Cermak (founder of the modern Cook County Democratic Organization), was looking for a black leader to consolidate and expand the support New Deal Democrats were attracting in the ghetto. When, shortly after Dawson's failure to win reelection, Kelly approached the one-legged Republican and offered to make him Democratic committeeman of the second ward, Dawson eagerly seized the opportunity and the patronage placed at his disposal. Shrewd in both dispensing jobs and selecting lieutenants, Dawson built a powerful political organization that kept him in Congress for more than a quarter of a century (from 1942 until his death in 1970), extended across a half dozen black wards by the mid-1950s, and earned him increasing influence in Democratic circles. At the height of his power he was secretary of the Cook County Democratic Central Committee and played a crucial role in ousting Martin Kennelly from the mayor's office in 1955 (after Kennelly displayed what Dawson felt was an overbearing concern with raiding policy wheels on the South Side).[100] It was William L. Dawson who acted as kingmaker for the soon-to-be kingmaker, Richard J. Daley.

Despite such power, however, the congressman refused to lead a racial confrontation over the issue of redevelopment. Dawson's rise – which coincided exactly with the emergence of the second ghetto – not only depended on the rapidly growing number of segregated black voters but was rooted in the brand of issue-free politics that characterized all "machines." Geared simply to winning office and dispensing tangible incentives to his followers, Dawson, by joining the reigning Democratic coalition, became a protector of the status quo. A black population still very much in need of the material

benefits a "boss" like Dawson could bestow supported the congressman despite his transformation from "an outspoken and courageous
champion of racial issues" into a politician who, according to Harold
F. Gosnell, "avoided public discussion of race goals" and subdued
potentially divisive racial questions. Moreover, whatever his politics, Dawson's stature and power in the larger community were
sources of pride to Black Chicago, and Dawson retained a good
following for that reason as well.[101]

When the New York Life project was proposed, Dawson opposed
it, but not very tenaciously and certainly not for its racial implications. Ira Bach went to Washington to try and mollify the congressman, and he recalled later that it was a "very strange, strange kind
of a meeting." Dawson became quite "emotional," Bach remembered,
but "his emotion had nothing to do with the project or with the
situation of Lake Meadows." Dawson's major concern was that "the
police were cracking down" on the policy wheels and jitney cabs
operating in his district. Dawson "didn't care whether Lake Meadows
came or not"; he was "only concerned with these two items." He
asked Bach to intercede with Kennelly on his behalf and offered to
drop his opposition if "the mayor did something" about the official
harassment. Nothing else showed quite so well what motivated
Dawson's machine or the services it rendered. Even more important, Bach's failure to sway Kennelly (he recalled getting only a
characteristic "blank stare" from the mayor when he presented Dawson's request) did not prove fatal to the project. Dawson's opposition – manifested largely in the delaying actions of Second Ward
Alderman William Harvey – stalled the project somewhat, but it did
not intend to kill it, nor was it capable of doing so. As for those black
critics who charged that Dawson was unresponsive to black needs,
the congressman replied simply that "I have tried to fight for civil
rights where it is the most effective, within the caucuses of my own
party." His power there was real and undisputed. Kennelly, whom
Chicago columnist Mike Royko characterized as having "as much
respect for blacks as the next self-made white businessman living on
the city's Gold Coast," paid for his indifference with his political
career. It remained, however, for nonmachine politicians – a rare
and endangered species in Chicago – to raise racial issues, such as
those embodied in the Carey Ordinance, openly in the city council.[102]

A second threat to Lake Meadows emanated from different sources.
By late 1950, as the clearing of the development area was well under
way, outlying white neighborhoods began to see and feel the impact
of the New York Life project. The people in these districts especially

feared the city's internal black migration southward. Their representatives seized upon New York Life's request to close Cottage Grove Avenue between 31st and 33rd Place as the means with which to kill the project. Approval of the necessary ordinance in the city council required thirty-eight affirmative votes out of fifty, and the company had clearly stated its intention to withdraw from the project should its request be denied.[103]

The most articulate spokesman for the affected neighborhoods was Cornelius Teninga, a realtor from the Roseland community. The people of Roseland, Teninga informed the Housing Committee of the Chicago City Council, "suddenly find that they have a vital interest in what is taking place near the heart of Chicago ten miles north of them." They detected not only a "disastrous financial burden" in the forced rehousing of thousands of displaced persons but also the "kindling of alarming racial tensions which will result from the wholly unnecessary dispersal of the colored inhabitants at the center of our City...into the outlying areas." Teninga did not try to hide the convenience of the political issue before the council. "The problems presented by the diversion of Cottage Grove Avenue... are not nearly as vital to the people of Chicago," he told the aldermen, "as the disastrous consequences of this suggested pattern of redevelopment."[104]

The support given Teninga's cause was rooted firmly in the city's South Side neighborhoods. A list of those opposed to the closing of Cottage Grove Avenue reveals organizational backing from the Oakland-Kenwood Planning Association, the 55th Street Businessmen's Association, the Woodlawn Property Owners' League, the Ninth Ward Safety Council, and others from Hegewisch, South Shore, East Side, Russell Square, Beverly, Rosemoor, Roseland, South Chicago, and Park Manor. Individuals involved in the battle displayed similar roots. Frank Rathje, president of the Chicago City Bank, was a key figure in the Southtown Planning Association, a group that tried to solve the problem of racial transition in Englewood by devising a scheme for the colonization of blacks in the suburb of Robbins. Also supporting the opposition was Newton C. Farr, a man known to Chicago's blacks as the city's most vigorous defender of restrictive covenants and one who would later figure prominently in the urban renewal of Hyde Park.[105] The leaders who struggled to kill the project clearly represented constituencies who felt their own existence was imperiled by the New York Life project.

Supporters of Lake Meadows rallied to the defense of the redevelopment program with a fervor born of needless desperation. The

closing of Cottage Grove Avenue was symbolic of the city's determination to clear slums by private enterprise, and the failure to pass
the vacation ordinance would, in Holman Pettibone's words, probably "be fatal to our program." With such grave issues at stake, the
forces that developed and enacted the state's housing program made
certain that their plans would not be thwarted.[106] Pettibone met with
Teninga and a delegation of project opponents but failed to win
their support. Realizing after the meeting that "their real objection is
to any redevelopment program which...tends to remove negroes
from where they now live to sections of the city in which there are
few or no negroes," Pettibone was perceptive enough to "doubt if I
made much impression."[107] Unable to sway the opposition, the developers defeated them in the council. The MHPC led the political
fight and assigned lobbyists to each alderman whose vote was in
doubt. The determination to apply "pressure from outside organizations and individuals" even led to the recruitment of a member of
the local Catholic hierarchy to talk to his co-religionists in the council. Other measures had to be taken as well. The chairman of a key
city council committee demanded a bribe from the CLCC's director
in return for a favorable outcome. Because Ira Bach felt himself in
"no position" to comply with the alderman, he "went back to
Pettibone." "Pettibone dealt with the chairman," Bach recalled more
than thirty years later, "without a payoff; he had other ways." The
city council approved the closing of Cottage Grove Avenue by a vote
of 44 to 4.[108]

After the defeat of the Carey Ordinance and the closure of Cottage
Grove Avenue, no one mounted any major opposition to the com-
pletion of Lake Meadows. The court cases challenging the 1947 legislation and the redevelopment process were also disposed of by the
end of 1952.[109] "One by one the hurdles are being surmounted,"
Pettibone wrote Bach. "All of us can now feel assured that the fundamental concepts of our Redevelopment Program are sound."[110]
The achievement was an intensely personal one for Mumford and
Pettibone. The chairman of the CLCC realized this and, even though
Mayor Kennelly had participated in the ground-breaking ceremony
for the city's first redevelopment project, Bach sent a shovel used on
that occasion to Pettibone. "I have put it in a corner of my office,"
the latter gratefully acknowledged, "so...I can enjoy looking at
it."[111]

As for the housing program itself, its significance lay in its precedents and its origins. Not only did the Illinois Blighted Areas Rede-

Ground breaking for Lake Meadows: (from left) Philip M. Klutznick, Na-
thaniel S. Keith, Michael J. Long, Mayor Martin Kennelly, T. K. Gibson, Sr.,
Otto Nelson, Reverend J. H. Jackson, Holman D. Pettibone. (© *Chicago
Sun-Times*, 1952. Photograph reprinted with permission.)

velopment Act provide a model for later federal legislation, but the
demand for public housing stimulated by the New York Life project
and the seizure of the site selection process by the city council had
grave implications for the future. Moreover, the demonstrated un-
willingness of William Dawson's "sub-machine" to make Lake
Meadows a major racial or political issue revealed the inability of
blacks to substantively shape, alter, or prevent the reconstruction of
the near South Side. If there was any force within the black community capable of exercising such influence, it was Dawson's organization. The black accommodation to the ghetto, however, produced a
brand of politics that precluded such action.

The framers of the program aided in this process by consciously
muting racial issues and dispatching them quickly when they did
intrude. A purposeful blend of private initiative and public power,
Chicago's postwar housing program was basically economic in motivation. An attempt to revivify the central city, it harnessed governmental power and resources to the needs and aspirations of large
private interests. As such it represented the successful adaptation of
the "business creed" to post–New Deal America.[112] If the plan lacked
racial motivation, however, it was not without racial consequences.

In producing both the need and the political support for a massive public housing program, it set the stage for the next round of ghetto-building. In scattering thousands of other blacks across the face of the city, it accelerated the pace of racial succession and helped trigger a scramble for survival among several outlying neighborhoods. It also led, consequently, to the next phase of the city's postwar reconstruction.[113]

5 A neighborhood on a hill: Hyde Park and the University of Chicago

Now, Bob, as president of the University of Chicago, I don't see how you can do right by the negro problem.

> Mr. [William B.] Benton to Mr. [Robert M.]
> Hutchins, April 8, 1941, Robert M. Hutchins
> Papers, Addenda I, Box 103, Folder 11, The
> University of Chicago Archives

Illinois Institute of Technology is embarking on a somewhat similar project. You will remember they announced a few years ago that they were abandoning their site but have since said they would remain where they are...Perhaps we can learn from them some techniques.

> Harold H. Swift to Herbert P. Zimmerman,
> October 16, 1944, Presidents' Papers, 1940–6,
> Folder: Housing, Community, and Real
> Estate Office, 1944, The University of Chicago
> Archives

In early 1952, one thousand members of Chicago's financial, political, and social "aristocracy" celebrated the progress of the New York Life Insurance Company's Lake Meadows project with a luncheon at the Conrad Hilton Hotel. Sponsoring the event, a critic noted, were organizations whose presiding officers lived in Lake Forest, Lake Zurich, Palos Park, Evanston, and Highland Park. With one exception, only Mayor Kennelly, whom the critic "presumed" still resided within municipal borders, represented Chicago's residents. Even the housing and redevelopment coordinator lived in Park Ridge. "Small wonder," the observer declared, "that there was so little expressed concern" for the economic and social costs of "Chicago's Success Story" (the theme of the luncheon). It was unknown, he concluded, how much "of the present difficulties in Hyde Park" were attributable to "these well meaning busy bodies from the outlands."[1]

135

The clearance of the Lake Meadows site by itself cannot account for the added black migration to Hyde Park, but it was evident that the demolition did accelerate a movement already under way. In the late 1940s and early 1950s, the traditional Cottage Grove Avenue barrier, which separated the Hyde Park-Kenwood area from the Black Belt, was shattered. With the creation of the citizen-oriented Hyde Park-Kenwood Community Conference (HPKCC) in 1949 and the University of Chicago's establishment of the South East Chicago Commission (SECC) in 1952, it was clear that the movement that culminated in the urban renewal of the Hyde Park area, despite generalized references to "slums," was primarily a response to threatened racial succession. Before the 1950s had ended, Hyde Park, using resources unavailable to other similarly affected neighborhoods, initiated the further expansion of governmental powers through the passage of additional state legislation and harnessed those powers in the attempt to preserve the area. And, as was the case with the Blighted Areas Redevelopment Act of 1947, the local program pioneered in Chicago later served as a model for the federal legislation that spread the concept of "urban renewal" across the nation.

Nowhere was the role of private initiative, power, and interest in the postwar reconstruction of Chicago more evident than in the city's rapid abandonment of slum clearance for a program of "conservation" in the early 1950s. The dust stirred up by the wrecker's ball had barely settled on the Lake Meadows site before influential institutions and individuals rooted in Hyde Park, pressed by the rapid racial transition of their area, directed public policy away from the destruction of slums and toward the preservation of sound but threatened neighborhoods. It was not as though the city had already destroyed all of its dilapidated structures and provided "decent, safe, and sanitary" dwellings for their inhabitants. These problems still remained. The forceful resort to legal and political solutions for its increasingly precarious status, however, placed Hyde Park in the vanguard of those compelling a reordering of the city's priorities.

The city council's approval of the Hyde Park-Kenwood Urban Renewal Plan in 1958 assured the community's success in preventing its annexation to the Black Belt. There were two reasons for that success. The first was the University of Chicago's commitment to the area. The second was the "liberal" ideology held by many Hyde Park residents that permitted a greater flexibility on racial issues than was possible in other parts of the city. Willing to bend under the weight of a limited black presence, the neighborhood was not broken by it.

The more important factor, by far, was the University of Chicago's stake in the area. The 1958 Urban Renewal Plan was the culmination of a quarter of a century of direct university involvement in community affairs. From the beginning, the University of Chicago sought to maintain a "compatible environment" for its operations. By the early 1950s, this meant not the preservation of the racial "integrity" of the area but the creation of a controlled, integrated environment. The alternative was to stand by and watch the community become the latest addition to the Black Belt. The university, through the SECC, subsequently tried to create an economically upgraded and predominantly white neighborhood. If the racial homogeneity of the area could no longer be maintained, class could still be used to assure the "quality" of those nonwhites permitted to remain. Rather than representing a sharp break from the era in which the university supported racially restrictive covenants, the events of the 1950s must be seen as the culmination of a generation-long struggle. Locked in a battle for its existence, the university was hardly engaging in a noble experiment on the viability of interracial communities. It did, however, make realistic and unavoidable concessions to its physical situation and then, with grim determination, used the urban renewal tool to restructure and control its neighborhood.

If the most powerful, the University of Chicago was not always the most visible agency concerned with racial succession. In November 1949, on the very night that Englewood's rioters were attacking "outsiders" around 56th and Peoria, a meeting of concerned Hyde Parkers was held. It led to the creation of the Hyde Park-Kenwood Community Conference. Intended to deal creatively with the prospect of a black "invasion," the conference sought the emergence of a stable "interracial community of high standards." Toward that end it welcomed blacks into the area and attempted to enlist their aid in maintaining a desirable neighborhood for residents of all colors. The institutional manifestation of the liberal sentiment found in the university community, the HPKCC could be characterized as the embodiment of the community's conscience, whereas the SECC and the university represented its interests. As such it complemented the SECC as a subordinate to it in the renewal process.

The HPKCC has been viewed as a successful demonstration of democracy in action, of citizen participation in urban renewal. In terms of enlisting and mobilizing recruits, organizing block clubs, and generating self-help activities, this was true.[2] In terms of attaining their goals, however, the conference alone was doomed to failure. The HPKCC lacked the power to lend substance to its assertions of goodwill. It was, in fact, the continued rapid in-migration of blacks, the increasing instability of the neighborhood, and the deteriorating conditions at the fringes of the area that immediately preceded the formation of the SECC in 1952. The power of Hyde Park's residents to make substantive changes in the eventual urban renewal plans through the offices of the conference was relatively insignificant. As for the HPKCC's actual role in the renewal process, it was not, as its leadership believed, so much supplemented by the university as it was supplanted by it. By 1958 the HPKCC's primary purpose was that of securing the requisite public support for the SECC program.

The HPKCC, however, was necessary for the successful reconstruction of the community. Its one indispensable function was its fervent espousal of the necessity of creating an interracial community. Without questioning the sincerity of Hyde Park's liberal phalanx, it was apparent that its public transformation of the inevitable into the desirable, or at least, the acceptable, slowed the pace of white out-migration, permitted the university to marshal its resources, and was largely responsible for fostering an atmosphere within which urban renewal could take place.

Yet, even here, the University of Chicago must be granted some measure of responsibility in creating and sustaining the community's public acceptance of integration. As the major property owner in the area, the university served as a buffer between most of Hyde Park's residents and the consequences of the "ghettoization" of the area. Nearly 88% of the neighborhood's dwelling units were renter-occupied in 1950 (compared with the South Deering community where 68.7% of the units were owner-occupied).[3] It was the university, in its role as property owner, that was in the front lines in the battle to preserve the area as "desirable." The university shouldered the main burden of local self-defense, made the difficult decisions it felt had to be made, and exposed itself to the criticism its position naturally attracted. The university, as the institution with the most to lose and the power to assure its own survival, thus afforded its neighbors the luxury of their liberalism. The demand for public housing as part of the urban renewal package, for example, was made by the HPKCC more out of the desire for ideological consistency than out of conviction. But the demand could be safely expressed because the university, as the keeper of the community interest, made the final decision. The good fight could be fought without the fear that it might be won. It was the property holder, whether the owner of a bungalow or a major university, who had to be *sure* of the future.

The University of Chicago's urban renewal plans, however, were not foisted upon an unwilling citizenry. To a great extent the university and its neighbors wanted the same things. The genius of the symbiotic relationship between the HPKCC and the SECC extended beyond the fact that one dealt with the "grass roots" and the other moved the levers of power. It was also that the latter staunchly defended the community's interests and permitted the former to articulate its highest ideals. If the ideals had to be sacrificed when they conflicted with the measures deemed necessary by the SECC, then local residents could still pride themselves on having raised important issues while placing the responsibility for the inequities inherent in the renewal plans on the university. When criticism of the final renewal plan came from "outside" sources, represented by the Archdiocese of Chicago, however, the community stood as one against all threats to its survival.

It was apparent by 1946 that the process of racial succession was beginning in western Hyde Park. Shortly thereafter, it also became evident that the city's redevelopment was placing additional pressures on the neighborhood. Harold M. Mayer of the University of Chicago voiced a common concern when he noted that the uprooting of people and businesses in slum clearance areas was "one of the reasons" neighborhoods such as Hyde Park were faced with their own crises. Where 573 blacks lived in Hyde Park in 1940, 1,757 were there in 1950. Significantly, most of that increase occurred after 1948.[4]

The first organized response to this challenge resulted in the creation of the Hyde Park-Kenwood Community Conference in late 1949. The 57th Street Meeting of Friends (Quakers) served as a catalyst in the formation of the group, and it was clear that the Quakers were responding to the prospect of racial succession, not the more innocuous problem of "deterioration." Julia Abrahamson, executive director of the HPKCC until mid-1956, recalled that the key question raised at the initial meeting of concerned groups and individuals was whether to meet the problems created by "changing population" through "conflict or cooperation."[5] The Hyde Parkers had the example of Englewood's rioters clearly before them as they deliberated the proper course of action. They thus consciously viewed their new organization as an alternative to the "type of disorder and violence which has disgraced other communities."[6] "The general purpose" expressed by those gathered at the November meeting was "to keep whites from moving away, to welcome the new Negro residents into all community activities, and to maintain community property standards."[7]

The Hyde Park-Kenwood Community Conference prided itself on being an organization of the "people" and most of its efforts centered on their mobilization. Literally thousands of individuals were organized into autonomous block clubs dedicated to the improvement of their community. To prevent whites from fleeing, the conference fought the rumors that inevitably appeared in all transition areas. Reports that blacks had a "secret alliance" to move at least one black family into every block were denied through vigorous educational campaigns; rumors concerning the rate of property turnover were similarly quelled, and growing concern over an allegedly skyrocketing crime rate was attacked as an "exaggeration."[8] To prevent the deterioration of local property, the conference received and acted on reports of illegal conversions, overcrowding, and other conditions that might prompt remedial city action. Having established a strong working relation with the city's Building Department, a main area of the HPKCC's endeavor was the prosecution of housing code violations.[9] The result was that blacks entering Hyde Park, especially in the conference's early days, were met not by howling mobs but by building inspectors.[10]

Yet, despite this flurry of activity, the conference was ill equipped to meet its goals. A basic problem stemmed from the HPKCC's status as a voluntary organization. Peter Rossi and Robert Dentler discussed the "dilemma of volunteerism" as it related to the HPKCC Planning Committee and concluded that there were "serious limitations" on what could be accomplished by those working "outside of their regular occupational commitments."[11] The conference's small professional staff was also overworked and, as the pace of neighborhood change accelerated after 1950, was immersed in day-to-day "crises" such as rumor control. The growing awareness of community problems that led alarmed residents to seek conference membership also absorbed staff energies and, paradoxically, impaired its effectiveness.[12]

There were also more fundamental problems. The HPKCC's isolation from local sources of power, for example, compelled it to take a legalistic approach in fighting deteriorating housing conditions. If the conference was willing to welcome blacks into Hyde Park, many of the area's businessmen, large property owners, and the University of Chicago were not. The conference's liberal stand on racial issues cut it off from potentially powerful supporters and, consequently, sources of informal pressure that could have been applied to the real estate operators seeking to "change" the area. In the battle against conversions, the conference was thus forced to use the cumbersome legal process.[13] Moreover, there were difficulties inherent in the law itself. Even after the community's vigilance succeeded in bringing illegal construction to a virtual halt, legal conversions remained a growing problem about which the conference could do little. Judges were also reluctant to enforce the code on overcrowding as there was no provision for the relocation of those evicted under the law. They knew, given the housing shortage, that strict enforcement would only create hardship and shift the problem from one locality to another. By late 1952, Julia Abrahamson was forced to observe that the spotty enforcement of minimum housing standards was "little or no deterrent" to worsening conditions.[14]

The failure to halt the physical decline in the neighborhood was, of course, merely a function of the conference's inability to significantly influence the process of racial succession. It was in confronting this basic problem that two of the HPKCC's more debilitating weaknesses were revealed. The first involved the conference's perception of the nature of their plight and the second involved the incompatibility of the organization's goals and assumptions.

Paradoxically, the very ability to comprehend the complex forces operating in Hyde Park led to paralysis and dependence rather than determined action. From the beginning, articulate Hyde Parkers and the HPKCC leadership perceived their own racial situation as only a part of a larger metropolitan problem. An early policy statement by the HPKCC Planning Committee declared that the conference's objectives "can be achieved only in the framework of an adequate and comprehensive planning program for Chicago and its region. The forces which are now changing the character of the Hyde Park-Kenwood area do not originate, and are not primarily subject to local control from within the area." "The long range solution to this problem for this community," the Planning Committee concluded, "depends in large part upon the opening of all parts of the city and suburbs to . . . [blacks] in order to relieve the population pressure on Hyde Park-Kenwood."[15] A forceful blend of principle and self-interest subsequently led the conference to advocate open housing for the entire region as a means of stabilizing Hyde Park's precarious racial balance.[16]

This citywide perspective and search for metropolitan solutions, although historically sound, was politically naïve and, worst of all, placed the fate of Hyde Park in the hands of those who did not live there. First, it was a virtual declaration of war against outlying white neighborhoods. During the Airport Homes dispute the Chicago Lawn Businessmen's Association expressed the view commonly held in such areas when it resolved that, for the sake of racial peace, the ghetto should be permitted to expand solely into neighborhoods "immediately adjacent to it." Those holding such views saw Hyde Park's sudden espousal of open occupancy as hypocritical or, at best, self-serving. They also saw it as a threat to their own stability. Second, by calling for both state and city enactment of open housing legislation, the conference placed Hyde Park at the mercy of political representatives whose primary allegiance lay elsewhere. Even if such legislation would be effective (and later events proved that it would not), the political and metropolitan approach to maintaining an interracial community in Hyde Park merely stressed the community's vulnerability by asserting its dependence.[17]

Throughout the early 1950s the pace of racial transition increased in the absence of effective countermeasures. The northwestern section of Hyde Park was experiencing the heaviest in-migration of blacks, and the repeated appointment of committees and attempts to devise "special projects" to stabilize the area exposed the conference's lack of a practical solution to the dilemma posed by racial succession. Finally, the desperate search for a means to prevent the total displacement of whites compelled the conference to confront the previously hidden tension between its goals and assumptions.[18]

In articulating the liberal ideal of creating an interracial community of high standards, the HPKCC not only embraced the principle of nondiscrimination but vigorously espoused its acceptance by the entire city. Yet, by 1956 it was apparent that nondiscrimination in Hyde Park was synonymous with "the destruction of the hope of an interracial community." The conference had fought to stabilize the area as one of mixed residence for years even as their most tenaciously held belief worked against their success. The continued in-migration of blacks and steady departure of whites led to the inescapable conclusion that the HPKCC was failing. An ongoing debate between the conference's Committee to Maintain an Interracial Community (which felt it was "morally indefensible to retreat from the original goal of open occupancy") and its Real Estate Committee (which was "particularly concerned with the rapidity with which the peripheral areas of our community have been changing into an extension of the adjoining all Negro neighborhoods") produced a proposal to establish a Tenant Referral Office, which would "carefully screen all persons seeking housing in Hyde Park-Kenwood and...make a conscious and deliberate effort to prevent the trend toward all Negro blocks by encouraging whites to rent apartments that became vacant in these areas."[19] "Efforts to obtain. . . open occupancy throughout the city so far have not been received sympathetically by other communities where the pressure of Negro in-migration is not as great as in Hyde Park," the committees reasoned in a joint statement. Their proposal for the Tenant Referral Office recognized both Hyde Park's deteriorating condition and the need to act independently if trends were to be reversed. Forced to choose between ideological consistency and their continued residence in the area, the HPKCC board chose the latter. Although the choice "deeply troubled" many, most concluded that "the demonstration of a really stable interracial community DOES justify the kind of manipulation that is required to achieve it."[20]

Although the full implications of the conference's policies did not become evident until mid-decade, the organization's inability to achieve its goals was apparent much earlier. By the spring of 1951, the *Defender* cited the "swift movement of whites" from Hyde Park as evidence of strained relations and lamented that the ghetto was "simply being extended" rather than "liquidated."[21] By 1952 the HPKCC itself recognized the unmistakable trend. "While it is true that cooperation and understanding have increased," Julia Abrahamson informed the conference's board of directors, "it is also true that slowly the pattern of segregation has been spreading." "This process is bound to continue," she stated in what amounted to an admission of helplessness, "unless adequate housing is provided throughout the city and it be made possible for people to live wherever they wish."[22] Established to maintain an interracial community and to preserve high living standards, it was evident within three years of its founding that the Hyde Park-Kenwood Community Conference could do neither.

No one was more aware of the conference's inadequacy than its executive director. For its first two and a half years, Julia Abrahamson wrote, the HPKCC tried to meet "the overwhelming flood of problems in a finger-in-the-dike operation." "What was needed," she concluded, "were massive resources, public as well as private, and an imaginative and long-term planning program."[23] The conference had always advocated systematic planning and had long urged the University of Chicago to take an active part. Finally, in early 1952, the Council of Hyde Park Churches and Synagogues encouraged six major local agencies, including the University of Chicago, to develop a concerted attack on the community's rising crime rate.[24] This effort culminated in the creation of the South East Chicago Commission and the vigorous assertion of University of Chicago power. Although Abrahamson celebrated the university's entry into the battle to preserve Hyde Park as a victory for the HPKCC, it is clear that the university did so for its own reasons. University of Chicago involvement in the urban renewal of Hyde Park was itself the culmination of two decades of constant interest in community affairs and was keyed, from the beginning, primarily to the area's fluctuating racial situation.

Contemporaries viewed the establishment of the SECC as the result of "public indignation about the rising crime rate."[25] There is evidence to suggest, however, that the community's perception of a growing crime problem (a most emotional and sensitive issue when related to middle-class white perceptions during racial succession) was more the opportunity for the university's intervention than its cause.[26] The HPKCC received reports that the March 27, 1952, mass community meeting in Mandel Hall was "engineered" by the university for the specific purpose of setting up a new organization.[27] A Committee of 5 was appointed at this gathering to study community problems and make recommendations. At a May 19 meeting the committee "announced" the creation of the SECC. "We used a rather sensational kidnapping and attempted rape case," Chancellor Lawrence A. Kimpton (who succeeded Robert Maynard Hutchins in 1951) wrote in reference to an abduction that threw local residents into a state of "near-panic" prior to the May meetings, "to bring the community together and announce a plan for the organization of the South East Chicago Commission." The plan itself had been developed earlier and had been presented by the university in previous meetings held at the suggestion of the Council of Hyde Park Churches and Synagogues. There was little doubt, at any rate, that the SECC was a university creation. Kimpton chaired the Committee of 5 that created it, and the university provided $15,000 as one-half of the organization's budget for the first year.[28]

The establishment of the SECC ended the University of Chicago's two-decade search for a satisfactory means to control black migration into its immediate environment. The university's "active participation and leadership in the work of stabilizing the neighborhoods surrounding the Campus" dated back to 1933 when Frank O'Brien, a University of Chicago alumnus and the vice-president of McKey and Poague Realtors, requested assistance in "financing" the expensive legal resistance to "the attempts of the colored" to enter the Washington Park Subdivision southwest of Hyde Park. Drawn into community affairs by a threatening racial situation, the university reorganized the local property owners' association into the Woodlawn Property Owners' League. It also quickly "called meetings of citizens in the Hyde Park-Oakland-Kenwood districts," which resulted in the creation of the Hyde Park Property Owners' Association and the Oakland-Kenwood Property Owners' Association. More than a passive supporter of these groups, the university was the spark and driving force behind them. Throughout the 1930s and 1940s the university subsidized these organizations and their legal efforts to bar blacks from the immediate area. From 1933 to 1947 (with the exception of a single year for which data could not be found), the university spent $110,923.72 on "community interests," $83,597.46 of which was apparently used in defending restrictive covenants. Before the fiscal year 1941–2, $69,150.12 was spent "principally" for such "legal services" and payments of $165.00 per month were made to the Woodlawn Property Owners' League for "protective work." By 1944 the university counted among its "accomplishments" the seven-year-delay in "the conversion of the Washington Park Subdivision from a white to a colored neighborhood," the eviction of "three groups of Mexicans, and other persons considered unassimilable in the community," and its services as "custodian of older restriction agreements and sponsor...[of] new block restriction agreements." A confidential memorandum to Robert Maynard Hutchins also revealed that the University of Chicago served "as headquarters for the Federation of Neighborhood Associations, the primary object of which...[was] to oppose efforts of the colored groups and social workers to secure the passage...of a bill declaring restriction agreements invalid and contrary to public policy."[29]

When attacked, the university staunchly, if unenthusiastically, defended its attempts to control its environment. The first notable debate on the university's restrictive actions came in 1937 as Robert Maynard Hutchins responded to charges in the *Defender*. "An examination of the University's record will, I am sure," Hutchins wrote, "convince any fair-minded person that, in determining the policies of the institution, neither the Trustees nor the administrative officers are actuated by race prejudice." However, Hutchins continued, the university "must endeavor to stabilize its neighborhood as an area in which its students and faculty will be content to live." "However unsatisfactory they may be," the chancellor concluded, racially restrictive covenants were legal instruments and Hyde Park's residents had the "right to invoke and defend them."[30]

The war years saw a reopening of the racial issue. Charges of discrimination in student admissions and services combined with those leveled against the university as a property owner to prompt Chancellor Hutchins to call for a "fresh and comprehensive attack on the whole thing."[31] His administrative colleagues advanced several policies, all of which suggested the use of quotas, "appropriate balances," or measures that would not push beyond the "limits of social tolerance."[32] In chiding his advisers for "missing the point of the racial problem," Hutchins wrote:

> The point is simply this: a university, of all institutions, cannot talk about the limitations of social tolerance. A university is supposed to lead, not to follow. A university may elect to push things only to the limit of social tolerance; but, if it does, it had better keep quiet about it. The ordinary excuse for social intolerance is that social tolerance would threaten the economic security of the tolerator. This excuse is not available to a university. A university is supposed to do what is right, and damn the consequences.[33]

His own inclination led Hutchins to advocate the "absolutely indiscriminate selection [admission] of all students who meet our intellectual and moral requirements." Hutchins could not reconcile, however, his desires for a blanket policy of nondiscrimination with the university's role in the community. "I have always been perplexed by the problem of our property on the south side," he wrote. For that reason, he advised the separation of the university's academic and real estate policies. "I think they are different," Hutchins helplessly concluded. "But don't ask me why."[34]

Tools other than restrictive covenants were also used by the university to control its environment, and, like the restrictive agreements, they were aimed primarily at manipulating the racial situation in the immediate area. By mid-1944 the Woodlawn community to the south of the campus was rapidly deteriorating and undergoing racial transition. The plight of the area was perceived almost entirely in racial terms. There was talk in administrative circles of the Washington Park Subdivision having "turned completely colored," of the advancing "dividing line between the colored and white neighborhoods," and that the main shopping center south of the Midway was "becoming darker day by day." By August, Chancellor Hutchins was presented with the option of whether the university, "solely as a matter of self-protection and irrespective of the so-called racial equality issue, should exert its utmost efforts to preserve its neighborhood communities."[35] The university selected two courses of action, which were of great significance for the future: It decided to expand its program of real estate investment and control; and it engaged in the process of urban planning.

The administration persuaded the board of trustees to establish a $500,000 revolving fund for "area protection" through rehabilitation after the latter had been taken on a bus tour "through typical colored neighborhoods so that they...[had] an opportunity to see conditions in all types of colored neighborhoods lying between the Loop...and the Campus."[36] A verse, written in Hutchins's own hand, revealed the purpose of the program as it praised the man responsible for purchasing local property:

> The Chancellor and the President gazed out across the park,
> They laughed like anything to see that things were looking dark.
> "Our neighborhood," the Chancellor said, "once blossomed like
>   the lily."
> "Just seven coons with seven kids could knock our program silly."
> "Forget it," said the President, "and thank the Lord for Willie."[37]

During the 1950s the trustees supplied another $4 million to, in Kimpton's words, "buy, control, and rebuild our neighborhood."[38]

The urban planning approach grew out of several neighborhood studies that were conducted by the university beginning in 1939 and culminated in the Chicago Plan Commission's publication of a conservation plan for Woodlawn in the mid-1940s. It had the same roots as the rehabilitation program. When the university initiated the study of Woodlawn, its former director of community interest work wrote that, "the chief fear was of negro invasion." Gradually the administration realized that there were "many more factors in the picture and there would be much less likelihood of racial invasion if the neighborhoods could be kept strong and desirable within themselves." This realization that racial succession and "blight" were inextricably bound up with each other pointed the way to future developments.[39]

After the war, and especially after redevelopment began, the situation in Hyde Park grew increasingly acute. But still, the pace of change in Woodlawn, Kenwood, and Hyde Park was measured not by the number of buildings falling into disrepair but by those passing into black ownership.[40] The university subsequently found itself pursuing activities that later characterized the SECC. "Outside influence" through the "right contacts," rather than the cumbersome legal process, was explored as a way to correct poor building conditions; both the Chicago Plan Commission and the Chicago Land Clearance Commission were contacted to see if the area around the campus might qualify for a redevelopment project; and the university administration inquired into the possibility of taking property "by the exercise of the power of eminent domain" under existing Illinois law. Several specific suggestions proposing the creation of a "Planning Office" within the university and the "stak[ing] out of a planning interest" between 43rd and 67th streets were also received.[41]

Most revealing of all, however, were the assessment and recommendations made by the Treasurer's Office in April 1949. Noting that the "forces of deterioration have been much greater than the efforts of the University and a small group of property owners to stabilize conditions," the report asserted that the decline and "invasion" of the area between 63rd and 67th streets had "advanced too far to be checked" and that the cost of successful remedial action in the sector between 60th and 63rd streets was "more than the University can assume." It recommended that the strip of property between 60th and 61st streets (including the south side of 61st) between Cottage Grove and Dorchester avenues be acquired to "serve as a buffer between the University and the deteriorating neighborhood to the south." As for controlling the area's population, it was hoped that the "problem of restriction might be avoided by the wrecking of undesirable buildings" and the development of attractive quarters that would be occupied by university faculty and employees. The area north of the Midway was another matter. The report recommended that $200,000 per year be spent "to eliminate the most undesirable buildings and residents" west of Ellis Avenue while the university prepared for the "eventual ownership of the entire area." The adjacent neighborhood between 55th and 59th streets east of University Avenue could be kept safe, the report concluded, with the removal of some small pockets of blight and the preservation of rent levels that would "maintain the white population." In its essentials, the report anticipated the university's creation of the South West Hyde Park Redevelopment Corporation to "renew" the area west of Ellis and the construction of the Hyde Park A and B developments in the mid-1950s. Its suggestion that demolition and rent levels be used as effective indirect means of controlling the area's population was also subsequently followed. Outlines of the university's eventual course of action were thus discernible by the late 1940s – at least half a year before the HPKCC was founded. The creation of the SECC was the culmination of two decades of continuous neighborhood involvement and, apparently, the immediate response to conditions as they rapidly changed north of the Midway between 1949 and 1952.[42]

If convinced of the necessity for action and, with the creation of the SECC, in possession of an agency strong enough to produce it, Hyde Park and the University of Chicago still lacked the necessary legislative tools. The 1947 Blighted Areas Redevelopment Act provided only for the clearance and reconstruction of *existing* slum areas. Hyde Park-Kenwood, despite its difficulties, hardly fell into that category. If the power of eminent domain and public funds were to be harnessed for the preservation of the University of Chicago area, earlier laws had to be amended and new ones written. As long as the public's attention and resources were committed to slum clearance, the rebuilding of Hyde Park was impossible.

There was no sinister "plot" to divert the city from a program of redevelopment to one of renewal. There was, simply, increasing concern over legitimate problems and the power to restructure "public" priorities. The elevation of Hyde Park's alderman, Robert E. Merriam, to the chairmanship of the Chicago City Council's Housing Committee in May 1951 was a key step. Merriam personally championed the cause of the basically sound, but threatened, middle-aged community. It was apparent, Merriam charged, that "many of the people being forced out of slum areas were moving to conservation areas, and that they and others were causing new overcrowding and problems in the vast middle belt of the city." New slums were being created faster than the old ones were being destroyed. It was much preferable, the alderman believed, to spend the comparatively small amounts needed to preserve sound communities than to wait for their decay and be faced with the prohibitively expensive task of massive demolition and redevelopment. Merriam subsequently waged a successful campaign to have the city council declare "conservation" a "major objective" of city policy.[43]

Even as Hyde Park's alderman was in the vanguard of those calling for a conservation program, other forces were laying the groundwork for necessary legislative action. In early 1952 the Metropolitan Housing and Planning Council established a Conservation Committee, which, in the following year, published a massive three-volume report entitled *Conservation*. Replete with suggestions for new legislation, the study selected Hyde Park-Kenwood as the pilot area in which to test fresh techniques and devices for renewal. The attention given the university community was no accident. The MHPC study was commissioned by Laird Bell, chairman of the university's board of trustees, and more than one-third of the council's board members either lived in Hyde Park or were University of Chicago graduates.[44] Most important of all, however, the committee's financial support came largely from Hyde Park. The University of Chicago provided $8,000 and other "interested concerns" contributed as well. The SECC, in fact, found itself in the position of "withdrawing unnecessary financial support while still expressing interest in and approval of the project." There was no doubt that the study was viewed as having more than academic significance. In discussing the undertaking, the Executive Committee of the SECC noted that a similar study had induced the New York Life Insurance Company to begin its Lake Meadows project.[45]

The final report was largely the production of Reginald Isaacs, head of the planning unit at Michael Reese Hospital, and provided a "technician's view of how to do things." It called for a legislative finding that slum *prevention* was a public purpose for which the city could exercise the right of eminent domain. If granted this power, the city would be able to "eliminate standard as well as substandard structures in those cases where their location or condition was inimical" to a local conservation plan.[46] This was entirely in keeping with Isaacs's determination that "something imaginative and revolutionary" had to be done to preserve threatened areas. In drafting a trenchant critique of the report, Nicholas von Hoffman noted that the proposed laws would give "technicians wide power that could only be checked by the public with great difficulty." "The leit-motif" of the study, von Hoffman wrote, was "coercive power wielded by the technocrats."[47]

The MHPC's proposals formed the basis for the Urban Community Conservation Act of 1953. Passed by lopsided bipartisan majorities, the act made slum prevention a public purpose that warranted the use of governmental power and funds. It not only expanded the municipality's authority to invoke eminent domain, but a companion measure empowered the Community Conservation Board (to be set up under the act) to make repairs on structures that owners were unwilling to bring up to minimum standards and take a lien on the property for the costs incurred. Finally, the act provided for community participation and approval of local conservation plans through an appointive Community Conservation Council.[48] Despite the trepidation in some quarters over the significant expansion of government power (Mayor Kennelly was "lukewarm" on the law), Sydney Stein, Jr., chairman of the HPKCC, expressed the reasoning of those most immediately concerned when he said that "the risk of granting these powers was far less than the risk of the alternatives considered."[49] The University of Chicago's stand on the measure was, of course, unequivocal. Chancellor Kimpton felt that the Urban Community Conservation Act "was of vital importance to the University and its community." Indeed, if anything, Alderman Clarence Wagner noted somewhat indelicately, it "look[ed] like a U[niversity] of C[hicago] bail-out."[50]

Passage of the Conservation Act and the lien law represented only two-thirds of the General Assembly's important work as far as Hyde Park was concerned. The University of Chicago, through the SECC and its aggressive executive director, Julian Levi, assumed the primary responsibility for amending the Neighborhood Redevelopment Corporation Act of 1941. The original measure permitted any three citizens and residents to organize a private corporation and, under the supervision of a mayorally appointed Neighborhood Redevelopment Commission, carry out a redevelopment plan. Once the corporation purchased or had under option 60% of a designated redevelopment area, it would be empowered to exercise eminent domain to obtain the remainder of the site.[51] Originally enacted as a device to keep blacks out of the 63rd and Halsted area, the measure was never used, as its 60% ownership requirement proved unworkable.[52] Julian Levi, however, proposed including conservation areas in the scope of the Neighborhood Redevelopment Corporation Act and, most important, the revision of the stipulation that required the corporation to own 60% of the designated site before obtaining the power of eminent domain. Levi suggested, instead, that the corporation need only secure the consent of the owners of 60% of the redevelopment site to be bound by the corporation's plans before eminent domain could be used. A determined lobbying effort by Levi and the SECC proved successful and the 1941 law was amended accordingly.[53]

With the passage of the General Assembly's 1953 renewal measures, the tools to preserve Hyde Park were at hand. As a solution to the community's problems, these enactments represented a totally different approach from that envisioned by the HPKCC in its call for an open housing law. First, the racial implications of the 1953 program were not readily apparent. Where the conference's proposal was conceived entirely in racial terms and guaranteed to raise vociferous opposition, the MHPC's Conservation Act and the SECC's amendments to the 1941 Redevelopment Act were measures that could benefit any community and, certainly, the city as a whole. The charge of pious hypocrisy could be leveled at Hyde Park's support of open occupancy but not at its endorsement of the latter laws. Most important, though, the MHPC and SECC approach avoided predicating Hyde Park's preservation on the peaceful resolution of the entire city's racial and housing problems. The 1953 laws provided the means with which Hyde Park and the University of Chicago could attack their own problems without regard for what occurred elsewhere. The Conservation Act and its companion legislation represented a declaration of independence for Hyde Park and marked the absolute reversal of the HPKCC approach, which placed the community's fate in the hands of distant, if not hostile, powers.

The subsequent reconstruction and preservation of Hyde Park-Kenwood proceeded in three major phases. First, the development of two projects, Hyde Park A and B, removed a badly deteriorated section of the community and provided a shopping center and new housing. Second, the university organized the South West Hyde Park Neighborhood Redevelopment Corporation, which conducted renewal activities to the west of its campus. Third, an urban renewal plan for the entire community was drawn up and approved in 1958. In each phase, the university, through the SECC, was the dominant force, and the HPKCC, effectively barred from the decision-making process in the first two phases, acted primarily as a communications link between the planners and the community when the latter's nominal approval was required in the third and final stage.

The primacy of the university in the urban renewal of Hyde Park is best illustrated by the key role played by the South East Chicago Commission. Created and largely supported by the university, the SECC was generally regarded as an appendage to Chancellor Kimpton's administration. The SECC's director also clearly viewed himself as an "agent of the university."[54] In the spring of 1954 the Marshall Field Foundation provided a grant of $100,000 to the university, which was used to set up a Planning Unit within the SECC. Subsequent to this, as Rossi and Dentler point out, "technical and administrative work ordinarily the province of municipal agencies was taken over by the University, the Commission, and the Planning Unit." This assumption of power was the result of the need for quick action, doubts as to the city's ability to produce a desirable plan, and the "embryonic stage of the municipal agencies in question." Ultimately the university contracted with the city to do its own technical planning and produce an Urban Renewal Plan for the entire area. Moreover, the board of citizens appointed by the mayor to review and approve the plan (the Community Conservation Council) used the staff of the SECC as its own. Thus those with the power to disapprove local renewal projects were served and advised by those having the most vital interest in the acceptance of university-drawn plans.[55] The university's overwhelming presence was also evident in the two earlier stages of renewal. The South West Hyde Park Neighborhood Redevelopment Corporation was established with university capital, and its officers and trustees included Julian Levi and a number of men prominent in the university's central administration.[56] The corporation's plans, as well as those originally devised for the Hyde Park A and B projects, were, in fact, produced by the SECC's Planning Unit.[57]

Given the university's dominating role in urban renewal, the views of two men – Chancellor Kimpton and SECC Director Julian Levi – were the key determinants in defining both the goals and nature of the urban renewal process.[58] Much has been made in the past about the community's participation in urban renewal through the offices of the Hyde Park-Kenwood Community Conference. It was clear, however, that in the two instances where the cooperation of the "people" could be legally dispensed with, the university and the SECC simply ignored the HPKCC. Bitter disputes arose over the plans for Hyde Park A and B and the South West Hyde Park renewal not because the conference was inexperienced or unable to build a "consensus" in the community but rather because the university was able to achieve its ends through the Blighted Areas Redevelopment Act of 1947 in the first instance and through a private redevelopment corporation in the second. Only in the last stage of the community's renewal, the formation of a comprehensive plan under the Urban Community Conservation Act of 1953, was the assent of the community required. It was, therefore, only in this last phase that the university and the SECC had need of the conference's services and found it useful in building necessary community support. At no time did the former regard the latter as a "partner" in the undertaking, and the role ultimately played by the HPKCC was determined more by the university's needs than anything else.

Publicly, Chancellor Kimpton denied that community deterioration was a "racial problem." Privately, the goals he stressed for the renewal of Hyde Park were clearly racial in nature. Kimpton explicitly sought an economically upgraded and predominantly white neighborhood. He viewed upper income housing as "an effective screening tool" and as a means of "cutting down [the] number of Negroes" residing in the area. He was also prepared to take more direct action. In preparing an outline for a board of trustees meeting he noted simply: "Tear it down and begin over again. Negroes."[59] In addition to his more general economic and racial goals, Kimpton specifically sought a buffer on the southern border of the campus and the maintenance of South East Hyde Park as a white enclave.

He believed that "many of his faculty members would move away if Negroes [were permitted] in SEHP." When widespread suspicion of the university's aims became apparent, Kimpton rejected the HPKCC's advice to publicly answer all questions. The "University's position was such that it would do more harm than good to go out and face the public," he felt. "If a U[niversity] representative honestly answered questions relating to these matters," he observed, "the University would be in a worse position than it is now."[60]

Whereas Kimpton discreetly expressed the goals of those directing the urban renewal of Hyde Park, Julian Levi, as director of the SECC, controlled the mode of operation.[61] Levi recognized that university expansion and the development of a "compatible environment" often placed the institution into "direct and even brutal collision with others." In a speech given at the Massachusetts Institute of Technology, Levi detailed his views on how that conflict should be handled by deprecating the HPKCC without naming it. Urban renewal, Levi explained, should not be approached as a human relations program, an exercise in participatory democracy, or a compromise between institutional and community needs. "If we are really serious about the needs of our institution," he continued,

> then our problem is not one of compromise; it is rather the establishment of priorities. If we are really serious about the next generation of teachers and scholars, lawyers and doctors, physicists and chemists, then we have got to worry about the adequate housing of the graduate student; about the clearing of land for a new laboratory; about the closing of streets to divert traffic from campuses; about the development of a "compatible environment" including substantial slum clearance...We cannot have it both ways. We are either going to have graduate students, who produce leadership for the next generation..., or we are not going to achieve these results because we are unwilling to disturb existing owners and populations.[62]

Levi obviously did not view the planning process as one consisting of "give and take" between the university and the community. It was only when planners became "weak-kneed," he believed, that poor compromises were made.[63]

Insofar as the race issue was concerned, Levi believed, as did the HPKCC, that it was a metropolitan problem. Unlike the members of the conference, however, he felt that the "grave issues of minority housing must be settled separately from conservation." Rather than being paralyzed by the scope of the problem, Levi wanted to "save" Hyde Park and leave the larger issue, even if in aggravated form, for the city to solve at some later date. Levi was aware that the "most

Julian Levi (left) and Lawrence A. Kimpton review maps and plans for Hyde Park. (© *Chicago Sun-Times*, 1953. Photograph by Bob Kotalik, reprinted with permission.)

bitter" of all urban renewal "dilemmas" involved minority groups. To call for comprehensive metropolitan planning as a prelude to renewal, however, was simply a means of avoiding the problems, not resolving them. "The bitter decisions will have to be taken anyhow," he concluded. Levi chose to make those decisions rather than be rendered impotent by their prospect.[64]

It is not surprising that Julia Abrahamson felt that friction developed with Levi's appointment and the evolution of an SECC program that "brought it into conflict with the work... [and] goals of the conference."[65] In day-to-day operations, such as handling housing code violations, a modus vivendi emerged that saw the HPKCC take the high road of persuasion and legal action, whereas the "bludgeon force" of the SECC was kept in reserve. When cases required pressure beyond that provided by the legal process, Levi "put the screws" to slumlords by convincing banks, insurance companies, and management firms to call in loans, cancel fire insurance, and cease tenant referrals.[66] When it came to the planning process or racial issues, however, the SECC remained aloof. The Conference Committee to Maintain an Interracial Community tried repeatedly to enlist SECC help but encountered only cold indifference.[67] As for renewal itself, the HPKCC was often placed in the position of being questioned about university policies "about which little [was] known."[68] One particularly embarrassing incident occurred when the conference, at Levi's request, testified in favor of creating a neighborhood park in conjunction with the Hyde Park A and B project. Led to believe that its action was merely a prerequisite to a necessary Park District inquiry, the conference was taken by surprise when the SECC followed with a specific and detailed plan for the park's construction. Unaware of the plan's existence and believing their testimony had not been connected with any concrete proposal, conference representatives were chagrined. The block groups affected by the plan charged the HPKCC with breaking its "commitment to community discussion." They did not know that the conference staff was as shocked as any at hearing the SECC's presentation.[69]

The most revealing glimpse of the nature of SECC-HPKCC relations was provided, however, by the operations of the Committee of 6. Originally formed as an advisory body to the SECC's Planning Unit, it had been of limited use until it was reconstituted and revived soon after the park proposal controversy. The committee consisted of two representatives each from the university (Kimpton and Vice-President William B. Harrell), the SECC (Levi and Newton Farr), and the conference (the executive director and the chairman of the board). It was nominally charged with formulating policy and coordinating efforts.[70] As Rossi and Dentler conclude, though, such coordination was "more a hopeful myth to the Conference... than a matter of practice." The Committee of 6 actually functioned as a "platform from which University and Commission intentions were announced, Conference suggestions entertained, and points of disagreement clarified." At best it was only an "apparent medium for policy negotiation" and a provider of "limited advance information" to the conference.[71]

Julia Abrahamson rebelled against this subordination of the HPKCC. She was unwilling to place the conference in the position of merely "selling" university plans to the community, and there was considerable fear within the HPKCC that it was simply being "used."[72] Yet there was little that could be done. The placement of the conference representatives on the outer ring of the inner circle of policy makers vitiated attempts to oppose the university. "How can we meet with the University administration privately each week to share thinking and negotiate differences," one conference member asked rhetorically, "while also engaging in public attacks?"[73] Thus the university's goals of a predominantly white and economically upgraded community guided the renewal process. Even the most liberal Hyde Parkers would have found the first goal congenial, if difficult to admit, but the conference had gone on record as favoring a community "of diversified structures for different types of family and income groups." It had even endorsed the inclusion of public housing as part of the renewal plan. Moreover, many residents feared being "priced out of the area" and "a move by powerful interests to create an upper-middle class community."[74] The conference, however, lacked the strength to do other than merely articulate these latter goals.

Unable to alter basic policy, the conference assumed as its primary function that which was left to it: the task of "explainer, clarifier, and mediator between the people of the community and the official planning unit." Once the SECC had seized the initiative, the HPKCC Planning Committee found itself simply "informing the community after changes and proposals have been announced by the Planning Unit, and dealing with crises."[75] After the park proposal incident, the committee decided to act as a "transmission belt" (the term is Rossi and Dentler's) in conveying Planning Unit intentions to the community and citizens' concerns back to the planners.[76] By 1957 James V. Cunningham (Julia Abrahamson's successor as executive director), perhaps more willing to "sell" plans than his predecessor had been, "had achieved an uninfluential yet satisfying rapprochment" with the SECC on the basis of the "transmission belt" function.[77]

Still, this sort of citizen participation emerged only with discussions over the comprehensive renewal program, which was finally approved in 1958. The first two phases of Hyde Park's reconstruction – the development of Hyde Park A and B and the operation of the South West Neighborhood Redevelopment Corporation – proceeded under legislation that did not require community assent to renewal plans. The result was that the conference had little impact on the proposals devised for these early programs and each precipitated bitter, but futile, resistance.

Conceived in the early 1950s, a primary reason for the Hyde Park

A and B project was the desire to show some tangible "progress" to dispel the pessimism infecting many of the area's whites and thus stabilize the existing population. It was known that the process of completing a comprehensive renewal plan would take years and that such efforts would be fruitless if current residents deserted the neighborhood before its completion.[78] Consequently, the desire for quick action led to the use of existing and already court-tested legislation. In late 1953 the Chicago Land Clearance Commission was asked to survey the most deteriorated sector of Hyde Park in the hope that it would be declared a "blighted" area and thus qualify for redevelopment under the Illinois Blighted Areas Redevelopment Act of 1947 and the federal Housing Act of 1949. Two sections within the surveyed area (53rd Street to 57th Street and Woodlawn Avenue to Lake Park Avenue) were officially designated as "blighted." The larger site (42.7 acres) was called Hyde Park A and the smaller one (4.6 acres) was Hyde Park B. Although the redevelopment area covered only 6% of Hyde Park-Kenwood, it included 40% of that community's deteriorated dwelling units.[79]

Redevelopment plans called for the construction of a shopping center to replace many small retail outlets that had clustered along 55th Street. Affected businessmen went along with the plans in the belief that they would be able to relocate within the community. Proceeding under the legislation that permitted the New York Life Insurance Company's Lake Meadows, however, meant that the decisions as to the size, nature, and tenancy of the new shopping center were determined by the private developers contracted to build it. Local businessmen found themselves permanently displaced and bitter over being "double crossed and taken for a ride on the 'Hyde Park A and B' plan."[80] Levi and the SECC were content with the plans as they assigned top priority only to visible progress. Thus the demolition of the first building to make way for the project was staged as the "climax" to an annual meeting of the SECC and secured wide publicity – despite the feeling of many HPKCC members "that it was unfortunate to have a public celebration centering around [an act] of destruction."[81]

The most acrimonious controversy, however, stemmed from the university's plans for "renewing" the South West Hyde Park area through the use of a private redevelopment corporation. Separated from the larger community encompassed by the general renewal plans being concurrently developed, the neighborhood immediately west of the campus was reconstructed under the one law that directly granted the power of eminent domain to private parties. It was the one phase of Hyde Park's revivification over which the SECC and the university exercised the most direct control. The HPKCC had no hand in the planning and participated, despite some internal divisions, only to support the redevelopment corporation's actions. The renewal of South West Hyde Park also entailed the most visible attempt to regulate the university's racial environment.

It was clear from discussions held by the Committee of 6 that the area's problem was conceived primarily in racial terms. Jack Meltzer, head of the SECC Planning Unit, warned the committee that "all the area North of 55th, and the area West of Ellis from 55th to 58th . . . was becoming 100% Negro so fast that he wondered if the whole urban renewal program was not endangered." Kimpton spoke of "trying to maintain the University's island from 55th to 61st," but Levi was less willing to surrender any ground. He felt that although things would "get worse for a while," it was possible to sustain a "holding action," and then, "as the urban renewal plan goes into effect, . . . [have a] 'rollback.' " The corporation's redevelopment site extended from 55th to 59th streets, from Cottage Grove to Woodlawn Avenue (excluding the University of Chicago campus). Most of the 54-acre site was marked for rehabilitation, but a 14.5-acre sector between 55th and 56th, from Cottage Grove to Ellis Avenue, was slated for clearance and university acquisition. The population of the entire redevelopment area was slightly more than 54% black; that of the acquisition site was 80% black.[82]

Equally important was the way in which the South West Hyde Park Neighborhood Redevelopment Corporation met the legal requirements necessary for it to obtain the power of eminent domain. The first prerequisite compelled the corporation to secure the signed consent of the owners of 60% of the redevelopment area. The HPKCC contacted fifteen of the twenty-five property owners who signed consent agreements and found that ten were upper-middle-class white homeowners who lived outside the acquisition site. Significantly, five of these were university employees. The university had bought local property in the name of its employees in the past, and the 1949 treasurer's report stated that the university already owned "about one-half" of the property west of Ellis between 55th and 59th streets. It thus needed the consent of owners of but a small portion of the redevelopment area in order to secure the power of eminent domain. Indeed, a major complaint of those living in that section was that they "were not even approached nor asked to sign consents." The extent of university property ownership and James Cunningham's private assertion that the redevelopment site was "gerrymandered" to produce the needed agreements explain the ease with which the consents were secured.[83]

The second requirement concerned the condition of the buildings in question. Those residing within the acquisition area strongly disputed the Redevelopment Corporation's classification of their area as "deteriorated." Others did as well. James Cunningham personally inspected eight structures marked as dilapidated on corporation maps and found them to be in "excellent condition." He felt, generally, that the information produced by the redevelopers was "weak" and that there had been considerable rehabilitation since the initial surveys, which had written off structures with minor and easily repaired defects. The Planning Unit, however, refused to reconsider its classification of the site and forcefully asserted that the area was still "headed for blight."[84] In subsequent hearings before the Neighborhood Redevelopment Commission, the corporation established the principle of "conversion by use." Even if structurally sound, many of the buildings in South West Hyde Park housed more families than they were originally intended to shelter. It was contended that this pattern of overuse "inevitably led to slum and blight" and that once under way the process could not be stopped.[85] The amended 1941 Redevelopment Act, of course, did not demand proof that an area was blighted – only that it was in danger of becoming so. The Neighborhood Redevelopment Commission accepted the corporation's argument, approved its plans, and, despite a later court battle, the South West Hyde Park Neighborhood Redevelopment Corporation obtained control of its designated site.[86]

Throughout the planning for South West Hyde Park, the university, the SECC, and the Redevelopment Corporation worked efficiently but quietly. The *Hyde Park Herald* complained in two pointed editorials that the university's use of public powers compromised its position as a private institution and that its "semi-public status in...community renewal work means that it cannot have 'private' freedom to do anything it sees fit." It demanded that the university administration give the community "a full picture of what they are doing."[87] The HPKCC was also totally locked out of the decision-making process on South West Hyde Park. It was precisely on this issue that Julia Abrahamson most strenuously objected to being placed in the position of "selling" the university's plans, and James Cunningham (who became executive director in the midst of this controversy) stated that the university presented its program on a "take it or leave it" basis. Yet the HPKCC supported the Redevelopment Corporation. Cunningham defended the proposal in a long letter to the *Herald,* and Julian Levi was permitted to "go over" the conference's testimony to the Neighborhood Redevelopment Commission and select the HPKCC's witnesses.[88]

The final phase of Hyde Park's reconstruction involved the adoption of a general urban renewal plan. First released for public discussion in February 1958, and approved by the City Council in November of that year, the Final Plan encompassed the entire area from 47th Street to 59th Street between Cottage Grove Avenue and the lake (with the exception of Jackson and Burnham parks, the Illinois Central Right of Way, and those areas already being redeveloped).[89] Of the 855.8 acres included in the project, 105.8 were subject to either total or spot clearance; 638 structures containing 6,147 dwelling units were marked for demolition. More than 4,000 families were slated for relocation (over a five-year period), and the construction of 2,100 new homes resulted in a net reduction of nearly 4,000 dwelling units for the entire area.[90]

North West Hyde Park endured the most extensive work under the Final Plan. There were three points at which the citizens of that area tried to alter the planners' designs. First, planners intended to clear an area to the north and west of the Kozminski school for a park and, later, institutional expansion. Local residents objected to the number of sound structures that would have to be demolished and suggested that the same purposes could be achieved if clearance took place east of the school. Their suggestion on this "matter of great local saliency but. . . small technical significance" was adopted by the Planning Unit. The other two areas of controversy, however, produced different results. One centered around the use of the site vacated by the Rodfei Zedek Temple. Planners wanted to clear additional land around the site and use it for a new school, park, and parking area. Citizens took exception to the extra demolition and the prospective use of the locale. Eventually the planners removed the future designation of the site and simply called it a "park." The amount of clearance was not reduced. The changes, as Rossi and Dentler conclude, were "very minor. . .but important enough to eliminate controversy." The final dispute revolved around a site centered at 55th Street and Maryland Avenue. There was a consensus that this sector should be cleared (among those living outside the two blocks to be demolished); but when planners proposed a Research Park for the site, the community objected to such institutional use. Most favored new housing on the site in the hope that more white families could be induced to live in the rapidly "changing" area. It is likely that the public furor over the Research Park caused it to be abandoned, but the Planning Unit simply substituted other institutional uses for the disputed site. Local suspicions that the university simply wanted to displace blacks by "institutionalizing" the area and creating a "racial barrier" subsequently developed. In each of these three cases the changes incorporated into the Final Plan were of little significance. What *was* of great moment was that even though the citizens "did not get what they wanted, they were. . . not alienated from the Final Plan." Thus, in the area of their greatest influence, Hyde Park's citizens shaped renewal plans only when the university's interest remained "general" and "did not require specific sites."[91]

If the planners were willing to accommodate the community on points that did not alter the overall configuration of the Final Plan, they remained adamant when challenged on questions of basic policy. The most controversial issue in Hyde Park's urban renewal was whether or not it should include public housing. Many in the community wanted to take "fair responsibility for relocation and to prevent the use of public funds to subsidize housing only for those who need it least."[92] The HPKCC provided institutional expression for this sentiment as its leadership repeatedly called for the provision of public housing in renewal plans and ultimately made a formal policy statement favoring the construction of 200 to 250 such units in Hyde Park.[93]

The university, the SECC, and Julian Levi, however, refused to soften their unequivocal opposition to public housing. When pressed on the issue in a Committee of 6 meeting, Levi objected to it "as something harmful to the neighborhood which the people did not want anyway." Even the demand for middle-income housing was enough to spark a Levi "tirade" against its advocates and lead him to denounce it as "stupid and unnecessary."[94] To underscore his hostility to all who threatened the goal of an economically upgraded community, Levi, according to Hyde Park alderman and public housing advocate Leon Despres, "engineered" the attempt to defeat the alderman when he ran for reelection in 1959.[95]

Despite the vehemence of his position, Levi's assessment of the community's temper was both cool and accurate. Many were thrown into a quandary on the public housing issue by their "theoretical favor of it and realistic concern over bringing a high number of indigents into the area."[96] "Many who call for public housing the loudest will be the quickest to move to Evanston when it comes next door to them," one of Leon Despres's constituents wrote. "One can be pushed too far," the writer added, "in living up to his liberal ideals." Others commiserated with blacks in need of good housing and even conceded the value of publicly provided units. They also felt, however, that the entry of low-income blacks would be the "handwriting on the wall" signifying the destruction of the community and that the liberal cause would derive no benefit "from the collapse of its mightiest stronghold – *our* Hyde Park" (emphasis added).[97] Indeed, Rossi and Dentler point out that the demand for public housing was made more out of the desire for ideological consistency on the part of the conference leadership than as a representation of "grass roots" support. If anything, they note, the "majority" of block groups were against conference testimony on this point and even the board members were divided. If public housing was made part of the Final Plan, knowledgeable observers commented, those on the HPKCC board would be "collectively pleased and individually disappointed."[98]

The timorous nature of the support for public housing was most glaringly revealed in the conference policy statement that called for it. In asking for 200 to 250 low-income units scattered over numerous small sites, the HPKCC hardly envisaged accommodating a unified 462-unit development such as that which confronted the people of South Deering in the Trumbull Park Homes. Furthermore, the conference felt that 50 to 100 of the units should be reserved for the elderly and suggested that other units be constructed to accommodate large families, as it was understood that the "waiting lists for large families include a larger proportion of white[s]. . . than do the lists as a whole."[99]

The fears of public housing's friends and foes were needless. Although a preliminary project report called for 500 public housing units, the Final Plan, initially, provided none. Finally, 60 units for the elderly and 60 for families were included. A full decade after the renewal plans had been approved, however, only 34 units had been constructed – and 22 of those were for the elderly. Even the violent accommodation in Trumbull Park permitted the presence of about 25 publicly housed low-income families; it was more than twice the number permitted in Hyde Park.[100]

Where public housing was concerned, the nature of the symbiotic relationship between the HPKCC and the SECC was not that of the "people's" organization working in conjunction with those moving the levers of power. The SECC was closer to the "people" on this issue than was the conference. Rather, the organizations represented the two sides produced by the major intellectual and emotional division on the matter. The SECC protected the community's "interests" as it took the "practical" view of the situation. The HPKCC, much less certain about its mission than its rival, appealed to the community's sense of justice and responsibility and formally articulated the liberal's theoretical acceptance of public housing. With the power to make the final decision in the hands of the former organization, however, the latter could safely represent the community's "conscience" and breathe a surreptitious sigh of relief when overwhelmed by the forces of the "real world."[101] The verbalization of an ideal, rather than its realization, became an end in itself.

Once the Final Plan was presented, a citywide debate ensued on its merits.[102] Leon Despres saw threats to the plan emanating from three sources. First, there was "some bitter Negro opposition because the plan reduces the total housing available to Negroes." Second, there was "some serious opposition to the failure to supply low income, middle income, and more abundant housing." The university, Despres noted, was "not greatly interested in encouraging devices for middle income housing nor in making sure the hoped-for rehabilitation of existing structures will keep rents low." Finally, there was "spotty die-hard opposition to specific individual provisions."[103] Despite his own misgivings, Despres testified in favor of the plan. As the city council had the power only to accept or reject the proposal, not amend it, the consequences of its deficiencies were not as alarming as those of not having a plan at all. The university knew this and, perhaps, counted on the considerable reluctant support that was forthcoming from those actually displeased with their plans. Especially revealing in this regard was the position taken by Robert Merriam, former Hyde Park alderman and a pioneer in the city's conservation movement. "My own reaction," Merriam wrote after considering the program's limitations, "is that a practical demonstration of the ability of a city and a community to rejuvenate itself is so vital that it is worth pushing even with the shortcomings." He concluded, however, that the "opportunistic attitude of the University administration" was "a sorry thing to watch."[104]

The most cogent critique of the Final Plan came from beyond Hyde Park's borders. Displaying a perspective that accepted the city as an organic entity, the Archdiocese of Chicago, through its newspaper, the *New World*, and the Cardinal's Committee on Conservation, spoke out against the Final Plan. In a series of articles and editorials that appeared in the *New World* throughout the spring and summer of 1958 the original objections of Hyde Parkers themselves were resurrected: There was too much demolition, good homes would be destroyed while there was still a housing shortage, the relocation envisaged would be disruptive, there was no provision for low- or middle-income families. The most perceptive arguments, however, were not those that went over old ground. In placing the Hyde Park-Kenwood Urban Renewal Plan in a citywide context, the *New World* and, especially, the Cardinal's Committee on Conservation and its spokesman, Monsignor John J. Egan, provided a forceful rebuttal to Julian Levi's independent action on behalf of a single community.[105]

In testifying against the program, most of the monsignor's objections revolved around the metropolitan theme. He implicitly attacked the shift from slum clearance to conservation by emphasizing the plight of Chicago's "hundreds of thousands" of poorly housed people who were "irrelevant" to the proposed plan and would not be helped by it. He also urged the members of the city council to remember that "you are not voting on a plan to build something; you are voting...to tear something down." The impact of demolition and relocation, Egan asserted, would be felt by all neighborhoods. Finally, he asked, after Hyde Park was "deftly swathed in 'green belts,' 'open spaces,' and 'parking lots,' what are we going to give everyone else?" Fearing the consequences of pouring all of the city's resources into a single community, the monsignor warned the alderman that "the anomaly you face is the city all slum but for one section, the one with those 'high standards.' " In sum, Monsignor Egan protested against Hyde Park's initiative, ability, and power to marshal resources on its own behalf – and the act of self-preservation that left the rest of the city to take care of itself.[106]

As with the HPKCC's espousal of open occupancy, the position taken by the Cardinal's Committee represented a forceful blend of conviction and interest. Viewing the city as an interdependent collection of communities, it was less willing than others to single out any one for special treatment. It was also, obviously, painfully aware of the broad implications of the actions taken by a single community and the subsequent costs extracted from its neighbors. Relocation from Hyde Park presented many surrounding Catholic communities, especially St. Leo's parish, with an in-migration of uprooted blacks. At one point, Monsignor Egan complained personally to Julian Levi that the Catholic Church, unlike more mobile Protestant churches, could not abandon its "cathedrals" and that Hyde Park's renewal was "creating too much of a problem for them." Other members of the archdiocese also felt that the "racial overtones of the *New World* editorials would give any sensitive and informed person grounds for believing that we were trying to keep Negroes from moving into other neighborhoods."[107]

Hyde Parkers, united by the "outside" attack on their plan, responded by dismissing Monsignor Egan's legitimate criticisms as being rooted simply in base interest. They pointed accusatory fingers at the exclusionary practices of Catholic communities and vigorously reasserted that Hyde Park's renewal, in contrast, would maintain a stable, integrated neighborhood as an example for all.

This counterattack represented a new, "evangelical" zeal. In the years between the founding of the HPKCC and the SECC, conference members were in "general agreement" that their actions should *not* be held up "as a model for other communities to follow." They felt that "every community must plan its own program on the basis of its own distinctive problems and resources."[108] With the establishment of the SECC, its Planning Unit, and the Ford Foundation "demonstration" grant, however, the activities in Hyde Park were given broader significance.[109] The liberal goal of creating a stable interracial community, of course, implicitly contained the idea that Hyde Park would show the rest of the city the proper way to respond to racial transition. But the significance of Hyde Park's example grew, seemingly, in direct proportion to the resources it demanded. Fears that Hyde Park was monopolizing the state's allotment of federal funds and receiving disproportionate municipal services were met with increased claims of local importance. "We will have to get used to the rather selfish act of spending 40 million dollars on our own neighborhood when it might appear that some or all of that money should go elsewhere," the *Hyde Park Herald* editorialized in 1957. The editors knew, certainly, that the entire city had "a great stake" in Hyde Park's success, but they were forced to admit that "this is a tough problem for Hyde Parkers with a conscience."[110] In using the idea that Hyde Park was an example for all to follow, the Final Plan's proponents seized upon the broadest possible public justification for the project. By the time the archdiocese had made public its objections, the *Hyde Park Herald*, apparently having resolved its pangs of conscience, asserted that a "demonstration that neighborhoods of all races can live in a community of peace and self-respect is worth whatever price must be paid."[111]

Despite the rhetoric, however, Hyde Park's singular treatment resulted more from political realities than the desire to create an interracial utopia. When the Community Conservation Board was first constituted, its energies were absorbed by the needs of those primarily responsible for its existence. By 1955 there was "growing alarm and concern" over complaints by less well organized communities that they were not receiving sufficient CCB attention. By 1957 there was "considerable resentment" that the board's only successful effort was the Hyde Park renewal program.[112] Hyde Park's possession of a well-financed Planning Unit and the considerable disorder afflicting the city's housing agencies also, according to Julian Levi, "play[ed] into our hands." Given the abundant resources in Hyde Park, that community was able to produce a renewal plan, whereas the rest of the city was "paralyzed." Levi knew that without "serious competition for the public's money" it would be "impossible" to cut funds designated for the university area. The absence of a comprehensive city plan, a cause for lamentation among most planners, similarly permitted the quick and the strong to seize available resources. Levi, in a rare and tactful bit of understatement before an audience of planners, simply noted that the absence of a comprehensive program "was not fatal."[113] Finally, the university's board of trustees secured the backing of Mayor Richard J. Daley in return for their political support and, according to Leon Despres, a promise "to leave city-wide policies to him."[114]

Thus the university remained cool to attempts by the HPKCC to enlist its aid in pushing for a metropolitan open housing law, and the mayor worked out the compromise that, in the wake of the archdiocese's critique, assured passage of the Final Plan. After a calming delay, Daley initiated some minor cutbacks in the proposal that were a "concession to the opposition – but a concession which was not harmful to the plan as a whole." Although the mayor felt that the airing of views was important, and that many of the criticisms were valid, he did not believe sufficient reason existed "to hold up the plan and permit the neighborhood to deteriorate."[115] Chancellor Kimpton expressed his gratitude by lauding Daley as "the greatest Mayor the City of Chicago ever had."[116]

In his inaugural address in the fall of 1951, Chancellor Lawrence A. Kimpton had noted that when the University of Chicago was founded sixty years before it was in "the most desirable residential district in the city." The "carriages of Chicago's elite moved sedately down Drexel Street and nobody dreamed of the process of decay that would set in over the next half century." Seven years later, testifying in support of the Hyde Park-Kenwood Urban Renewal Plan, Kimpton asserted that "it is not possible to operate and maintain a great university in a deteriorating or slum neighborhood." "Accordingly," he informed the aldermen, "the very life of the University is at stake."[117] More than anything else, these statements explain the needs to which Hyde Park's urban renewal was addressed, the rationale that guided the program, and the forceful methods used to achieve it.[118]

Engaged in a literal struggle for survival, the university was neither indulging in a "noble experiment" nor setting an example for others. Julian Levi, in fact, felt that Hyde Park's image as a nascent interracial utopia was a detriment to the renewal effort. The "perpetual discussion of the joys of interracial activities will cause men and women of good will. . . to applaud the 'noble experiment' while at the same time they caution their daughters not to go to the University of Chicago lest they be raped on the streets," Levi wrote.[119] He knew that much of the interracialist rhetoric, however satisfying to a liberal community in the process of reducing its nonwhite population, bore little relation to what he and the university were trying to accomplish. Moreover, the university's use of the private redevelopment corporation in South West Hyde Park was, as one knowledgeable observer commented, a "one crack operation." The difficulties in using the corporation, the obvious problems of granting the power of eminent domain to private parties, and the friction it produced meant that the tool could not easily, if ever, be used again.[120] In terms of the broader renewal plan as well, the Hyde Park experience was more unique than trend-setting. Monsignor Egan's 1958 claims that the Final Plan was surrounded by "pretense" and that city officials had privately stated that the program would be both the first and last of its kind also proved accurate.[121] The urban renewal of Hyde Park was an undertaking launched by particular interests for specific purposes. As such, and in the tools it employed, it was sui generis.

Central to an understanding of the nature of the program is the race issue. It was, of course, not the only factor; there were legitimate concerns about the aging of the area, its gradual deterioration, and the provision of necessary room for institutional expansion that existed independently of racial considerations. The prospect of *racial* succession, however, called both the HPKCC and the SECC into being and initiated the movement that culminated in urban renewal. The attempt to control, alter, or reverse this process and its attendant consequences spurred the reconstruction of Hyde Park and provided the context within which the other problems were resolved.

Two arguments have been advanced to deny that Hyde Park's urban renewal was "aimed" at blacks. The first states that since the goal of the plan was to create an integrated community, blacks could hardly be considered a "target." It would, however, be more accurate to conceive of the integration of Hyde Park simply as a necessary by-product of its renewal rather than the purpose behind it. Those controlling the rebuilding process viewed the presence of blacks as more inevitable than desirable and, accordingly, set out to produce an accommodation on their own terms. By the mid-1950s, the question was not whether there would be any blacks in Hyde Park but rather would there be any whites? The maintenance of a white presence around the University of Chicago subsequently meant, by definition, integration. It was more the product of a tenacious defensive reaction than that of an adventurous step forward; as such it could only be a result, not a goal.

The second argument pointed to the many whites forced to relocate as a consequence of renewal activities and thus successfully refuted charges, made largely by the black press, that the plans simply represented a process of "Negro clearance." That all blacks were not rooted out of the community (that was an impossibility) and that some whites were, however, still does not dispose of the race issue as it manifested itself in Hyde Park. Most of the whites dispossessed during renewal were uprooted by either the A and B project (72% of the 892 families relocated were white, 18% were black, 10% other) or the Final Plan (40% of the relocatees were white, 60% were nonwhite).[122] Authorized under the 1947 Blighted Areas Redevelopment Act, the Hyde Park A and B development was undertaken to dispel fears of rapid succession, restore confidence in the community, and slow the pace of white out-migration. Using the only legal tools immediately available, it was necessary to begin work in already "blighted" areas. Ironically, the only "blighted" sectors in Hyde Park were predominantly white. Moreover, 46.1% of the white families (166 out of 360) and 48.8% of the white individuals (198 out of 405) uprooted by the A and B project were relocated within Hyde Park-Kenwood; only 16.6% of the black families (30 out of 181) and 13.8% of the black individuals (5 out of 36) found similar accommodations.[123] Insofar as the Final Plan was concerned, some whites may have been forced to move to deflect charges of racial manipulation. Julian Levi was thus reluctant to respond to local protests over the clearance of a particular sector because it was the "only clearance area in an all white neighborhood." In any event, the willingness to dispossess whites, especially lower-middle-class whites, is hardly evidence of a benevolent attitude toward blacks.[124]

Claims that class was substituted for race as the crucial variable separating Hyde Parkers from their neighbors similarly overlook the complexity and subtlety of the race issue in this neighborhood. "The fluidity of race relations in America has changed the whole character of the relations and made the issues in some places matters of class and proportions of Negroes rather than the presence of Negroes *per se*," wrote St. Clair Drake, co-author of *Black Metropolis* and a leader of the South West Hyde Park opposition. "And this," Drake stated unequivocally, "*is* involved . . . in Hyde Park's renewal effort."[125] The key question, James Cunningham asserted in reference to the university's racial policies, was: "How do you tell desirable from undesirable Negroes?"[126] Chancellor Kimpton pointed toward the use of class, not as a *substitute* for race but as a *back-up* for it, when he articulated the desire for a community of people of "similar tastes and standards." Apparently able to tolerate greater economic heterogeneity before the racial homogeneity of the community was shattered, the inability to keep blacks out necessitated the economic upgrading of the area as a form of "insurance" intended to regulate both the number and "quality" of blacks remaining after renewal. The "pricing out" of whites who were unable to keep up with the economic pace in Hyde Park was yet another necessary by-product of the reconstruction process and, coincidentally, additional proof that the program was not merely one of "Negro removal." Such whites were viewed, apparently, as gangrenous appendages that had to be sacrificed to preserve the health of the larger organism. If permitted to remain, their relatively cheap housing would, eventually, provide an entree for lower-class blacks.[127]

Despite the centralization of the decision-making process, the university's goals of a predominantly white and economically improved community were not imposed upon an unwilling citizenry. In the main, by fulfilling its own needs, the university acted in accordance with the wishes of most local residents. The one time a major policy matter became an issue of public concern, the "realistic" decisions made by those in power enjoyed more support than the "idealistic" course charted by the "people's" organization. Still, the willingness to tolerate a significant black presence in the community (with or without public housing), for whatever reasons, separated Hyde Park from other neighborhoods facing similar situations. This willingness, carefully cultivated by the HPKCC, gave the community the resiliency and the time it needed to respond to the challenge without being overwhelmed. In acting in what it perceived to be its own defense, the university employed no half measures, refused to compromise its self-defined interests, and permitted others the satisfaction of participating in a "noble experiment."

6 Divided we stand: white unity and the color line at midcentury

> Most of us were born here; most of us have lived here and here only; most of us had some very deep roots in this local soil that just couldn't be uprooted very easily.
>
> *South Deering Bulletin*, May 21, 1955

> The whites of the North from whatever descent have had to make their own way. Those of Anglo-Saxon descent who were early settlers naturally set patterns agreeable to themselves. The subsequent coming of other nationalities...resulted in many difficulties of adjustment – and yet there was adjustment. A real American white has been evolved and should be permitted to evolve further.
>
> *South Deering Bulletin*, September 10, 1955

The people who shouted in heavily accented English around the Trumbull Park Homes seemed little more than barbarians to the more enlightened elements in Hyde Park. Indeed, recoiling from the specter of racial violence, Hyde Park's Leslie Pennington begged for a peaceful solution to South Deering's confrontation. "We worked it out together [in Hyde Park]," Pennington stated. "Can't you South Deering people call a council with the Negroes there to work out your problems so all can live happily together?"[1] Trumbull Park's whites, however, were little inclined to take such advice. They viewed the Hyde Park rhetoric and renewal as an exercise in rank hypocrisy and perceived that all were working within a white consensus.[2]

Nothing would have shocked Hyde Parkers more than the assertion that they were part of a generalized "white" effort to control the process of racial succession in Chicago. The imputation of brotherhood with the ethnic, working-class rock throwers would have been more than they could bear.[3] Yet, there was just such a consensus. Each of the various white groups or interests agreed on the fundamental undesirability of racial succession. Each of them were, for their own reasons, unable or unwilling to flee the city, and each believed that the process had to be controlled to protect their self-

171

defined interests. There was certainly wide divergence in the means deemed acceptable to manage succession, but the Hyde Park proclivity for sending building inspectors rather than debris into the homes of new black residents stemmed from the same fears that called forth crowds elsewhere.[4] Similarly, there might be perceived differences as to the numbers of blacks that could be "safely" permitted in a given area, but nowhere were whites willing to relinquish control of their "turf." Although the rhetoric of integration was in sharp contrast to the virulent racist diatribes that were offered in some quarters, the justifications given for actions taken reveal the differences among the various white groups to be more in the vehemence of language and the sophistication of the resistance than in fundamental assumptions.

If there was general agreement on the need to defend oneself against the prospect or consequences of racial transition, however, there was deep division over how that should be done. Moreover, these intrawhite disputes were more than mere debates over tactics. With a rapidly growing black population in their midst, Chicago's whites found themselves engaged in a desperately competitive struggle with each other. The successful "defense" of one neighborhood increased the problems of the others.

The web of existing interrelationships and conflicting interests virtually compelled acrimonious confrontations among various local white groups. The cordon of hostility that had done so much to produce the ghetto was largely responsible for the overcrowded, decaying, and economically debilitating status of the city's core. The whiteness of many of the city's outlying neighborhoods was thus maintained only at the expense of centrally located communities. The attempt to alter this condition by Loop interests uprooted thousands of blacks and multiplied the pressures felt in surrounding areas. Whites in outlying neighborhoods, including Hyde Park, subsequently protested the closing of Cottage Grove Avenue in the attempt to prevent the construction of the Lake Meadows project. Ultimately responding in kind, the Hyde Park community managed, as the Archdiocese of Chicago painfully noted, to "save" itself without regard for the consequences beyond its borders. Moreover, the redevelopment of the near South Side and the renewal of Hyde Park, in addition to taking territory out of black hands and compelling at least its partial replacement elsewhere, necessitated a massive public housing program. The result was that whites in other communities were left to face the possibility of a substantial and sudden in-migration of low-income black families. At a minimum, even if such areas were not compelled to accept public housing, they had to pay taxes for their construction elsewhere. In this context, opposing white factions, sensing the conflict in their interests, viewed each other as the "enemy."

Aggravating the situation was the fact that the divisions separating the white adversaries were rooted in more than geography. Class and cultural antipathies also played a significant role in this acrimonious intrawhite dispute. The quick resort to political and legal measures and the willingness to expand public power for private ends set the Loop interests and the Hyde Park community apart from the ethnic, working-class, and heavily Catholic neighborhoods that witnessed the worst postwar violence. The deep cultural fissures dividing these various groups became particularly noticeable with the creation of the South East Chicago Commission, the planned renewal of Hyde Park, and the contemporaneous explosion in South Deering. Hyde Park was, of course, a relatively well-to-do, significantly Jewish area, which prided itself – as the home of the University of Chicago well might – on its intellectual character. As such, it was a community largely alien to the Irish in Englewood and the Slavs in South Deering. The peculiar nature of its own response to racial succession, with its celebration of integration and vigorous condemnation of violence, was seen as both selfserving and threatening by these concerned outside observers. For their part, Hyde Parkers often displayed a prejudice of their own against the "unenlightened" and a cultivated sense of moral selfrighteousness.[5] Conflicts of interest were thus reinforced by conflicts of class and culture, which animated and emphasized intrawhite differences.

These rivalries and hostilities, which were often buttressed by feelings of disdain on the one hand and deep suspicion on the other, were nowhere more evident than in the disputes over the use of governmental power. It is perhaps ironic that the enormous expansion of official power in Chicago during the heyday of Senator Joe McCarthy took place at the behest of the city's corporate and institutional elite. It was their plans that required the widespread use of eminent domain, the forced movement of thousands of individuals, and the growth of such government agencies as the Chicago Housing Authority (CHA). Moreover, this increase in the scope of government operations occurred at precisely the moment when selfconscious authorities were beginning to prove susceptible to pressures brought by blacks and their advocates. The post–World War II triumph of liberal environmentalism thus added to the anxiety of people who sensed the breakdown of traditional neighborhood insularity in the face of political and social forces beyond their control. The intrusion of government into the day-to-day life of Chicago's neighborhoods in an unprecedented fashion, the overwhelming nature of racial change in the postwar city, and the growth of strong ideological currents, which would soon culminate in the "civil rights revolution," all contributed to a second strong reaction by the city's ethnics. Bitter against black movement into their communities, they were no less so against the intellectuals and the city planners. The attack against the latter, with its antiradical, anti-Communist rhetoric had all the trappings of "McCarthyism" well before the Wisconsin senator became nationally prominent. This antisubversive movement provided the most dramatic evidence of the intrawhite struggle that was rooted in local racial issues and the expanding use of government power.

Chicago's housing battles were fought at a time when American race relations were becoming more fluid. The context within which they were waged was especially conditioned by the impact of World War II on the nation's social structure and beliefs. The war disrupted "traditional patterns of racial behavior" and broke down "many barriers to equality." Scholars debated whether the war crisis should be characterized as the "forgotten years" of the civil rights revolution, but few doubt that it served as a "catalyst" for the changes that followed.[6]

Perhaps the most significant alteration in America's racial situation was one of mood and belief. It was during the 1940s that the most important change in white racial thinking since the Great Migration occurred. Liberal environmentalism, championed by Franz Boas and a few others during the 1920s and 1930s, found a growing, enthusiastic public as the United States waged war on Nazi Germany. Gunnar Myrdal, in what has been called a "full codification of the new egalitarianism," hailed the routing of the hereditarian racists in *An American Dilemma* (1944). Although some question may remain as to whether the commitment to liberal environmentalism was firmly rooted in its overwhelming ideological force or in more mundane considerations, such as the growth of the Northern black electorate, the desire for social stability, and the needs of the United States as an emerging world leader, the increasing acceptance of the belief and its implications were clear. An ideology that denied the existence of significant differences between the races led directly to the assertion of the desirability of the complete integration of blacks into American society. Racism – at least among intellectuals, clergy, and policy makers – was placed on the defensive.[7]

Deeply rooted patterns of discrimination, however, were slow to change. Critics have consequently, and rightly, taken issue with Myrdal's "almost naïve" overoptimism concerning the course of post-war race relations.[8] If Myrdal underestimated the virulence and depth of American racism, however, he was at least partially correct in identifying the nature of the postwar struggle for equality. In noting the growing role of government, Myrdal saw that public regulation and "social engineering" were in increasing demand.[9] As a political problem, America's racial "dilemma" was thus less a cause for individual self-scrutiny (although there was much of that) than it was for intrawhite confrontation. The meaningful battles over racial issues in postwar America were not fought in the psyches of tortured individuals; they were waged between the engineers and the engineered.

Nationally, growing public concern with persistent racial injustice and inequality manifested itself in the appointment of President Truman's Committee on Civil Rights in December 1946 and the publication of its report, *To Secure These Rights*, the following year. The strong civil rights recommendations included in the report were made part of Truman's 1948 legislative program, and even though few of the measures were immediately implemented, their symbolic value was not lost. The *Defender* called the report "magnificent" and praised Attorney General Tom Clark's public announcement that his office was filing "friend of the court" briefs in the restrictive covenant suits pending before the Supreme Court.[10]

Locally, forces had already been active along the civil rights front for several years. Two articulate spokesmen who persistently and publicly inveighed against invidious racial beliefs were University of Chicago sociologist Louis Wirth and the Most Reverend Bernard J. Sheil. Wirth felt that the war, by throwing society "out of gear," provided an opportunity to remold traditional "ideas, sentiments, and attitudes."[11] Sheil stressed similar themes and asserted that it was "the most dangerous kind of hypocrisy to wage a war for democracy and at the same time...deny the basic benefits of democracy to any group of citizens." Sheil also captured the militant, uncompromising, and crusading mood that characterized much of the growing liberal sentiment in Chicago and the nation. "I hate the hate which tries to twist and pervert the American spirit into an unlovely, unloveable thing," Sheil declared. "I am nauseated by our native Fascists, who use racism as a weapon of political and economic discrimination."[12]

Nor were these mere voices in the wilderness. Others began to organize into action groups. The Christian-pacifist Fellowship of Reconciliation established a cell at the University of Chicago in October 1941, which immediately became deeply involved in the local race relations situation. Out of this cell emerged the Chicago Committee of Racial Equality (the first CORE group), an organization dedicated to fighting racial injustice through the application of Gandhian principles.[13] The wave of violence that shook the nation in 1943 provided further impetus to the coalescence of the liberal phalanx in Chicago. The Chicago Council Against Racial and Religious Discrimination (whose name was later shortened to the Council Against Discrimination [CAD]) was formed in the weeks following the Detroit riot.[14] Similarly, the Catholic Interracial Council (CIC) also sought to "educate and mold public opinion... in matters calling for the application of the Catholic principles of interracial justice" after its formation in 1945.[15]

Such fledgling combinations joined more established groups rooted in Chicago's black community. A more militant tone was already evident in the Black Belt by the late 1930s, and such organizations as the Urban League and the NAACP reflected it. The NAACP, particularly, led a frontal assault on discrimination in public accommodations and, even before the war, gained black access to the swimming pool at Armour Square, won judgments against numerous restaurants, and sponsored several campaigns to increase local job opportunities. In terms of housing, these groups demanded and got the federally supported Ida B. Wells housing project (at a time when a "fair share" of such housing seemed more important than its location) and the appointment of Robert R. Taylor to the Chicago Housing Authority. Equally significant, the NAACP was also pressing its legal campaign against restrictive covenants, pursuing the Lee v. Hansberry case in the ultimately successful attempt to open up the Washington Park Subdivision. The coming of the war simply intensified the existing movement. The Urban League worked quietly, but assiduously, behind the scenes to secure thousands of jobs previously unavailable to Chicago's blacks. The NAACP assembled the Chicago contingent for the March on Washington Movement in an effort to press the demand for jobs on the national level. By the war's end, St. Clair Drake and Horace R. Cayton were able to note that the very nature of the struggle added additional weight to black demands. "They were liberating people from Fascism abroad," the co-authors of Black Metropolis wrote, and America's native sons were now "expecting to be liberated from Jim-Crow at home."[16]

Black pickets protest segregation at the White City Roller Rink (63rd and South Parkway, now Martin Luther King, Jr., Drive) on Chicago's South Side, 1946. (Chicago Historical Society, Negative ICHI-17209.)

Such hopes were no doubt fed by the increasingly active role taken by local government. In the panic-filled days following the Detroit explosion, Chicago was the first of many cities to create a municipal agency to improve the racial situation: the Mayor's Committee on Race Relations. More than a superficial response to the prospect of bloodshed, the committee soon changed its name to the Chicago Commission on Human Relations (CHR) and by the end of 1947 was elevated into a permanent and independent city department.[17]

From the beginning, the commission's primary purpose was to prevent the outbreak of racial violence. Given the prevailing assumption that such outbursts were primarily due to black dissatisfaction with the dogged persistence of racial injustice, the CHR, in its early years at least, became a reforming agency of some zeal. The CHR reviewed and acted on complaints of discrimination (accusations that the CHR found justified were turned over to the newly created

Civil Rights Unit of the City Law Department), worked closely with the Board of Education to expand intercultural programs and teacher training in human relations, and aided private groups in their own endeavors to promote interracial amity.[18] The CHR also organized four citywide conferences between 1944 and 1952 to keep the subject of discrimination before the public. The second of these meetings, the Chicago Conference on Home Front Unity in May and June of 1945, issued a Chicago Charter on Human Relations, which called for the end to discrimination in nearly every phase of city life. Indeed, by the time the Truman committee's *To Secure These Rights* was issued, the executive director of the CHR was able to accept it as a document that "undergirded and reinforced" local efforts already in motion.[19]

This outpouring of liberal energy in both the private and public sectors was intended to produce the "moral atmosphere" within which racial inequities would be quickly eliminated. It produced two complementary crusades, both designed to alter, or at least control, traditional attitudes and animosities. The first campaign involved the efforts to get Chicago newspapers to refrain from "race labeling" in their daily reporting. Believing that such reporting developed "stereotyped thinking," aroused antagonism against minorities, and produced a "sense of shame and suffering" in the minds of blacks, the CHR fought vigorously to end the practice of race labeling "except where necessary to identify an escaped criminal." By the end of 1947 only the recalcitrant *Chicago Tribune* refused to change its policy.[20] The second crusade, which was of greater symbolic than practical importance, was the attempt to "make race hate illegal." Reminiscent of the fervent post–World War I movement to outlaw war, Chicago was one of several American cities that tried to legally prohibit the publication or circulation of material that tended to "incite religious or racial hatred." Finally, in 1947, the city council passed an ordinance (by an overwhelming 43 to 5 vote) making the anonymous publication or circulation of hate literature an offense punishable by fine or up to six months' imprisonment.[21]

In terms of the housing issue, this swelling of liberal sentiment manifested itself in two key areas. First, even as the war was in progress, restrictive covenants began to fall under withering ideological attack. They were denounced as "uneconomic, undemocratic, and unethical," and the city's black press wondered aloud if Americans were going to "de-nazify" their racial beliefs by doing away with such agreements.[22] The mobilization of anticovenant feeling peaked as the war drew to a close and culminated in a series of large public gatherings. The Chicago chapter of the NAACP, the CHR, and the CAD each organized anticovenant parades and conferences.[23] As a result, although covenants were still legally enforceable until May 1948, their open or tacit support became a risky proposition for those in the public eye. Even young Richard J. Daley posed as the "progressive-minded" anticovenant candidate in black areas during his unsuccessful race for sheriff in 1946.[24]

The pressure of liberal public opinion also made itself felt in a second key area: the administration of the city's public housing program. Traditionally, the Chicago Housing Authority had used the "neighborhood composition rule" as the cornerstone of its racial policy. Accepted by black leaders and public housing advocates since the mid-1930s, it meant that no public housing project was permitted to alter the racial character of its surrounding neighborhood. During the war, however, it became apparent that blacks were in the greatest need of CHA housing and that they could hardly be accommodated within the existing Black Belt. Of the 4,881 units included in the CHA's war program, 4,147 were allotted to blacks. Moreover, partly out of necessity and partly out of the desire to produce biracial projects, sites beyond the Black Belt's borders were used.[25] The concessions to wartime exigencies, however, gave way in the postwar era to similar measures, which had, by that time, become ideological imperatives.[26]

The key to the CHA's postwar shift in racial policy was found in its temporary housing program for veterans. As these emergency units were needed rapidly and as Mayor Edward Kelly wished to avoid placing further burdens on the city's budget, vacant sites already in possession of the Park District, the Sanitary District, and the Board of Education were used. Almost by definition, this meant that the veteran's projects were located in outlying, all-white residential districts. Because more than 20% of the veterans seeking emergency housing were black, however, and because federal rules demanded that blacks receive a fair proportion of this federally aided housing, it proved necessary to circumvent the old neighborhood composition guideline. Despite their caution in instituting this change in policy (the CHA commissioners decided to integrate only the largest projects with a very few blacks), violence erupted at the Airport Homes and the Fernwood Park Homes. The emergence of the integration of CHA-operated housing as a burning public issue subsequently found the housing authority, in the words of Martin Meyerson and Edward C. Banfield, "hailed by pro-Negro and damned by anti-Negro organizations for its 'aggressive leadership' in the struggle to end racial discrimination." Reluctant revolutionaries, the CHA commissioners never formally proclaimed the new policy. Once embroiled in public controversy, however, they found it impossible to back away from the principle of nondiscrimination.[27]

The CHA's program, whatever the reasons behind it, simply reflected what was, as least nominally, the "official" attitude in Chicago. The Commission on Human Relations, in the wake of the *Shelley* v. *Kraemer* decision, articulated a policy on living space that was enthusiastically antisegregationist. Even Mayor Martin Kennelly, who personally valued the city's peace over its integration, was compelled in the aftermath of a 1950 Park Manor disorder to flatly declare that "there is no such thing as a white community in Chicago." Obviously intended as the articulation of an ideal rather than a factual assertion, Kennelly's public declaration was praised by the *Defender* as a "historic statement," which "made it clear . . . that democratic principles will not be sacrificed to appease the racial prejudices of any group." This compelling public attitude provided a fragile context for the city's ensuing housing battles.[28]

Least affected by these ideological currents were the architects of the city's 1947 redevelopment program. As successful businessmen, Milton Mumford and Holman Pettibone were pragmatic enough to accommodate themselves to public pressures as long as their plans were not threatened. In framing the legislation that permitted the construction of Lake Meadows, they strained mightily to avoid agitating the race issue. When racial considerations did intrude, they consistently worried more about their self-interest than their ideological consistency. Thus, when Governor Green insisted upon the use of a Land Clearance Commission rather than the Chicago Housing Authority as the proper agency to clear land for private redevelopment, they went along. Unaffected by public protests, their only fear was that the mayor, as a politician, might feel compelled to back away from their legislation. Similarly, when controversy arose over the sites of relocation projects, Pettibone and Mumford opted to do only what was necessary to see their proposals through the General Assembly; they let the state's black legislators decide the issue. Finally, given the aroused state of public opinion, they permitted the ban on restrictive covenants to be written into their proposals.[29]

When they felt threatened, however, Pettibone and Mumford reacted strongly. The introduction of the Carey Ordinance in the city council, for example, led Mumford to denounce the "fanatics" who endangered the Lake Meadows project on purely ideological grounds.

Always the businessman, he believed the passage of the nondiscrimination law would frighten investors and end the chances for
private redevelopment in Chicago. He exhibited thinly veiled con-
tempt for idealists who pursued their goals without considering the
consequences of their actions when he publicly denied that the goal
of integration could be achieved in housing units that "never get
built."[30]

Less able to ignore ideological considerations was the University
of Chicago. Painfully aware of the need to arrest the racial transition
of Hyde Park, the university's administration found itself at odds
with many in the community who were the staunchest advocates of
the new racial outlook. Indeed, the Hyde Park-Kenwood Community Conference, in its fervent desire to produce an "interracial community of high standards," initially defended principle as much as
community survival. Also, the university, as Robert Maynard Hutchins well knew, could not move as boldly – or at least as coldly – as a
large business to maintain its security. The very nature of a university, Hutchins affirmed, compelled it "to do what is right and damn
the consequences." Hutchins's inability to reconcile the university's
needs and its obligation to do "what is right" led only to inaction.
His departure in 1951 enabled his successor, Lawrence Kimpton, to
lead the University of Chicago in the forceful assertion of its control
over its immediate environment.[31]

Once the renewal of Hyde Park was under way, the task of recon-
ciling the university's needs and ideals did not disappear. Many
Hyde Parkers were truly troubled by the demolition of large portions of their community and the forced removal of thousands of
neighbors. That most of those compelled to leave were black simply
added to their unease. One result was the repeatedly expressed
concern with the purity of the community's motives. If the actions
associated with the renewal of the area were questionable, or at least
subject to conflicting interpretations, it was essential, the uncomfortable survivors felt, that the *reasons* for them be unassailable.
Thus the claim that Hyde Park was participating in a "noble experiment" to create an integrated community was repeated with fervor
by those who needed to be sure that they were doing what was
"right." If the distinction between having their buildings torn down
by hate or demolished by love somehow escaped those who were
forced to flee, the need of those who maintained it was certainly
understandable.[32]

But even the idea of the "noble experiment" was not enough. If
that concept could be used to justify the renewal program, it hardly

explained the community's all too common reaction to the in-migration of large numbers of blacks. The fears of neighborhood deterioration, economic loss, and violent crime – common to all white districts facing racial transition – manifested themselves clearly in Hyde Park and enabled calculating university leaders to establish the South East Chicago Commission. Such a response to racial change in an area where invidious racial beliefs were being most vigorously attacked proved disconcerting to say the least. It therefore also became necessary to prove, somehow, that the community's defensive reaction was *not* related solely to the color of its new inhabitants. An environmental explanation had to be found for the reactions that flowed from racial perceptions.

Lawrence Kimpton, in a speech delivered shortly after Christmas in 1953, articulated the university's and the community's rationale for forceful action. It is significant that in beginning his talk, Kimpton was careful to set himself apart from the "other" whites dealing with similar problems. "I abhor discrimination," Kimpton assured his listeners, "and I am appalled by...incidents of [racial] violence." He also felt compelled to assert that the university was simply doing what was "right." There could be no justification for the school's desertion of the area, he declared. Having thus prepared his audience, Kimpton then discussed the specific nature of Hyde Park's plight.[33]

The difficulty the community was experiencing was "only incidentally a race problem," according to Kimpton. The real culprits were the "brute economic and social facts which underlie and create the problem." Impersonal historical forces were fueling the migration that increased Chicago's black population. Moreover, Kimpton noted, the newcomers' problems of adjustment were greatly complicated by their "place of origin." "By far the greatest part of the Negro in-migration has come from relatively backward Southern agricultural communities," Kimpton asserted, "and they have entered a highly industrialized, Northern urban community." Not only did the migrants face a difficult transition to city life, but the ghetto itself, now the site of severe overcrowding and "physical and...moral deterioration," could not accommodate the swollen black population. Border areas, such as Hyde Park, which justifiably feared "annexation and engulfment," were thus reacting not to the color of the new residents but rather to their habits of life. It was the "southernness," or the environmentally induced "moral deterioration," not the blackness of the new residents that inspired fear among the old settlers.[34]

The chancellor's emphasis on the rural southern background of the black migrants and their need to be acculturated to a "completely industrialized civilization" before they could be accepted as urban neighbors was part of a larger theory that was gaining increasing popular and academic support in the 1950s. Kimpton himself provided the optimistic corollary to the proposition that cultural, not racial, differences were all that separated blacks and whites. "There is a remarkable similarity here," he wrote, "to the problems of absorption that have been faced in the history of our country with the immigrant from Europe. To be sure, the Negro faces the difficult barrier of color, but the European immigrant faced the tangible hurdle of language and alien culture." The implication, of course, was that time and patience would "melt" away cultural differences and that the blacks, as the immigrants before them, would be fully integrated into American life.[35]

If Kimpton was eloquent in bringing such ideas to his Hyde Park constituency, University of Chicago sociologist Philip H. Hauser became their leading academic advocate. Testifying before the United States Civil Rights Commission in 1959, Hauser both echoed and amplified Kimpton's earlier statements. The problems facing blacks, Hauser asserted, were "essentially the same kinds of problems which confronted our immigrant groups in the past." Hauser admitted, of course, that the "adjustment" blacks had to make might be rendered "more difficult" because of race prejudice, but this was merely a complication. Moreover, Hauser concluded, there were "other forces at work" that would "accelerate this process in comparison with that of the foreign-born." Blacks did not "waste a generation switching from a foreign to the American tongue," the "general economic climate" would permit blacks to rise more rapidly, and the assistance of government "will probably go far beyond what the immigrant had." The outlook, in short, called for the inevitable, if not the rapid, acculturation of the black migrants.[36]

There were, however, several problems with the theory as it was applied to Hyde Park. First of all, the university's concern with the changing complexion of its environment antedated Kimpton's expressed fear of the Southern migrant by nearly twenty years. There had been consistent university acknowledgment of the problems posed by the encroaching black community (never in the 1930s or 1940s was it described as being either "rural" or "southern"), and the treasurer's memorandum of 1949, which anticipated the later renewal program, paid overwhelming attention to the simple fact of color. When class differences among black in-migrants were recognized, it was not to assert that the more well-to-do were more acceptable; it was only to note that the acquisition of the area in which they lived could be achieved more leisurely than elsewhere because "the threat of deterioration...[was] not so serious."[37] Even as the Committee of 6 debated policy in the mid-1950s, it was evident that the key issue was color. Despite the easy availability, by that time, of the rhetoric of the acculturation theory, there was no indication that the parties involved considered "Southern" blacks a special problem.[38] The "rural" or "unacculturated" black was merely a palatable coded reference to all blacks, which neatly combined environmental predilections and racial perceptions – especially since no differentiation ever affected renewal policy. Edwin C. Berry of the Chicago Urban League did, in fact, make that charge before the United States Civil Rights Commission shortly after Professor Hauser testified. There was a tendency, he noted, to "simply equate Negroes with newcomers, indigents, and slum dwellers. This is done to Negroes no matter how long they have lived here, how great their educational and cultural achievement, or their ability to pay [for good housing]."[39]

Most revealing in this regard was the treatment given black sociologist St. Clair Drake, a Hyde Park resident and co-author of *Black Metropolis*. Drake had attempted to buy a house in the all-white enclave in South East Hyde Park. After experiencing some difficulty, Julian Levi of the South East Chicago Commission admitted to him that he had personally intervened to kill the transaction because he felt Drake "didn't have enough money" to properly repair the property. Yet, when a white prepared to purchase the same home, even though Drake knew him to be "more of a poverty-stricken church mouse than I," Levi did not interfere. Only when it was apparent that Drake was leading the spirited opposition to the South West Hyde Park Neighborhood Redevelopment Corporation was he offered a home in the restricted area. Drake refused the house, as he believed it was merely a ploy to get him to "sell out" his neighbors in the sector slated for redevelopment. It appeared, Drake concluded, that "when they got under pressure due to my being in Southwest Hyde Park, they were willing to slide a point and let me in Southeast." Hardly a recent Southern migrant, Drake's experience revealed that only the most severe pressures could produce even the token integration of South East Hyde Park.[40]

A second problem with the acculturation theory was that the facts of black in-migration to Chicago and Hyde Park did not support it. First, despite the renewed black migration to Chicago, the propor-

tion of Southern-born blacks in the city was declining steadily. Where
72% of the blacks born in the United States and living in Chicago
were Southern natives in 1930 (a time when their "southernness"
was not seen as a particular problem), only 64% were Southern-born
in 1940, and only 59% were in 1949. Also a significant proportion of
the black migrants to Chicago after World War II already had an
urban background before coming to the city. Second, blacks who
had lived in Chicago for some time, not newcomers, typically led
the movement into previously all-white areas. The North Lawndale
community on the West Side was the Southern migrants' main port
of entry during the 1950s – not Hyde Park. Finally, a survey conducted of those forced to relocate because of the demolition associated with the Hyde Park A and B projects revealed that of the 162
uprooted black families, 94% had their last previous residence within
the Chicago metropolitan area – no other group had proportionately
as many longtime local residents so affected. Only 88% of all those
displaced had their last previous residence in the Chicago area, and
only 87% of the whites could make that claim. In this instance, at
least, not newcomers but established black Chicagoans were removed
from the area.[41]

The acculturation theory, as applied to Hyde Park, had its primary value in the psychological comfort it provided its adherents
rather than in its descriptive accuracy. As did the "noble experiment" concept, it also justified the defensive action taken. Yet, despite the fashionable environmentalism of the first idea and the
rhetoric of integration associated with the second, Hyde Park's role
in the "white" reaction to racial succession was clear. The celebration of the community's integration merely elevated an unwanted
fait accompli into a daring achievement. Ultimately, it was Julian
Levi, the architect of Hyde Park's renewal, who accurately perceived
and acted upon the community's membership in the "white" consensus. He boldly dismissed public housing as something the people of Hyde Park did not need and did not want. And he understood
that those who applauded the "noble experiment" would be among
those who refused to send their daughters to the Midway should it
be taken too seriously. Levi's ability to gain overwhelming support
for his plans should have been enough to convince the most sympathetic observer that in Hyde Park, as elsewhere, what was done was
more important than what was said.[42]

The acculturation theory that was employed so delicately in Hyde
Park was used as a bludgeon in South Deering. Adopting the "lib-

eral" framework utilized by their fellow Chicagoans, Trumbull Park's residents stood in the vanguard of the white consensus and emphatically declared that they did not want the "savage, lustful, immoral standards of the southern negro" thrust upon them. Believing that blacks were "hyper-sexed, immoral, and dangerous," the *South Deering Bulletin* substituted crudities for sophistries when, much as Chancellor Kimpton did, it asked for time. When blacks are "educated to behave and act like civilized people," the *Bulletin* magnanimously editorialized, South Deering might be willing to consider integration. Until then, it concluded, Trumbull Park would vigorously defend itself and watch "spineless communities raped, robbed, and murdered."[43]

The *South Deering Bulletin*'s outburst was significant, though, for more than its easy acceptance of the Hyde Park sociologists' paradigm. Above all else, it was an expression of racial solidarity. The varied ethnic backgrounds of the protestors who gathered around the Trumbull Park Homes did not prevent them from joining together as one to assert their "whiteness," their badge of rank and status in their adopted home. As two elderly couples, one "Italian, the other...Slavic," told the pastor at St. Kevin's: "We built this church. It's our church and the Niggers can't come here."[44] Indeed, if anything was clear from the examination of the housing mobs of the 1946-57 era, it was their character as ethnic amalgams. Nowhere was a single ethnic group fighting for its own homogeneous neighborhood or nationality.

This merging of the "ethnics" who shared a common American past and – especially in neighborhoods like South Deering, which was tied to the South Chicago steel mills – a common working-class culture demonstrated the malleability of ethnicity in the absence of striking color differences. The *South Deering Bulletin* celebrated the fact that the community was "settled by our ancestors" and also that the current population was but a generation or two removed from the European-born Serbs, Poles, Croats, Italians and Irish who developed the community. "The foreigners...built this country," the *Bulletin* declared, and are "making it what it is through their many varied experiences. They are not tearing down – they raise families, buy homes, beautify their little neighborhood. Can the negro compare with that?" Indeed, the whites around Trumbull Park constructed their own immigrant/black analogy, which adhered more closely to their own perspective. Nobody was "poorer" than the European immigrants, the *Bulletin* claimed, and yet their accomplishments were achieved without government aid; they "just worked like hell and saved for a rain[y] day." Let the blacks, it was concluded, do the same.[45]

When the Howards "accidentally" integrated the Trumbull Park Homes, they thus found a community welded together by an intense race consciousness. The *South Deering Bulletin* submerged nationality and stated the case plainly: "White people built this area [and] we want no part of this race mixing...Race pride has come to the fore as a new set of values."[46] Throughout the Trumbull Park disorders, each apparent "attack" on the community was viewed as a racial affront that called for an appropriate "white" response. Additionally, the array of organized civil rights forces operating in the area led members of the defensive-minded community to repeatedly call for the creation of a "white" organization to represent their interests in much the same way the NAACP and others advanced those of blacks. Significantly, this deep concern for "white," not "ethnic," rights was often heard in taverns where Polish remained the primary language.[47] Nor was the common denominator of color peculiar to Trumbull Park. The disturbances in Cicero, Park Manor, and Englewood were, above all, viewed as the results of black incursions into "white" areas. Airport Homes protestors denounced the blacks' insistence on "living with white people," and the spokesman for the Fernwood Park opposition firmly asserted that "we live in a white community and we intend to keep it white."[48]

This common antipathy toward blacks, however, does not mean that ethnicity had become either unimportant or irrelevant by the 1950s. As John Higham, a historian whose commitment to the assimilationist tradition is unquestioned, noted, the immigrants and their descendants had the ability to "shed outward marks of foreign origin without undergoing total assimilation." "Some differences of world view," Higham continued, "linger after the group itself has ceased to figure largely in a person's consciousness."[49] In particular, distinctive "ethnic" attitudes toward homeownership, neighborhood and communal solidarity, and the value of stability (as opposed to mobility) not only brought these "whites" into sharp conflict with blacks but also heightened differences between them and other whites – especially the native-born planners and businessmen – whose actions had grave consequences for the central city.

Historians who have very often agreed on little else have all noted the "ardent ambition to own a lot and a home" on the part of Irish, Italian, and Slavic immigrants.[50] This transfiguration of the ancient peasant land hunger occurred in the context of the immigrants' quest for security, respectability, community, and status in a society that questioned both their ability and worth. The purchase of a new home, the Lithuanian newspaper *Lietuva* subsequently editorialized in 1913, was not only "one of the best ways to get ahead," it was also a means of "honoring" your nationality; it was a patriotic as well as a profitable practice.[51] So intense was this desire to own a piece of real property that native-born observers like the settlement house workers were confounded by it. Sophonisba P. Breckinridge, Mary McDowell, and Jane Addams were all concerned that the sacrifices made by the newcomers to enable the purchase of a home caused many of their problems. They worried that, in Addams's words, the "immigrants had been so stirred by the opportunity to own real estate and their energies had become so completely absorbed in money-making that all other interests had apparently dropped away." Addams seemed to fairly bristle at the fact that they "would rather be uncomfortable in a little house than to start out in some reasonable way in...[an] apartment"; and she questioned the utility of tying down a workingman to "a given piece of ground." "If his property had been in some other form, let us say stocks or bonds," she sensibly, rationally concluded from her own perspective, "it would have allowed him much more mobility in regard to his labor, and he would have a better chance of adjusting himself to the changing conditions of his trade."[52]

The immigrants, however, persisted in their "unreasonable" attitude, and, Jane Addams notwithstanding, they were mobile as well. The exceptional movement of urban populations has been well documented for the nineteenth and early twentieth centuries, but the link between migration and assimilation has been more effectively asserted than proven. The encroachment of industry on inner-city neighborhoods, the simple desire to escape congested, perhaps squalid, living conditions, the existence of needed jobs in outlying districts, and the regular arrival of successive waves of newcomers all compelled residential mobility, but not, necessarily, the easily assumed acculturation of the foreign-born.[53] Some undoubtedly did wish to flee from their past. But others, apparently, moved in order to *retain* old values. A key force pulling immigrant Italians to the outlying districts of West Englewood and Melrose Park, for example, was the abundance of cheap land and the opportunity to own a lot and house. Flight to these areas can perhaps best be viewed as the articulation, rather than the abandonment, of old ideals.[54] Chicago's Czechs experienced a similar movement for similar reasons. The immigrants who originally settled in the crowded district east of Halsted moved to new "semirural" sections toward the southwest "so that they

might invest in more land and thus afford the luxury of a garden."
Indeed, rather than causing the dispersal of "assimilated" immigrants,
this sort of movement, through the Pilsen community and out to the
"new brick and stucco dwellings" in Cicero and Berwyn, according
to one Czech source, symbolized the "arrival," not the "disappear-
ance," of the Czechoslovak in America.[55] The opening up of such
new areas and the opportunities they afforded combined to produce
both mobility *and* more stable ethnic concentrations.[56]

It is thus possible that much of the movement detected in the late
nineteenth and early twentieth centuries was not incompatible with
the establishment of neighborhood or communal ties. The Dillingham
Commission found that of 2,024 foreign households studied in Chicago, 86.7% spent their entire period of residence in the United States
in Chicago; whereas only 17.3% of the total spent their whole residence in a single apartment, 76.1% spent the entire period in a
single neighborhood. Of the 810 families who spent ten years or
more in the United States, 83% spent their entire sojourn in Chicago, 65.1% spent it in a single neighborhood, but only 6.5% spent it
in a single apartment. By the mid-twentieth century, sociological
"participant-observer" studies conducted in working-class neighborhoods in Chicago and elsewhere captured the persistence of tenacious neighborhood ties among the less assimilated members of the
"new" immigration.[57]

The increased stability of at least some of the immigrants and their
attachment to their neighborhoods was apparent by the beginning
of World War II. Throughout 1939, the Chicago Plan Commission,
as part of a Works Progress Administration project, employed a field
staff of approximately 1,500 persons to enumerate every parcel of
property on each of the city's 19,455 assessor's blocks. One of the
more striking contrasts revealed by the survey involved rates of
homeownership. Only 21.7% of the city's native-born white residents owned their homes; 78.3% were tenants. In comparison, 41.3%
of Chicago's foreign-born owned their homes and only 58.7% rented.
Of the various foreign-born groups, the Italians, Scandinavians, Poles,
Lithuanians, Germans, and Irish, listed here in ascending order,
owned between 40% and 50% of the homes in which they lived.
Immigrants of British birth lagged somewhat behind, owning only
35.9% of their dwelling units, and the largely Jewish Russians had
the lowest homeownership rate of all the white groups – a mere
17.1% (Table 7). If anything, the gross comparison between the
native- and foreign-born whites *understates* the difference between
the largely Catholic "ethnics" and the native-born because the

Table 7. *Homeownership by race and nativity, 1939*

Race and nativity	Total units	Owner-occupied	Tenant-occupied	% Owner-occupied	% Tenant-occupied
Native white	603,603	131,170	472,433	21.7	78.3
All foreign-born white	264,952	109,479	155,473	41.3	58.7
British	11,849	4,255	7,594	35.9	64.1
Scandinavian	25,307	11,107	14,200	43.9	56.1
Irish	14,271	7,082	7,189	49.6	50.4
German	61,502	30,010	31,492	48.8	51.2
Polish	58,915	25,919	32,996	44.0	56.0
Italian	33,370	13,232	20,138	39.7	60.3
Russian	24,837	4,256	20,581	17.1	82.9
Lithuanian	9,792	4,628	5,164	47.3	52.7
Other	25,109	8,990	16,119	35.8	64.2
Black	70,986	6,355	64,631	9.0	91.0

Source: Chicago Plan Commission, *Residential Chicago.*

American-born children of the former group purchased homes more readily than other natives but were included in the latter group by the Plan Commission. Also, the Russian Jews, as immigrants, were included in the foreign-born category and acted as a "drag" on the homeownership rate for the group as a whole. (This was also true of other subgroups. The presence of Polish Jews in the general Polish category also undoubtedly depressed the homeownership rate for the entire group.)[58]

The foreign-born also showed a greater inclination to endure at a single address than did the native-born (Table 8). Nearly four out of every ten immigrants were found living in the same home for more than a decade; only one out of every five native whites and only one out of every ten blacks could make that claim. Moreover, if only homeowners are considered, the relative stability of the immigrants is even more apparent (Table 9). Nearly three out of every four immigrant homeowners lived in the same house for a minimum of ten years by 1940; one in four lived in the same dwelling for more than two decades. Not only did native whites and blacks own proportionately fewer homes, but they left them more quickly. Only about two out of every three individuals in these two groups spent as many as ten years in their own homes.

An examination of several selected community areas further reveals that those suffering violence in the postwar era tended to have

Table 8. *Duration of residency, 1939, by number and percentage*

Duration of residency	Native white		Foreign-born white		Black	
Less than 6 mos.	79,420	(13.2)	19,281	(7.3)	10,721	(15.1)
6 mos.– 11 mos.	54,622	(9.1)	13,811	(5.2)	7,534	(10.6)
1 yr.– 1 yr., 11 mos.	92,009	(15.2)	26,183	(9.9)	10,997	(15.5)
2 yrs.– 2 yrs., 11 mos.	76,798	(12.7)	25,906	(9.8)	9,449	(13.3)
3 yrs.– 4 yrs., 11 mos.	97,668	(16.2)	39,326	(14.8)	13,107	(18.5)
5 yrs.– 9 yrs., 11 mos.	85,318	(14.1)	43,010	(16.2)	11,579	(16.3)
10 yrs.– 19 yrs., 11 mos.	79,374	(13.2)	67,811	(25.6)	6,079	(8.6)
20 yrs. or more	38,339	(6.4)	29,627	(11.2)	1,516	(2.1)
Total	603,548	(100.1)	264,955	(100.0)	70,982	(100.0)

Source: Chicago Plan Commission, *Residential Chicago.*

Table 9. *Duration of residency in owner-occupied units, 1939, by number and percentage*

Duration of residency	Native white		Foreign-born white		Black	
Less than 6 mos.	4,535	(3.5)	2,310	(2.1)	168	(2.6)
6 mos.– 11 mos.	2,965	(2.3)	1,752	(1.6)	125	(2.0)
1 yr.– 1 yr., 11 mos.	5,752	(4.4)	3,473	(3.2)	206	(3.2)
2 yrs.– 2 yrs., 11 mos.	6,959	(5.3)	4,672	(4.3)	265	(4.2)
3 yrs.– 4 yrs., 11 mos.	10,551	(8.0)	7,344	(6.7)	451	(7.1)
5 yrs.– 9 yrs., 11 mos.	14,807	(11.3)	10,869	(9.9)	849	(13.4)
10 yrs.– 19 yrs., 11 mos.	53,321	(40.7)	52,584	(48.0)	3,169	(49.9)
20 yrs. or more	32,278	(24.6)	26,472	(24.2)	1,121	(17.6)
Total	131,168	(100.1)	109,476	(100.0)	6,354	(100.0)

Source: Chicago Plan Commission, *Residential Chicago.*

Table 10. *Homeownership and duration of residency for selected community areas, 1939*

	Hyde Park	North Lawn-dale	West Lawn	Rose-land	Engle-wood	South Deering[a]
Total units	15,956	25,190	2,550	11,648	25,277	1,725
% Owner-occupied	7.3	18.7	72.3	49.1	26.9	46.3
% Tenant-occupied	92.7	81.3	27.7	50.9	73.1	53.7
Duration of residency less than 6 mos.	15.5	10.5	8.6	10.1	12.2	10.2
6 mos.– 11 mos.	8.9	7.5	6.5	5.9	8.2	4.1
1 yr.– 1 yr., 11 mos.	17.8	13.8	9.2	11.6	13.1	10.3
2 yrs.– 2 yrs., 11 mos.	13.5	12.6	11.0	9.6	11.3	9.3
3 rs.– 4 yrs., 11 mos.	17.3	18.4	12.5	13.7	15.4	13.6
5 yrs.– 9 yrs., 11 mos.	15.5	17.9	16.1	14.3	13.6	13.3
10 yrs.– 19 yrs., 11 mos.	8.3	13.1	29.5	22.9	14.5	25.6
20 yrs. or more	3.3	6.3	6.7	11.9	11.6	13.6

[a] The South Deering figures were adjusted to account for the opening of the Trumbull Park Homes in 1938. The adjusted figures represent the community *outside* the public housing project.
Source: Chicago Plan Commission, *Residential Chicago.*

relatively high rates of homeownership and persistence (Table 10). Englewood, Roseland (the site of the Fernwood Park Homes), West Lawn (locale of the Airport Homes), and South Deering had between 26.1% and 39.2% of their residents living in the same home for at least ten years. The Englewood community, which contained many apartments, was lowest among the riot areas with 26.9% of its units owner-occupied and 26.1% of its residents located at the same address for ten or more years. South Deering, Roseland, and West Lawn had owner-occupancy rates of 46.3%, 49.1%, and 72.3%, respectively. These latter three areas also had between 34.8% and 39.2% of their residents situated at a single address for more than a decade. Although these data were gathered before the war, the depression-induced housing shortage made a drastic revision of these figures unlikely for at least a decade. If anything, it is more likely that a relatively stable core population or nucleus of residents remained entrenched through the war period and into the era of racial violence.[59]

The most interesting contrast is with the heavily Jewish Hyde Park and North Lawndale communities. The former had a mere 7.3% of its units owner-occupied and only 11.6% of its residents lived there more than ten years. Only the commitment of its institutional anchor, the University of Chicago, prevented its rapid racial transition. On the West Side, North Lawndale provides an even more illuminating comparison. Black in-migration to this area began in the late 1940s and gained momentum through the 1950s. As in Hyde Park, this movement was not violently resisted. By the end of 1947, more than 1,400 black families had purchased homes in North Lawndale – a movement that went uncontested save for two "minor" incidents. A longtime observer of Chicago's racial situation praised the character of the "only two areas" of the city where "real liberal leadership" avoided the violence that was so prevalent elsewhere on the South Side and in "non-Jewish areas of the West and North sides."[60]

At this point, however, the Hyde Park and North Lawndale experiences diverged. As in Hyde Park, citizens' organizations were started in the West Side community; first the North Lawndale Citizens' Council, then, its successor, the Greater Lawndale Conservation Commission (GLCC), which was consciously modeled after Hyde Park's South East Chicago Commission. Julian Levi's advice was solicited in setting up the GLCC, but no level of expertise could make up for the West Side's more serious shortcoming: the University of Chicago's location in Hyde Park and not North Lawndale. Although supported by major local interests (most notably by Sears, Roebuck and Company), the GLCC was plagued by recurrent financial problems, passive leadership, and growing divisions within the community. Sears was always interested in the GLCC and backed it both financially and with personnel; but it was still only a supporter of an independent organization. The University of Chicago *was* the SECC and had, in fact, staked its very survival on the commission's success. Consequently, a conservation program for North Lawndale's whites was merely a vain hope. Both willing and able to move quickly (only 17% of the area's units were owner-occupied), North Lawndale's Jews left the community. The rapid and relatively peace-

ful transition of North Lawndale established Chicago's West Side as
a major ghetto in its own right. Only 380 blacks lived there in 1940;
13,146 did so in 1950, and 113,827 did so by 1960. In that same
period, the community's white population declined from 102,048 to
10,792. Where a bitter house-by-house guerrilla war was waged on
the South Side, an orderly retreat ensued on the West Side.[61]

By 1950 there was no denying that many of the predominantly
Catholic descendants of the "new" immigration were less mobile
and less willing to leave their communities than were North Lawndale's Jews. In the wake of the Cicero riot, the Reverend Daniel M.
Cantwell of the Catholic Interracial Council rendered a judicious
judgment:

> The town is an enviable picture of order and peace. Czech house-
> wives are second to none in the care of their homes...Indeed,
> what has gone wrong in Cicero is something good. The home-
> making virtues of these people have been oversown...by national
> exclusiveness, by middle class materialism, by the drying up of
> human compassion and sympathy for other families in need.
> They have acquired homes, but they made them the golden calf
> to be worshipped and possessed at all costs.[62]

Nor was this simply an outsider's view. A local clergyman similarly
alluded to the suburb's mixture of the sacred and the profane. "The
god worshipped in Cicero," he was quoted as saying, "is the unencumbered deed and...the town's real churches are its savings and
loan associations."[63]

This elevation of property holding to an "almost sacred frame of
reference" was not confined to Cicero. Other troubled areas such as
Trumbull Park exhibited it as well.[64] Although the argument that the
community's residents were simply fighting to preserve property
values was frequently expressed, it was clear that something more
than economic concern was at work. Trumbull Park's whites were
fighting for "the preservation of the neighborhood," the *South Deering
Bulletin* editorialized, its property values, its morals, its children's
future,...[and] the future of the older set who...cannot run away
to a new neighborhood and start all over again." Moreover, the
community itself was referred to in reverential tones, as a place of
familial birth and death, as a place where many residents had "very
deep roots."[65]

The reference to a Chicago neighborhood as an ancestral home
may seem incongruous coming, as it did, from people who were
resident here for perhaps fewer than two or three generations. Yet
there was something to it. Many of the areas resisting racial succes-

sion were neighborhoods that were brought into being by groups who now found their traditional insularity disrupted by one of the great population movements of the twentieth century. If the founders, as individuals, were no longer present, there was at least a lasting sense of community, if not ethnic proprietorship, which embraced the "turf" in question.[66] A Cicero resident of Czech descent emphasized the point that the first Czechs found a "wilderness" when they settled there in the 1890s. The community building and sense of in-group feeling that was cultivated was so intense that a serious protest was mounted against the attendance at church of the first Catholics of German descent to move into the area. Such a community could not meet the challenge of race a generation later.[67] Similarly, Poles settled around Calumet Park and began buying property there when the area was "still a wood"; the original settlement was, in fact, called Sobieski Park. In less than a year in the early 1890s "almost all" the lots were sold, all the trees were cut down and removed, streets had been cleared, and sidewalks laid. The pride in these achievements and the construction of "beautiful residences" was surpassed only by the sense of accomplishment that attended the residents' own, literal, construction of the new Polish Catholic Church.[68] The Irish apparently had identical feelings about their Visitation parish, which was established in Englewood when much of the surrounding area was merely a swamp.[69] Nor were these feelings of proprietorship restricted to Catholics or the "new" immigrants. An informant from the Fernwood community, the site of the one riot that supplied significant numbers of participants of Dutch ancestry, stated that the Dutch were the "oldest inhabitants of the area" and that, despite their current minority status, they still exercised "the lead in community affairs" and expressed the "most provincial attitudes." "Many of the women and even some of the men," it was added, "live their entire life without once stepping outside of the boundaries of the community."[70]

As trying as the immigrants' ordeal was – they were, during World War II, still less than a generation removed from the bitter and humiliating struggles against Prohibition, immigration restriction, and other nativistic assaults – they were generally successful, by the postwar era, in achieving some stability. First came "bread and a home," a modicum of economic security. Second, and especially important after being seared by the brand of racial inferiority in the 1920s, was their status as "whites." Racial succession, from the standpoint of the "ethnics," challenged both. Threats to their homes, the "respectability" of their communities, or their own precarious status were thus capable of provoking violence. Their shared experiences, values, and color all led to a common frame of reference in interpreting the meaning of neighborhood change.

Their fear of losing their identity as "whites" was clearly revealed by their overwhelming concern with the prospect of interracial marriage or sexual assault in transition areas. Local residents told American Friends Service Committee counselors that the fear of intermarriage was "what caused the intensity of the feelings" in Trumbull Park. Some events, such as the black attempt to use the park's swimming pool, were interpreted primarily as acts of sexual aggression that aimed directly at promoting intermarriage.[71] Most revealing, however, was the reaction noted by the ACLU's observer in the "ethnic" South Chicago taverns in the wake of the Supreme Court's 1954 desegregation ruling. No one mentioned, he reported, that the decision referred to schools, particularly southern schools. Tavern habitués viewed the *Brown* decision instead as the means for "moving ...niggers into every neighborhood" where they would occupy homes, destroy property values, and intermarry with whites and thus send the "whole white race...downhill." Indeed, given their view of the "community" (intimate contact was a necessary corollary to entry into the neighborhood), the one naturally flowed from the other.[72]

The fears conjured up by images of black sexual aggression were surpassed only by those concerning the disintegration of traditional neighborhoods. Supporters of the communal uprisings against integration continually referred to the "protection" of their homes, "homes that they paid for with good sweat-filled dollars." But if financial security could be found in homeownership, it was a precarious kind of security in the twentieth-century city. Tied to the land, the ethnics sought stability rather than mobility. The trek to the suburbs, for them, would be a forced march made at great sacrifice; it would represent the end rather than the fulfillment of a dream. Haunted by their own racial beliefs, South Side homeowners saw "years of toil and sacrifice" coming to naught. Moreover, the security provided by the home was even greater than the monetary value attached to it. Communities like South Deering displayed close ties between residence and jobs, and the loss of the former, many steelworkers believed, meant the loss of the latter. And the dispersal of the traditional neighborhood threatened extended kinship networks (especially the links between aging parents and their children) and provided the prospect of "isolation, loneliness, and insecurity." Thus, the neighborhoods fearful of succession fought for their "turf" as well as their homes; they were defending much more than an aggregation of individual houses.[73]

The special saliency of the housing issue is striking when compared to other points of racial contact. Not only were territorial confrontations still capable of producing violent interracial clashes in the mid-twentieth century (the bitter labor and political disputes that contributed so heavily to the outbreak of violence in 1919 were no longer sources of overt conflict), but their persistence – indeed, their aggravation – at the dawning of the civil rights revolution was in sharp contrast to the emergent civility found in other areas. Even Joseph Beauharnais, founder of the racist White Circle League, was able to assert in 1951 that "no white person objects to extending semi-courtesy to negroes when he encounters them in transportation or industry." It was only when it came to intimate social contact, he affirmed, that "normal white people" reacted strongly. The Cicero Civic Commission reiterated the point, stating with pride that "over 50,000 people of every race, creed and color [came to Cicero] daily to work in its factories." Indeed, the willingness to work with blacks and the general absence of conflict in areas such as public transportation (where the shroud of urban anonymity could be pulled around oneself) made the violent reactions on territorial issues all the more striking.[74]

The ethnics' defensive yet militant espousal of their "whiteness," however, and the demand for privilege on that basis, was a flawed defense in the context of post–World War II race relations. First, their assertion of what they held in common with the majority society, and the acceptance of that assertion, led, by the 1950s, to their "invisibility." When the United Councils of the Polish Roman Catholic Union requested that the Polish community be represented on the board of the Metropolitan Housing and Planning Council, the MHPC replied that it did not "recognize national groups as such, but only individuals or groups having an interest in housing." Having become "white," ethnic interests merited no distinct consideration. Complacent observers also assumed the luxury of benignly comparing the immigrant and black experiences to the detriment of both. Not only was the immigrant/black analogy cavalier in its assessment of the impediments imposed by color (Saul Alinsky felt the concept was "unfortunate in that it induces a sedative effect, when the situation calls for intrepid, aggressive action"), but it took for granted the eventual integration of the latter into American society on the basis of the former's experience. In so doing, the theory assumed that the immigrants' struggle had been successfully concluded. In presuming that the immigrants – or their descendants, the "ethnics" – had been fully assimilated, the immigrant/black analogy accomplished in a single stroke what was only haltingly, painfully, and often incompletely done. More, it dismissed their experience as unimportant and made their reactions seem simply pathological, the tortured products of the more "backward" elements of a monolithic "white" population. Unlike the intellectuals in Hyde Park (who went to great lengths to demonstrate their sincere motivations and benign intentions), or the blacks now caught in the glare of the environmentalists' spotlight, these people were granted neither the complexity, nor even the significance, of their own history.[75]

Second, the immigrants and their children displayed the poor judgment of becoming militantly white at the precise moment prerogatives of color were coming into question. If they were successful in finally linking their identity to that of the natives, they were left not simply with the natives' privileges of rank but also with the bill for past wrongs that the "whites" were now expected to pay. As the more mobile and well-to-do fled to the suburbs, those still tied to the city were left to face a rapidly expanding ghetto and an increasingly hostile government with anachronistic racial slogans as their primary defense. What could ring more hollow in 1955 than the *South Deering Bulletin*'s proud assertion that a "real American white ha[d] been evolved" out of the various nationalities?[76]

The irony of their situation was neither lost nor completely understood by those confronting racial succession in the 1950s. In groping for an explanation, vulnerable communities and individuals often saw themselves besieged by uncontrollable and malevolent forces. A sense of desperation accompanied an articulated belief in their weakness before powerful conspiratorial agents. For the ethnics, this anxiety was fed, perhaps, by a lasting sense of persecution, a remnant of the age of intense nativism.[77] In any event, the major population movements of the age, the discrediting of racial theories even as many of Chicago's neighborhoods sought to defend their "whiteness," the increase in civil rights activity, and the actual involvement of some "Progressives" and Communists in local disorders, all contributed to the belief that the traditional order was being "subverted." Particularly frightening in this regard was the increasingly visible role of local government in community affairs. The activities of the Chicago Housing Authority, the Commission on Human Relations, and the omnipresent police guard, which not only surrounded disputed housing projects but also accompanied the first blacks moving into private homes in white communities, seemed tangible proof that a social and political coup was being mounted in the postwar city. A piece of racist doggerel circulating at the time summarized the fear and bitterness evident in many neighborhoods:

> Tell all the chillun to git on the bus,
> Kennelly done give the town to us!
> Old Urban League they planned the war
> And whites don't live here any more.
> They give us all we ask for and then some too;
> Chicago's police force belongs to you.
> So buy them tickets and come along,
> Chicago's the place where we belong![78]

Betraying all the outrage of those who have finally mastered a game only to find the rules suddenly changed, the ethnic, working-class communities waged ideological war against their perceived enemies.

The plethora of new and existing organizations that engaged in civil rights activity in postwar Chicago gave whites who were adamant about maintaining the racial "integrity" of their "respectable" communities the impression that vast forces were arrayed against them. Nearly two years after the Trumbull Park disorders began, Louis Dinnocenzo, president of the South Deering Improvement Association, told his followers that "the nation [was] astounded that a community so small has dared to fight...against such organizations as the NAACP, the Urban League, the CIO Packinghouse Union, the Anti-Defamation Council [sic], the B'nai B'rith, the Catholic Interracial Council, and several human relations groups." It was a case, the *South Deering Bulletin* agreed, of people with a "burning desire to keep their homes" being challenged by brute force. Outside pressures were clearly felt by the "man in the street" – *something* was disrupting the traditional peace of the neighborhood – even if those forces were not always clearly identified.[79]

Nor were these suspicions of fomented racial disorder peculiar to Trumbull Park. The Chicago Urban League (CUL), in particular, became the target of rumors from all portions of the city. The most damaging claimed that it purchased property in white neighborhoods and generally subsidized black movement into previously all-white areas. The charges were so widespread that both the Urban League and its primary financial backer, the Community Fund, sustained serious economic losses. The CUL was, in fact, according to its executive director, "not too active" in the Trumbull Park matter because it had "been lambasted in all of these situations in such a manner that we've lost contributors."[80]

The very process of racial succession itself inspired conspiratorial explanations. The speculators who were so instrumental in "changing" an area did not live in the communities in which they did business, and the property they sold to blacks was often held in trust until a given block was "broken." The result was that transition areas felt that they were caught in the grip of unseen forces they could not control. The immediate black occupation of several homes after one or two "block-busting" sales simply added weight to the belief that they were being manipulated. Charges were continually being made that "Jews," "smart niggers," or some other rapacious brokers were out to make a fortune at the homeowner's expense.[81] Ultimately, these views received legal expression as the Cook County Grand Jury investigating the Cicero disorder ignored the more than 100 arrested rioters and indicted the 3 blacks and 1 white involved in the rental of accommodations to blacks. Significantly, a white Communist who distributed leaflets at the riot scene was also indicted. All were charged with conspiring to lower Cicero's property values.[82]

Suspicions that Communists were somehow involved in racial succession were, in fact, raised years before the Cicero riot. During the Park Manor riot of July 1949, a number of Young Progressives and representatives of the Illinois Civil Rights Congress tried to cross police barricades so that they might "protect" the home under attack. Their presence, their arrest, the provision of their bail by an admitted Communist, and their later invitation to one of the beleaguered black residents to speak at a rally were proof enough to Park Manor whites that a subversive left-wing plot existed to disrupt their neighborhood.[83]

The suspected connection between "subversive" political groups and racial disorder became even more apparent after the Park Manor riot. When the disturbance at 56th and Peoria erupted in November 1949, Mayor Martin Kennelly seized upon the "subversive" explanation for the continued disorder in the city, and the local courts gave the conspiratorial view further official sanction. Complicating matters here, as at Park Manor, was enough "evidence" to lend credence to the "Communist plot" theory. First, the host of the interracial union meeting that sparked rumors of a prospective house purchase by blacks was both Jewish and a Communist. Additionally, Young Progressives from the University of Chicago entered the riot area as observers and provided the Englewood crowd both with targets and "proof" of subversive involvement. Mayor Kennelly's first public statement on the incident subsequently attacked elements that fed on "disorder." Official approval for the mob's actions was more boldly provided by Sixteenth Ward Alderman Paul Sheridan who asserted that the violence was properly motivated by "anti-communist" sentiments. The most glowing defense of the community, however, came from Judge Joseph H. McGarry who freed the rioters brought before him. "To speak or write of these incidents as race riots or religious disturbances is a gross and unwarranted insult to the residents of this peaceful neighborhood," McGarry wrote. It was the "considered opinion" of the court, he went on,

> . . . that the original incident in front of the Bindman home. . . as well as all the incidents which followed on the four succeeding days, was the result of a miserable conspiracy, hatched and put into effect by a small but highly organized and highly vocal band of subversive agents, professional agitators and saboteurs bent upon creating and furthering racial and religious incidents in this neighborhood for the purpose of discrediting the City government, the Police Department and the Court and the people who reside in this district.[84]

Civil rights forces were understandably dismayed by this turn of events. The justification of antiblack violence with antiradical rhetoric, one CAD official complained, "can only result in giving a hunting license to every hooligan inspired by race hate."[85]

There were deeper reasons, however, for the fusion of the fears of racial succession and domestic subversion. More important than the visible, though insignificant, activity of avowedly radical groups was the growth of government involvement in neighborhood affairs and the twin clashes of interest and culture between the social engineers and the engineered. The breakdown of traditional neighborhood isolation and the nature of the contacts between local people, government agencies, and urban planners greatly aggravated an already tense situation.

The fear of government, rather than of a radical fringe, was first evident during the construction of the emergency veterans' housing projects. The opening of the Chicago Housing Authority's Fernwood Park Homes in Roseland in 1947 brought about the first real confrontation between local sentiment and metropolitan government. The community's alderman, Reginald DuBois, accused the CHA of engaging in "ideological experiments" by insisting on an integrated development. Local organizations, churches, and ministers were virtually unanimous in their opposition, and attempts to enlist their aid in assuring a peaceful opening failed. Even an attempt to reassure the community by CHA Executive Secretary Elizabeth Wood ended abysmally. In response to pointed questioning, she was left asserting that "we are the government and we do what we do." "The result," according to a Community Relations Service study, was a riot that "grew out of a clash between an aroused community...and forces outside the community which sought to carry through the [nondiscriminatory] policy in spite of local neighborhood opposition." The community reacted violently, it was concluded, when it "found itself helpless to guide its own destiny."[86]

There is no doubt that the community viewed the "intrusion" of government into local affairs as the primary cause of the disorder. The *Calumet Index* singled out the CHR and decried the fact that, even with the "tragic example of the Airport Homes" before them, they used "thoughtless force" to bring about "overnight" change. The *South End Reporter* agreed, claiming that it was the action of the city government that "kindle[d] and produce[d] racial hatred, mob violence, and death." The CHR's budget and very existence was, in fact, subsequently challenged by local organizations and their supporters in the city council who saw it as a "headquarters for zealots sowing the seeds of unrest and turmoil."[87]

Seeking explanations for this "destructive" government action, local residents soon found "Communist infiltrators" stirring up trouble. Especially as the war of attrition between the CHA and South Deering dragged on, it became clear to many South Siders that the housing authority was "filled with Reds," and it became common practice for the South Deering Improvement Association to attack its antagonists for their subversive character. By the early 1950s, the local press was calling for the "complete investigation of the CHA by Senator McCarthy's group" and, particularly, the careful scrutiny of Elizabeth Wood, who, it was believed, "made no determined effort to weed out Housing Authority employees and tenants who have been described as Communist sympathizers." Miss Wood herself was called a "pinkie" by Alderman DuBois and was said to have a "sympathy for Socialism."[88]

Nowhere, however, was the breakdown of traditional neighborhood insularity in the face of growing government operations more apparent than in the implementation of the city's redevelopment program. Cornelius Teninga, a lifelong Roseland resident, was the most articulate spokesman for those who wished to halt the Lake Meadows project by opposing the closing of Cottage Grove Avenue. Outlying white communities were taken by surprise, Teninga claimed, by the impact of inner-city redevelopment. The implications of poorly publicized plans were not understood until thousands of dispossessed blacks began looking for new homes. It was in this manner, Teninga testified in 1950, that "we recently became aware of a new pressure which we had not previously experienced." He protested the new redevelopment law that permitted the condemnation of an individual's property and its conveyance to another private individual or group as despotic. He also claimed that redevelopment was an unwarranted burden on uprooted blacks. But most important, of course, was the "gratuitous and unnecessary policy of displacement," which compelled the people of Roseland to see that they had "a vital interest in what [was] taking place in the heart of Chicago ten miles north of them." Like his realtor father before him (who had worked to restrict the same far South Side district in the 1920s), Teninga was primarily concerned with the racial purity of his previously undisturbed community.[89]

The proposed Carey Ordinance for nondiscrimination, also closely associated with the New York Life Insurance Company's development, offered a similar opportunity but a more complex problem. Passage of what was viewed as a "pro-black" measure might have ended the project. Yet whites in outlying communities, as exemplified by Ninth Ward Alderman Reginald DuBois, were more concerned with growing government sensitivity to black demands and subsequently urged its defeat. In an emotional plea, which would seem ludicrous if not viewed in the context of the raging intrawhite dispute over the city's changing racial geography, DuBois denounced the proposal as an act of "persecution." With rhetoric reminiscent of the "personal liberty" battles of the Prohibition Era, DuBois contended that crusading dreamers "brought the moral issue into the political arena; and now morality [was] made to justify any oppression of one part of the public by another." His constituents believed that "pressure groups" and "organized minorities" were trying to control the "whip-hand of our government" and that rule of the people was rapidly becoming "rule of a faction." In their defense, DuBois ironically concluded his argument against the nondiscrimination ordinance with a plea for tolerance. "Nothing destroys liberty," he warned the city council in a phrase that must have reminded some of his listeners that the Founding Fathers were also slaveholders, "so surely and quickly as the spread of intolerance."[90]

But if DuBois and other South Side whites asked for tolerance from their perceived antagonists, they were much more likely to be greeted with indifference, disdain, condescension, or hatred. Nothing better demonstrated the yawning chasm separating the backgrounds, values, and perceptions of the planners from those of the planned. Where the protesting neighborhoods were largely working class, Catholic, and ethnic, the architects of the redevelopment program were overwhelmingly professional, Protestant and Jewish, and native American. Pettibone and Mumford were members of Congregational and Methodist churches, respectively, and were virtual models of upward and outward mobility in their professional and personal lives. Residence in the suburbs to them was both desirable and possible; it was certainly not a prospect to be dreaded, even if one was "pushed" there by changing inner-city realities. Pettibone, moreover, was a captain in the American Protective League during World War I, an organization that "snooped through German neighborhoods looking for enemy agents," and, in the words of Edward F. Dunne, onetime mayor of Chicago and Illinois's only Catholic governor, "goaded and insulted persons whose only offense was the possession of a German name." Even if such 100% Americanism was due to nothing more sinister than a young man's ardent patriotism (Pettibone was in his twenties at the time), it betrays, at the very least, a certain insensitivity toward those of different backgrounds. Similarly, the moving forces behind the Hyde Park renewal – Chancellor Lawrence Kimpton, businessman and lawyer Julian Levi, and planner Jack Meltzer – hardly identified with working-class Catholics. Even the nemeses of the white resistance, the CHA's Elizabeth Wood, the CHR's Thomas Wright, and the CAD's Homer Jack, came from roots that almost guaranteed clashes of values and perspective with the antiblack protestors. Each displayed a reforming zeal that was undoubtedly related to their strong religious backgrounds; Wright was educated for the ministry, and Wood, born in Japan, was the daughter of a lay Episcopal missionary. Jack was a co-founder of CORE at the University of Chicago and at the time of the Trumbull Park uprising was minister at the Unitarian Church in suburban Evanston. It was Wood, though, with her bachelor's and master's degrees from the University of Michigan, her teaching experience at Vassar College, and her influence in the Chicago Housing Authority who epitomized the perspective and power of those public figures who sought changes for which ethnic Chicago was not prepared. Such officials and policy makers contrasted sharply with the ringleader of the Trumbull Park resistance, Carl Buck, whom ACLU investigators described as "making a nominal amount per year" in the auto towing business and as an individual who had trouble paying his bills. And even though Buck himself was apparently a "native-American of Anglo-Saxon ancestry," the inner circle of South Deering Improvement Association activists identified by the ACLU consisted entirely of people named

Nahirney, Santucci, Salvatore, Lalich, Mistovich, Bogdanovich, Kral, Kelly, Dorio, Robish, Michalik, Jarmusz, Landini, Diclemente, Barnowski, and Sickick.[91]

The planner's attitude toward those who occupied the withered urban landscape was revealingly demonstrated by Reginald Isaacs, head of Michael Reese Hospital's planning unit and primary author of the Metropolitan Housing and Planning Council's study, *Conservation*. Two years before the completion of the MHPC's 1953 report, Isaacs was arguing for the creation of a conservation "Authority," which would have the power of eminent domain and the ability to "force owners to maintain minimum standards with the threat of seizure if they do not comply." As for the local groups most affected by the proposed agency's actions, Isaacs felt they "should be merely advisory at best," with the task of comprehensive planning left in the hands of the "centralized authority." More, according to Isaacs, the agency "should be autonomous,...not responsible to the city council, [and] completely free of politics" – which is to say free of democratic controls and, especially, free from the dictates of Chicago's political machine and the interests it represented. The people in the neighborhoods, Isaacs declared, "don't know themselves what is good for them much less for the city as a whole."[92]

Isaacs's views were not idiosyncratic. D. E. Mackelmann, housing coordinator in the early 1950s and later a special consultant to the city's planning department, also stressed the dangers of "too much we the people." Reserving the task of urban reconstruction to the "professionals," Mackelmann would tolerate independent voices only if they "consulted the people who could see the problem with practical knowledge and know-how." Nor was Julian Levi, who revised the Neighborhood Redevelopment Act of 1941 so that the power of eminent domain could be effectively used by private parties, disposed to take a vote before making either policy or "technical" decisions. Citizen participation in the renewal of Hyde Park – though mandated by law – was passive and consisted primarily of the acquiescence in plans drawn by "technocrats" (Nicholas von Hoffman used the phrase to describe those working under the Urban Community Conservation Act) acting in the interests of the University of Chicago.[93] And those living outside Hyde Park had no input whatsoever. On questions of power, then – its locus, scope, and exercise – the pro-renewal forces staked out positions that brought them into conflict with Chicago's ethnic neighborhoods.

The mere presence of such power, however, was not enough. There also had to be the willingness and determination to employ it despite opposition, despite the tensions it generated, and despite its imperfections. Julian Levi was the personification of the tenacity needed to see the process through. Indeed, it was Levi's recollection that Kimpton selected him to head the South East Chicago Commission because he was "fed up with his sociologists who could diagnose the problem world without end, but couldn't quite tell him what to do." "No one either knew or wanted to fuss with the nasty nitty-gritty." Levi did. He was committed to creating an environment within which the university could fulfill its academic mission and was convinced that a "failure to act" would have constituted an affirmative decision to annex Hyde Park to the Black Belt. When confronted with white opposition, however, and questioned about the impact Hyde Park relocatees were having on "white parishes," Levi replied simply that the discussion was "out of bounds" and that he was "not about to cut up this town with anybody." The other communities would have to fend for themselves.[94]

When it came to questions of racial policy, there was greater disagreement among the pro-renewal forces, but their differences were of little consequence for the antiblack resistance. First, there were members of the liberal phalanx such as Elizabeth Wood and Thomas Wright. Wishing to end racial discrimination and segregation, Wood, particularly, could be every bit as tenacious and unswerving as Levi in pursuit of her goals and her willingness to use official power. On the local level, these forces were represented by the Hyde Park-Kenwood Community Conference whose interracialist rhetoric was particularly alarming to the anti-integrationists. Next, there were some officials and businessmen like Ira Bach and Ferd Kramer who were eager to develop integrated projects like Lake Meadows and Prairie Shores even as they settled for segregated public housing as a solution to their relocation problems. "Practical" individuals, they were willing to break existing racial patterns but were unwilling to jeopardize the postwar reconstruction for the sake of ideals. And then there were people like Mumford, Pettibone, and Levi, for whom racial issues were simply political problems demanding the proper management. Mumford and Pettibone tried to mute the race question by ignoring it, even as they pursued plans with grave racial implications. Levi similarly ignored white protests from Hyde Park's neighbors and tried to defuse pro-black opposition by integrating his Planning Unit. Revitalizing the Loop and preserving the University of Chicago were not intended to solve either the city's housing or racial problems; as such, controversial racial issues (once they were dispatched as threats to renewal) were left for others to face.[95]

The local white resistance gained little comfort, however, from the apparent divisions among the pro-renewal forces. It made little difference in Roseland that Elizabeth Wood chose to talk about integration and that Holman Pettibone did not. The former might choose to introduce a handful of blacks in the Fernwood project, but the latter's plans were no less alarming. Cornelius Teninga knew that 15,000 blacks lived on the Lake Meadows site and that redevelopment plans accommodated but 5,000. "Where," he asked the Chicago Plan Commission, "will these people go?" Similarly, the people of Trumbull Park were aware that the University of Chicago was attacking "blight" around its campus, evicting blacks, and, according to the *South Deering Bulletin*, erecting "new glass and steel palaces" to be occupied by "selected tenants." It seemed clear to the editors that university officials were creating a "buffer zone" to "save their own hides" at the expense of less well-to-do South Side communities. Roseland's Teninga summed up the frustrations and perceptions felt in the outlying neighborhoods. "What sinister masterminds have conceived this great iniquity upon the taxpayers of our city?" he asked. "How long will they be permitted to operate behind the scenes and oppose the will and good sense of the great majority of the home and property owners of our city whose thrift and industry have helped to make ours one of the finest in the world?" He regretted also that the "fair name" of New York Life was linked to a venture that would "forever brand them as being antagonistic to the Negroes living within the area and to the whites who live away from it; as being in favor of the prodigal waste of the taxpayers' money; and as being the dupes of an element of our country temporarily enjoying a bolshevistic authority."[96]

As implied by Teninga's inability to see New York Life acting in its own interest for its own reasons, it was not the business community but the presumed Bolshevist "element" that attracted the greatest ire. The most bitter disputes, because they were the most visible, were those that erupted between the growing liberal phalanx and the white resistance. Part of the problem stemmed from the conception of prejudice that prevailed in the wake of the struggle against nazism. Viewed more as a psychological than a social problem, it was seen by many as being simply "irrational," a sign of "serious mental deficiency" or even "bleak stupidity."[97] Antiblack rioters were characterized as "hysterical," "berserk," and the "dupes of bigots." Moreover, the mobs themselves were seen as being aberrations, collections of a "few unstable and misinformed Americans," rather than as representatives of the communities of which they were a part.[98] And these were passionately held views. South Side whites were frequently compared to the German people under Hitler, and Chicago Housing Authority staff members bitterly cursed "the bastards...in Trumbull [Park]." If anything tempered these emotions, it was condescension. Some concerned observers felt, for example, that the people of Cicero realized they were wrong and that they were "frustrated" by this knowledge. They prescribed a "spirit of understanding and forgiveness" as a necessary condition for progress.[99]

There were prescriptions for peace as well. Most often, education was called upon to produce a "new climate of opinion." But this was no easy task. R. Sargent Shriver, president of the Catholic Interracial Council, spoke for many when he said that "the apostle of interracial justice among highly prejudiced fellow citizens resembles...the missionary conversing with a foreign people accustomed to ancient tribal customs and taboos." Yet, it had to be done. "The false idols will fall," Shriver concluded, "only when people have become sufficiently enlightened to wish to remove them themselves."[100] This missionary approach manifested itself most clearly in both a joint CIC-American Friends Service Committee project to promote better race relations in Cicero and the western suburbs and an AFSC proposal for civilizing Trumbull Park. Just as the ACLU sent in an undercover operative to gather information, some AFSC leaders suggested "underwriting" a "Catholic, Eastern European descent, working-class" family to live in South Deering for two years, during which they would work to change local racial attitudes.[101] If bringing the "word" failed to convert the heathen, however, some were willing to experiment with more drastic alternatives. Ninety of the arrested Fernwood rioters were sentenced to "compulsory group therapy" as part of their rehabilitation.[102]

The split between the "liberals" and the white resistance erupted into open confrontation during a 1956 meeting between representatives of the South Deering Improvement Association and the Hyde Park community. In a forum sponsored by the Channing Club and held on the University of Chicago campus, president Louis Dinnocenzo and lawyer Patrick Allman set out to refute claims that the people of South Deering were simply "ignorant foreigners and illiterates." Charges and countercharges were hurled in an acrimonious debate, which left each side convinced of its own righteousness and its opponent's dubious sanity. Dinnocenzo's performance, one Hyde Parker wrote, simply proved to a "justifiably disgusted audience" that "bigots are...ignorant and pathetic creatures." Enlightened individuals, she concluded, could only "feel sorry for [the people of Trumbull Park] and pity their sickness." For their part, South

Deeringites were similarly appalled by their first chance "to see and hear the so-called intellectuals in action." It was clear that the university was filled with radicals, the *South Deering Bulletin* editorialized, who were "sick in mind and spirit." "To try to reason with these perverted people," it lamented, "is like beating your head against a stone wall." The two sides had nothing in common save their color.[103]

There was one attempt to reconcile the black need for living space with the ethnics' desire for stability. Testifying before the U.S. Commission on Civil Rights in 1959, community organizer Saul Alinsky proposed a 5% quota on blacks who would be given entry to all-white neighborhoods scattered throughout the city. "Let there be no mistake about it," Alinsky told the commissioners, "no white Chicago community wants Negroes, and that also includes those... which publicize themselves as interracial." He knew that the closely knit ethnic districts bordering the Black Belt bred both "warm, communal ties" and an "isolationism" that resisted the entry of new populations that "might upset the status quo." "We can ignore these facts and continue to blow the trumpet for moral reaffirmations," Alinsky concluded, "but unless we can develop a program which recognizes the legitimate self-interest of white communities, we have no right to condemn them morally because they refuse to commit hara-kiri."[104]

The proposal was controversial and arguable on several grounds. First, the morality of imposing a quota was questioned and Alinsky, a Jew, recognized the irony of his suggesting such action. He felt, however, that what was "an unjust instrument in one case can serve justice in another." Further addressing his critics in an aside Julian Levi would have appreciated, Alinsky also proclaimed that those who "state a moral principle and avoid the hard, grimy reality of implementation [had] a museum mentality where morality is nothing more than a showpiece." A second problem involved the white acceptance of even a 5% quota. Alinsky's assessment that whites would "jump" at the guarantee was debatable, and his plan was attacked in communities where cooperation would have been vital (the quota certainly had little appeal to distant white neighborhoods not immediately threatened by ghetto expansion). Finally, the plan's intent was to preserve white communities and institutions. It relegated blacks to permanent minority status in the new areas that would be opened up and said nothing about *their* institutions, needs, or aspirations. In any event, even though Alinsky's "benign quota" tried to address realistically the problems posed by the dual housing market and the housing shortage, it never attracted more than a brief flurry of attention. Black, ethnic, and institutional interests would not be reconciled.[105]

There was a time when the community of interest between Hyde Park and its less well-to-do neighbors was apparent. As the demolition for Lake Meadows was carried out, as the black movement into Hyde Park assumed significant proportions, but *before* the South East Chicago Commission was created, Newton Farr issued a detailed critique of the New York Life Insurance Company's project that contained many of the complaints later made against the Hyde Park renewal plans. First among his dozen points was the claim that the acquisition of inner-city property for redevelopment drove blacks "to other parts of the city."[106] In the scramble for "survival" that followed (which pitted not only whites against blacks but whites against each other as well), each community used the best means at its command to advance its own interests. In pioneering renewal legislation and finding a suitable legal alternative, the Hyde Park community simply illustrated the unity of race and the persistent divisiveness of class and ethnicity. Moreover, its approach was both a cause and an effect of the passing of the isolation characteristic of Chicago's neighborhoods. Responding to the impact of major postwar population movements, which eroded traditional insularity, Hyde Park acted independently to enlist the aid of every level of government in plans that had serious consequences for those living beyond its borders. The environmentalism that helped justify the action taken within those borders, however, was conveniently forgotten when dealing with the "other whites" who resisted their efforts and the racial transition of *their* neighborhoods. Clashes of interest and culture precluded the application of "environmental" explanations to the actions of adversaries who were, by their own vigorous assertion, simply "white."

The obliteration of old racial borders and the novel role of government in shaping new boundaries found other South Side communities less able to respond than Hyde Park. "A working man purchases a home..., secures a mortgage, improves the property and enjoys the fruits of his labor and then, all of a sudden," the *South Deering Bulletin* complained, "city planners and do-gooders decide that they are going to dump a project in his back yard and resettle the entire community." More, the wives and daughters of these "do-gooders" were "safe in the suburbs while the common people who cannot afford to live in these communities have to live the hazardous lives of city-dwellers [and] pay city taxes so the civic-leader suburbanites are paid." For many, this unprecedented imposition of "outside force" was beyond comprehension.[107] To ward off blacks, a virulent, but increasingly disreputable, brand of racism was used. As evidence of related intrawhite struggles, a host of antisubversive conspiracy theories linked volatile racial and political realities.[108] In a rapidly changing urban environment, the erosion of provincialism and the intrusion of a hostile "outside" world sparked bitter neighborhood battles. Significantly, those organizations with a citywide orientation – such as the Commission on Human Relations, the CHA, and private citizens' groups such as the Catholic Interracial Council – were arrayed against agencies that were firmly rooted in local soil. Just as the housing authority and the CHR had to fight recalcitrant local "improvement associations," the CIC had to deal with an "uncooperative and hostile clergy" at the parish level.[109] The resolution of these disputes produced the second ghetto.

7   Making the second ghetto

You can't call Stateway [Gardens] a ghetto. It is beautiful.

> Alvin Rose, executive director of the Chicago
> Housing Authority, U.S. Commission on
> Civil Rights, *Hearings: Chicago* (Washington,
> D.C.: Government Printing Office, 1959),
> p. 726.

[The] idiocy of Rose's remarks is quite apparent.

> Typewritten notes, n.d., Leon Despres Papers,
> Chicago Historical Society

In May 1953, Earl Kribben, a Marshall Field and Company vice-president, asked Governor William Stratton to make the proposed Urban Community Conservation Act an administration bill. The measure was bold in asking for powers "no mayor or alderman had ever dared" to request and was designed to "establish a national pattern in dealing with urban problems." Less than eight weeks later, Kribben again wrote the governor, this time appealing for his signature on the renewal legislation that had sailed through the General Assembly. He also implored Stratton to veto a bill that provided for local referendums before public housing could be built. The passage of the latter measure, he advised, would "only make the slum job in Chicago that much harder by effectively choking off the supply of relocation housing which must be provided if private capital is to rebuild slums." "Furthermore," he added, local referendums were "quite needless, as the City Council [had] the public housing site problem very well in hand."[1] The governor granted both of Kribben's requests.

The opponents of the renewal legislation claimed that the powers it bestowed upon the city were "unprecedented" encroachments upon "property rights and individual rights." One critic branded the new measures "undemocratic" and "paternalistic," claiming that there would be "no need for the communists to overthrow this government by force and violence because... the powers given in [the Urban Community Conservation Act] will enable any group of com-

212

munists to do most anything they care to do." Perhaps amused at
this placement of Marshall Field and Company in the vanguard of
the revolution, and supremely confident that renewal plans were
well on their way to realization, Earl Kribben, when handed a copy
of the critic's remarks, simply scrawled "Tsk! Tsk!" in the margin.[2]

This sequence of events clearly demonstrated the combination of
forces that produced the second ghetto. First, the larger "downtown" interests and some powerful institutions situated outside the
Loop found themselves confronted, after the war, with threats to
their survival that were beyond even their considerable means of
control. Unable to flee the city, they realized that the power of the
state – not as it then existed but in greatly augmented form – would
have to be enlisted in their aid. The result was that those economic
and institutional interests that had the money, time, personnel, and
influence to conduct surveys, make plans, draft legislation, and implement renewal did so. They exerted *positive* power by guiding the
machinery of government. To be sure, the rhetoric of the "public
interest" accompanied each new legislative proposal and the wed-
ding of private interest and public power did serve, in some instances, a broadly defined "public interest." And there is no question
that these powerful interests perceived themselves to be laboring for
the good of the city; they were not mere cynics manipulating "the
system" for their self-aggrandizement alone. But the fact remained
that Chicago's postwar rebuilding was privately conceived to protect those who directed it. The public benefits were by-products of a
desperate struggle for individual survival and never the primary
force behind the program.

Second, those who violently resisted the movement of blacks into
their neighborhoods and were discomfited by growing government
power and its impact on racial affairs were never able to exert the
sort of influence that their white antagonists did. At most, they
exercised a *negative* power, never able to thwart plans they opposed
but able to extract concessions when they viewed their interests as
too severely threatened. Although not "veto groups" in the literal
sense, pockets of local resistance did influence public policy and lent
their distinctive imprint to the second ghetto. Most significantly,
whites in outlying residential neighborhoods were able to shape the
policies of the Chicago Housing Authority and transform that agency
from one that tinkered with the status quo into one that served as a
bulwark of segregation. Essentially, however, the position of such
white neighborhoods was still one of relative weakness compared to
the forces that were creating the postwar reconstruction program.

Unable to do anything in a positive sense *for* themselves, they could only, to a limited extent, prevent things from being done *to* them. The way in which the city's "ethnics" made their voices heard and their power felt was through violence. Although not universally efficacious – some neighborhoods successfully employed violence to prevent racial succession, whereas others simply endured it as part of the transition process – local disorders *were* instrumental in molding both CHA site selection and tenant selection policies. In the first instance, the city council responded to local pressures by obtaining the power to veto the housing authority's selection of prospective project sites. Thus Earl Kribben was able to assure Governor Stratton that the council had the situation "well in hand" and advise against the passage of legislative restraints that would threaten the program. In the second case, the housing authority itself proved responsive to the violent pressures placed upon it. Moreover, by the mid-1950s there were significant changes in CHA personnel, which also indicated its inability to overcome hardened white resistance. Most important among these was the replacement of Elizabeth Wood as executive secretary during the Trumbull Park disorders. The personification of the CHA's nondiscriminatory postwar policies, her removal marked a turning point in the process in which the housing authority was first subdued and then enlisted in the struggle to maintain the racial status quo. More political than pathological, Chicago's housing violence, if limited in scope, was nonetheless effective.

The decade of disorder that followed the end of the war had other effects as well. Members of the previously vocal liberal phalanx were similarly cowed. The Chicago Commission on Human Relations apparently went through a metamorphosis identical to that of the housing authority, and where it was excoriated for its "race-mixing" policies in the 1940s, it was denounced – from opposite quarters – for its "do-nothing" stance in the 1950s. The convergence of local and national waves of reaction in the antisubversive campaigns of the era also served to splinter liberal forces. Groups such as the Council Against Discrimination and the Chicago Urban League were placed on the defensive by charges of subversive affiliations or activities. Split internally and weakened by the loss of economic support, both groups sank into inactivity.

The desiccated state of the liberal cause during the 1950s was, however, merely symptomatic of a larger problem: the isolation of blacks in Chicago. If certain whites had "positive" power, and others had "negative" power, at least the claim could be made that they all had *some* power. Despite the massive impact that redevelopment and renewal had on Chicago's blacks, they were effectively locked out of the decision-making process. True, black opposition developed to the Lake Meadows and Hyde Park projects, but it represented little more than verbal protestation. Where the New York Life Insurance Company's project was concerned, the black community was fragmented, uncertain, and easily ignored. Hyde Park's plans sparked greater black unity, but internal divisions persisted and the very nature of the legislation under which renewal proceeded made black opposition fruitless.

The process of urban reconstruction, which saw blacks treated as objects rather than as participants, revealed their powerlessness. In an era that saw the massive expansion of the Black Belt, no fundamental alteration in the pattern of segregation occurred. If anything, that pattern was reinforced by government sanction and public funds. The apparent shift in racial attitudes accompanying the war and the seemingly increased government responsiveness to black demands proved incapable of altering Chicago's racial accommodation. Where liberal forces massed around the principle of nondiscrimination in the 1940s, tenacious white resistance compelled a fundamental redefinition of the problem by the 1950s. The desire to do away with all forms of discrimination in the war decade gave way, in less than ten years, to talk about the more "practical" principle of integration. Affirmations of the need to produce a color-blind policy were replaced by the practice of tokenism and the satisfaction provided by the symbolic breaching of previously underestimated barriers. As civil rights forces mobilized in the South and as the *Brown* v. *the Board of Education of Topeka, Kansas* decision of 1954 was hailed as a new beginning in race relations, Chicago moved in the opposite direction by institutionalizing a greatly enlarged black ghetto and turning away from the ideals that seemed so compelling during the fight against nazism.

Violence and politics have long been associated. Although most evident in periods of revolutionary upheaval, the significant impact of lesser disturbances on day-to-day decision making has been less well noted. In Chicago during the 1940s and 1950s, the role played by the press contributed to the undeserved obscurity of the racial disorders of those years, but there were other reasons as well. It was crucial that the violence did not seem to "change" anything. The ghetto existed before the riots, and it certainly persisted after they had ended. Yet that is precisely the point. The maintenance of the status quo was an act of great force. The preservation and expansion of Chicago's ghetto was due not to inertia but to the continuous application of old and new pressures. The "invisible" violence of the postwar era, judiciously applied by those having some measure of influence, set the stage for the more spectacular, but less effective, black upheavals of the 1960s.

Chicago's white-initiated riots represented both a rejection of the city's political system and the deepest involvement in it. The violent resistance to black in-migration in Bridgeport, Englewood, and Park Manor and the rigid control of community facilities in South Deering were rationalized as necessary acts of self-defense. As conservative, communal acts undertaken as a "last resort," they bore all the characteristics of vigilantism run rampant along the modern city's racial frontier. Yet the disorders at the Airport Homes, Fernwood Park, and South Deering had deeper implications. These incidents precipitated and complemented the organized, peaceful efforts in the political arena that led to the subjugation of the CHA and the quiet retreat of the CHR. Given the growing government involvement in neighborhood affairs and the increasing sensitivity to racial issues, these struggles reflected shifting demographic and political realities in the postwar city. Local white interests, if placed on the defensive, were not yet ready to succumb to either new voices in the political arena or the increasing centralization of the political system.[3]

The vigilante approach to neighborhood control, keyed closely to changes in the private housing market, produced mixed results. In Park Manor, the outbursts of violence in 1949 and 1950 and the creation of the White Circle League were ineffective in preventing racial succession. By August 1953 the *Defender* was able to proclaim that all was "calm and peaceful in the former embattled area." The whites who remained were resigned to the area's transition and were preparing to leave.[4] Similarly, the efforts of the Southtown Planning Association, the Southtown Land and Building Corporation, the rioters at 56th and Peoria, and the unknown bombers of black-owned homes failed to maintain Englewood as a white preserve.[5]

But it would be a mistake to classify the use of violence as universally ineffective. One community where it enjoyed considerable success was Bridgeport. This area had a long tradition of animosity toward blacks. The Lowden Commission investigating the 1919 race riot characterized both Bridgeport and the Back of the Yards district – which stretched southward for more than 4 miles from 22nd Street (now Cermak Road) just west of Wentworth – as one in which "hostility to Negroes is so marked that the latter not only find it impossible to live there, but expose themselves to danger even by passing through."[6] Racial friction remained high here even after World War II. In 1946 Thomas Wright, executive director of the Commission on Human Relations, singled out the Bridgeport area as one of almost chronic violence and, in the rhetoric of the age, called it a "symbol of grassroot Ku Klux Klanism in Chicago." Succeeding years brought similar reports.[7] Consequently, despite its proximity to the Black Belt, ghetto residents displayed little desire to move into such hostile territory.[8]

There is no clear reason why such tactics had such variable success, although there are suggestive possibilities. Class seems to be a significant factor here. Of those communities violently resisting racial succession, those that were slightly more well-to-do or middle class (like Park Manor or Englewood) were those that changed most rapidly. Perhaps related to the greater housing alternatives provided for the middle class and the possibility of flight, the working-class districts of Bridgeport and Back of the Yards (which stabilized itself largely through Saul Alinsky's vigorous organizing efforts) successfully resisted transition pressures because they had no choice. Significantly, it was also precisely those areas *not* covered by restrictive covenants (generally a middle-class tool) that were most successful in maintaining their racial homogeneity. A map published in the *Defender* in the wake of the *Shelley* v. *Kraemer* decision made it clear that much of the South Side below 55th Street was covered by such covenants, whereas the working-class districts immediately west of the Black Belt were not. Since the covenants were being ignored even before they were declared unenforceable by the Supreme Court, it is doubtful that the court's decision alone accounts for the Black Belt's southern movement. It seems more likely that those neighborhoods that had to reduce their sense of mutual obligation to a written contract displayed a fragile sense of community that could not, ultimately, withstand racial pressures. Those communities that failed to produce restrictive covenants were certainly not less race conscious than those that had them; it was simply that they felt no need for them. Communal traditions and institutions were still strong in these comparatively stable residential areas and their sense of reciprocal obligations and duties made such covenants superfluous. In other words, any district that felt compelled to have the legal machinery of the state support its communal solidarity was revealing a weakness that became glaringly apparent when the pressures of the dual housing market were brought to bear upon it.[9] Chronic violence on a small scale in Bridgeport did more to discourage black in-migration than did restrictive covenants and the infrequent large outbursts that betrayed cracks in white unity elsewhere.[10]

If the major disorders in Park Manor and Englewood failed to stem the tide of black movement, however, the disturbances at the Airport, Fernwood, and Trumbull Park homes had considerable political impact. Indeed, more significant than Chicago's eruption of postwar "neovigilantism" was the violence that occurred as a part of the ongoing debate on the government's role in racial affairs. These latter episodes of violence were instrumental in shaping the city's approach to racial issues and were directly responsible for the abandonment of the housing authority's tentative flirtation with policies that challenged the status quo.

Race had always been a central concern of Chicago Housing Authority policy. In implementing its neighborhood composition rule in its earliest projects, the housing authority displayed a literal-mindedness that testified to both the significance and the sensitivity of racial issues. In the Addams Homes, the lone public housing project among those taken over from the federal government to house both whites and blacks, CHA Executive Secretary Elizabeth Wood restricted the number of black families so that it corresponded to the number living on the project site before it was cleared. This unofficial black quota was modified only by the threat of legal action, and then only slightly. Moreover, as long as whites predominated, blacks remained segregated within the project. Given their choice of apartments, the first blacks admitted to the new development gathered around the same entry way. Two years later, even though whites and blacks necessarily shared the same buildings and entrances (they did not share the same stairwell when the project opened in 1938), the blacks were kept on one side of the project as a matter of policy "because... that was where they lived" before the development was built.[11]

Significantly, tenacious adherence to the neighborhood composition rule made the CHA, especially when confronted with violent resistance, less tractable than some of the neighborhoods it entered. Open conflict swirled about the Cabrini Homes when its status as a slum clearance project was changed to defense housing at the start of the war. Determined to maintain a preclearance site tenancy that was 80% white and 20% black, the CHA was left with a project for which local whites were largely ineligible. Neighborhood hostility subsequently compelled Elizabeth Wood to be "very careful" in moving in the "proper proportions" of whites and blacks. The housing authority also took pains to maintain some "solid white sections" in the project in the hope of attracting additional whites. Aware of the bitter local opposition, Wood made that concession because she feared "extreme violence from the Italian neighborhood." Ultimately, however, the 4 to 1 ratio of whites to blacks had to be abandoned. A dearth of white applicants, an overabundance of black applicants, and the embarrassment of holding units vacant in a time of dire shortage compelled revision. By 1949 blacks occupied 40% of the apartments in the Cabrini development – a quota that, by that time, meant there were proportionately more whites in the project than in the changing neighborhood surrounding it.[12]

Chicago Housing Authority policy shifted with the veterans' emergency housing program after the war.[13] Economic imperatives compelled the placement of temporary veterans' housing on scattered sites in overwhelmingly white neighborhoods, and federal guidelines necessitated the evasion of the neighborhood composition rule. Cautiously, the CHA tried to integrate the larger projects. It was this program that provoked the violent reactions at the Airport Homes and Fernwood Park. Significantly, it was the last attempt (until the 1980s) to implement a public housing program that employed both scattered sites and at least an apparently nondiscriminatory tenant selection policy.[14]

The CHA was able to embark on this limited experiment only because of its independence from the Chicago City Council. Legally, it was not responsible to the council for its site selections or its policies. Politically, it enjoyed the sponsorship of Mayor Edward J. Kelly until the spring of 1947. With the protests at the Airport Homes, though, the first calls for the curtailment of the housing authority's power were heard. Alderman Michael Hogan, representing the people surrounding the Airport site, presented a petition to the city council just days before violence erupted asking that the CHA be brought under the authority of the mayor and the council. People in the community also clamored for an investigation of the CHA and the dismissal of Elizabeth Wood. Supporters of the housing authority warned Mayor Kelly of this attempt to "absorb" the CHA into the city's government and were apparently reassured by Kelly's declaration that the CHA was "a responsible, efficient, public agency whose commissioners and staff...are giving the highest type of devoted service." Saved for the moment, the CHA nonetheless suffered each of the indignities presaged by this 1946 list of local demands.[15]

Ironically, the succession of "Boss" Kelly by the "clean" Martin H. Kennelly in April 1947 found the CHA losing its important source of political support. Kelly, despite his position as leader of the powerful Democratic machine, was the protégé and heir of Pat Nash and other "new breed" politicians who unified the party and won public support not only through the traditional use of patronage and corruption but also by adopting reform-type administrative procedures and, in the words of the latest analyst of the Chicago machine, by "professionalizing government" – a blend of tactics and technique later elevated to an art form by Richard J. Daley. Maintaining a tenacious hold on the party apparatus, Kelly controlled the ward organizations and kept the "heat" off the CHA. Under this protective mantle, Elizabeth Wood ran a "clean" agency, supplied no patronage to the organization, and experimented (however timidly) with integration. When scandal (and rebellious party operatives) forced Kelly into early retirement and local Democrats found businessman Martin Kennelly's image just what they needed to retain control of City Hall, the CHA lost its political guardian. Instead, it had to deal with a political neophyte who was neither willing nor able to control the reigning ward bosses. The Fernwood riot, occurring a few months after Kennelly took office, showed the housing authority how vulnerable it now was. Rumors flew, even as the fighting was in progress, that Fernwood's alderman, Reginald DuBois, would introduce a resolution "to liquidate or severely criticize" both the CHA and the Commission on Human Relations. DuBois failed to offer his proposal only because of the danger continued rioting posed for the city. Black Alderman Archibald J. Carey, Jr., and DuBois "declared a truce" during the August 18 city council meeting to prevent controversial measures from coming "up on the floor." After a cooling-off period of two months, however, DuBois finally did offer the resolution that led to the subordination of the CHA.[16]

DuBois charged the CHA with inefficiency and mismanagement and called for an official investigation. His main complaint, though, was that the CHA "persist[ed] in theories of housing which are shared by no other representative local governmental agencies...and are not in accord with those of a great majority of citizens." It was evident that DuBois's charges were, as CHA chairman Robert R. Taylor testified, "a smokescreen for a demand that the Authority enforce racial segregation." The *Defender* denounced the "little bund of rabid racists" seeking the investigation, and Alderman Carey warned that the "basic purpose" of the inquiry was to effect "a change in the racial policy of the Authority." Nor were these black critics alone in their concern. Even the genteel board of governors of the Metropolitan Housing and Planning Council was informed that "racism is an important factor to those who oppose the Chicago Housing Authority on the plea of inefficiency." The agency thus had to defend itself not only against the formal charges raised but also against the "undercover purposes" of those whose motivation, according to Robert Taylor, would not "stand the light of day."[17]

The source and the timing of the anti-CHA accusations revealed other ulterior motives as well. As the housing authority became more active and the weight of government was increasingly felt in the neighborhoods, local improvement associations began to federate and become more politically involved. The CHA subsequently became a prime target of such organizations. The leadership of one such group working in the Fernwood area, the Calumet Civic Council, claimed, in fact, that DuBois's call for an investigation was made at their insistence.[18] Moreover, DuBois's resolution was introduced on October 15, 1947, less than a month before the election in which the bond issues for slum clearance and relocation were to be voted upon. The city's entire 1947 housing program, which required a vigorous CHA effort, was thus threatened.

The apparent vulnerability of the redevelopment package stemmed from the fact that there were two distinct bond issue referendums on the November ballot. The first provided money for slum clearance and land assembly; the second was for the relocation efforts of the CHA. The proposals were interdependent. Given the city's desperate housing shortage, it was obvious that the city's plans would, in Holman Pettibone's words, "rise and fall on public housing for relocation." Presentation of the legislative proposals in this fashion was a calculated risk, but Pettibone and Mumford knew that private developers needed public housing. They hoped that the presentation of private redevelopment and public housing as a "package deal" would cause the widespread public support for the first measure to carry the second. Those suspicious of redevelopment, however, knew that they had only to defeat the bond issue funding the CHA to bring the whole program to a halt.[19]

Consequently, when Kennelly learned that DuBois intended to request an investigation of the CHA in October, he called the Ninth Ward representative and more than a dozen other aldermen to his office. The mayor tried to persuade DuBois to hold off his resolution until after the November 4 election but succeeded only in sparking a "violent disagreement." DuBois refused to yield and, after making his charges, shrewdly claimed that the CHA was already surveying sites in three South Side wards, which would be integrated after the bond issues were approved.[20] The housing authority was "being. . . smeared with half-truths and falsehoods before having a chance to be heard," CHA commissioner Wayne McMillen complained. "It has been apparent to everyone," he added, "that such headline frauds are unsubstantiated and were designed to defeat the bond issues." Thus aroused, the CHA ignored the opinion of the corporation counsel that the city council had no authority to investigate it. Once the charges were made, the housing authority itself demanded that the council conduct the inquiry so that the organization could be vindicated in full public hearings.[21]

The city council, however, did not hold its hearings until late November. The campaign for the bond issues was subsequently carried out in the acrimonious atmosphere of charges and countercharges. Local organizations and neighborhood newspapers rallied against the proposals. The *Southtown Economist* was "astonished" that Kennelly could admit that an investigation of the CHA might "well be warranted" and yet ask for its postponement. Similarly, the Fernwood-Bellevue Civic Association claimed that a "yes" vote on the relocation referendum was a vote of confidence in the CHA – the very agency that, in the association's eyes, had "provoked violence, riot, bloodshed, juvenile and adult delinquency, discrimination, and [the] destruction of friendly and harmonious understanding between the races."[22]

Ultimately, however, the Pettibone-Mumford strategy proved sound. Neighborhood groups were cut adrift as traditionally conservative institutions with citywide constituencies reluctantly supported both referendums. The *Chicago Tribune* stated the case for all such organizations:

> In good conscience we cannot recommend the adoption of the land clearance bond issue and the defeat of the housing authority issue. You can't tear down the old houses as long as there is no place into which the occupants can move; that is the justification and only justification for the second bond issue.[23]

The Citizens' Association likewise agreed to support both referendums even though it continued "to question the general principle of public housing." The bond issues passed easily.[24]

With the bond issues out of the way, the city council was able to quickly conclude its investigation of the CHA. The indirection employed by the housing authority's critics almost returned to haunt them as the council subcommittee conducting the inquiry deftly sidestepped the race issue. The subcommittee was cognizant of some "vague criticisms" of the CHA's racial policies, but it elected not to investigate them since "these accusations have not been put forward directly."[25] This refusal to confront the problem of race, however, merely removed it from public consideration – it was hardly over-looked. In its report to the Housing Committee of the city council, the subcommittee also made a series of recommendations. The CHA's failure to "work closely with the city" was a "major criticism" of the housing authority's past actions, and the report stressed the "necessity for the CHA to function as a part of the city team." Consequently, the subcommittee recommended that the city council "declare it a matter of policy" that it should be given the power to approve "all sites utilized by the Chicago Housing Authority."[26]

In its own final report (issued on March 15, 1948), the Housing Committee adopted its subcommittee's recommendations. Without dissent, the aldermen cleared the Chicago Housing Authority of the charges of mismanagement and inefficiency. Similarly, they refused to deal directly with the question of the housing authority's racial practices. Buried within that report, however, was the crucial statement of council policy. As suggested, the council explicitly sought the power to veto sites selected by the CHA, "including redevelopment projects for private use and possible sites of. . .future Federally-aided public housing programs."[27]

This assertion of council power over the CHA had far-reaching implications. There was no immediate need for the state legislature to respond to the city council's plea as the council, under the provisions of the Relocation Act of 1947, was granted the power to approve the sites selected by the CHA for public housing financed by city and state funds. It was significant, however, that the city council specifically sought a legislative mandate to extend that power to cover housing authority operations that were *not* locally financed. At the time the report was made, it was clear that the federal government would soon be passing legislation that would provide for a massive new public housing program. It was also clear that unless the state law under which the housing authority operated was amended the city council would exercise no control over this new program.

The result was that in 1949, shortly before the federal Housing Act of that year became law, the state legislature (ever hostile to the CHA) granted the Chicago City Council the powers it sought without a dissenting vote. In requiring city council approval for public housing sites in cities of more than 500,000 residents, the new measure was clearly aimed at Chicago, and the CHA became the only housing authority in the state to have its prerogatives so restrained. The CHA commissioners knew at the time the law was passed that it meant "the end of public housing sites in good residential areas." Ex-commissioner Robert R. Taylor said later that he knew the battle to distribute public housing throughout the city "was lost" when the General Assembly of Illinois acceded to the council's request – a request resulting from the desire to "prevent the influx of Negroes into white neighborhoods" and from the pressure of public opinion.[28] The result was that the selection of relocation sites in 1948 and the first slate of federally funded project sites in 1949–50 established a pattern that saw public housing located primarily in existing ghetto areas.

The housing authority's dilemma was apparent. Relocation housing had to be built on vacant land if it was to facilitate redevelopment. Choosing sites that were occupied would merely compound the already difficult problem of rehousing those uprooted by new construction. Suitable vacant land, however, was primarily located in outlying white districts, whereas those dispossessed were overwhelmingly black. Thomas Wright, executive director of the CHR, thus realized that the sites eventually selected would arouse antagonism "no matter where they [were]." Chicago's blacks were well aware that a "crucial" decision was being made that could "seal" them even more tightly in their existing ghettos. Yet, sites in all-white communities would be "violently opposed."[29]

Racial considerations were, consequently, paramount in the deliberations that produced a Chicago City Council-CHA agreement on relocation housing sites. The housing authority submitted its first list of sites in December 1947 and a second six months later after Mayor Kennelly and council leaders had rejected the initial proposal. Kennelly praised the second list but recanted shortly thereafter. His reconsideration followed the overt and "violent opposition" of aldermen Anthony Pistilli and John F. Wall and the gathering of 5,000 white protestors at one of the larger vacant land sites. Despite the fact that this second slate of sites was already unpalatable to some "pro-housing" forces, five weeks of intense negotiations and further compromise ensued. CHA commissioners Robert R. Taylor and Wayne McMillen met with a group of key aldermen and agreed to nine new sites, which the housing authority staff futilely disapproved. Acceptance of this new "package" by the whole council proved a mere formality as the aldermen ratified the compromise by a 40 to 5 vote.[30]

At first glance it might seem as though the CHA staff had little to complain about. Five of the nine sites, after all, were located in "white" areas. Yet this was a step that could hardly have been avoided (at least with the first group of relocation sites), and there were other extenuating circumstances as well. The city council agreed to accept those locations only after striking a "deal" with the housing authority's commissioners. A 10% quota on black occupancy in the projects in white areas was the price of the council's acquiescence. Moreover, despite the fact that they were in technically "white" communities, the controversial sites were smaller than the housing authority's staff would have preferred and they were often in undesirable locations, isolated from nearby residential concentrations by major traffic arteries, railroad tracks, canals, and industrial districts.[31]

Such mixed results produced predictably mixed reactions. The Public Housing Association, a strong supporter of the CHA, felt that the sites were "largely bad" and that the housing authority, "worn out by the overwhelming pressure exerted upon them," had surrendered long-held positions. Others similarly suspected that "political factors and local pressures played at least as large a part as the principles of sound city planning." However, even Homer Jack, representing the Council Against Discrimination, was compelled to admit that "concessions have been wrung from the racist politicians" and that the program was "perhaps the best one obtainable." Ultimately, the most common judgment was rendered by the Metropolitan Housing and Planning Council and the *Defender*. There were problems with the site package, the MHPC acknowledged, but they were not enough to "outweigh the tragedy of continued inaction in starting housing in Chicago." Reasserting the vital link between relocation in public housing and the city's redevelopment program, the MHPC urged acceptance of the package (as did the CHR), warts and all. For its part, the *Defender* noted that the "race question was at the bottom of the choices" and that the sites were "carefully selected in areas that would present little racial friction." Despite their placement near "buffer" zones such as factories and railroads, the *Defender* still proclaimed them a "Gain For [the] Race" and concluded that they represented "about the best plan on which business, political, and racial interests can agree."[32]

If necessity dictated the city council's acceptance of some relocation housing in white areas in 1948, the selection of the first slate of sites for projects funded under the federal Housing Act of 1949 revealed its desire to contain the city's black population. This time, however, the supporters and staff of the CHA – certain that the housing authority's commissioners would again "capitulate" if permitted to negotiate with the council – succeeded in persuading the housing authority to go "public" with the fight to locate its projects on predominantly vacant sites.[33] The city council's final approval of a second group of public housing sites in August 1950 was not the product of surreptitious dealings – it was a raw display of political power. Unfortunately, from the CHA's perspective, it was the power of the council and not that of the housing authority that dictated the final selection of sites.

The CHA submitted its first list of seven sites (containing a projected 10,000 units) in November 1949. After some bitter argument and public hearings (Louis Wirth declared that the "seven hills of Rome had caused less discussion than these seven sites"), the aldermen rejected five of the locations and accepted two slum sites adjacent to existing CHA projects.[34] Shortly thereafter, several members of the council, out to "get" their recalcitrant colleagues who supported the CHA package, took a bus tour of the city and developed their own list of prospective sites. Shaped by "whim, prejudice, and revenge," their offerings were pared, in part, from a list of fifteen sites contained in the two wards of the aldermen most friendly to the housing authority.[35] Clearly unacceptable, the "bus-tour sites" did little but enhance the housing authority's public stature vis-à-vis the city council and provide the opportunity for a new CHA initiative. Quickly, the housing authority submitted a second list of sites. Before this new list could be voted upon, however, Mayor Kennelly intervened and urged the creation of a council subcommittee to negotiate with the housing authority. With this opening, aldermen John J. Duffy (the reigning power in the council since Ed Kelly's retirement), William J. Lancaster (chairman of the Housing Committee), and a few other council notables, including Clarence Wagner and Tom Keane, dropped consideration of the CHA's proposal and began selecting sites to meet their own criteria.[36]

Unalterably opposed to placing public housing in "virgin" territory, Duffy insisted that the new projects be placed in the slums – especially those in which some public housing already existed. Given these guidelines, the "Duffy-Lancaster compromise program" provided for 10,500 units on slum land and only 2,000 units on vacant land. Eight slum sites – including the two previously approved – were selected. All of these were located in black communities. There were also seven vacant sites, but the construction envisaged here was small compared to that slated for black areas. The plan would uproot 12,465 families (virtually all black) and provide relocation housing (that built on vacant land) for but 2,112. Moreover, because of the extensive demolition required in occupied areas, the entire program represented a net addition of only 47 units to Chicago's housing supply.[37]

Negative reactions were not long in coming. Robert C. Weaver voiced his "vigorous disapproval" of the program, and the Chicago

Urban League called it "dishonest in intent" and "hypocritical in nature." The *Defender* was even more strident. The plan was "dangerous," the newspaper declared. It was "calculated to continue the ghetto and strengthen the spirit of segregation," and, as such, it contained the seeds of "serious racial conflict." "The hate-mongers are determined to confine the Negro population of Chicago within a walled city" was the *Defender's* inescapable conclusion.[38]

White critics were similarly appalled. The CAD felt that the Duffy-Lancaster proposal "might be worse than no housing" at all, and even the Metropolitan Housing and Planning Council voiced objections. Deeply concerned about the redevelopment of the near South Side, the MHPC believed that the thousands of families displaced by construction on slum sites would overburden the local agencies "already throttled by relocation difficulties" and thus impede, rather than expedite, the reclamation of blighted areas. Moreover, the MHPC feared the chilling effect such public developments would have on private investment in the South Side. Such investment was essential to the success of redevelopment, and "the logical place for it to go," Ferd Kramer wrote the CHA, was adjacent to the "investments of the Illinois Institute of Technology and Michael Reese Hospital." "In the interest of a total housing program," Kramer implored, "it would be much better if a wall of high density public housing projects does not box in IIT."[39]

Those who wished to modify or even kill the Duffy-Lancaster program turned to Washington, D.C., for aid. Guidelines established by the federal Housing Act of 1949 provided for the equitable treatment of the races and considerable care in relocating those displaced by slum clearance. The Chicago plan was obviously vulnerable on both points, and it still had to secure Public Housing Administration (PHA) approval. PHA officials were informed, however, that the Chicago City Council would accept only the Duffy-Lancaster proposal and no other. Faced with the choice of a poor program or none at all, PHA officials hesitated. Clearly they would have preferred a better selection of sites, but they also wished to avoid the political embarrassment of seeing one of the Fair Deal's much publicized programs killed in the Democratic stronghold of Chicago. To the surprise of CHA officials, the federal authorities were conciliatory and extracted only minor concessions from Chicago's political leadership. The PHA demanded the selection of an additional "white" slum site and suggested that more vacant land be added to ease the relocation problem – although it did not threaten rejection of the program if more vacant land was not added.[40]

To meet these objections, Ralph Burke, a consulting engineer hired by City Hall to advise the aldermen on the technical aspects of the housing program, took two steps. First, he selected an additional "white" slum site as requested. This was easily accomplished, however, only because the designated location, although technically "white," was actually an area undergoing racial succession. "White" for planning purposes, the site was nearly all black by the time it was developed. Second, Burke issued a report that attempted to solve the problem of relocation. He called for the construction of public housing in "stages." If construction was started on vacant lots, alleys, and "other interstices of the slum sites," no homes would have to be destroyed until after new units, within the development areas, became available. In this fashion, the blacks living on construction sites would be relocated within their own communities. Although the plan called for extremely high population densities and violated both CHA and Chicago Plan Commission standards, it proved attractive to the city council because it promised to contain the city's black population. CHA officials criticized the plan, of course, but time was now working against them. Their press and public support eroded as the debate dragged interminably on. Ultimately, the housing authority, as the PHA before it, found itself confronted with the choice of accepting the council's package or obtaining no public housing at all. After the PHA recommended acceptance of the "compromise," the housing authority's commissioners voted their approval.[41] With CHA backing, the city council approved the Duffy-Lancaster slate of public housing sites in August 1950.[42]

A reluctant accomplice in the development of a public housing program that reinforced the city's pattern of segregation and placed its greatest burdens on the black population, the CHA was compelled to endure yet further indignities. After the program was accepted, actions by the Sanitary District Board and a railroad removed two of the few vacant sites from the list of locations available for CHA development. Moreover, it was also discovered that not only was the "white" slum site no longer predominantly white but also that it was hardly a slum. Most of the homes in the area required only minor repairs. Some CHA officials tried again to prevent final PHA approval of the program. Despite such efforts, however, final federal authorization for the program was obtained in November 1951.[43]

Sharp fluctuations thus characterized the CHA's policy between 1946 and 1950. In its emergency veterans' housing program, the housing authority tried to circumvent its old neighborhood composition rule and integrate small projects scattered throughout the city. The disturbances associated with the veterans' program, however, compelled the CHA to confront the problem of race even as they provided the impetus for the city council's acquisition of power over it. The incidents at the Airport and Fernwood homes consequently were, in Elizabeth Wood's opinion, "important out of proportion to their quantitative contribution to integrated housing," because they set the stage for the 1950 program "whose impact on Negro living and concentration [was] tremendous." At the end of the struggle over the first slate of federally funded projects in 1951, Wood thus correctly asserted that the housing authority's "present racial policy" was unceremoniously "forced" upon it. By 1952 she was referring to the CHA as a "captive Authority" whose opponents "have won hands down."[44] Caught in a wave of reaction, the CHA was unable to withstand the popular and political pressures that now guided its actions. Moreover, the housing authority was also in the anomalous position of having an executive secretary who was, by temperament, a "fighter" at a time when fighting did little good. At most, Elizabeth Wood could serve only as an "agitator" when peace rather than justice was being demanded. As such, her days at the housing authority were numbered.

Changes in personnel had been frequently associated with political and policy shifts affecting the CHA. In 1948, for example, Milton Shufro, the housing authority's assistant executive secretary and liaison to the mayor's office, was compelled to resign. As Elizabeth Wood's principal staff adviser, Shufro was one of those who had convinced Mayor Kelly to wrap a protective arm around the agency. When Kelly left office in 1947, however, Shufro, as a Kelly protégé, felt the enmity of those forces in the city council who were reasserting their own power and who also resented Kelly's heavy-handed support of CHA proposals. With the removal of Kelly's protective presence and the overnight transformation of Shufro into a political liability, the assistant secretary had no choice but to resign. Similarly, John Ducey, CHA director of planning, also left the housing authority in 1948. Ducey attempted to get the CHA to deal explicitly with the problem of Chicago's expanding black community by proposing the preparation of a set of maps delineating the consequences of various patterns of black community growth. After failing to get the city's agencies to consciously consider the future pattern of black settlement in Chicago and after his experience with the relocation program, Ducey also tendered his resignation.[45]

It was clear that political pressures, especially those stemming from the housing authority's racial policies, were instrumental in driving both Shufro and Ducey out of the CHA. At a 1949 testimonial luncheon held to show that their policies still enjoyed "strong citizen support," Elizabeth Wood contended that the "tragic result" of their departure was that "cowardice, mediocrity, and timidity" were replacing "what was once our pride – our leadership, our knowledge that we fought for what was needed for the poor people of this city." Already reacting against the pressures that threatened the sound implementation of the federal program, Wood resolved to fight on against "the forces of timidity."[46]

The issue that now became the source of much debate was the CHA's tenant selection policy. The housing authority's oldest projects, which had been built in white communities and tenanted under the neighborhood composition rule, remained all white in the early 1950s. Thus, the Addams Homes, except for the fewer than 75 apartments allocated to blacks, and the Trumbull Park, Lathrop, Bridgeport, and Lawndale developments were "reserved" for whites. There was a like number of all-black projects, and the remaining CHA developments (all occupied during or after World War II) had mixed racial occupancy. The integrated projects were carefully managed and maintained their interracial character only through the placement of quotas on black occupants and the "maximizing" of white occupancy. This became increasingly difficult with time, however, as slum clearance and new construction uprooted large numbers of blacks who were then given a high priority on CHA waiting lists. The result was that the housing authority was compelled to accept "non-priority white families" in preference to high-priority black families in order to maintain both their all-white and integrated projects. Proportionately fewer white applicants meant that they were admitted soon after application, whereas the growing number of black applicants were placed on rapidly lengthening waiting lists. Moreover, in both the "white" and the integrated projects, apartments were held vacant until white occupants could be secured. To assure the smooth functioning of this system, the forms filled out by prospective tenants were coded to indicate their race.[47]

The most controversial aspect of the CHA's tenant selection procedures involved the maintenance of its four all-white projects. Elizabeth Wood and her staff continually prodded the policy-making CHA commissioners by providing lists of qualified black applicants who requested apartments in the restricted developments. The staff carefully researched these prospective tenants and provided short lists of "model" families who had already had some experience with integrated living. Elizabeth Wood further pushed the applications by attaching them to copies of the resolutions on nondiscrimination that the commissioners had passed since the end of the war. She was, however, careful not to place such items on the agendas of the commissioners' regular meetings because she presumed that they would "not like to have it discussed in open session."[48]

Wood's deference, though, had its limits, and she was not above using outside pressure. When, in April 1952, she was visited by representatives from liberal groups seeking her advice on desegregation measures, "she suggested," one of her visitors recalled, "that we start with the Housing Authority." She informed her listeners that the CHA maintained four all-white projects despite the fact that the "great majority of applicants are Negro." This was due, she added, to the demands of "politicians" who contended that such was the price for city council approval of the next slate of prospective sites. So informed, two representatives of the Council Against Discrimination wrote the CHA commissioners a week later, requesting a conference on housing authority racial policy and asking for a denial of a "rumor that there is an order prohibiting occupancy of certain of the Chicago Housing Authority projects by Negroes."[49]

This request to discuss the persistence of all-white public housing projects in Chicago initiated a year of negotiation in which threats of making the dispute public and legal action were countered by seeming acquiescence and delay on the part of the housing authority. The CHA originally agreed to hold a meeting in response to the April 1952 CAD inquiry but refused to set a date. When informed in August, however, that the CAD felt "compelled" to go public with their complaints, the housing authority agreed to meet the following month. The September 1952 meeting made it clear that the commissioners feared the outbreak of violence should they try to integrate their traditionally white projects, but it also produced a "reclarification" of CHA tenant selection policy and a promise that changes would be forthcoming "within a reasonable time." After a long winter of inaction, however, the Chicago chapter of the NAACP publicly charged the CHA with practicing discrimination in April 1953. A second round of discussions ensued, but the commissioners again expressed their fear of violence. James Downs, the city's housing and redevelopment coordinator and adviser to the mayor, pointedly refused to pressure them into changing their policy. Indeed, once the charge of persistent segregation was made public, the CHA simply hired a consulting firm to study its procedures. Further vague promises to alter prevailing practices assuaged no one, and a lawsuit seemed imminent. It was at this point that Betty Howard "passed" for white in applying for an apartment at the Trumbull Park Homes. The subsequent outbreak of disorder in South Deering – not the continued arguments of CHA critics – finally compelled CHA action.[50]

The very violence that the housing authority feared forced it to extend, at least verbally, its policy of nonsegregation to all of its projects. A brief flurry of disorder achieved what sixteen months of tedious negotiation could not.[51] More, the violence at Trumbull Park precipitated an internal crisis, the resolution of which transformed that policy statement into a mere paper declaration. It also produced the dismissal of Elizabeth Wood. Eager to maintain a bold front in the face of mob violence, the CHA carried on a war of words. Its actions, however, belied its pronouncements. For all its protestations, CHA policy *was* made in the streets.

As the rioting in South Deering dragged on, it became evident that the people of that community were firmly convinced of the efficacy of violent resistance. Just as the rioters at Fernwood were aware of the "redemption" of the Airport Homes, the people of Trumbull Park frequently pointed to the Cicero riot of 1951 as evidence that violence paid. South Deering residents admired the "guts" of Cicero's fighters, talked of importing a few of them "to show us how to get rid of these damn niggers," and openly hoped Trumbull Park would become "another Cicero."[52]

The CHA, its proclamations notwithstanding, did little to dissuade the rioters. The disorder that greeted Donald Howard and his family quickly produced a "freeze" on further move-ins for nearly three months. When crowds greeted the second group of black tenants in October 1953, the placement of such families in the Trumbull Park Homes was again halted – this time for almost four months. In a maze of perhaps intentional bureaucratic confusion, the CHA commissioners instructed Elizabeth Wood (verbally – they were careful not to put such orders in writing) not to admit additional black families until she received "clearance" from the police commissioner and Housing Coordinator James Downs. Downs claimed that his approval would be "automatic" once that of Commissioner Timothy O'Connor was secured, but O'Connor asserted that it was not within his authority to grant such "clearance." This confusion tied Wood's hands and the executive secretary had no choice but to halt the movement of black families into the project and "return the matter to [the commissioners] for further discussion."[53]

The CHA accommodated itself to the violent resistance in other ways as well. Special criteria were established for potential black Trumbull Park residents in the hope of minimizing white recalcitrance. At first only families without school-age children were permitted, and, later, only those with children in the lower grades and none with children in parochial school were allowed to enter. The presence of both parents and a local work address were also demanded. "Such artificial selective factors," the American Friends Service Committee concluded, "reduce[d] the opportunities for a natural increase in the number of Negro families...or even [the] maintenance...of Negro occupancy in the project." That, however, was part of the "armed truce" that existed in South Deering in the mid-1950s.[54]

If the whites of Trumbull Park learned that violence paid, they also knew that it could be even more effective when coupled with political pressure. The South Deering Improvement Association was especially active in promising political reprisals for continued inaction. Through such pressure, and the cooperation of Tenth Ward Alderman Emil Pacini, the SDIA was able to extract several concessions. When black use of the community's parks became an issue in the summer of 1954, an unmistakable display of force through mob action and simultaneous negotiation prompted the city to refuse black requests for "permits" to use South Deering's facilities. The reduction of the omnipresent police detail, always a source of irritation to the local white populace, was similarly achieved by such SDIA pressure. Threats of political reprisal also succeeded in isolating the CHA from potential sources of support. Other city agencies declined to back the housing authority, and even Mayor Kennelly refused to display a "strong attitude upholding a non-discrimination policy in public housing."[55]

The combination of violence and political pressure produced other significant results as well. Seeking relief after a full year of chronic disorder, city fathers took two important steps. First, they set a quota on the number of black families permitted in the Trumbull Park Homes. Precipitated by the escalating violence of the summer of 1954, the "deal" was denied by the city, but there is no doubt that a bargain between community and city leaders was struck after the rioting in Trumbull Park in early July. On July 16 representatives of the South Deering Improvement Association met with the mayor, James Downs, and the police commissioner "to discuss the Trumbull Park Homes situation." This gathering and a second meeting with Downs apparently produced the settlement. In early August Carl Buck, president of the SDIA, informed his neighbors that he "had made a deal with the Housing Authority...for just so many [blacks]." Although the quota was originally reported to be nineteen or twenty families in the 462-unit project, the limit was apparently marginally flexible, as thirty-one black families occupied the development at one time in 1955. This total soon declined, however – and declined precipitously in the wake of the riot in nearby Calumet Park in 1957 – and the working quota seemed to range between twenty-five and thirty black families. Indeed, Edward H. Palmer, director of Community and Tenant Relations at the Trumbull Park Homes between 1960 and 1962 testified that the CHA established a quota of twenty-five black families, which was made explicit to housing authority personnel through "oral instructions...rather than by written order."[56]

The second step taken to help bring peace to the city was the ouster of Elizabeth Wood as executive secretary of the CHA. Soon after the Howard family occupied its Trumbull Park apartment, Alderman Emil Pacini renewed the demands first heard in 1946 by calling for Wood's removal.[57] Yet, even though her dismissal came just weeks after the culmination of the quota "deal," voices were heard denying that racial issues had anything to do with her separation from the housing authority. And there was something to their contentions.

Relations between Wood and the commissioners who directed the CHA had been strained for some time, and there had been, during the preceding year, some bitter controversies over issues other than race. Most acrimonious was the dispute over the hiring of a new general counsel in the spring of 1953. Mayor Kennelly, futilely pursuing Cook County Democratic Party Chairman Richard J. Daley's support for a third mayoral term, wanted the CHA to hire John M. Daley, the chairman's second cousin. The housing authority's commissioners went along. Oddly enough, it was Kennelly's own use of civil service that had reduced the patronage available to the machine and led to increased pressures on the CHA, a heretofore untapped source of jobs. Elizabeth Wood, however, publicly protested the "political nature" of the proposed appointment and noted that the candidate had but five years of legal experience (CHA regulations demanded at least eight) and that he ranked 183rd in a class of 191 at his law school. The candidate soon withdrew his name from consideration, but the controversy did not die. The bitter dispute over the appointment of a general counsel continued to poison relations between Wood and the commissioners. The latter, by resolution, moved "to attack the administrative authority of the executive secretary" and undermine her influence within the agency.[58]

Although it is evident that such disputes earned Wood many powerful enemies (not the least of which had to be Richard J. Daley), the timing, nature, and consequences of her removal from office reveal that it was a combination of problems – racial, political, and personal – that came together in the summer of 1954 to force her dismissal. She was initially eased from a position of power when, on August 23, the commissioners made public, and implemented, recommendations for the housing authority's reorganization made by Griffenhagen and Associates, a private consulting firm. The Griffenhagen study called for the abolition of Wood's position of executive secretary and the creation of a new office – that of executive director – to oversee the day-to-day operations of the housing authority. Simultaneously, the commissioners announced the selection of General William B. Kean, a retiring commander of a Midwest military area, as the new director, effective on October 1. Obliquely indicating a shift in basic policy, John Fugard, chairman of the CHA's board of commissioners, simply explained that "business considerations had finally overridden the 'social aspects' of CHA" operations and that sound management would "henceforth. . . be of first importance." Sensing a fundamental change in the CHA's approach to its job, the *Sun-Times* agreed with the reorganization. Wood's temperament was suited to the job when the CHA was a struggling new agency, the *Sun Times* declared; then, it needed a "fighter." Now, however, the agency was well established and it needed an "administrator," not a "propagandist."[59]

Elizabeth Wood, as had to be expected, reacted strongly. The commissioners' action, Wood publicly charged, was taken "without notice or prior consultation." The study upon which it was based was largely prepared while she was away on an extended leave and it was not made available to her before the commissioners announced their action. Furthermore, the study left Wood's future at the housing authority undefined, although Fugard suggested that she might stay on as an assistant to Kean and an adviser on the now deemphasized "social aspect of housing." Wood took the latter suggestion as a personal affront and felt that she had been treated in a "deliberately insulting manner," which was little more than a "calculated attempt. . . to make my continued stay at the Authority impossible." In issuing her public statement, however, Wood also attacked the commissioners and their motives. It was this verbal assault, made a week after the commissioners' original announcement, that finally prompted her outright dismissal.[60]

There were two basic charges in Wood's indictment of her superiors. The first, obviously drawing on the past year's experience, claimed that she was being attacked by those who objected to her refusal to show "personal or political favoritism" in running the housing authority. More significant, however, at least in her own mind, was the hostility generated by her "single-minded devotion to carrying out the spirit and letter of policies adopted by the Commissioners." "The truth," she claimed, was that "the differences that have arisen between the Commissioners and the Executive Secretary have been related primarily to the issue of the elimination of segregation in public housing and the opening of all...projects...to Negro and white persons without discrimination or segregation." She charged further that the commissioners merely paid "lip-service" to their announced policies while they "privately issu[ed] instructions thwarting those policies." "My views on such ambidexterity," she tersely told the press, "have been no secret." She then recounted the history of the Trumbull Park Homes dispute and the commissioners' vacillating response to conditions in South Deering. "The long and short of the Authority's racial relations policy," she finally concluded, "is that the Commissioners are either unwilling, unable, or afraid to come to grips with it." It took less than a day for the commissioners to respond by firing her.[61]

There is little doubt that Wood's political problems and her dispute with the commissioners over racial policy prompted her removal – although it is difficult, if not impossible, to assess precise degrees of responsibility. Cora M. Patton, president of the Chicago Chapter of the NAACP and an Elizabeth Wood sympathizer, reported widespread rumors that the executive secretary was the victim of an "expertly engineered coup...masterminded" by Housing Coordinator James Downs. There was, apparently, some basis for the allegation. It was Downs who suggested to the CHA commissioners that they hire the Griffenhagen firm as part of a general review of public housing operations, which would result in some unspecified "basic recommendations." Although cryptic, Downs suggested to Fugard in April 1954 that the firm be retained to conduct a study as "a means of implementing our broader thinking on this subject." The "subject" was never explicitly defined in the letter, although it is likely that they contemplated some sort of reorganization. Downs added, again with tantalizing obscurity, that he had consulted with the mayor who agreed that such action was "desirable." Griffenhagen and Associates was hired by the housing authority shortly thereafter, and Elizabeth Wood, who initially refused to accept the sixty-day leave granted her by the commissioners (May 15–July 15, 1954), went on an extended vacation when promised that she would be called back when the Griffenhagen staff interviewed top CHA personnel.[62]

Whatever the initial motivation behind the Griffenhagen study – whether "sinister plot" or legitimate self-scrutiny – the violence at the Trumbull Park Homes made certain that it became the vehicle for Wood's ouster. As the periodic disturbances grew in intensity over the summer of 1954, the city grew more responsive to the demands of the SDIA – hence the "deal" setting up a quota on black tenancy in the development. In early August, however, nearly three weeks before the Griffenhagen investigation became public knowledge and shortly after the SDIA's "victory" in limiting black access to the Trumbull Park Homes, the SDIA leadership spoke of pressuring the "proper people" to have Elizabeth Wood "removed from office." Throughout August it was common knowledge in South Deering that there was another "deal in the making" and that Trumbull Park's whites "should be careful in the meantime." On August 7, still more than two weeks before the commissioners stripped the executive secretary of her power, the ACLU's observer in South Deering reported that a settlement was expected "very soon" and that for the first time in a year the people of Trumbull Park, like those in any other neighborhood, were "working on their lawns or cleaning their cars. There was not a bit of tension." Finally, after Wood's authority was taken away, the SDIA leadership explained to the community that she was dismissed because she "tried to fight" the "original deal" setting a quota on the black presence in the Trumbull Park Homes. She simply "would not go along with the politicians" and, consequently, "they arranged for her to be ousted." Indeed, Elizabeth Wood herself later claimed that her firing was part of an arrangement between City Hall and the SDIA.[63]

Obviously, the fact that the Griffenhagen study was ordered several months before the quota was established at Trumbull Park raises the question as to how closely developments there were related to Wood's downfall after seventeen years in office. But the murky origins of the investigation, and the lack of any clear indication that her removal was contemplated that far in advance of the actual event, lead to the conclusion that it was the combination of pressures that produced her separation from the housing authority. Her political vulnerability and the CHA's deteriorating position in the community made it possible, perhaps, for the "politicians" to go further than they would have originally dared and thus attempt to solve several problems at a single stroke by removing her from office. At any rate, the racial implications of her departure were very clear even if such considerations were not totally responsible for the purge itself.

Indeed, the most common interpretation given Elizabeth Wood's departure assigned primary significance to the race issue and expressed concern over future CHA policy.[64] Aware of the strong public reaction along these lines, the commissioners emphasized their own commitment to nondiscrimination and General Kean's "liberal" record as an army commander. Engaging in some overzealous public relations, the commissioners reported, apparently erroneously, that Kean was the man responsible for integrating American troops in Korea. The CHA's publicity, however, was so effective that some Trumbull Park residents actually feared that Kean might be a larger problem than Elizabeth Wood. It was, in fact, a growing sense of confusion and despair in that community that compelled the SDIA to come forward with its pacifying "explanation" of events. Soon, the people of South Deering were further reassured by the news that Kean "made some kind of a deal before he got the job" as a condition of his appointment. Later events proved that the whites of Trumbull Park had little to worry about.[65]

When the Trumbull Park uprising began, the usually perceptive Elizabeth Wood viewed it as the "last stand" of the forces opposed to integration. Misreading the trend of the preceding five years, she was only half right. It *was* a "last stand" of sorts – but hers, not theirs.[66] With Wood out of the way, the CHA no longer fought the pressures that impinged upon it. The change in housing authority leadership – which was later paralleled by a large turnover of staff – presaged the institution of new tenant and site selection procedures that turned the CHA into a bulwark of segregation in Chicago. Before, the housing authority had given ground only grudgingly. Now, it joined those forces that had previously assaulted it.

Tenant selection policies under General Kean and his successor, Alvin E. Rose, were marked by both change and continuity. First, in 1955, new instructions were issued regarding the selection procedures for tenants in those developments that had been carefully managed to preserve their integrated status. Before, the staff had been instructed to "maximize" white occupancy in these projects by expediting all white applications regardless of their normal "priority status" and by sustaining high vacancy rates and subsequent economic loss when sufficient numbers of white applicants were not available. General Kean ordered the staff to cut the losses. In the parlance of the racial coding system used on CHA applications, the staff was still instructed to maximize "A" (white) families in these developments, but they were "no longer to hold vacancies for them and were to assign "B" (black) families if no "A" families were available.[67] Given the composition of CHA waiting lists, these projects rapidly became increasingly black.

The policies that remained unchanged, however, were as significant as those that were altered. The racial coding system on CHA applications remained in force throughout the period, and, as late as 1959, Executive Director Alvin Rose (who succeeded the retiring Kean in 1957) was "prepared to admit the worst" regarding housing authority applications. Not only did the forms designate the race of the applicant, but the information was used to "select, or not select, tenants for certain projects." These projects, of course, were the four that remained all white until the Trumbull Park Homes project was "accidentally" integrated in 1953. If Elizabeth Wood could do little to change the status of these developments while she was in office, however, they retained an almost timeless quality after she was gone.[68]

Nowhere was the link between violence and public policy more clearly established than in the maintenance of the character of the Trumbull Park, Bridgeport, Lawndale, and Lathrop projects. As of mid-1953, each remained all white. The subsequent dispute and publicity centering about the Trumbull Park Homes, however, made their status the subject of considerable discussion. Obviously operating in violation of state nondiscrimination statutes, great changes seemed to loom in the offing. More than a decade later, though, their character was altered but slightly. The Trumbull Park and Lathrop projects endured only token integration. In 1965 Trumbull Park maintained its unofficial quota of twenty-five black families, and the Lathrop Homes housed but thirty-two such families in its 925 units. If progress was minimal in these projects, it was virtually nonexistent in the Bridgeport and Lawndale developments. The latter contained two black families in its nearly 130 apartments, and the former still failed to house any blacks at all in 1965.[69]

There was no doubt that the fear of violence prevented more significant changes. Alvin Rose repeatedly expressed the determination merely to maintain the number of black families that lived in the Trumbull Park Homes when he took office. This meant a total of twenty black families throughout the 1950s and, under what he later termed an "elastic quota," the addition of five more families in the 1960s. When asked, he told listeners that he did not "want to take any further steps in integration at Trumbull Park or in the other projects in question until he was sure it could be done without violence." He spoke of nondiscrimination as a "goal" rather than a policy and wished to avoid anything that would cause another "flare-up." Nor were assaults on CHA property and tenants his sole concern. Episodes of racial violence unrelated to public housing in Bridgeport led him to "back off" plans for integrating the project in that community. It was thus evident that in terms of tenant selection, the link between violent reaction and government response was clear and direct: As long as whites were willing to fight to keep blacks out of the projects already established in their areas, the CHA was unwilling to integrate them.[70]

More important than tenant selection procedures, however, were the informal arrangements made concerning the method of choosing proper sites for CHA development. The accommodation finally established between the housing authority and the city council provided, in effect, the same sorts of controls on CHA operations envisaged by the anti-public housing Larson bills, which were periodically proposed in the state legislature. The Larson bills called for local referendums before the CHA would be permitted to build on any given site. Although the working relationship between the housing authority and the council did not call for formal elections, it empowered local communities to veto the selection of public housing sites within their borders.

The agreement on procedure was established in discussions held between General Kean and Alderman W. T. Murphy, chairman of the council's Housing and Planning Committee, in early 1955. Kean proceeded on the assumption that the city council was the "governmental agency which is most vitally interested in the exact location of projects" and that the CHA's primary considerations were merely "economic and developmental." Without specifically raising the race issue, Kean restricted the housing authority's concern to the aforementioned subjects and claimed that the CHA staff could not "fully evaluate various other factors, which must be determined by the City Council." It was an abdication of responsibility inconceivable just a few years before. Kean then proceeded to outline a new site selection procedure, which necessitated obtaining the consent of the aldermen of the wards in which proposed sites were located. Without aldermanic "clearance," the sites would be withdrawn from consideration. Neighborhood groups cheered this development, and the *South Deering Bulletin* applauded the fact that aldermen, and through them the residents of the communities involved, were being consulted in the site selection process. The aldermen and the voters now had a "strong voice" in deciding where public housing would be built, the *Bulletin* concluded, and the new arrangement assured that communities would "not be faced with the problem of unwanted neighbors."[71]

Proof of the *South Deering Bulletin*'s contentions was not long in coming. The next slate of sites for proposed CHA developments came before the city council in 1955–6. This program contained eleven prospective sites, six of which (including the five situated in outlying areas) were rejected by the aldermen. All of the sites finally approved were located along State Street, Cottage Grove Avenue, or South Park Avenue between 38th and 63rd streets – all well within the main South Side Black Belt. Personally, General Kean asserted, he "held no brief for the choice of sites," but, he added resignedly, "it was the business of the CHA to build low rent housing and...they could build only where the city permitted them to." The "most obvious effect" of this new slate of sites was, in the protesting words of Ferd Kramer, "to create further concentration of high density... segregated housing on the Central South Side." Some of the sites, the Metropolitan Housing and Planning Council spokesman added, fell "so far short of accepted criteria as to create grave new social and economic problems for the city." "We hope," Kramer concluded in a letter to James Downs, "that you will work for a program scattering small public housing developments throughout the city, instead of great colonies of racially, socially, economically, and politically segregated housing."[72]

With the succession of Richard J. Daley's man, Alvin Rose, to the executive director's chair of the CHA, even the mild reticence expressed by General Kean disappeared. Indeed, there is some evidence that as late as 1956 the CHA staff, at least, was willing to investigate all possible sites for public housing and recommend certain locations "even though they felt the City Council would not approve them."[73] Rose's administration, however, raised CHA-city council cooperation to new levels and eliminated all hints of discord. Now, "as a courtesy," aldermen were contacted *before* the housing authority would even seriously consider a site so that they could test their community's reaction. If the people and the alderman of a given ward objected to public housing in their area, it stood, in Rose's words, "no chance of getting through." CHA commissioners echoed these views. "We have gotten to the place," one declared, "where we do not even try to sail non-ghetto sites past the City Council." Only those sites certain of approval were fully investi-

These houses on the west side of Dearborn Street between 34th and 35th streets were demolished to make way for the Stateway Gardens public housing project. (Photograph courtesy of the Chicago Housing Authority.)

gated (it would be a waste of CHA money to prepare elaborate site reports on locations that were sure to be rejected) and submitted for council action – the housing authority acted as its own censor. In so doing, the CHA was fulfilling the role Rose sketched for it in a January 1958 speech before the Planning and Housing Committee of the City Club of Chicago. "We are not going to use public housing as a wedge," Rose declared (after asserting that "too much has been made over this interracial business"); "our role must be one of friend to the community." In playing that role, the CHA's subservience to the city council was simply overlooked. When asked, Rose failed to recall any discussion over the housing authority's lack of autonomy because "this condition was just part of our daily life. We didn't discuss that any more than we discussed how the room was furnished."[74]

Given these conditions, the site selection process for public housing units was unmarred by controversy throughout much of the 1950s and early 1960s. Of the thirty-three projects approved between 1950 and the mid-1960s, twenty-five and a "substantial portion" of

Demolition and construction of Stateway Gardens proceeds along the rail-road tracks between 35th and 39th streets, 1959. (Chicago Historical Society, Negative ICHI-17210. Photograph by Clarence W. Hines.)

another were located in census tracts containing a black population in excess of 75%. Of the remaining seven developments, six were located in areas undergoing racial transition. By the time the projects were actually completed, only one of the thirty-three was situated in an area that was less than 84% black; and all but seven of the developments, when actually completed, were located in census tracts that were at least 95% black.[75] In terms of the apartments themselves, this meant that more than 98% of the 21,010 family units constructed since 1950, and more than 99% of the 10,256 built after the 1955 Kean-Murphy "deal," were located in all-black neighborhoods.[76] There was little doubt that the CHA, as critics later charged, was building "almost a solid corridor of low rent housing along State Street and nearby streets from Cermak Road (22nd Street) to 51st Street." This policy of "intensive centralization" led simply to the "pyramiding of existing ghettos" and the concentration of a host of urban ills.[77]

Stateway Gardens at dawn, 1981. The massive Robert Taylor Homes public housing project begins at the point where Stateway Gardens fades into the background. (© *Chicago Sun-Times*, 1981. Photograph by John H. White, reprinted with permission.)

The only exception to this pattern does more than prove the rule. Those few projects located in white areas were virtually all designated as housing for the "elderly" and, as such, came fully equipped with their own special tenant selection procedures. These projects were filled under a "proximity" rule, which gave highest priority to those living closest to them. Given the degree of segregation in Chicago, this meant that those located in white areas would remain white. Hardly an accident, this special admission policy for the elderly was demanded as a precondition to city council approval of the sites involved. Interestingly, Alvin Rose expanded General Kean's restricted view of CHA abilities and obligations in order to justify the practice. Ignoring the fact that it was the housing authority's "sociological experiments" that generated so much opposition in the 1940s, Rose now declared that the CHA had "the legal right as well as the responsibility to act on sociological considerations in the housing of elderly persons and families of low income." To compel the elderly to break the ties of family, friends, and religion, which they had established over a long period of time in a single neighborhood, Rose asserted, was needlessly destructive. By the 1960s, "sociological" considerations thus enjoyed new support as they were implemented to uphold prevailing patterns of segregation.[78]

In defending the CHA's program before the U.S. Commission on Civil Rights in 1959, the executive director could only stress expediency, the CHA's progress in tearing down slums, and his perception of the beauty of south State Street.[79] Held "captive" by the city council at the end of Elizabeth Wood's tenure in office, the CHA was domesticated under her successors.

If the white resistance found government responsive to its needs, the beginning of the postwar period seemed to find blacks in a similar position. The creation of the Chicago Commission on Human Relations in the wake of the 1943 Detroit riot and its postwar crusades to rid the city of race labeling in the mass media, scurrilous hate literature, and restrictive covenants were clear evidence of unprecedented government concern with racial issues. The Chicago Housing Authority's attempt to establish integrated projects for veterans and its rhetorical support for the principle of nondiscrimination also indicated that government was no longer able to ignore black demands. The publication of the report of President Truman's Committee on Civil Rights in 1947 and the Supreme Court's emasculation of restrictive covenants the following year appeared as national confirmation of local trends. Yet the gains for blacks were largely symbolic, and the government concern that seemed so promising was ephemeral. Indeed, the process of urban reconstruction in the postwar era was characterized as much by the absence of black input as it was by the overwhelming force of local institutions and the marginal influence of white ethnics. The emergence of the second ghetto was grave testimony to the persistence of black powerlessness in Chicago.

The wave of violent reaction in the decade after World War II was instrumental in isolating the black community from potential and timid sources of support. Chief among those whose ardor for civil rights cooled noticeably in the 1950s was the Chicago Commission on Human Relations. At first glance, it appears as though the CHR went through a reactionary metamorphosis analogous to that of the CHA. Such, however, was not the case. There was an underlying consistency of purpose in the commission that simply led to attempts at reform in the 1940s and to a greater appreciation for the status quo in the succeeding decade.

Since its inception, the CHR was primarily devoted to the preservation of racial peace in Chicago. Created as the nation reeled under the impact of a succession of racial disturbances, the commission turned to reform in the 1940s as it believed that racial violence resulted primarily from the injustice suffered by the black community. An end to discrimination would produce greater understanding between the races and, it felt, an end to racial violence. The growth of white resistance to the expanding black community in the late 1940s and 1950s, however, led the CHR to revise its working assumptions. As long as it believed that the cause of peace could best be served by eliminating racial inequities (as long, in other words, as the CHR viewed black dissatisfaction as the most likely source of disorder), the commission played the role of reformer. By the 1950s, though, it was clear that embittered and frightened whites posed the strongest threat to the city's stability. It was at this point that it became evident that the commission's first commitment was to maintaining the city's racial peace, not the transformation of racial relationships.

In the 1950s, consequently, the CHR tended to support, rather than attack, the current state of affairs. The housing authority consulted it when considering the integration of its projects, and the commission refused approval of any activity that threatened violence.[80] By the last half of the decade, agency officials not only wished to avoid any "precipitous action" but actively defended the city against charges of extreme segregation and advised against the release of information that would "influence people in a negative way." By the 1960s Saul Alinsky was calling them "highly paid professional propagandists for the status quo." They were nothing more, Alinsky sneered in his inimitable style while addressing an annual meeting of race relations officials, than "zoo keepers" who were "trying to keep the animals quiet."[81]

Nor was the Commission on Human Relations the only organization deeply affected by the wave of reaction sweeping the city. Virtually every group involved in race relations had its motives questioned, its support weakened, and its membership and leadership fragmented in the early 1950s. One especially telling episode involved an ad hoc group, the Committee to End Mob Violence (CEMV), which was created by Chicago Urban League executive Sidney Williams after the Peoria Street riot in late 1949. Organized because Williams felt that there was no black agency "doing anything to stem the tide of violence," the CEMV attacked the "shameful failure" of Mayor Kennelly and the police commissioner and questioned the role played by the more "responsible" human relations organizations in sponsoring a "hush-hush press policy." The committee's attack on mob violence, however, was soon overshadowed by its "open door policy" in admitting new members. The presence of "leftists" and "communists" in its ranks left the CEMV open to attack.[82]

The committee was quickly painted with a "red brush," and, revealingly, most of the charges came from other race relations leaders and groups. Homer Jack claimed that only "disillusion and confusion can result from cooperating" with the CEMV and acknowledged that the "heart" of his charge was "ideological." Feeling the full weight of the "red scare," groups like the Council Against Discrimination – after bitter internal wrangling over the application of "loyalty standards" to the CEMV – asked the committee to withdraw its request for support so that the CAD would not have to confront the issue. After that action, one CAD board member commented coldly that "perhaps Chicago needed a Council Against Communism – we are in error to misuse an organization to fight Communism under the guise of fighting racism." For his part, Sidney Williams denounced the apparent paternalism of white "supporters" who, in his view, were attacking the group because they were not "master-minding it."[83]

The impact of this dispute reached far beyond the CEMV alone. Not only was that group neutralized, but the clash precipitated a series of crises in related organizations. The CAD, which had already lost the support of some conservative church groups because of Homer Jack's "militant" leadership, now suffered an ideological split with some adherents backing the CEMV. Fragmented further by black suspicions of its heavily Jewish support, the council sank into inactivity and disappeared by the end of the decade.[84] More significant, however, was the devastation of the Chicago Urban League. Sidney Williams's close affiliation with the "radical" CEMV brought the league into "disrepute." His charges of Catholic involvement in the Peoria Street disorder brought on a mass resignation by the league's Catholic board members. Moderate blacks and conservative labor leaders also left the CUL's board. Finally, the CEMV controversy dealt a staggering blow to the league's already delicate financial condition. The Community Fund, which supplied 50% or more of the league's annual budget, lost $300,000 per year in contributions at mid-decade because of its support of the CUL. Several large industrial supporters (who kept their own file on Sidney Williams's activities) also neglected to make their customary donations. After an internal investigation, the league closed its doors for six months, fired its staff, and dismissed Sidney Williams. When it resumed activity, it had both the support of the business community and a more conservative leadership.[85]

Those groups that seemed to support the black community in the days after World War II thus either altered their policies or crumbled under the pressure of the 1950s. Left alone, that community simply lacked the resources to influence public redevelopment or renewal policy on its own behalf. The one remaining black organization, the local NAACP, had no regular staff, was torn by factions, and could attract but twenty or thirty people to its meetings. And when, despite such problems, it did threaten to seriously agitate racial issues, William L. Dawson simply had his precinct captains and political operatives become voting members of the organization. A moderating change in leadership soon followed.[86] Moreover, as shown by the dispute over the Lake Meadows project, Chicago's blacks were themselves divided and unable to muster a clear voice in opposition. Later, although greater public unity was achieved in the battle against the Hyde Park-Kenwood urban renewal plans, deep divisions persisted, and there was a similar inability on the part of blacks to become participants in, rather than the objects of, urban renewal.

Most vociferous in their objections to the Lake Meadows development, of course, were those blacks living on or near the project site. A host of local organizations such as the Champions, the Vigilantes, and the Park Lake Council, among others, appeared to protest the city's redevelopment plans.[87] And the Snowdenville Community Council (organized between 39th and 43rd streets, South Parkway to Cottage Grove) voiced the concerns of many when it claimed that "high rents will replace restrictive covenants as means of keeping out Negro masses." Local leaders articulated their position before the Commission on Human Relations. "Because Negroes have had to struggle so continuously for every section they now occupy," one of them informed the CHR, "there is hesitancy to give up any part of their community until they know what plans are in store for them. This history is accentuated by the fact that much of the property on the South Side is irreplaceable for Negroes." The Snowdenville Community Council concluded simply that they had "better organize and keep alert."[88]

The call for unity went unheeded, however, and near South Side residents soon found themselves isolated within the larger black community. The *Defender*, for example, at first took a noncommittal attitude, running articles on both sides of the controversy.[89] The sponsors of Lake Meadows, though, saw that the South Side was "about to split itself wide open" over the issue and subsequently engaged in a vigorous public relations effort, which included a large advertising campaign in the *Defender*. The newspaper, which was published by John Sengstacke, then became a strong supporter of redevelopment and ran a series of articles extolling the project and dismissing the opposition. Only a "few of those who would have to be moved" and the "landlords who are greedily lining their pockets with outlandish rents" objected to the program, the *Defender* charged. By early 1949, the *Defender* ignored a full day of city council hearings devoted to the opposition, and Alderman Archibald Carey learned that the Land Clearance Commission had "Sengstacke sold on all out support." Finally, the paper lent its pages to pro-development forces within the black community who claimed that the dread of "Negro clearance" was unfounded and that "our lesser fears do not extend across the community." "These little fears are simply the immediate and individual concerns of this group and that," the project's supporters declared, "and ought not be permitted to stand in the way of public progress." It was time to "tear the foul, rotting, vermin infested buildings to the ground and build housing which will give the people living in that area the chance to live like human beings."[90]

An agitator of racial issues under founder Robert S. Abbott early in the century, the *Defender* was now controlled by Abbott's nephew, John Sengstacke, who was both a personal and political acquaintance of Congressman William L. Dawson, "boss" of Chicago's black sub-machine. Like Dawson in the political arena, the paper went through a metamorphosis that saw it deemphasize racial crusades and strike a more moderate tone by the 1940s. Where, in the Abbott era, the *Defender* was supported largely by its black circulation, it now found circulation declining, and it became dependent on advertising – especially that bought by whites and the Democratic party in election campaigns. It also turned more to sensationalism (particularly in reporting crime) than racial agitation in an effort to bolster its readership. Being in the forefront of "racial" causes helped launch both the *Defender* and Bill Dawson's political career a generation earlier. Now, both were established entities whose interests were better served by avoiding, rather than stirring, such controversies. When the Lake Meadows dispute erupted, the city's major black newspaper hesitated ever so slightly and then came down firmly in the developers' camp. As Frayser T. Lane told a meeting of the Champions: "Big money cannot be stopped easily by prayers and petitions."[91]

It was Dawson's political organization, though, that gave the people in the redevelopment area what little support they did receive.

Even here, however, the dependence of the black sub-machine on its white counterpart meant that the black politicians were unable to challenge the program in a fundamental way. More concerned about police harassment of South Side policy wheels and jitney cabs, Dawson tried to use his leverage not to influence public policy (which, in all probability, would have been futile) but to extract tangible benefits from the political system. His backing enabled site residents to stall the project, and it maximized the prices they received for their condemned properties. Accepting the "inevitable," the black politicians did not fight the program; but they did engage in a delaying action to the benefit of those who "stuck with" them.[92]

The debate over the Hyde Park-Kenwood renewal plans found the black community far more united but just as powerless. William Dawson was convinced that a "hostile force" was acting against black interests, but Richard J. Daley's support for the project forced Dawson to remain silent. The charges of "Negro clearance," however, which had become a cliché by this time, made the University of Chicago's plans an unavoidable "race issue" and the black press joined the opposition. Acting as a catalyst in this regard was the university's treatment of South West Hyde Park. The most blatant attempt to reduce black population near the campus, the university's use of its own neighborhood redevelopment corporation for such purposes aroused considerable resentment – not only by site residents but by the black community as a whole. In this instance, however, renewal was carried out under the Redevelopment Act of 1941 as amended by Julian Levi and the SECC in 1953 – the one piece of renewal legislation that granted the power of eminent domain to private parties. No matter how spirited the opposition, the university had the law on its side. A lawsuit and subsequent litigation delayed renewal plans for two years, but there was never any doubt that the university would win.[93]

There was a broad spectrum of black opposition to the more general 1958 renewal plans for Hyde Park, but it was neither as vigorous nor as united as that aroused previously. Once the project was publicly defined as a "race issue," of course, the *Defender* and groups such as the NAACP lined up against it, but their opposition was halfhearted. Indeed, the introduction of class as well as race as a salient variable in determining residence in Hyde Park fragmented the community's black population. Almost every black leader in the community, St. Clair Drake asserted, was nearly "driven schizophrenic trying to decide whether to act as a 'Race Man' or in terms of his social class position." Such indecision often led to publicly held "race" positions and private support for renewal – a combination clearly not designed to foster determined resistance. Indeed, the NAACP, after stating its public disapproval, merely "went through the motions" in opposing the Hyde Park plans. In the eyes of blacks who supported renewal, their stance was "purely *pro forma*" and not taken out of conviction. The most serious attack on the plan was subsequently carried out not by the black community but by the Archdiocese of Chicago.[94]

These divisions were symptomatic of a deeper fissure in Chicago's black community. In his *Negro Politics*, James Q. Wilson described the split between those black leaders advocating the pursuit of "status" goals and those seeking tangible "welfare" ends. "Status" goals, according to Wilson, were those that sought to integrate "the Negro into all phases of the community on the principle of equality" and were generally sought by "race" organizations like the NAACP. The black leaders seeking "welfare" ends – such as William L. Dawson – were less concerned with principle and argued simply for the provision of "better services, living conditions, or positions."[95]

This split manifested itself in virtually every housing issue raised in the 1940s and 1950s. When Lake Meadows was first proposed, a number of black-owned insurance companies planned to pool their resources to invest in the project. It was a textbook example of the sort of self-help and black business development that Charles Duke, an advocate of better black housing and later co-sponsor of the Ida B. Wells Homes, had in mind when he suggested the improvement of the ghetto in 1917. But in the post-World War II era, suggestions that the insurance companies themselves would be assisting in "Negro clearance" forced them to drop their plans. The provision of new housing could not be discussed apart from its overall impact on the black community and questions of principle. And when the Lake Meadows plans were openly discussed, the split between those fearing removal and those demanding improved housing effectively neutralized the opposition, save for its chilling effect on black investment.[96] Should redevelopment be supported only if it furthered integration? Or was the clearance of slums and the construction of new housing reason enough for ghetto residents to back it? The black community never spoke with a single voice on this issue.

The contrast between "welfare" and "status" ends appeared most starkly, however, in debates over public housing. In the early post-war era public housing drew strong support from all segments of the black community. The implementation of the program on a segregated basis, though, led many to reassess their commitment in the

1950s. Some even debated, inconclusively, whether or not to oppose the desperately needed units because they could only be had at the cost of furthering segregation. According to one black newspaper editor:

> We think that public housing is wrong the way it's being handled ...But on the other hand, we can't oppose it too much because we don't want to penalize people who need housing somewhere of some kind...The whole thing is bad...But if we come out against it hard, then they'll just not build it anywhere, and that would be worse. So what do we do? We just mumble about it.[97]

Theoretically, there need not have been a choice implied in the pursuit of either "status" or "welfare" goals. Practically, however, the inability to resolve the conflict between the two – more housing would be provided *only* on a segregated basis – paralyzed the black community and precluded any serious efforts to influence public policy.

Unable to do anything to alter the plans that shaped their lives, Chicago's blacks responded viscerally, charging the planners with conspiracy and reviving an old strain of nativism in response to their ethnic antagonists. The dimensions of the conspiracy varied. Some believed the "plan" was to drive all blacks out of the area between 12th and 63rd streets; others stretched the territory to be "reclaimed" by whites down to 67th. The same new governmental agencies and powers that frightened white ethnics similarly affected blacks – only the latter saw no communists or subversives. "Land-grabbing" realtors, bankers, businessmen, and institutions provided explanation enough. There were as many reasons for the perceived conspiracy as there were villains: Blacks were to be pushed out of their desirable inner-city locations and herded to the outskirts of the city or to undesirable suburbs such as Robbins to make way for Loop workers (there was at least some truth to this – not all conspiracies were fantasies); the dispersal of black population was designed to dilute that community's political strength; the use of eminent domain was intended to reduce black property owners to tenancy. Whatever the validity of these contending explanations, the blacks employing them – as the whites who discovered their own conspiracies – were responding to the fact that large forces beyond their influence were controlling their lives, a perception as accurate as it was distressing.[98]

As for those who physically assaulted blacks, the latter's response addressed the attackers' weakness as much as their strength. "Nearly every man or woman arrested thus far in the Trumbull Park area," the *Defender* asserted, "bore names that very few Americans can pronounce. . . It would appear that the people with (zuktjorsljp) names like this in parentheses should be advised by their leaders to live peacefully – the American way." Suggestions made in the wake of the Trumbull Park and Calumet Park uprisings that violence could be averted if black migration to Chicago were halted prompted derisive references to European "DPs" in the black press. "Are responsible leaders of the displaced persons from Europe discouraging inflow of their people?" the *Defender* queried. "They should. Their folks cause most of the racial friction."[99] Although not nearly as serious as earlier manifestations of black nativism, the revival of anti-immigrant, anti-ethnic feeling in the second half of the twentieth century in the black community furnished persistent proof of deep strains in the social order as well as evidence of both the ethnics' power and vulnerability.

By 1960 the growth and development of Chicago's black areas of residence confirmed the existence of the city's second ghetto. The city housed nearly eight blacks for every one that lived there in 1920. The main South Side Black Belt was several times larger than it had been during the city's disastrous 1919 race riot, and it was more isolated as well. Its older, northern end was now almost solidly institutionalized and frozen in concrete. Slums had been torn down (as well as some areas that were not slums), their occupants sent to feed the swelling movement of blacks into newly occupied provinces farther South or on the city's West Side. Middle-class housing projects, rapidly expanding institutions such as Michael Reese Hospital and the Illinois Institute of Technology and – as a symbol of deference to the power of the city's white neighborhoods – a growing row of low-rent, high-rise public housing projects occupied the ground formerly taken by an older black community. On the West Side a minor enclave had grown into a major ghetto in its own right as black migrants from the South and displaced urban natives dispersed by the wrecker's ball filled the vacancies left behind by a Jewish population in exodus. The vastness of Chicago's black community and the numbers housed within it, however, were merely the quantitative measures separating this ghetto from its predecessor and hardly its most distinguishing characteristics.

Quantitative measures alone do not justify calling Chicago's modern black metropolis its "second ghetto." There are, however, two key features associated with this second period of ghetto formation that do necessitate the distinction. First, a host of fresh decisions, not merely the acquiescence in old ones, redrew and reinforced the ghetto's boundaries. There is no denying the burden of the past, but Chicago's neighborhoods and leadership sustained the actions of past generations with a passion that went beyond the grudging consent given to "inevitable" developments. Entering a period of massive growth in the post–World War II era, the ghetto, in effect, was re-created and reshaped by *new* pressures, not old ones. Chicago's second ghetto is a dynamic institution, not a dead inheritance from the past.

As such, there was a sense of an opportunity lost. In 1948 Robert Weaver believed that the nation's urban centers, Chicago prominent among them, stood on the threshold of an era that promised the destruction, rather than the revivification, of the ghetto. Less than five years later, however, knowledgeable observers saw that chance rapidly slipping away. There was "no greater problem" facing race relations workers, the conference of the National Association of Intergroup Relations Officials warned in 1952, than slum clearance and redevelopment. The "way in which these programs are conceived and carried out will. . .largely determine the physical framework and. . .greatly influence the socio-psychological atmosphere in which the anti-discrimination struggle must take place for decades to come." Yet, the speaker noted forlornly, "as the bitter displacement experiences of racial minority groups have led them to fear, too many city officials are disposed to employ slum clearance and urban redevelopment projects to preserve and extend, rather than to loosen up, the city's racial pattern in housing." Federal legislation provided some statutory safeguards, of course, but it was already apparent that local officials were likely "not only to overlook constructive approaches which are permitted but even to attempt evasion of mandatory requirements."[100]

The comments of these concerned critics point to the second key characteristic that distinguishes the "second ghetto": the deep involvement of government. Previously, white hostility had been expressed primarily through *private* means – violence, voluntary agreements among realtors, and restrictive covenants were the most powerful forces determining the pattern of black settlement. Before the Depression, government involvement was generally limited to the spotty judicial enforcement of privately drawn restriction agreements. With the emergence of redevelopment, renewal, and public housing, however, government took an active hand not merely in reinforcing prevailing patterns of segregation but also in lending them a permanence never seen before. The implication of government in

the second ghetto was so pervasive, so deep, that it virtually constituted a new form of de jure segregation.

The development and implementation of these governmental programs was carried out within a white consensus. The fruits of these
programs, as shown by the massive wave of both public and private
construction on the South Side, were the result of a combination of
violent and legal actions carried out by private groups engaged in a
desperate struggle for survival with each other as well as with the
exploding black metropolis. The chronic violence that helped preserve the Black Belt's border with Bridgeport was paralleled by the
determined invocation of the urban renewal tool by the University
of Chicago in maintaining a white presence in Hyde Park, thus
limiting the Black Belt's expansion to the east or west and increasing
its southern movement. Trapped between persistent "ethnics" and
dogged "renewers," the Black Belt followed the path of least resistance through those communities that were neither. Moreover, the
redevelopment of the near South Side and the subsequent massive
placement of public housing nearby – much to the chagrin of developers and local institutions – stood as mute testimony to the power
of private enterprise to shape public policy and the efficacy of violent resistance. It was a compromise between the "interests" and the
"ethnics," which left neither totally satisfied but proved, at bottom,
acceptable to the "white" community as a whole.

The conditions of that compromise, furthermore, had a deep impact on the lives of thousands of black individuals. The need for
relocation units to house those displaced by slum clearance meant
that the sponsors of those programs became the most significant
supporters of public housing. The dominance of the CHA's utilitar-
ian function in the early 1950s meant that many families, some of
them broken by renewal and relocation, found cold sanctuary in the
housing authority's developments. There were, consequently, in
the words of the assistant manager of one large project, "some people living at the [Robert] Taylor Homes. . .who. . .harbor deep-felt
resentments, hostilities, and bitterness and are overtly distrustful of
management and the Housing Authority." "And," he concluded, "I
don't doubt that some project youngsters vent their hostilities and
resentments by destroying CHA property."[101]

Although such actions may have served to convince Alvin Rose
that it would be foolish to construct apartments of the quality *he*
would like to live in, it had more dangerous consequences for the
tenants of the projects themselves. Accepting the first slate of ghetto

sites out of sheer expediency, planners and developers proved unable to alter the pattern of site selection for public housing later on. The statutory cost limitations on such construction and the repeated selection of expensive inner-city property meant that public housing, of necessity, was of the most economical sort: high-rise elevator buildings. Such an environment, when filled with tenants nursing "deep-felt resentments," provided daily inconvenience and danger.[102]

The key decisions influencing this pattern of events were all taken by the early 1950s. The resort to government power and resources to stem the tide and the consequences of racial succession was completed locally by 1953 and nationally by 1954. Similarly, the wave of violence that engulfed the city following the end of the war was almost wholly contained within Mayor Martin Kennelly's two terms in office (1947–55). Ironically, there was but a single violent incident (the Airport Homes riot) under the corrupt Kelly administration, and only one other serious territorial disorder (the Calumet Park disturbance of 1957) under Kennelly's successor, Richard J. Daley. It was during the Kennelly administration, in other words, that the "interests" and the "ethnics" successfully pressed their demands that eventually reshaped the racial geography of the city.

Kennelly's political style was conducive to the private exertion of power and the competitive struggle for survival in which localized interests acted forcefully in their own behalf. A "reform" candidate and a purposely "weak" mayor, Kennelly proved receptive to the large businesses and institutional interests that asked him to adopt their housing programs as his own. Moreover, both unwilling and unable to dictate to the local Democratic "machine" as his predecessor had done, Kennelly allowed the aldermen, ward committeemen, and the local interests they represented to take advantage of the power vacuum at the top of the political structure and successfully extract concessions from an administration that valued peace above all else. Indeed, it was precisely the power vacuum created by Kelly's retirement that permitted the "interests" and the "ethnics" to flex their political muscles and reach their eventual accommodation. As early as 1949, in fact, the "public housers" were denouncing Kennelly for his failure to provide firm leadership and, ironically, were so disgruntled with the reform-minded mayor that they openly longed for the protected status they had enjoyed under the much tougher Kelly.[103]

This meant, of course, that Richard J. Daley – who has assumed "larger than life" proportions in the eyes of both admirers and ene-

mies – was hardly the architect of Chicago's latest racial accommodation. He was simply its keeper. Its terms were laid out before he
took office and there was probably little he could do to alter them.
The CHA had already been subdued by the city council. Elizabeth
Wood had already been fired (although there is a possibility that
Daley, as chairman of the Cook County Democratic Organization,
might have had something to do with this), and the pattern of
selecting ghetto sites for public housing was firmly established. When
Ferd Kramer met with the mayor and informed him that it was "bad
planning" to "relegate all low rent housing projects to the South
Side," Daley took note of the argument but "made no commitments."
Kramer was later informed that, given the state of local opinion,
"the Mayor cannot help very much to reverse the situation."[104]

In assuming his caretaker role, however, Daley worked efficiently
to end the messy public disputes that had characterized his predecessor's administration. The site selection procedure for public housing was raised to a fine art in city council chambers. Objectionable
sites were not rejected by recalcitrant aldermen; action on them was
simply deferred at the request of Housing Coordinator James Downs.
The first time this maneuver was witnessed by neophyte independent Alderman Leon Despres, it left him "perplexed" – the "deferred" sites simply disappeared and were never brought up again.
As for the CHA itself, Daley made certain that it would never again
be a source of controversy by filling it with "his people." Appointments to the CHA board of commissioners were made part of Daley's
"political apparatus" and the commissioners themselves became noted
for their ability to take "political orders" and not "rock the boat." It
was also Daley who personally directed the selection of Alvin Rose
as General Kean's successor as CHA executive director – a move that
obviated future maneuvering in the city council over CHA site selections. When, finally, in 1969, a federal court decision found the
CHA guilty of discrimination and ordered that future public housing units be constructed in white areas, public housing construction
in Chicago simply ceased. Nothing would be permitted to shake the
city's new racial accommodation.[105]

The implications of this racial settlement for the turbulent 1960s
are clear, if in need of further explanation. Most important, perhaps,
the black uprisings of those years can now be viewed as a "backlash"
to concrete events and not simply as random acts of aggression.
Also, the "neo-ethnic revival," which appeared, seemingly, largely
as a response to those riots and related developments, may be seen

as part of a much longer chain of events. Ethnics found their hard-earned "whiteness" of the 1950s an increasingly vulnerable status in the civil rights and post-riot era. The rediscovery of ethnicity was, perhaps, thus an effective new tactic in fending off advances made by politically aggressive blacks. Further research is needed here, but it is evident that the "second ghetto" has a history all its own. Born of the struggles between planners and politicians, racists and liberals, ethnics and institutions, it was the product of all; none could have done it alone.

Epilogue: Chicago and the nation

Unquestionably Chicago is far ahead of any other city in providing the legal and conceptual framework of an effective conservation program.

> Jack M. Siegel and C. William Brooks, *Slum*
> *Prevention Through Conservation and*
> *Rehabilitation* (Washington, D.C., Government
> Printing Office, 1953), p. 69

Do you wonder or are you indifferent as to how long attacked groups can continue to "turn the other cheek," as to how long they will rely on judicial and protective agencies? How long can they be expected to keep faith in the face of an unrelieved, maiming menace? I swear I don't know. I only know that my chain has been shortened so that I begin to choke and I am fast losing patience.

> Carl C. Elliott, Jr., to the *Chicago Defender*,
> October 25, 1958

Once the laws were passed, the building began. In the Douglas neighborhood on the near South Side, the Lake Meadows project led the way. The Chicago Land Clearance Commission purchased and cleared the site for $16 million and sold it back to the New York Life Insurance Company for $3.4 million (at $.50 per square foot for residential property and $1.75 for commercial). The investment sparked considerable new construction. Michael Reese Hospital, already expanding, supported the Prairie Shores apartment complex immediately north of Lake Meadows, the Illinois Institute of Technology continued to grow, the Mercy Hospital – once almost certain to leave the community – cast down its bucket and revitalized itself as well. By 1970 the results were apparent. Twenty years earlier the population of the Douglas area stood at 78,745, 97.1% black. After redevelopment, its residents were reduced to 43,705, and the proportion of blacks had declined to 86.5%. Integration, though, was not extensive. Whites clustered largely in the Prairie Shores apartments, and a few, in the Lake Meadows complex. Poor blacks remained in the

259

public housing, which accompanied the privately sponsored projects. The Ida B. Wells extension, Prairie Avenue Courts, Stateway Gardens, and other Chicago Housing Authority projects replaced the earlier slums.[1]

In Hyde Park a new shopping center at 55th and Lake Park, the Harper Court development, and new residential construction stretching westward along 55th Street were visible indications that renewal was also under way around the University of Chicago. By their own standards, the school and the South East Chicago Commission were successful. Between 1960 and 1970 the number of dwelling units in Hyde Park was reduced by 20.1% and its population had shrunk by 26.4% (from 45,577 to 33,559). Median income was up, blacks were down. The former jumped from $6,772 to $11,515 (which included the area's traditionally hard-pressed student population), and 55% of Hyde Park's families earned more than $10,000 per year. The black population declined from 17,163 to 10,427, a drop of nearly 40%. Most important, the neighborhood had stabilized itself as an integrated, middle-class community. University ownership of 150 parcels of Hyde Park property (not including those accommodating instructional buildings) and the persistent demand for good housing by university faculty and middle-class blacks prevented future deterioration. By 1970 the mean value of owner-occupied units in Hyde Park was $40,332, and the average monthly rent was $144; the comparable figures for the city as a whole were $22,752 and $115, respectively.[2]

A major result of urban renewal was thus the creation of integrated enclaves on the fringes of a still-growing ghetto. The presence of lower-class blacks, or the threat of ghetto engulfment, was used, in effect, to extract housing gains for the black middle class. The poor were relegated to existing slums or public housing – and they were kept at arm's length. Hyde Park, for example, has only twelve family-style public housing units and another twenty-two for the elderly scattered within its borders. And, by the 1980s, the small steps made toward integration were, in some instances, coming undone.

Ferd Kramer, president of the Metropolitan Housing and Planning Council, manager of Lake Meadows, and developer of Prairie Shores, tried desperately to integrate his projects. He was determined that the "fine modern apartment development which would be replacing a Negro slum should not in turn become a Negro ghetto." Lake Meadows, the first project, was the most intractable problem. It rose "out of a sea of rubble with part of the slums nearby still standing and occupied." Consequently, it was "almost impossible" to attract whites, and only a dozen or so occupied the first 500 units. And, Kramer believed, he was successful in attracting "self-respecting Negroes" only because they "were so desperate for decent housing." Later, newspaper ads touting the sparkling new high-rises, their view of the lake, and rents 40% below anything comparable ran without mentioning the development's location in the attempt to lure whites. Some marginal, temporary success resulted, with the later buildings attracting 25% and 50% white occupancy. Normal attrition, however, and the failure to reattract white families soon made Lake Meadows a middle-class black complex. In the summer of 1980 Kramer said simply that he "was always disappointed that we weren't able to integrate Lake Meadows. It was impossible." Holman Pettibone's and Milton Mumford's original vision of an all-black project south of the Loop was fulfilled.[3]

The short-run experience of the Prairie Shores apartments differed from that of Lake Meadows – in large part because of the latter's existence – but it, too, seemed to be moving in the same direction. To assure white occupancy here, the developers held an open house for the staff at Michael Reese Hospital before showing the apartments to the public. Some forty-five of the first fifty applicants were white, and the managers then used that to reassure later prospective tenants. The first building was 77% white when rented, and the four later buildings – each a bit easier to rent than the first tower – also developed an 80% white occupancy rate. Kramer claimed that the complex could have easily been *more* than 80% white, but that he was determined to maintain an integrated project. In effect, he placed quotas on both races as the demand for desirable apartments remained high. There was, however, a persistent white majority. Kramer felt that the whites "needed some feeling of security" and "would not want to be in the minority in an apartment building." "We have learned," he finally announced in 1962, "that it is possible to operate a mixed occupancy project in a city which has historically segregated its minority groups." By 1980, though, Kramer and Prairie Shores had been sued for discrimination, and lacking the support of the major local institutions, they settled out of court. "We're taking them as they come," Kramer said afterward, "first come, first served, and that means that the chances are that sooner or later [Prairie Shores will]...become a ghettoized project." Not distinguishing between quotas used as floors and those imposed as ceilings, it seemed "ridiculous" to him that they could be permitted in "school systems, labor unions, everything but housing." Yet it was also clear that, at least for those who filed suit, the demand for good housing super-seded experiments in integration. Middle-class black housing op-portunities will surely grow as a result, but, as Kramer noted, when Congress passed open housing legislation it did so to "promote integration and not to expand the ghetto."[4]

Even in Hyde Park, where many now defended integration as the raison d'être of renewal, there were limits. And Julian Levi recog-nized those limits in preventing racial transition. "You have in Hyde Park," Levi believed, "a definite segment of people who pride them-selves on their great conviction about liberal theories of one sort or another, but when the chips go down will behave like anybody else." Clearance and reconstruction had reduced the black presence in the community from 37.6% in 1960 to 31.0% in 1970 – still a significant proportion, to be sure. But the remaining blacks were not randomly distributed. The three census tracts clustered in North West Hyde Park, adjoining the ghetto, had black populations of 81.6%, 88.1%, and 94.7% in 1970. The university area and South East Hyde Park, however, contained five census tracts whose black presence ranged from a mere 3.7% to 6.6%. Six centrally located tracts where the black population ran as low as 15.6% and as high as 50.2% bridged the gap between these two largely black and white enclaves. The gradual scaling of the black population in Hyde Park, with its heaviest concentrations nearest the ghetto, has proven a stable arrangement.[5]

Perhaps the most striking feature of the citywide accommodation after World War II was the extent to which it adhered to the restric-tions laid down a generation before. In the aftermath of the 1919 riot, Governor Lowden's investigatory commission called not for integration, as Thomas Philpott has shown, but simply for a peace-ful settlement of the territorial issue through the provision of more and better black housing. It proposed "building up," expanding, and improving the ghetto, not abolishing it. As the black middle-class moved into Lake Meadows and other near South Side renewal proj-ects, portions of Hyde Park, and new areas of single-family homes (such as Park Manor), the Lowden commission's report seemed almost prophetic. As substandard units disappeared and poor blacks moved into public housing concentrated in existing ghetto areas, the commission's report appeared less a prophecy than a blueprint. And it was all symbolized by the construction of the Robert Taylor Homes between 1960 and 1962. Initially comprised of 4,415 units in twenty-eight identical sixteen-story buildings, the Taylor project has cast the shadow of the original Black Belt in concrete. Two miles long, barely a quarter of a mile wide, hemmed in by railroad tracks and the Dan Ryan Expressway, the development housed, when completed, some 27,000 residents (20,000 of them children), all poor and virtually all black.[6] As a prescription for interracial peace, it may have paid off. When the riots came in the 1960s, the newer West Side ghetto exploded, not the old Black Belt.

There were other links to the past as well. The housing experiments of the 1920s, which grew from Progressive Era roots, provided a foundation of experience for the post–World War II developers. Housing reform legislation in 1927, for example, conceived of government assistance only in negative terms and simply removed certain restrictions that had previously limited the activity of private real estate corporations. It was not enough, by itself, to inspire new development. Similarly, the construction of the Michigan Boulevard Garden Apartments (Rosenwald Gardens) and the Marshall Field Garden Apartments at the end of the decade were also instructive failures. As attempts to prove that private industry could provide good, moderately priced housing and turn a neat profit as well, both the Rosenwald and Field ventures simply highlighted the difficulties involved. Ferd Kramer remembered later that the "problem of trying to acquire land without the right of eminent domain was so expensive and tedious that no one else in Chicago had the nerve to try it again." Equally significant, the Rosenwald and Field experiments were small efforts, according to Kramer, whose "influence went little further than their own doorsteps." Hoping to inspire later projects through the force of their example, the Rosenwald Gardens initially earned but 2.4% on its $2.7 million investment, and the Field apartments made less than that on land that cost three times the original estimate. Potential imitators were not impressed.[7]

After World War II, however, the private sector *was* willing to try it again. Now, the negative approach to government was replaced with a call for positive aid. Developers asked for, and got, expanded powers of eminent domain, relocation assistance, and subsidies via the "write-down" formula. More, the 5- and 6-acre projects undertaken by the most ambitious World War I era reformers were now replaced by developments like Lake Meadows, which cleared more than 100 acres by itself and was yet but a part of larger renewal plans. In both its scope and in the tools needed to bring it into being, Lake Meadows was the culmination, in Ferd Kramer's estimation, of "more than twenty years of trial and error." In the 1920s private enterprise had been unleashed to provide low- and moderate-income housing with little effect. In the 1950s it talked the government not only into giving it new bootstraps but also into hauling them up two-thirds of the way. The results, even down to the open spaces and green areas that embraced the new high-rise ghetto, were tailored more to Progressive Era concepts than to late twentieth-century realities.[8]

Finally, there were two other Progressive Era remnants that survived in modified, but clearly recognizable, form in the post–World War II years. First, there was the "business creed" that approved of constructive housing reform as long as it was profitable. This tenet remained inviolate in the modern age. Both redevelopment and renewal were dependent upon private capital; investors were enticed by the prospect of profit, and their needs determined not only whether a project got off the ground but its ultimate form as well. Remaining less intact was the business creed's definition of government's proper role. The Progressive Era notion that government might concern itself only with city planning, restrictive legislation, and zoning ordinances was replaced by a more expansive conception of legitimate government functions. The building and management of housing, previously reserved for private enterprise, now became – at least in part – a proper sphere for government action. Public housing, however, won its greatest support as relocation housing, as the vital link permitting private business to begin the postwar reconstruction of Chicago, not as a social reform providing subsidies to the poor. One principle of the business creed, in other words, was sacrificed so that another – reform at a profit – could be salvaged. The second major remnant of the Progressive Era, the color line, also remained largely in place. It had been breached, briefly and with little lasting effect, on the near South Side and bent out of shape, under the crushing pressure of necessity, in Hyde Park. Otherwise, it persisted. Black and white Chicagoans remained at least as separate as they had been two or three generations earlier.[9]

The city, and the nation, formally recognized the emergence of the second ghetto by the mid-1960s. In the summer of 1966 Dr. Martin Luther King, Jr., brought his Southern Christian Leadership Conference to Chicago, established a headquarters in a West Side tenement, and led a series of open housing marches into the heavily ethnic, white areas that circled the massive black districts. King had discovered, in journalist Mike Royko's words, "the city's soft underbelly." The marchers fell under a withering rock and bottle assault – King himself was struck while walking through Gage Park on the Southwest Side – and the city seemed to teeter on the edge of disaster. Mayor Richard J. Daley obtained a court injunction limiting the demonstrations and then convened a summit conference with King to discuss open housing.[10]

Even as King was marching against persistent segregation in Chicago, other forces came into play. On August 9, 1966, Dorothy Gautreaux and three other black CHA tenants filed a class action suit in federal court charging the housing authority with discrimination. They also sued the federal government for its financial support of the existing accommodation. Attacking the government's open reinforcement of the ghetto, the black tenants refused to make a choice between "status" and "welfare" goals. In 1969 Judge Richard B. Austin found that CHA family housing was 99% black-occupied and that 99.5% of its units were in black or racially changing areas. The judge's final decision, moreover, was a public indictment of the CHA. He decreed that the next 700 units built by the housing authority had to be placed in white areas and that succeeding construction be undertaken on a quota basis, with 75% of all units (later reduced to 60%) also being placed in white neighborhoods.[11]

The recognition of the second ghetto, however, and even the call for remedial action did little to alter it. The Summit Agreement on open occupancy reached between King and Daley was a vaguely worded statement of principle that promised little action over an indefinite period. Commentator Len O'Connor noted that few could specify the precise terms of the agreement, and a Daley lieutenant, Tom Keane, later denied its existence. Mike Royko concluded that it "wasn't worth the paper it was printed on." All could agree that open housing was a desirable goal; beyond that, there was nothing.[12]

Little more came of the Austin decision. The immediate impact of that judgment was to virtually halt the construction of public housing in Chicago. If blacks were no longer willing to choose between "status" and "welfare" ends, there were whites who had both the power and the will to choose for them. Between 1969 and 1980 a total of 114 new subsidized apartments were built – an average of slightly more than 10 per year. Finally, on June 17, 1981, years after Dorothy Gautreaux herself had died, Judge John Powers Crowley approved an agreement that brought more than fourteen years of continuing litigation to a close. The agreement divided the city into three segments, where the earlier Austin decision had recognized only two, white and black. Crowley added "revitalizing" districts, racially mixed areas undergoing gentrification (the displacement of urban poor by middle-class back-to-the-city renovators), to the others. The agreement required the federal government to grant rent subsidies to 7,100 black families over the next decade, enabling them

to move out of the ghetto. Up to two-thirds of the subsidized apartments, however, could be located in the "revitalizing" neighborhoods of Uptown, South Shore, Hyde Park, or the near West Side.
Only one-third need be located within the white sectors of the Southwest and Northwest sides.[13]

The agreement was a retreat from the earlier Austin order and was,
as the *Tribune* noted, an "acknowledgment of the new realities of
race in Chicago." Primary among these "new realities" was the realization that integration would not occur simply because a federal
court had ordered it. The weight of the second ghetto, when added
to the first, represented a burden generations in the making, and it
was one the city could neither quickly nor easily surrender. Second,
growing black needs were once gain forcing compromises with principle. Even as the CHA virtually ceased new construction in the
1970s, the city was losing 6,000 units per year to fire and abandonment. By the 1980s, blacks were not only questioning the value of
moving into all-white neighborhoods but beginning, once again, to
demand more decent housing without further qualification. Finally,
gentrification in the 1970s displaced many inner-city residents much
as renewal had done earlier. There was, consequently, a revival of
the black fear of being "pushed out" of desirable central city locations. For all these reasons, the plaintiffs eventually agreed, in effect, to reduce the pressure for integration and take what they could
get. The final agreement signed by Judge Crowley was, in the ju-
rist's own words, "not perfect" but "fair, reasonable, and adequate."[14]

There was a final irony here. The agreement did not affect public
housing per se, but, rather, concerned itself with subsidized private
housing and Housing and Urban Development allocations. Only the
prospect of further legal action (Judge Crowley threatened to place
the CHA in receivership) prompted the housing authority to embark
on a new, scattered-site, low-income housing program. By this time,
however, financial stringencies at both the national and local levels
threatened the implementation of the new programs. Future HUD
allocations were certainly questionable under the Reagan administration and, as a state official observed, "the one thing a federal
judge can't do is make appropriations." Moreover, the CHA had its
own difficulties. It began a new $100 million building program only
to have Mayor Jane Byrne announce her intention to cancel the bulk
of it so that the funds earmarked for new construction could be used
to meet the agency's operating expenses. As the *Tribune* stated: "The
irony of all this is tragic. After 15 agonizing and frustrating years the
Gautreaux suit has finally produced results, only to run into the

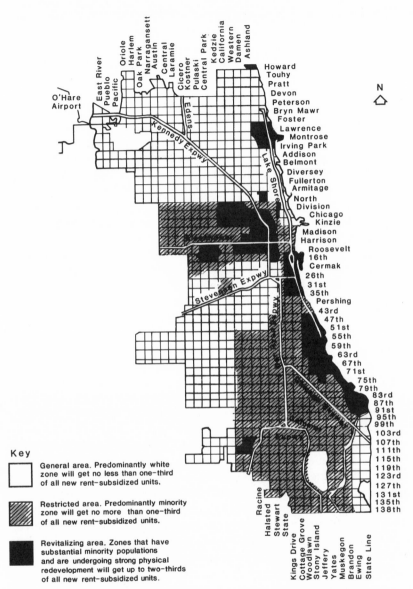

Map 5. Chicago low-income housing sites, 1981 (Gautreaux case settlement). (*Source*: U.S. Department of Housing and Urban Development.)

CHA's fiscal crisis and the mayor's desire to solve it with a fund diversion." Possessing the cash to build new units, the CHA lacked the wherewithal to maintain thousands of existing ones, some of them, by this time, more than forty years old. Whatever the outcome, it seemed certain that there would be no radical alterations in the city's racial geography.[15]

Perhaps most important of all, Chicago established a pattern of post–World War II development. Throughout the period, the needs of significant private interests shaped the debate on urban problems and, ultimately, established public priorities. The sense of vulnerability felt by Marshall Field and Company, Chicago Title and Trust Company, Michael Reese Hospital, Illinois Institute of Technology, and the University of Chicago – to cite only the most significant – led to their aggressive resort to the political arena. As a result, private initiative made Illinois a persistent leader in the enactment of renewal legislation. The Redevelopment acts of 1941 and 1947, and the Urban Community Conservation Act of 1953 each placed Chicago and the state of Illinois in the vanguard of the movement to rebuild American cities.[16] Moreover, the evolution of the Illinois legislative program reflected the peculiar needs of particular interests at specific times. Thus, in the immediate aftermath of World War II, the large Loop concerns, worried about suburban flight and their growing isolation in a ring of slums, embarked upon a vigorous redevelopment operation designed to clear them out, reattract solvent population to the central city, and strengthen the city's tax base. When, in the early 1950s, it became apparent that slum clearance added to the pressures felt by outlying communities, it was the University of Chicago and the Hyde Park neighborhood that then seized the initiative and focused public attention on the "conservation" of endangered, but not yet decayed, areas. Within a few short years, the broader concept of conservation replaced the more narrowly conceived one of slum clearance as the city's top priority.

This shift from redevelopment to renewal in Chicago paralleled events on the national level. An early preoccupation with slum clearance (as manifested in the Housing Act of 1949) was similarly replaced, during the Eisenhower administration, with a concern for slum prevention and the economies of scale and operation attendant upon the saving of basically sound communities (the major focus of the Housing Act of 1954). As a mirror image of the federal program, local operations in Chicago revealed many of the same problems that subsequently plagued the national effort: Relocation difficulties, charges of "Negro removal," the creation of vast new slums even as small sections of the old ones were destroyed, and the use of these programs by strong private interests for their own ends were all present.[17]

But, and this is the crucial point, the Chicago experience provides much more than a microcosmic example of a controversial federal program. First of all, in a literal sense, there was not a "federal" renewal effort at all. National legislation simply provided federal assistance, economic and otherwise, for innumerable local programs. As such, any serious examination of urban renewal must view local variations in detail. Compilations of aggregate national data have produced distorted views of the program. Similarly, a perspective rooted in Washington, D.C., is fragmentary at best and misleading at worst. Thus, claims that the government entered into competition with private enterprise, that its intrusion was both unwarranted and ineffective, and that downtown business interests opposed public housing lose force on the local level. The Chicago experience shows that it was the champions of private enterprise who first demanded and then controlled government "interference." It was private enterprise, in fact, that insisted that the government be made "bigger" so that it might be used more profitably. And not only were the city's largest businessmen in favor of public housing; they were the supporters who *counted*. It was pragmatic businessmen like Milton Mumford and Holman Pettibone, representatives of two of Chicago's leading economic and real estate interests, who won reluctant approval of public housing from the General Assembly of Illinois as part of the state's redevelopment program. Indeed, the national focus, which so often portrays the creation and evolution of urban renewal as the products of a continual struggle between "reformers" and "conservatives," has little application in the Windy City.[18]

Significantly, the Illinois program did more than just parallel the federal effort: It antedated its federal counterpart in both its redevelopment and renewal phases. There is evidence, moreover, that the Illinois Redevelopment Act of 1947 and the Urban Community Conservation Act of 1953 served as virtual models for the federal Housing acts of 1949 and 1954. The sources and nature of Chicago's policies are thus of more than passing interest as local variants in a broad program – they were of truly national significance.

It is, of course, impossible to trace the exact origins of the concepts embodied in the national Housing acts of 1949 and 1954. The major outlines of the 1949 act, however, appeared at least as early as 1941 when the National Association of Real Estate Boards (NAREB) issued a report on "Housing and Blighted Areas" and Alvin H. Hansen and Guy Greer published the pamphlet *Urban Redevelopment and Housing – A Plan for Post-War*. Both documents considered federal aid essential, and the problems of land assembly and cost were confronted in ways clearly visible in the 1949 legislation. A key innovation, however, was the legislative enactment of the "write-down" formula for reducing the cost of land sold to developers. This last feature was, of course, an integral part of the 1947 Illinois program – a program considered by its sponsors to be a "pioneering combination" of public and private power, which represented a "milestone" in redevelopment legislation and which transformed Chicago into a "laboratory" for the rest of the nation.[19]

The source of the "write-down" formula remains somewhat obscure. In searching for possible solutions to central city decay, Holman Pettibone assiduously scoured the nation for plans, laws, and concepts that could be applied in Chicago. His papers are filled with observations on early attempts at redevelopment in other cities. Pettibone was thus aware that the Home Builders Association of Washington, D.C., had proposed a slum clearance program in the 1930s as a response to the federal government's creation of the National Capital Housing Authority and its efforts to clear the Capital's back alley slums. The HBA's "Washington Plan" demanded that government assistance be limited to the exercise of eminent domain in acquiring slum property and the absorption of the difference between acquisition costs and the revenues brought in by then leasing or selling such land (after clearance) to private redevelopers. It was nearly identical to the "write-down" formula Pettibone later inserted into the Illinois Redevelopment Act of 1947.[20]

But Ferd Kramer had also experimented locally with a "write-down" procedure of his own. Responding to a request by University of Chicago Chancellor Robert Maynard Hutchins to provide faculty housing, Kramer offered to "build a building" for the university if Hutchins provided the land. "So we made a deal," Kramer recalled, "whereby he bought the church at the northwest corner of 56th and Dorchester, razed it, and sold it to us at its re-use value." In return for the $12,000 subsidy provided by the university, Hutchins received a building of more than 100 units, which gave first priority to university personnel. Although the contract to build at 5550 Dorchester was not formally signed until 1948 – a year after the passage of the Redevelopment Act – Kramer's conversations with Hutchins antedated the legislative initiative and, according to Kramer, was "the first time...there was a write down of the land, a subsidy in fact, to build a renewal project." Whatever its origins, the "write-down" formula found its way into the MHPC West Side study and the realm of public debate. Eventually, it made its way into the federal Housing Act of 1949.[21]

Even more significant was Chicago's role and experience in passing the Housing Act of 1954. This important legislation produced several notable changes in federal policy. What had previously been called "slum clearance and redevelopment" was now called "urban renewal" – a change that indicated the "shift in emphasis away from primary concern about the slums." The new approach was justified, the National Commission on Urban Problems later concluded, "as a broader design to rebuild the cities, and not primarily to help the poor." The new legislation placed greater stress on the rehabilitation of existing structures and neighborhoods, rather than on their demolition, and, for the first time, it became possible to use federal funds for other than "predominantly residential" purposes.[22]

The basic provisions of this legislation were contained in the December 1953 report of the President's Advisory Committee on Government Housing Policies and Programs. The committee's recommendations for increased federal "assistance to communities for rehabilitation and conservation of areas worth saving" were based on an appendix to its report co-authored by Jack M. Siegel. Siegel was an attorney for the Metropolitan Housing and Planning Council and a former staff member of the Chicago City Council Committee on Housing. More important, in 1952 he was appointed assistant director of the staff conducting the MHPC's "conservation" study, which, when issued in three volumes in early 1953, argued that slum prevention was a "public purpose" and that "present official agencies and powers were inadequate" to save "conservation areas." The MHPC's recommendations produced the Urban Community Conservation Act, a bill originally drafted by Jack M. Siegel. Based on a study of Hyde Park and fully intended to aid the University of Chicago in maintaining its environment, the Urban Community Conservation Act enabled the university and the city to set up the administrative machinery that would later take advantage of the aid offered by the 1954 federal legislation. Aware that local resources were insufficient and that federal aid would be needed, the University of Chicago Law School then assisted in the legal research preliminary to the passage of the later federal law. Siegel subsequently served on the President's Advisory Committee and was instrumental in suggesting changes in federal policy that strikingly resembled those contained in the Illinois law he had authored just months before. In his appendix to the influential report of the President's

Advisory Committee, Siegel stated flatly that Chicago had been the "pioneer in developing the concept of conservation" and was far ahead of all other cities in devising new legal tools for urban reconstruction. The Housing Act of 1954, in short, was the Illinois Urban Community Conservation Act writ large. When finally enacted, the City of Chicago – as had been the case after the passage of the Housing Act of 1949 – was well prepared to meet the legal requirements for aid and was first in line for the federal largesse.[23]

This chain of events again emphasizes the difficulty in assessing urban renewal from Washington, D.C. Traditional interpretations, whether favorable or unfavorable, take such a perspective, however, and have thus generated considerable confusion in the heat of historiographical battle. Viewing urban renewal "from the top down" creates at least two problems. The first entails discerning its goals and the establishment of a standard against which the program's success or failure can be measured. Bitter ideological critics such as Martin Anderson and even more realistic ones such as Charles Abrams have all taken seriously the statements of legislative intent contained in the federal laws as the proper bases from which to gauge the program's achievements.[24] In terms of the Housing Act of 1949, this meant living up to the standard of providing "a decent home and a suitable living environment for every American family." Given that goal, the federal effort could only be measured in degrees of failure. Yet, in a locally initiated and controlled program, the intentions of legislators in Washington are of less consequence than those of the people directing the various local endeavors.

This confusion over the program's real goals (as opposed to the rhetoric that surrounded it) has led several analysts to claim that it was "distorted" or "perverted" in implementation. The most unqualified assertion of this position came from the National Commission on Urban Problems. Believing that the sole purposes behind the federal legislation were those expressed within it, the commission declared the first eighteen years of the program a "failure" and claimed that its major goals were either not understood or simply not taken seriously. The legislation, with its articulated social goals, was "good." It was merely exploited by self-serving forces.[25] All of this, however, ignores the fact that local initiative and power not only controlled urban renewal efforts but also helped frame the laws under which it proceeded. The legislation merely did what it was intended to do. If anything was distorted, it was the judgment of those who attributed goals to the program that were not contemplated by the powers directing it.[26]

The second problem in viewing urban renewal "from the top down" involves a misreading of the significance of the shift from redevelopment to renewal as embodied in the Housing acts of 1949 and 1954. The transition from redevelopment to renewal has been alternately attributed to the success of the "planners," who finally won federal assistance for other than "predominantly residential" purposes, the shift in political climate with the ascension of Dwight D. Eisenhower and the Republican party, and the "failure" of the original program itself.[27] All of these factors were important, but they present only an incomplete picture by themselves. Again, a look at local conditions and especially those in Chicago is illuminating.

The Chicago experience is doubly important because of the role it played in shaping subsequent federal legislation. Although, from a national perspective, it might appear that the redevelopment effort started in the late 1940s lay "in the dumps," it was the success, not the failure, of slum clearance programs that sparked the conservation movement in Chicago and led directly to the Illinois Urban Community Conservation Act of 1953 – the local link and counterpart to the federal Housing Act of 1954. The demolition necessary for the Lake Meadows project uprooted thousands of blacks and helped accelerate their movement into the Hyde Park community. It was largely in the attempt to stem the tide of racial succession that the University of Chicago and its supporters moved so forcefully to enact new state legislation to provide the tools needed to preserve a "compatible environment." It was, consequently, the massive shifting of nonwhite population attendant upon the successful implementation of Chicago's slum clearance operation that fostered the demand, and the acceptance, of "slum prevention" as a top urban priority. Racial issues, in other words, were instrumental in shaping Chicago's "conservation" movement and, hence, the nation's.

Given this view of significant motivations (the University of Chicago's goal, after all, was to create a predominantly white and economically upgraded neighborhood), some ramifications of the national program become more explainable. The charges so often leveled at the federal effort – that it neglected the poor; that it was actually anti-poor because of its demolition of low-rent housing and inadequate relocation procedures; that it simply subsidized those who needed aid least; and that it was transformed into a program of "Negro clearance" – were hardly evidence of a plan gone awry. These were not "perversions" of the enabling legislation, they were the direct consequences of it. Indeed, the indictment made of the national program in the mid-1960s was virtually unchanged from that heard a decade or more earlier on the near South Side and in Hyde Park. Thus, as Scott Greer notes, nearly 70% of the dwelling units condemned for urban renewal projects were occupied by blacks. This was primarily due, Greer felt, to their "central locations and deteriorated conditions, but the effects [were] the same as they would be if dehousing Negroes were the goal."[28] Yet, in some instances at least, that was precisely the goal. Indeed, in a recent study, Michael J. White found that for two of the four cities he examined in detail (Chicago and Cleveland) race was still a factor in selecting renewal areas even after controlling all other variables. This does not mean, of course, that the laws *had* to be used in this fashion; but it should be no surprise that they were.[29] If the University of Chicago could use state and federal assistance for such purposes under legislation and plans of its own devising, it was perhaps inevitable that those same tools could be similarly employed elsewhere.

Indeed, in New York, as Robert Caro pointed out in *The Power Broker*, Robert Moses eagerly used the expanded power of eminent domain granted by Title I of the Housing Act of 1949, a power "new in the annals of democracy." The results would be familiar to any Chicagoan. Slum clearance, which relied on public housing for partial relocation and the manipulation of data to minimize problems, soon devastated nearby areas and produced new pockets of deterioration even before the old ones were rebuilt. Nonwhites were hit hardest by Moses' plans and techniques, and using the legislation in a novel way, New York permitted private interests to milk the seized property and profit from it without development. The scandals that subsequently shook the nation's largest city were due to greed, a certain measure of ingenuity, and a legislative framework ripe for exploitation.[30]

Perhaps even more tragically, the legislation defeated even the best intentions of public-spirited officials who took the mandate to clear slums seriously. In Newark, the local housing authority tried to replace crumbling tenements with decent housing. Clearance in poor black areas, however, merely left the Newark Housing Authority (NHA) in possession of considerable vacant land – private developers were not eager to invest in such areas. To make renewal work, the NHA discovered it had to jettison its original goals and become more "flexible" in dealing with private business. Rather than "peddling vacant land," the NHA decided, in the words of one official, to "let the redevelopers tell us where they want to build." "Choice sites" and standard structures subsequently fell before the wrecker's ball, luxury apartments went up near the central business district, and much of the unmarketable vacant land in black areas was, for lack of suitable alternatives, devoted to public housing. As in Chicago, the ghetto was reinforced by new government-sponsored projects with indeterminate life-spans. Subsidies and profits flowed, as the business creed ordained, to the developers.[31]

The full implications of this pattern of redevelopment were not immediately apparent. As the civil rights revolution gained momentum, however, it became increasingly clear that the destruction of the urban ghetto would not be counted among its victories. If anything, government building programs gave old enclaves a permanence never seen before, and new ones were created by the uprooted thousands who mingled – as on Chicago's West Side – with a like number of recent migrants seeking their fortune within cities still sharply divided by color. Martin Luther King, Jr., recognized the irony and dramatized it by moving into that West Side tenement in 1966. At his death, less than two years later, Richard J. Daley was observing the smoke and flames enveloping much of that district from a helicopter. The electronic media carried the mayor's orders to shoot arsonists on sight and to maim or cripple looters. The second ghetto could be ignored no longer.

Notes

1. The second ghetto and the dynamics of neighborhood change

1 Chicago Commission on Race Relations (hereafter cited as CCRR), *The Negro in Chicago* (Chicago: University of Chicago Press, 1922), pp. 6, 18–19; William M. Tuttle, Jr., *Race Riot: Chicago in the Red Summer of 1919* (New York: Atheneum, 1970), pp. 33–4, 40.

2 CCRR, *The Negro in Chicago*, pp. 6–7, 19–20, 31–2, 655–67; Tuttle, *Race Riot*, pp. 41, 46.

3 Of the injured, 342 were black and 195 were white. See Tuttle, *Race Riot*, p. 64.

4 *Report of the Riot Study Committee to the Honorable Richard J. Daley* (Chicago: City of Chicago, 1968), passim.

5 Ibid., pp. 5–20, 27, 36–8, 66.

6 Morris Janowitz, "Patterns of Collective Racial Violence," in Hugh Davis Graham and Ted Robert Gurr, eds., *Violence in America: Historical and Comparative Perspectives* (New York: New American Library, 1969), pp. 412–44; August Meier and Elliott Rudwick, "Black Violence in the 20th Century: A Study in Rhetoric and Retaliation," in ibid., pp. 399–412.

7 Janowitz, "Patterns of Collective Racial Violence," pp. 424–5.

8 Allan H. Spear, *Black Chicago: The Making of a Negro Ghetto, 1890–1920* (Chicago: University of Chicago Press, 1967), pp. 223–4; St. Clair Drake and Horace R. Cayton, *Black Metropolis: A Study of Negro Life in a Northern City*, 2 vols. (New York: Harcourt, Brace, 1945; reprint ed., New York: Harper & Row, Harper Torchbooks, 1962), 2:xvi.

9 David A. Wallace, "Residential Concentration of Negroes in Chicago" (Ph.D. dissertation, Harvard University, 1953), p. 64; Thomas L. Philpott, *The Slum and the Ghetto: Neighborhood Deterioration and Middle-Class Reform, Chicago, 1880–1930* (New York: Oxford University Press, 1978), pp. 119, 121, 130, 146.

10 Spear, *Black Chicago*, pp. 142, 146; CCRR, *The Negro in Chicago*, pp. 106–8; Otis Duncan and Beverly Duncan, *The Negro Population of Chicago* (Chicago: University of Chicago Press, 1957), p. 92; Wallace, "Residential Concentration of Negroes," p. 69, claims no new communities came into being between 1910 and 1920.

11 Duncan and Duncan, *The Negro Population*, pp. 95–6; Wallace, "Residential Concentration of Negroes," p. 111; Philpott, *The Slum and the Ghetto*, p. 121.

12 Duncan and Duncan, *The Negro Population*, pp. 95–7.
13 Drake and Cayton, *Black Metropolis*, 1:184–7; Frederick Burgess Lindstrom, "The Negro Invasion of the Washington Park Subdivision" (M.A. thesis, University of Chicago, 1941); Wallace, "Residential Concentration of Negroes," pp. 79–80.
14 Drake and Cayton, *Black Metropolis*, 1:174.
15 Wallace, "Residential Concentration of Negroes," pp. 85, 88, 148, 149n.
16 Spear, *Black Chicago*, pp. 223–4; Wallace, "Residential Concentration of Negroes," p. 113; Duncan and Duncan, *The Negro Population*, pp. 96–7; Chicago Commission on Human Relations (herefter cited as CHR), *Fourth Chicago Conference on Civic Unity: Abridged Report of Proceedings* (Chicago: CHR, 1952), p. 7.
17 Duncan and Duncan, *The Negro Population*, pp. 95–6.
18 The previously mentioned works of Spear and Philpott, which were both written in the aftermath of the 1960s riots, have clear implications for contemporary race relations but halt their analysis at 1930 – or earlier. The same is true for Gilbert Osofsky, "The Enduring Ghetto," *Journal of American History* 55 (September 1968): 243–55, and idem, *Harlem: The Making of a Ghetto; Negro New York, 1890–1930* (New York: Harper & Row, 1966); David M. Katzman, *Before the Ghetto: Black Detroit in the Nineteenth Century* (Urbana: University of Illinois Press, 1973); and Kenneth L. Kusmer, *A Ghetto Takes Shape: Black Cleveland, 1870–1930* (Urbana: University of Illinois Press, 1976).
19 Robert C. Weaver, *The Negro Ghetto* (New York: Harper & Row, 1948), pp. 275, 324, 369.
20 For the impact of white hostility on black residential patterns in Chicago, see Spear, *Black Chicago*, pp. 6–8, 20–3, 26, 201, 208–13, 219–21; Tuttle, *Race Riot*, pp. 157–83; CCRR, *The Negro in Chicago*, pp. 113–35; Drake and Cayton, *Black Metropolis*, 1:213–74; Philpott, *The Slum and the Ghetto*, pp. 146–200; Kusmer similarly emphasizes white hostility in restricting the choices of black Clevelanders; see his *A Ghetto Takes Shape*, pp. 46–7, 165, 167–70; see also Katzman, *Before the Ghetto*, pp. 69–80, and Osofsky, *Harlem*, pp. 46–52, 81. It also should be noted that Spear and Wallace feel that the blacks' weak economic position was relatively unimportant as a cause for their segregation. See Spear, *Black Chicago*, p. 26, and Wallace, "Residential Concentration of Negroes," p. 195.
21 Kenneth T. Jackson, "Race, Ethnicity, and Real Estate Appraisal: The Home Owners Loan Corporation and the Federal Housing Administration," *Journal of Urban History* 6 (August 1980): 419–52; Mark I. Gelfand, *A Nation of Cities: The Federal Government and Urban America, 1933–1965* (New York: Oxford University Press, 1975), p. 123.
22 *Chicago Defender*, October 26, 1940, has a special section devoted to the Ida B. Wells Homes. For the Cleveland experience, see Christopher G. Wye, "The New Deal and the Negro Community: Toward a Broader Conceptualization," *Journal of American History* 59 (December 1972): 621–39.

278   Notes to pp. 12–17

23 *Chicago Defender,* June 12, 1943; Horace R. Cayton and Harry J. Walker, Memorandum to Mr. Blandford and Mr. Divers, National Housing Agency, January 14, 1944; Metropolitan Housing [and Planning] Council (MHPC), Minutes of the Executive Committee Meeting, November 21, 1944, both in the Metropolitan Housing and Planning Council Papers (hereafter cited as MHPC Papers), Manuscript Collection, The Library, University of Illinois at Chicago (UIC). The Metropolitan Housing Council changed its name to the Metropolitan Housing and Planning Council in 1949. To avoid confusion, the amended name will be used throughout this study.

24 *Chicago Bee,* May 14, 1944; Eugene O. Shands to John Blandford, n.d.; Metropolitan Housing [and Planning] Council, Minutes of the Executive Committee Meeting, November 21, 1944; Metropolitan Housing [and Planning] Council, Minutes of the Regular Meeting of the Board of Governors, April 4, November 1, 1944; Ferd Kramer to Robert Taylor, May 19, June 2, 1944; Ferd Kramer to Louis Wirth, May 31, 1944; Robert R. Taylor to Ferd Kramer, May 24, 1944, all in the MHPC Papers.

25 Devereux Bowly, Jr., *The Poorhouse: Subsidized Housing in Chicago, 1895–1976* (Carbondale: Southern Illinois University Press, 1978), pp. 17–54, 221.

26 Philpott, *The Slum and the Ghetto,* pp. 209–27; 244–69; *Chicago Defender,* October 26, 1940.

27 For the willingness of Chicago Progressives to observe the color line, see Philpott, *The Slum and the Ghetto,* pp. 271–347.

28 Spear, *Black Chicago,* pp. 71–89; 91–126; 181–200.

29 Ibid., pp. 111–26; Milton Rakove, *Don't Make No Waves – Don't Back No Losers: An Insider's Analysis of the Daley Machine* (Bloomington: Indiana University Press, 1975), pp. 256–81; James Q. Wilson, *Negro Politics: The Search for Leadership* (New York: Free Press, 1960); Harold F. Gosnell, *Negro Politicians: The Rise of Negro Politics in Chicago* (Chicago: University of Chicago Press, 1935; reprint ed., 1967); Ira Katznelson, *Black Men, White Cities* (New York: Oxford University Press, 1973); Charles Branham, "Black Chicago: Accommodationist Politics Before the Great Migration," in Melvin G. Holli and Peter d'A. Jones, eds., *The Ethnic Frontier: Essays in the History of Group Survival in Chicago and the Midwest* (Grand Rapids, Mich.: Eerdmans, 1977), pp. 211–62.

30 For the city as a whole, the demand for new housing was even greater than the raw population data would indicate. Between 1940 and 1949 the number of families increased at more than *twice* the rate of the general population. The formation of new families, deferred during Depression and war, accelerated rapidly in the postwar era. See "A Factual Report on Housing" (mimeographed, April 15, 1950), p. 1, MHPC Papers.

31 Drake and Cayton, *Black Metropolis,* 1:90–1.

32 The difference in total growth for the two periods was due to natural

increase. This was calculated at 5,900 per year between 1940 and 1950 and at 17,200 per year between 1950 and 1956. See Chicago Community Inventory, *Population Growth in the Chicago Standard Metropolitan Area* (Chicago: n.p., 1958), p. 12.

33 Carl Condit, *Chicago, 1930–1970* (Chicago: University of Chicago Press, 1974), p. 286; Metropolitan Housing [and Planning] Council, Minutes of the Meeting, October 27, 1937, MHPC Papers.

34 Illinois State Committee on the Condition of the Urban Colored Population, *Report* (n.p., n.d.), p. 81; U.S., Congress, House, Interstate Migration Committee, *Hearings Before the Select Committee to Investigate the Interstate Migration of Destitute Citizens*, 76th Cong., 3d sess., 1940, pt. 3, pp. 1098–9, 1102 (hereafter cited as the Interstate Migration Committee, *Hearings*); *Chicago Defender*, May 18, June 15, 1940; May 10, 1941.

35 Interstate Migration Committee, *Hearings*, p. 1098; *Chicago Defender*, May 11, 1940; Illinois State Committee on the Condition of the Urban Colored Population, *Report*, pp. 81–9.

36 "Housing News," June 1941; April, June 1942, all in the Graham Aldis Papers, Manuscript Collection, The Library, UIC.

37 *Chicago Bee*, July 4, 1943; May 14, 1944; August 5, 1945; *Monthly Summary of Events and Trends in Race Relations* 2 (November 1944): 94.

38 Metropolitan Housing [and Planning] Council, Minutes of the Regular Meeting of the Board of Directors, April 1, 1943, MHPC Papers; *Chicago Bee*, May 23, June 6, 1943; October 15, 1944; April 25, 1945; *Chicago Defender*, March 6, June 5, 1943; April 7, 1945; May 27, 1950; January 5, 1952.

39 *Chicago Defender*, November 27, 1943.

40 Chicago Plan Commission, *Residential Chicago* (Chicago: City of Chicago, 1943); City of Chicago, *Report to the People* (Chicago: City of Chicago, 1947), pp. 155, 157; Dr. Louis Wirth, "Statement of the MHC-MEHC Meeting, City Council Chambers, April 7, 1947," pp. 1–2, MHPC Papers.

41 Of the veterans registered at the center, approximately 75% were white and 25% were nonwhite. Metropolitan Housing [and Planning] Council, Minutes of the Meeting with the NHA and Veterans Information Center, July 30, 1945; Leonard R. McDonald, "The Truth – Real Facts About the Veterans' Housing Problems," n.d., both in the MHPC Papers; CHR, "Monthly Report of the Executive Director, February 1947," (mimeographed, n.d.), Chicago Urban League Papers (hereafter cited as the CUL Papers), Manuscript Collection, The Library, UIC.

42 Black resistance to "temporary" units, which it was feared would become permanent additions to the ghetto, contributed to the reluctance of the housing authority to use them. See Ferd Kramer to Robert R. Taylor, May 19, June 2, 1944; Robert R. Taylor to Ferd Kramer, May 24, 1944; Ferd Kramer to Louis Wirth, May 31, 1944, all in the MHPC Papers. See also "Temporary Housing Need Confirmed by Survey"

(mimeographed, n.d.); Metropolitan Housing Council to James Downs, Jr., June 5, 1946; James Downs to Howard E. Green, June 6, 1946, all in the MHPC Papers; CHR, "Memorandum on the Airport Homes," (mimeographed, n.d.), CUL Papers, p. 11; John Bartlow Martin, "Incident at Fernwood," *Harper's Magazine* 198 (October 1949): 88.

43 U.S. Commission on Civil Rights, *Hearings: Housing* (Washington, D.C.: Government Printing Office, 1959), p. 672; Condit, *Chicago*, p. 287; "Report on Survey of Conversion Program" (mimeographed, February 25, 1947), p. 1; "Chicago Housing Center Closes After Providing Living Accommodations for 400,000 People in 6 Years" (mimeographed, n.d.), pp. 2–3, both in the MHPC Papers.

44 Tabulations of the Chicago Urban League's "social problems" cases were found in the CUL Papers; *Chicago Defender*, July 3, 1948; *Chicago Bee*, April 21, August 11, September 1, 1946; "General Housing Situation in Chicago" (mimeographed, n.d.), p. 4, MHPC Papers.

45 Innumerable editions of the *Chicago Defender* from February 1947 through at least May 1954 contain examples of such operations.

46 Duncan and Duncan, *The Negro Population*, p. 80.

47 Leonard Z. Breen, "Chicago: Its Housing Supply and Its Population Change, 1940–1950" (mimeographed, February 29, 1952), pp. 2–4, Aldis Papers; Chicago Community Inventory, "Census Statistics on Housing for Chicago, 1950, 1940" (mimeographed, May 1954), pp. 22, 30–1, The Library, UIC.

48 These figures meant that in 1940 the ratio of nonwhite- to white-occupied overcrowded units was 4 to 1; in 1950 it was 6 to 1. As nonwhites also had a higher proportion of one-person households, the ratio would have been even higher had it been calculated for multi-person households alone. See Duncan and Duncan, *The Negro Population*, p. 79.

49 Breen, "Chicago: Its Housing Supply," pp. 1–12; Chicago Community Inventory, "Census Statistics," pp. 22, 30–1.

50 When broken down by race, it was found that 13% of the white-occupied dwelling units were deficient in plumbing facilities, whereas 40% of the units occupied by nonwhites were similarly lacking. See "A Factual Report on Housing," n.d., p. 5, MHPC Papers; Breen, "Chicago: Its Housing Supply," p. 12.

51 Metropolitan Housing [and Planning] Council, *Biennial Report of the Metropolitan Housing Council: Activities in 1943–1944* (Chicago: n.p., 1944), p. 3.

52 Metropolitan Housing [and Planning] Council, *The 1942 Annual Report* (Chicago: n.p., 1943), pp. 8–9.

53 Metropolitan Housing [and Planning] Council, *Biennial Report . . . 1943–1944*, pp. 14–15, and "Report of the Committee on Substandard Housing to the Board of Governors of the Metropolitan Housing Council," June 24, 1940, pp. 14–15, MHPC Papers. The housing council also put out a pamphlet in 1954 entitled *The Road Back*, which reprinted a series of articles on slum conditions published in the *Chicago Daily News* from June 10, 1953, through the rest of the year.

54 Samplings taken from the *Chicago Bee* and the *Chicago Defender* provide numerous examples. See the *Bee* for February 2, 9, 1947, and the *Defender* for November 5, 12, 26, 1949, to cite just a very few. See also the *Chicago Daily News*, December 9, 1950; September 17, 1953; *Chicago Sun-Times*, December 10, 1950; January 30, February 20, May 14, 1958; *Chicago Tribune*, September 8, 1958; Metropolitan Housing [and Planning] Council, Minutes of the Regular Meeting of the Board of Governors, February 1, 1944, and Minutes of the Executive Committee Meeting, January 31, 1958, both in the MHPC Papers; "Report on 215–219 E. 31st Building," July 1949, CUL Papers; Joel D. Hunter to Mrs. Frederick H. Rubel, March 24, 1944, MHPC Papers.

55 *Chicago Sun-Times*, November 13, 1950; *Chicago Defender*, November 18, December 16, 1950.

56 John Bartlow Martin, "The Hickman Story," *Harper's Magazine* 197 (August 1948): 40–8.

57 Metropolitan Housing [and Planning] Council, *Biennial Report . . . 1943– 1944*, p. 3.

58 Condit, *Chicago*, pp. 286–7.

59 Ibid.; Office of the Housing and Redevelopment Coordinator, *Residential Construction: City of Chicago, Chicago Metropolitan Area, 1953* (Chicago: n.p., n.d.); *Residential Construction: City of Chicago, 1950 Through 1954* (Chicago: n.p., 1955); *Residential Construction: City of Chicago, 1956* (Chicago: n.p., 1957).

60 Chicago Community Inventory, *Population Growth*; Mayor's Committee on Race Relations, *Race Relations in Chicago* (Chicago: n.p., 1944), p. 13; Illinois Inter-Racial Commission, *Fifth Report of the Illinois Inter-Racial Commission* (Chicago: n.p., 1953), p. 26; Evelyn M. Kitagawa and Karl E. Taeuber, eds., *Local Community Fact Book: Chicago Metropolitan Area, 1960* (Chicago: Chicago Community Inventory, 1963), pp. 8–9.

61 Wallace, "Residential Concentration of Negroes," p. 264n; *Chicago Defender*, September 4, 1954. See also Karl Taeuber and Alma Taeuber, "The Negro as an Immigrant Group: Trends in Racial and Economic Segregation in Chicago," *Journal of American Sociology* 69 (January 1964): 379.

62 CHR, "Monthly Report of the Executive Director, October 1950" (mimeographed, n.d.), p. 8, CUL Papers; see also Metropolitan Housing [and Planning] Council, Housing Committee, Draft of Statement on the Minority Housing Problem in Chicago, n.d., pp. 9–10, MHPC Papers; U.S. Commission on Civil Rights, *Hearings*, p. 687; Duncan and Duncan, *The Negro Population*, pp. 71–3; "The Growing Negro Middle Class in Chicago," *Human Relations News* 4 (October 1962): 2–3.

63 The rental for a two-room furnished apartment, which shared a kitchen and a toilet, in a tenement converted to black occupancy was $78 per month. In contrast, the rent for an apartment in Mayor Martin H. Kennelly's Gold Coast building, unfurnished but including an in-a-door bed, refrigerator, private bath, and kitchenette, was $74.50. See Weaver, *The Negro Ghetto*, p. 104n.

64 "The Growing Negro Middle Class," p. 2.
65 Illinois Inter-Racial Commission, *First Biennial Report* (Chicago: n.p., 1945), p. 58; CHR, *Fourth Chicago Conference*, p. 49; Duncan and Duncan, *The Negro Population*, pp. 9, 15–16, 252, 275; Rose Helper, *Racial Policies and Practices of Real Estate Brokers* (Minneapolis: University of Minnesota Press, 1969), p. 50; U.S. Commission on Civil Rights, *Hearings*, p. 729; "The Growing Negro Middle Class," p. 2; Metropolitan Housing [and Planning] Council, Housing Committee, Draft of Statement, p. 10; Stanley Carlson Stevens, "The Urban Racial Border: Chicago, 1960" (Ph.D. dissertation, University of Illinois at Urbana-Champaign, 1972), pp. 87–90.
66 Drake and Cayton, *Black Metropolis*, 1:184–7; Earl Dickerson to T. K. Gibson, October 29, 1952, CUL Papers; *Chicago Defender*, September 14, November 16, 1940; *Chicago Bee*, March 17, 1946.
67 *Chicago Bee*, November 21, 28, 1943; *Chicago Defender*, November 20, 1943; December 1, 1945; June 1, 1946; December 6, 1947. For the refusal to evict after a pro-covenant ruling, see the *Bee*, April 23, 1944.
68 *Chicago Defender*, October 10, 1942; February 5, 1944; March 10, 1945; February 9, 1946; April 5, 26, May 24, June 14, 21, August 2, 9, October 11, December 6, 1947; March 13, April 24, May 8, 15, June 5, 1948; *Chicago Bee*, April 2, 16, 23, 1944; May 13, September 23, 1945; April 2, June 15, 1947; CHR, *Report for 1945* (Chicago: n.p., 1946), p. 28; Minutes of the Housing Committee Meeting, May 12, 1948, Lea Taylor Papers, Chicago Historical Society (CHS); *Against Discrimination* 1 (June 1948), MHPC Papers.
69 Helper, *Racial Policies*, p. 35; U.S. Commission on Civil Rights, *Hearings*, pp. 684–5.
70 Helper, *Racial Policies*, pp. 172–6.
71 Ibid., pp. 166–8; U.S. Commission on Civil Rights, *Hearings*, pp. 740–2, 746–7, 753–4, 759, 882.
72 Norris Vitchek, "Confessions of a Block Buster," reprint of a 1962 *Saturday Evening Post* article, Leon M. Despres Papers, CHS.
73 Mark J. Satter, "Land Contract Sales in Chicago: Security Turned Exploitation," Saul Alinsky Papers, Manuscript Collection, The Library, UIC; CHR, *Selling and Buying Real Estate in a Racially Changing Neighborhood: A Survey* (Chicago: n.p., n.d.), pp. 5, 8. See also E. F. Schietinger, "Racial Succession and Changing Property Values in Residential Chicago" (Ph.D. dissertation, University of Chicago, 1953), pp. 208–9, passim.
74 CHR, *Selling and Buying Real Estate*, pp. 9–10, Table 1, and passim; Helper, *Racial Policies*, pp. 177–80; CHR, "Questions and Answers on Housing (Preliminary Draft)," January 1958, Greater Lawndale Conservation Commission Papers, CHS.
75 CHR, *Selling and Buying Real Estate*, p. 10.
76 U.S. Commission on Civil Rights, *Hearings*, pp. 685–6.
77 Lea Taylor to Fred Hoehler, October 12, 1949, Chicago Commons Papers, CHS.

78 Metropolitan Housing and Planning Council, *The Road Back*, p. 17.
79 Lucille Sproggins to Sidney Williams, September 3, 1954, CUL Papers.
80 Duncan and Duncan, *The Negro Population*, pp. 133–236, 238–40.
81 Metropolitan Housing [and Planning] Council, *Report of the Activities for 1941* (Chicago: n.p., 1942), p. 3; Metropolitan Housing [and Planning] Council, Minutes of the Meeting, July 6, 1943; Metropolitan Housing [and Planning] Council, *Biennial Report . . . 1943–1944*, pp. 8–9, all in the MHPC Papers; *Chicago Bee*, January 14, 1945.
82 *Chicago Tribune*, July 2, 1953; *Housing News* 2 (November 1942), Aldis Papers; Metropolitan Housing [and Planning] Council, *The 1942 Annual Report* (Chicago: n.p., 1943), p. 7, MHPC Papers; Statement for *Daily News* by Alderman Robert E. Merriam, June 16, 1953, Robert E. Merriam Papers, the Department of Special Collections, University of Chicago Library; Memorandum of Meeting with General Smykal, October 15, 1953; Metropolitan Housing and Planning Council, Minutes of the Meeting of the Committee on the Reorganization of the Building Department, November 19, 1953; Memorandum from Jack Siegel to Earl Kribben, July 2, 1954; Metropolitan Housing and Planning Council, *The Road Back*, p. 29, all in the MHPC Papers.
83 Metropolitan Housing and Planning Council, "Report on the Major Violators of the Housing Code" (mimeographed, n.d.), pp. 1–2, 9, 24, 27, and passim; Memorandum from Jack Siegel to Dorothy Rubel, July 14, 1954; Miscellaneous Comments and Questions about the Housing Violations and the Court, November 15, 1958; Joseph Pois to Richard J. Daley, August 25, 1955; Memorandum from Mary Wirth: Comments on the Court Hearings in Branch 31 of the Municipal Court, December 5, 1958; Memorandum from Mary Wirth to Dorothy Rubel, n.d.; Metropolitan Housing and Planning Council, Minutes of the Meeting of the Reorganization and Enforcement Committee with Mr. James Downs, Jr., January 31, 1955; Memorandum from Mary Wirth to the Committee on Enforcement, January 9, 1959, all in the MHPC Papers.
84 Vitchek, "Confessions," not paginated; *Chicago Daily News*, October 13–17, 19–22, 1959; Helper, *Racial Policies*, pp. 41–2, 182–4, and passim; U.S. Commission on Civil Rights, *Hearings*, p. 741.
85 *Chicago Defender*, September 11, 1943; March 22, 1947; Alvin Winder, "White Attitudes Towards Negro-White Interaction in an Area of Changing Racial Composition" (Ph.D. dissertation, University of Chicago, 1952), pp. 37–8, 42–3, 58, 87–8, 91, 98–9.
86 Lea Taylor to Dorothy Rubel, June 16, 1945, MHPC Papers; U.S. Commission on Civil Rights, *Hearings*, p. 685.
87 The use of violence and legal maneuvering did not constitute the full range of white reaction. In the Back of the Yards neighborhood, labor, parish, and other local organizations supported the Back of the Yards Council, which successfully led the community in a series of stabilizing self-help and rehabilitation projects. The Back of the Yards experience was unique, however, and the resort to violence and urban planning

remained both the most common reactions and those with the greatest impact on the city as a whole. For the Back of the Yards experience, see Martin Millspaugh and Gurney Breckenfeld, *The Human Side of Urban Renewal* (New York: Washburne, 1958), chap. 4.

88 Lea Taylor to Robert Weaver, March 20, 1944; [Lea Taylor] to Mr. Kennedy, July 12, 1945; "Survey of Negro Population in the Chicago Commons Area, 1946," n.d., p. 2 and passim; Lea Taylor to John Joseph Ryan, May 2, 1946; Glenford W. Lawrence, Notes on Community Situation for Annual Report, November 1943; "Analysis of Neighborhood Needs," n.d.; Survey of Negro Families in the Neighborhood of Chicago Commons undertaken May-November 1946, all in Chicago Commons Papers.

89 Lea Taylor to Robert Weaver, March 20, 1944; "Houses West of Morgan Street Which Have Been Damaged or Destroyed in the Inter-Racial Situation," December 3, 1946; CHR, "Monthly Report of the Executive Director, November-December 1947" (mimeographed, n.d.); Lea Taylor to Don Jefferson, October 13, 1947; Statement by Mrs. Lillian Joiner, n.d.; typed notes on telephone call from Mr. [Samuel] Homan, November 1, 1947; Lea Taylor to Katherine (?) and Florence (?), October 16, 1947, all in the Chicago Commons Papers.

90 Interview with Fred Henderson, Southtown Planning Association, June 29, [1951], Merriam Papers; Memorandum from J. Cassels to File regarding visit with Fred Henderson, September 11, 1952, American Friends Service Committee Papers, Manuscript Collection, The Library, UIC; Memo: To Alinsky from Nicholas von Hoffman, November 30, 1959, Alinsky Papers.

91 *Chicago Defender*, May 3, 1941; April 12, July 5, 1947; CHR, "Monthly Report of the Executive Director, November-December, 1950" (mimeographed, n.d.), p. 13, CUL Papers; Summary of Meeting of Planning Advisory Committee to Robbins, Illinois, July 10, 1945, held in office of the Southtown Planning Association (SPA); Cook County Housing Authority, "Robbins, Illinois – An Immediate Problem" (mimeographed, June 17, 1947), all in the MHPC Papers; Wallace, "Residential Concentration of Negroes," pp. 257, 257n, 258n, 297, 297n.

92 *Chicago Bee*, November 28, 1943.

93 Metropolitan Housing [and Planning] Council, Minutes of the meetings of June 13, 17, 24, and July 1, 1947; Minutes of the Oakland-Kenwood Community Conservation Meeting, April 23, 1948; May 7, 1948; CHR, Memorandum on Community Conservation Agreement, January 20, 1948; Metropolitan Housing [and Planning] Council, Minutes of the Board of Governors Meeting, December 3, 1947; all in the MHPC Papers; CHR, "Monthly Report of the Executive Director, September 1950" (mimeographed, 1950), Appendix A, CUL Papers; *Chicago Defender*, January 24, 1948; Zorita Wise Mikva, "The Neighborhood Improvement Association: A Counter-Force to the Expansion of Chi-

cago's Negro Population" (M.A. thesis, University of Chicago, 1951), p. 68 and passim.

94 Handwritten note, n.d.; Minutes of the Meeting of June 13, 1947; Jack O. Ackermann to Metropolitan Housing Council, April 14, 1949; Evert Kincaid and George Hutchinson, "A Development Plan for Oakland-Kenwood," n.d., all in the MHPC Papers.

2. An era of hidden violence

1 On the causes of Chicago's 1919 riot, see Chicago Commission on Race Relations (CCRR), *The Negro in Chicago* (Chicago: University of Chicago Press, 1922); William M. Tuttle, Jr., *Race Riot: Chicago in the Red Summer of 1919* (New York: Atheneum, 1970); and Allan H. Spear, *Black Chicago: The Making of a Negro Ghetto, 1890–1920* (Chicago: University of Chicago Press, 1967). On the decline of black militancy in the wake of World War II, see August Meier and Elliott Rudwick, "Black Violence in the 20th Century: A Study in Rhetoric and Retaliation," in Hugh Davis Graham and Ted Robert Gurr, eds., *Violence in America: Historical and Comparative Perspectives* (New York: New American Library, 1969), pp. 399–412; Harvard Sitkoff, "Racial Militancy and Inter-racial Violence in the Second World War," *Journal of American History* 55 (June 1968): 661–81.

2 CCRR, *The Negro in Chicago*, pp. 124–9; Tuttle, *Race Riot*, pp. 157–83.

3 Detroit suffered a notable riot of this type in 1925. For details of the Ossian Sweet case, see Kenneth Jackson, *The Ku Klux Klan in the City, 1915–1930* (New York: Oxford University Press, 1967), p. 140.

4 Alfred M. Lee and Norman D. Humphrey, *Race Riot* (New York: Dryden Press, 1943); Tom Shogan and Robert Craig, *The Detroit Race Riot: A Study in Violence* (Philadelphia: Chilton, 1964); and Harvard Sitkoff, "The Detroit Race Riot of 1943," *Michigan History* 53 (Fall 1969): 183–94.

5 *Newsweek* 22 (July 5, 1943): 35–6; *Christian Century* 60 (June 30, 1943): 759–61; Lee and Humphrey, *Race Riot*, p. 63; *Nation* 157 (July 3, 1943): 4.

6 *Public Management* 26 (July 1944): 211–12; *Monthly Summary of Events and Trends in Race Relations* 3 (November 1945): 116.

7 Shogan and Craig, *The Detroit Race Riot*, p. 90; *New York Times*, July 7, 1943; *Chicago Defender*, July 3, 1943. Kelly hesitated slightly before making his public statement as he felt that "too much emphasis" on the riots would only "agitate" things further.

8 *New York Times*, July 6, 1943.

9 Ibid.

10 *Chicago Defender*, July 3, 1943; Louis Wirth to Clyde Hart, June 29, 1943, Louis Wirth Papers, University of Chicago (UC) Archives; St. Clair Drake and Horace R. Cayton, *Black Metropolis: A Study of Negro Life in a Northern City*, 2 vols. (New York: Harcourt, Brace, 1945; reprint ed., New York: Harper & Row, Harper Torchbooks, 1962), 1:91.

11 Drake and Cayton, *Black Metropolis*, 1:91; *Chicago Bee*, July 18, 1943; *Monthly Summary of Events and Trends in Race Relations* 1 (February–March 1944): 10; Mayor's Committee on Race Relations, "Statement of Aims and Programs" (mimeographed, n.d.), Municipal Reference Library (MRL), City Hall, Chicago. The Council Against Discrimintion (CAD) was originally named the Chicago Council Against Racial and Religious Discrimination; the amended name will be used hereafter.

12 Chicago Commission on Human Relations (CHR), *The People of Chicago, Five Year Report, 1947–1951* (Chicago: CHR, 1951), p. 3; Illinois Inter-Racial Commission, *First Annual Report* (Chicago: Illinois Inter-Racial Commission, n.d.), p. 7.

13 Drake and Cayton, *Black Metropolis*, 1:91.

14 Louis Wirth to Clyde Hart, June 29, 1943; CHR, *The People of Chicago*, p. 3.

15 *Chicago Defender*, August 23, September 6, 1941.

16 Metropolitan Housing [and Planning] Council, Minutes of the Regular Meeting of the Board of Directors, May 4, 1943, Metropolitan Housing and Planning Council Papers (hereafter cited as MHPC Papers), Manuscript Collection, The Library, University of Illinois at Chicago (UIC); Chicago Housing Authority (CHA), *Bulletin* 1 (March 25, 1941): 2; Louis Wirth to Clyde Hart, June 29, 1943; *Chicago Defender*, November 14, 1942.

17 Metropolitan Housing [and Planning] Council, Minutes of the Regular Meeting of the Board of Directors, May 4, August 3, 1943, MHPC Papers; Memos to Wilfred S. Reynolds from Lucy P. Carner, March 30, April 2, 1943, both in the Welfare Council of Chicago Papers, Chicago Historical Society (CHS); Louis Wirth to Clyde Hart, June 29, 1943.

18 *Chicago Defender*, March 27, September 18, October 9, 1943; Metropolitan Housing [and Planning] Council, Minutes of the Regular Meeting of the Board of Directors, April 1, August 3, October 5, November 2, 1943, all in the MHPC Papers; *Monthly Summary of Events and Trends in Race Relations* 1 (September 1943): 7. Other points of tension included Hyde Park, Back of the Yards, South Chicago, and the Hull House area. See the Minutes of the Council of Social Agencies, Chicago, Informal Meeting, Friday, June 25, 1943, in the Welfare Council of Chicago Papers.

19 *Chicago Defender*, October 11, 1941.

20 Ibid., December 13, 1941.

21 Drake and Cayton, *Black Metropolis*, 2:745.

22 Louis Wirth to Clyde Hart, June 29, 1943.

23 *Chicago Defender*, December 13, 1941.

24 Harold H. Swift to Pierce Atwater et al., May 23, 1942, Robert Maynard Hutchins Papers, UC Archives.

25 Louis Wirth to Clyde Hart, June 29, 1943. For remedial action after the Detroit riot, see Wirth to Clyde Hart, July 24, 1943, in the Wirth Papers.

26 *Chicago Bee*, June 6, 20, 27, July 4, 1943.

27   Louis Wirth to Clyde Hart, June 29, 1943.
28   *Chicago Defender*, August 7, 1943; *Chicago Bee*, August 8, 1943.
29   *Chicago Defender*, July 25, 1942; Louis Wirth to Clyde Hart, June 29, 1943. For the black-and-tan cabarets, see CCRR, *The Negro in Chicago*, pp. 323–5, and Tuttle, *Race Riot*, pp. 193–4.
30   *Chicago Defender*, May 22, 29, June 12, 19, 26, 1943.
31   Drake and Cayton, *Black Metropolis*, 1:91–2; John Bartlow Martin, "Incident at Fernwood," *Harper's Magazine* 198 (October 1949): 87.
32   Martin, "Incident at Fernwood," p. 87; *Chicago Bee*, January 21, 1945.
33   Martin, "Incident at Fernwood," p. 87.
34   Malcolm Ross, Untitled address delivered October 1, 1944, before the Chicago Urban League, Chicago Urban League Papers (herefter cited as CUL Papers), Manuscript Collection, The Library, UIC; CHR, *The People of Chicago*, p. 3; Martin, "Incident at Fernwood," p. 88; Chicago Conference on Home Front Unity, *Human Relations in Chicago* (Chicago: n.p., n.d.), p. 6; Mayor's Committee on Human Relations (hereafter cited as MCHR), *Human Relations in Chicago: Report for the Year 1946* (Chicago: CHR, n.d.), pp. 7, 9, 73; MCHR, *Race Relations in Chicago: Report for the Year 1945* (Chicago: CHR, n.d.), pp. 40–2; Chicago Urban League, Notes on the Special Meeting of the Board of Directors, December 5, 1949, CUL Papers; Illinois Inter-Racial Commission, *First Annual Report*, p. 42.
35   CHR, *The People of Chicago*, p. 29; Tuttle, *Race Riot*, pp. 47–9; CCRR, *The Negro in Chicago*, pp. 25–33; Welfare Council of Chicago, Minutes of the Meeting on [the] Interracial Situation held Friday, June 25, 1943, Welfare Council of Chicago Papers.
36   CHR, *Fourth Chicago Conference on Civic Unity: Abridged Report of Proceedings* (Chicago: CHR, 1952), pp. 77–8; Lawrence Rieser, "An Analysis of the Reporting of Racial Incidents in Chicago, 1945 to 1950" (M.A. thesis, University of Chicago, 1951), pp. 15, 15n.
37   [CAD], "Arson-Bombings and Other Terrorism Against Negro Households in Chicago, Documented Memorandum No. VII" (mimeographed, August 3, 1946), MHPC Papers.
38   Rieser, "An Analysis of the Reporting of Racial Incidents," p. 33.
39   These findings contradict the "leap-frog" hypothesis, which states that violence occurs only when the black population attempts to "leap-frog" nearby transition areas to settle in outlying white districts. The hypothesis overlooks the hidden, but chronic, violence at the edges of the ghetto. See Joseph Parot, "Ethnic vs. Black Metropolis: The Origins of Polish-Black Housing Tensions in Chicago," *Polish American Studies* 29 (Spring-Autumn 1972): 5–33.
40   Rieser, "An Analysis of the Reporting of Racial Incidents," p. 61; Illinois Inter-Racial Commission, *First Annual Report*, p. 47; CHR, "Monthly Report of the Executive Director, August 1948" (mimeographed, n.d.), p. 3, CUL Papers; Chicago Conference on Civic Unity, *Human Relations in Chicago, 1949* (Chicago: CHR, n.d.), p. 54.

41 These assaults represented one attack every two weeks and one arson-bombing every four weeks. [CAD], "Arson-Bombings"; *Chicago Bee*, April 7, June 17, 30, July 14, 21, August 25, October 31, 1946; September 8, 1948; *Chicago Defender*, July 6, 13, 20, September 28, December 7, 1946; January 4, July 5, August 30, October 18, November 22, 1947; February 28, April 10, 17, 1948; *Monthly Summary of Events and Trends in Race Relations* 1 (June 1944): 5; CHR, "Monthly Report of the Executive Director, October 1946" (mimeographed, n.d.), p. 8, The Library, University of Illinois at Urbana-Champaign; MCHR, *Human Relations in Chicago: Report for the Year 1946*, pp. 61–7; Herman H. Long and Charles S. Johnson, *People vs. Property* (Nashville, Tenn.: Fisk University Press, 1947), pp. 74–6.

42 Arvarh E. Strickland, *History of the Chicago Urban League* (Urbana: University of Illinois Press, 1966), p. 159.

43 Allen Day Grimshaw, "A Study in Social Violence: Urban Race Riots in the United States" (Ph.D. dissertation, University of Pennsylvania, 1959), p. 289.

44 Arnold Forster and Benjamin Epstein, *The Troublemakers* (Garden City, N.Y.: Doubleday, 1952), pp. 277–84; Strickland, *History of the Chicago Urban League*, p. 161; *Chicago Daily News*, July 12, 1951; *Chicago Sun-Times*, July 13, 1951; *New York Times*, July 14, September 15, 1951.

45 Forster and Epstein, *The Troublemakers*, p. 282; *New York Times*, August 1, 1951; *Chicago Defender*, August 11, September 15, 1951.

46 *Chicago Daily News*, July 17, 1951.

47 William Peters, "The Race War in Chicago," *New Republic* 122 (January 9, 1950): 12.

48 CHR, "Memorandum on the Fernwood Park Homes" (mimeographed, n.d.), passim, CUL Papers; CHR, *The People of Chicago*, pp. 9–10; Martin, "Incident at Fernwood," pp. 86–98; Strickland, *History of the Chicago Urban League*, p. 160; Homer Jack, "Chicago Has One More Chance," *Nation* 165 (September 13, 1947): 251–2; Metropolitan Housing [and Planning] Council, Minutes of the Board of Governors Meeting, August 16, 1947, MHPC Papers; Archibald J. Carey to Dorothy C. Patton, August 8, 1947, Archibald J. Carey, Jr., Papers, CHS.

49 CHR, "Peoria Street Incident" (mimeographed, n.d.), passim, MRL; Peters, "The Race War in Chicago," pp. 10–12; American Civil Liberties Union, "Report" (mimeographed, n.d.), Russell Ward Ballard Papers, Manuscript Collection, The Library, UIC.

50 Peters, "The Race War in Chicago," p. 12.

51 CHR, *The Trumbull Park Homes Disturbances: A Chronological Report August 4, 1953 to June 30, 1955* (Chicago: CHR, n.d.); Frank Brown, *Trumbull Park* (Chicago: Regnery, 1959); CHR, "Memorandum on the Airport Homes," (mimeographed, n.d.), passim, CUL Papers.

52 CHR, "Monthly Report of the Executive Director, October 1946," p. 8; [CAD], "Arson-Bombings."

53 MCHR, *Human Relations in Chicago: Report for the Year 1946*, p. 68;

Memo to Mayor Martin H. Kennelly from CHR, October 29, 1948, Daniel M. Cantwell Papers, CHS; *Chicago Bee*, July 14, 1946; *Chicago Defender*, July 6, 1949.

54 Approximately 300 questionnaires were turned in.

55 MCHR, *Human Relations in Chicago: Report for the Year 1946*, p. 69.

56 Philip A. Johnson, *Call Me Neighbor, Call Me Friend* (New York: Doubleday, 1965), p. 13.

57 Memo to Mayor Martin H. Kennelly from CHR, October 29, 1948.

58 CHR, "Monthly Report of the Executive Director, August 1948" (mimeographed, n.d.), p. 15, CUL Papers; Memo to Mayor Martin H. Kennelly from CHR, October 29, 1948; *Chicago Defender*, October 30, December 11, 1948; Alvin Winder, "White Attitudes Towards Negro-White Interaction in an Area of Changing Racial Composition" (Ph.D. dissertation, University of Chicago, 1952), pp. 18–19.

59 CHR, "Documentary Report of the Anti-Racial Demonstrations and Violence Against the Home and Persons of Mr. and Mrs. Roscoe Johnson, 7153 St. Lawrence Ave., July 25, 1949" (mimeographed, n.d.), CUL Papers.

60 David A. Wallace, "Residential Concentration of Negroes in Chicago" (Ph.D. dissertation, Harvard University, 1953), pp. 353, 353n.

61 "Park Manor Community Background," n.d., and "Notes and Comments on Urban League Work in Park Manor," n.d., both in the CUL Papers. See also the numerous reports filed by the various individual block clubs working with Urban League representatives in the CUL Papers.

62 [CAD], Memo on the Renewal of Conflict in Park Manor – July-August 1950 (mimeographed, n.d.), pp. 1–2; Transcript of the January 7, 1950, Meeting of the Conference to End Mob Violence, pp. 5–8, 51–2; Waitstill Sharp to Affiliates of [CAD], August 15, 1950, all in the CUL Papers; CHR, "Documentary Report on the Recurrence of Anti-Racial Disturbances in the 7100 and 7200 Blocks on St. Lawrence Avenue" (mimeographed, n.d.), p. 10, MRL; CHR, "A Documentary Memorandum, The White Circle League" (mimeographed, February 6, 1950), passim, American Civil Liberties Union–Illinois Division Papers (hereafter cited as ACLU Papers), the Department of Special Collections, University of Chicago Library; CHR, "Monthly Report of the Executive Director, November-December 1950" (mimeographed, n.d.), p. 33, CUL Papers.

63 *Chicago Tribune*, December 6, 1946; *Chicago Daily News*, December 6, 1946; *Chicago Sun*, December 4, 7, 1946; MCHR, *Human Relations in Chicago: Report for the Year 1946*, p. 91.

64 CHR, "Memorandum on Fernwood Park Homes," pp. 5, 8, 13, 18; *Chicago Tribune*, August 15, 1947.

65 *Chicago Sun-Times*, July 27, November 12, 1949; *Chicago Daily News*, July 27, November 11–14, 1949; *Chicago Tribune*, July 27, November 11, 12, 1949.

66 CHR, "Documentary Report of the Anti-Racial Demonstrations," p. 26; *Chicago Defender*, July 25, 1949.

67 CHR, "Memorandum on the Fernwood Park Homes," p. 44; *Chicago Defender*, November 12, 19, 1949. As a rule, however, the *Defender* provided much better coverage of such events than did its white counterparts. See the Transcript of the January 7, 1950, Meeting of the Conference to End Mob Violence, p. 36.

68 Sidney Williams to Homer Jack, December 19, 1949, Carey Papers; Sidney Williams to Mayor Martin H. Kennelly, November 29, 1949, Catholic Interracial Council Papers (CIC Papers), CHS; Strickland, *History of the Chicago Urban League*, pp. 172–5; Transcript of the January 7, 1950, Meeting of the Conference to End Mob Violence, pp. 53–5; *Chicago Defender*, November 17, 1951.

69 Louis Wirth to Curtis D. McDougall, January 17, February 8, 1950; Curtis D. McDougall to Louis Wirth, January 14, February 14, 1950, all in the Wirth Papers.

70 CHR, "Documentary Report of the Anti-Racial Demonstrations," p. 26.

71 Edward H. Meyerding to Violet Robbin, August 1, 1940, ACLU Papers.

72 *Chicago Daily News*, July 12–17, 1951; *Chicago Tribune*, July 13–14, 1951; *Chicago Sun-Times*, July 13, 1951.

73 Charles Abrams, *Forbidden Neighbors* (New York: Harper & Row, 1955), p. 105.

74 CHR, *The People of Chicago*, p. 12; Maynard J. Wishner, "Gains in Human Relations, 1952," address given at the 7th Annual Awards in Human Relations Luncheon, Chicago, December 9, 1952, MRL.

75 CHR, "Monthly Report of the Executive Director, November-December 1950," p. 35.

76 For the attacks on Dr. Percy Julian, see the *Chicago Defender*, November 25, 1950; January 20, June 16, 1951. For later assaults, see the *Chicago Defender*, July 5, 1952; July 2, 1953; March 6, August 7, 1954; CHR, "Monthly Report of the Executive Director, July-August 1953" (mimeographed, n.d.), p. 1, CUL papers.

77 This chronological sequence of interracial conflict differed from that of the World War I era. During the earlier period, the black ghetto was in the process of creation and the battles for housing and the use of public facilities were carried on simultaneously. After World War II, the black community had already established "black" facilities and institutions, which served even those who had moved away from them. Thus the battles over the use of "white" public conveniences did not occur until blacks were in sufficient strength to challenge for control of them. Consequently, a cleaner chronological division between the types of interracial conflict existed in the 1940s and 1950s than was the case earlier. See Vincent Giese, *Revolution in the City* (Notre Dame, Ind.: Fides, 1961), pp. 30–1, 44–7, and passim, for an illustration of the sequential nature of resistance in one area.

78 By mid-1957, the CHR noted an "apparent trend" toward increased attacks on persons as contrasted with earlier attacks against property. Not only did confrontations at parks, beaches, and other public areas involve personal conflict, but a number of attacks, including at least one bludgeon-style murder, occurred as victims simply passed through hostile territory. It is at this point that the distinction between social violence and criminal violence becomes blurred (if, indeed, a clear distinction can be made at all). After the killing of Alvin Palmer at 59th and Kedzie by a gang of whites, the CHR reported an "unusual number of assaults" throughout the city; twelve whites and five blacks were victimized in apparently "retaliatory" attacks and indicated, for the CHR, the "trend towards physical violence." The struggle for "turf" may thus be reflected not only in highly visible demonstrations but also in day-to-day "criminal" acts. See CHR, "Six-Month Report, January 1, 1957–June 30, 1957" (mimeographed, n.d.), pp. 9–10, Immigrants' Protective League Papers, Manuscript Collection, The Library, UIC; *Chicago Daily News*, March 13, 1957.

79 Mayor's Conference on Race Relations, *City Planning in Race Relations* (Chicago: Mayor's Committee on Race Relations, 1944), p. 53.

80 Mayor's Committee on Race Relations, *Human Relations in Chicago* (Chicago: Mayor's Committee on Race Relations, 1945), p. 6; MCHR, *Race Relations in Chicago: Report for the Year 1945*, p. 35; *Human Relations in Chicago: Report for the Year 1946*, pp. 56–7; CHR, *The People of Chicago*, p. 43. When measured against the violence directly related to the housing issue, these rare outbursts were truly insignificant. Of the 485 reported racial incidents in Chicago between 1945 and 1950, only 3.9% occurred within the recreational areas under the jurisdiction of the Park District Police; 73.6% of those incidents were directly related to housing or residential property. See Rieser, "An Analysis of the Reporting of Racial Incidents," p. 61.

81 The park is situated between 90th and 91st streets and between South Parkway (now Dr. Martin Luther King Drive) and St. Lawrence; South Parkway was the dividing line between the white and black communities.

82 The rancorous dispute over the project, which included significant black middle-class opposition, can be followed in great detail in innumerable editions of the *Chicago Bee* from February 27, 1944, to March 11, 1945.

83 MCHR, *Human Relations in Chicago: Report for the Year 1946*, pp. 70–1; *Chicago Defender*, October 12, 1946.

84 One black mother who had recently moved near Odgen Park "thought it rather peculiar never seeing any Negro children in the pool, especially in view of the fact that so many live in the immediate area." The efficiency of white hostility and the availability of alternative sources of recreation to allow such facilities to remain "white" even though the area around the park was changing was evident in the park policeman's suggestion that blacks use the Washington Park Pool. See CHR,

"Monthly Report of the Executive Director, July-August 1953" (mimeographed, n.d.), p. 9, CUL Papers.

85 MCHR, *Human Relations in Chicago: Report for the Year 1946*, pp. 70–1; *Chicago Defender*, October 12, 1946; April 24, 1954; CHR, "Monthly Report of the Executive Director, January 1947" (mimeographed, n.d.), p. 28, The Library, University of Illinois at Urbana-Champaign; CHR, "Monthly Report of the Executive Director, October 1950" (mimeographed, n.d.), CUL Papers. Attacks on blacks in Tuley Park occurred at least as late as 1957. See CHR, "A Preliminary Report on Racial Disturbances in Chicago for the Period July 21 to August 4, 1957" (mimeographed, n.d.), pp. 24–5, MRL.

86 These strikes were possibly triggered by similar incidents in Gary, Indiana. For the Chicago events, see MCHR, *Race Relations in Chicago: Report for the Year 1945*, p. 15; *Chicago Bee*, November 4, 11, 1945; *Chicago Defender*, September 29, October 6, 1945; for the Gary strikes, see *Chicago Defender*, October 6, November 3, December 1, 1945; *Monthly Summary of Events and Trends in Race Relations* 3 (December 1945): 145–52.

87 A. J. Neely to Sidney R. Williams, March 8, 1949; Statement of Marilyn I. Anderson, May 2, 1949; Complaint of Discrimination at Morris B. Sachs Store, 6638 South Halsted Street, n.d., all in the CUL Papers; *Chicago Defender*, June 21, 1941.

88 Events surrounding the White City Roller Rink are described in MCHR, *Human Relations in Chicago: Report for the Year 1946*, p. 51; *Chicago Bee*, December 23, 1945; January 13, February 3, 17, 24, March 3, 10, May 12, June 2, 1946; August Meier and Elliott Rudwick, *CORE: A Study in the Civil Rights Movement* (Urbana: University of Illinois Press, 1975), pp. 7–8, 12, 17, 32. For the Trianon Ballroom incident, see the *Chicago Defender*, June 5, 1954; CHR, "Monthly Report of the Executive Director, July 1950" (mimeographed, n.d.), pp. 14–18, MRL; for the Metropole Theater disorder, see CHR, "Metropole Theater Incident Numbers 1 and 2" (mimeographed, n.d.), passim, MRL.

89 Rainbow Beach extends southward along the lakefront from 75th Street; Bessemer Park is bordered by 89th Street on the north, Muskegon Avenue on the east, and South Chicago Avenue on the south and west; Calumet Park extends southward along the lakefront from 95th Street.

90 Stephen S. Bubacz, *Diary*, 1961, entries for July 9, 15, 17-19, 25, 29-30, 1961; Memo from Stephen S. Bubacz to Tony Sorrentino, July 25, 1961, both in the Stephen S. Bubacz Papers, Manuscript Collection, The Library, UIC; Clippings from the *Daily Defender*, July 5, 10, 17, 1961; *Southtown Economist*, July 9, 27, 1961; *Chicago Daily News*, July 10, 19, 27, 1961; *Chicago Tribune*, July 16, 17, 1961; *Christian Science Monitor*, July 20, 1961, all in the Saul Alinsky Papers, Manuscript Collection, The Library, UIC.

91 CHR, "A Report on the Bessemer Park Disturbances, July 25-August 16, 1960" (mimeographed, n.d.); Stephen S. Bubacz, *Diary, 1960*, entries for July 25-29, 1960, both in the Bubacz Papers.

92   By the early 1960s it was apparent that use of the public parks sur-
     passed housing as the city's most explosive issue – and not all the
     disputed parks were located on the Southeast Side. Surveys of tension
     areas in 1962 and 1964 revealed the parks' virtually uncontested status
     as sources of difficulty in the citywide distribution of trouble spots.
     See Ed Marciniak to CHR, May 10, 1962, and May 12, 1964, Ely Aaron
     Papers, Manuscript Collection, The Library, UIC.
93   *Daily Calumet* clipping, n.d., CIC Papers; "Chicago: Where Whites and
     Negroes Battle Again," *U.S. News & World Report* 13 (August 9, 1957):
     31–3; CHR, "A Preliminary Report on Racial Disturbances," passim.
     Violence again broke out in Calumet Park in 1973 as the accommoda-
     tion established in earlier years was threatened by continued popula-
     tion movements. See the *Chicago Daily News*, June 19-20, 1973; *Chicago
     Sun-Times*, June 13, 18, 1973.
94   CHR, "Press, Radio and Television Coverage of Racial Disturbances in
     Chicago from July 28 to August 15, 1957" (mimeographed, n.d.), MRL;
     New World, August 2, 1957; *Daily Calumet* clipping, n.d., in the CIC
     Papers.
95   "A New Approach to Residential Segregation: The East Side Civic
     League," n.d., p. 21, American Friends Service Committee Papers,
     Manuscript Collection, The Library, UIC.
96   *The Bulletin*, August 3, 1961, clipping, Alinsky Papers.
97   "A New Approach," pp. 1, 17.
98   Ibid., pp. 22–3.

3. Friends, neighbors, and rioters

1   Thomas L. Philpott, *The Slum and the Ghetto: Neighborhood Deterioration
    and Middle-Class Reform, Chicago, 1880–1930* (New York: Oxford Uni-
    versity Press, 1978), pp. 114, 162–80.
2   Morris Janowitz, "Patterns of Collective Racial Violence," in Hugh
    Davis Graham and Ted Robert Gurr, eds., *Violence in America: Histori-
    cal and Comparative Perspectives* (New York: New American Library,
    1969), pp. 412–44.
3   Philpott, *The Slum and the Ghetto*, pp. 160–1, 167–8, 194; Gilbert Osofsky,
    Harlem: The Making of a Ghetto; Negro New York, 1890–1930 (New York:
    Harper & Row, 1966), pp. 46–52; Kenneth L. Kusmer, *A Ghetto Takes
    Shape: Black Cleveland, 1870–1930* (Urbana: University of Illinois Press,
    1976), pp. 170–1. See also William M. Tuttle, Jr., *Race Riot: Chicago in
    the Red Summer of 1919* (New York: Atheneum, 1970) and St. Clair
    Drake and Horace R. Cayton, *Black Metropolis: A Study of Negro Life in a
    Northern City*, 2 vols. (New York: Harcourt, Brace, 1945; reprint ed.,
    New York: Harper & Row, Harper Torchbooks, 1962), 1:42–3, 66, 110.
4   Janowitz, "Patterns of Collective Racial Violence," p. 416.
5   Ibid., pp. 418–19.

6 The five riots occurred at the Fernwood Park Homes in August 1947, at 71st and St. Lawrence (Park Manor) in July 1949, at 56th and Peoria (Englewood) in November 1949, at the Trumbull Park Homes starting in August 1953, and at Calumet Park in July-August 1957.

7 Chicago Commission on Human Relations (CHR), "Peoria Street Incident" (mimeographed, n.d.), pp. 32, 35, Municipal Reference Library (MRL), City Hall, Chicago; Chicago Urban League, Notes on Special Meeting of the Board of Directors, December 5, 1949, Chicago Urban League Papers (hereafter cited as CUL Papers), Manuscript Collection, The Library, University of Illinois at Chicago (UIC).

8 *Daily Compass*, November 11, 1949, noted the beatings administered to University of Chicago students and other outsiders and claimed that sixteen nonrioters were arrested. *National Guardian*, November 21, 1949, also reported sixteen Progressive party members arrested at 56th and Peoria.

9 Edward H. Meyerding to Robert Ludlow and Tom Sullivan, September 20, 1951, American Civil Liberties Union–Illinois Division Papers (hereafter cited as ACLU Papers), the Department of Special Collections, University of Chicago Library.

10 CHR, "Documentary Memorandum, The White Circle League" (mimeographed, n.d.); Edward H. Meyerding to Arnie Matonta, April 12, 1950; Edward H. Meyerding to Walter White, July 30, 1951; *White Circle News*, June 19, 1950, all in the ACLU Papers.

11 George Rudé warns against treating violent crowds as "militant minorit[ies] to be sharply marked off from the larger number of citizens" and notes that a "bond of symapthy and common interest" may link the "active few with the inactive many." *The Crowd in History: A Study of Popular Disturbances in France and England, 1730–1848* (New York: Wiley, 1964), pp. 211–12.

12 The CHR produced aggregate, but not individual, data on the ages of the Calumet Park rioters. Of the 120 persons arrested, 15 (12.5%) were 17 and under, 58 (48.3%) were ages 17 to 21, 23 (19.2%) were between 21 and 30, 18 (15%) were 30 or older, and age was not found for the remaining 6 (5%). See CHR, "A Preliminary Report on Racial Disturbances in Chicago for the Period July 21 to August 4, 1957" (mimeographed, n.d.), Appendix, MRL. The data produced in the text are derived from information obtained on 51 individual rioters known through press accounts.

13 CHR, "Documentary Report on the Recurrence of Anti-Racial Disturbances in the 7100 and 7200 Blocks on St. Lawrence Avenue" (mimeographed, n.d.), pp. 15–16, 22, MRL.

14 William Gremley, "Social Control in Cicero, Illinois" (mimeographed, n.d.), p. 8, Catholic Interracial Council Papers (hereafter cited as CIC Papers), Chicago Historical Society; ACLU Observer's Report for July 13, 1951, ACLU Papers.

15 CHR, "Memorandum on the Airport Homes" (mimeographed, n.d.),

p. 4, CUL Papers; CHR, "Documentary Report of the Anti-Racial Dem-
onstrations and Violence Against the Home and Persons of Mr. and
Mrs. Roscoe Johnson, 7153 St. Lawrence Avenue, July 25, 1949" (mim-
eographed, n.d.), p. 2, CUL Papers; Thomas E. Rook, Report, No-
vember 17, 1949, CIC Papers; Elizabeth Wood to Members of the CHA
Advisory Committee on Race Relations, May 6, 1954, Business and
Professional People for the Public Interest Papers (hereafter cited as
BPI Papers), Chicago Historical Society (CHS).

16 Rook, Report, p. 1; ACLU Observer's Report, passim.
17 CHR, "Memorandum on the Airport Homes," p. 14; Homer Jack,
    "Documented Memorandum VIII, The Racial Factor in the Veterans'
    Airport Housing Project" (mimeographed, n.d.), pp. 2, 4, Welfare
    Council of Chicago Papers, CHS; *Chicago Tribune*, December 12, 1946.
18 CHR, *The Trumbull Park Homes Disturbances: A Chronological Report,
    August 4, 1953 to June 30, 1955* (Chicago: CHR, n.d.), pp. 12, 19, 23, 30,
    32, 40; Catholic Interracial Council, Memorandum Re Proposal of Pro-
    gram Services for Tenants of Trumbull Park Homes, December 1, 1954,
    CIC Papers.
19 Joseph Parot, "Ethnic vs. Black Metropolis: The Origins of Polish-Black
    Housing Tensions in Chicago," *Polish-American Studies* 29 (Spring-
    Autumn, 1972): 5–33; Pierre de Vise, *Chicago's Widening Color Gap* (Chi-
    cago: Social Research Committee, 1967), pp. 71–3. De Vise shows that
    Poles and Italians were the "whites" found in the greatest numbers in
    areas adjacent to the expanding Black Belt.
20 American Civil Liberties Union, "Report" (mimeographed, n.d.), Rus-
    sell Ward Ballard Papers, Manuscript Collection, The Library, UIC.
    Visitation Parish, *Diamond Jubilee* (Chicago: Visitation Parish, n.d.), p.
    23.
21 Gremley, "Social Control," p. 39. As of 1951, one mass per day in
    Cicero churches still used the Czech language out of respect for the
    "old people."
22 "Defeat in Cicero," *Christian Century* 68 (July 25, 1951): 862–3; Daniel
    M. Cantwell, "Postscript on the Cicero Riot," *The Commonweal* 54 (Sep-
    tember 14, 1951): 544; Confidential Memo to File from David McNa-
    mara, November 13, 1951, CIC Papers.
23 Report on Trumbull Park: Interview with Win Kennedy, Project Man-
    ager, August 5, 1955, CIC Papers.
24 Daily reports filed by the ACLU operative are deposited in the ACLU
    Papers, Box 11, Folder 9, and Box 12, Folder 1.
25 Operative L. G., Confidential Report, June 24, 1954, ACLU Papers;
    Albert G. Rosenberg to Elizabeth Wood, November 12, 1953, CUL
    Papers.
26 *Chicago Defender*, July 28, 1951.
27 CHR, "Report on Press, Radio, and Television Coverage of Racial
    Disturbances in Chicago from July 28 to August 15, 1957" (mimeo-
    graphed, n.d.), pp. 5–6, MRL.

28 *Chicago Defender*, April 18, 1957.
29 Chandler Owen, "A Program for the Solution of the Trumbull Housing Conflict" (1954?), p. 13, Robert E. Merriam Papers, the Department of Special Collections, University of Chicago (UC) Library; A. L. Foster to Reginald DuBois, March 11, 1954, Archibald J. Carey, Jr., Papers, CHS.
30 It is understood that such a method is imprecise at best. It was simply deemed appropriate to go beyond the *assumption* that the local residents arrested during a riot were ethnically representative of the community involved and that the attempt to establish, in broad terms, the general ethnic composition of the various mobs was thus desirable. The arrest lists were surveyed independently by the author (a Jew), and two colleagues (a Polish-American and a scholar of French-Irish extraction) who are specialists in urban history. The results, which were highly corroborative in virtually every case, were then combined to minimize possible error. The percentages in Tables 3, 4, and 5 represent the averages produced by that collaboration.
31 "New" immigrant stock refers to those of Slavic, Polish, or Italian ancestry as well as those of uncertain Southeast European provenance. All subsequent references to the "new" immigration in the text and the tables refer to these groups.
32 The descendants of the "old" immigration are considered those of Dutch, Swedish, or German origin; those of apparent Anglo ancestry are kept separate throughout this study. All subsequent references to the "old" immigration thus refer only to the former three groups.
33 *Chicago Defender*, April 18, 1957. Little analysis could be attempted with "Anglo-sounding" surnames for there was persistent evidence that many "ethnics" had Anglicized their names by the 1940s. As it was impossible to tell how large a group this was, the figures reported tend to underestimate "ethnic" riot participation and overstate that attributable to "Anglos."
34 Evelyn M. Kitagawa and Karl E. Taeuber, eds., *Local Community Fact Book: Chicago Metropolitan Area, 1960* (Chicago: Chicago Community Inventory, 1963), pp. 112, 116, 118, 150.
35 Catholic Interracial Council, Memorandum Re Proposal of Program Services for Tenants of Trumbull Park Homes, December 1, 1954.
36 Chicago Urban League, Research Department to Executive Director, September 13, 1957, Saul Alinsky Papers, Manuscript Collection, The Library, UIC.
37 Typed notes, CIC Papers; CHR, "Memorandum on the Airport Homes," p. 13; CHR, "Documentary Report of the Anti-Racial Demonstrations," pp. 4, 9.
38 Rook, Report; ACLU, "Report"; typed notes, CIC Papers; CHR, "Peoria Street Incident," passim; David McNamara to Stuart (?), January 21, 1950, CIC Papers.
39 William Gremley, "Scandal of Cicero," *America* 85 (August 25, 1951):

195; CIC to His Eminence Samuel Cardinal Stritch, October 27, 1956, CIC Papers; Lloyd Davis to David F. Freeman, April 9, 1956, CIC Papers.

40 *The Worker*, November 27, 1949, clipping in the CIC Papers; *Pittsburgh Courier*, November 26, 1949.

41 Betty Jallings to Lloyd Davis, May 21, 1954; Davis to Jallings, May 22, 1954, both in the CIC Papers.

42 South Deering Methodist Church, *Newsletter*, No. 3, Thanksgiving, 1957; Lloyd Davis to Rev. David K. Fison, December 9, 1957; Fison to Davis, January 28, 1958, all in the CIC Papers.

43 Lloyd Davis to Thomas E. Colgan, November 2, 1953, CIC Papers.

44 Catholic Interracial Council, Report of the Organizational Committee, June 7, 1945, CIC Papers.

45 Catholic Interracial Council, Minutes of the Second Meeting of the South Cook County Chapter of the Catholic Interracial Council of Chicago, September 12, 1957, CIC Papers; Bayard Rustin, Memo to Joint Committee of the American Friends Service Committee and the CIC, September 11, 1951, CIC Papers.

46 Catholic Interracial Council, Grant Proposal Prepared for Ford Foundation, February 2, 1954, CIC Papers.

47 CHR, "Memorandum on the Airport Homes," pp. 13–14.

48 CHR, "Memorandum on Fernwood Park Homes" (mimeographed, n.d.), pp. 2–5, CUL Papers; Community Relations Service, "Housing and Race Relations in Chicago" (mimeographed, September 22, 1948), pp. 50–1, Carey Papers.

49 CHR, "Documentary Report of the Anti-Racial Demonstrations," p. 1 and Appendix A.

50 CHR, "Peoria Street Incident," passim.

51 CHR, "A Preliminary Report," p. 6.

52 Operative L. G., Confidential Report, May 7, 1954, ACLU Papers.

53 CHR, *The Trumbull Park Homes Disturbances*, pp. 10–11; *Chicago Daily News*, April 10, 1954.

54 *National Guardian*, November 21, 1949; *Daily Compass*, November 21, 1949; CHR, "Peoria Street Incident," p. 26.

55 CHR, "Documentary Report of the Anti-Racial Demonstrations," p. 13; Gremley, "Social Control," p. 17.

56 Gremley, "Social Control," p. 17.

57 CHR, "Memorandum on the Airport Homes," p. 14.

58 Homer Jack, "Chicago Has One More Chance," *Nation* 155 (September 13, 1947): 251.

59 CHR, "Documentary Report of the Anti-Racial Demonstrations," p. 1; for Cicero, see Homer Jack, "Cicero Nightmare," *Nation* 173 (July 28, 1951): 64–5; and Mary Yedinak, "Cicero: Why It Rioted" (B.A. thesis, University of Illinois at Urbana-Champaign, 1967), p. 13.

60 Despite the proximity of the Black Belt and the apparent availability of black targets, there were reports of only three cars being stoned by

white teens and only a single injury was recorded. CHR, "Documentary Report of the Anti-Racial Demonstrations," pp. 11–12.

61 CHR, "Emerald Street Incident" (mimeographed, n.d.), pp. 19–20, MRL.

62 ACLU, "Report"; the ACLU report on the Englewood disorder noted that the neighborhood around 56th and Peoria "has been known for some years as one of the most dangerous spots" in the city in terms of black–white conflict. The black enclaves of Morgan Park, Lilydale, and the wartime developments in Princeton Park surrounded white Roseland residents. See Metropolitan Housing [and Planning] Council, Minutes of the Regular Meeting of the Board of Directors, April 1, 1943, p. 2, and August 3, 1943, Metropolitan Housing and Planning Council Papers (hereafter cited as the MHPC Papers), Manuscript Collection, The Library, UIC.

63 Although Leonard Richards took the placement of candles in windows for similar reasons as evidence of prior planning, it appears that such actions were more the result of common sense than conspiracy. These actions were similar to those taken by blacks who wrote "Soul Brother" on the windows of their stores during the riots of the 1960s. No one has seriously claimed that this attempt to avoid personal injury or damage to property was evidence of a broadly based conspiracy. See CHR, "A Preliminary Report," p. 11; Leonard Richards, *Gentlemen of Property and Standing: Anti-Abolition Mobs in Jacksonian America* (New York: Oxford University Press, 1970), p. 120.

64 CHR, "Peoria Street Incident," p. 31; ACLU, "Report," passim.

65 CHR, "Peoria Street Incident," p. 35.

66 ACLU, "Report," p. 3.

67 CHR, "Memorandum on the Airport Homes," p. 26; *Chicago Daily News*, December 11, 1946.

68 Waitstill Sharp, "Annual Report Essentials for the Year 1949" (mimeographed, n.d.), p. 1, CUL Papers; CHR, "Documentary Report of the Anti-Racial Demonstrations," p. 5.

69 ACLU, "Report," passim; *Chicago Maroon*, November 18, 1949; *Chicago Defender*, November 19, 1949; *Chicago Sun-Times*, November 18, 1949; *Chicago Daily News*, November 16, 1949; *Pittsburgh Courier*, November 26, 1949.

70 CHR, "Memorandum on Fernwood Park Homes," pp. 5, 8.

71 Archibald J. Carey to Dorothy C. Patton, August 8, 1947, Carey Papers.

72 *Chicago Bee*, February 23, 1947; CHR, *The People of Chicago: Five Year Report, 1947–1951*, of the Chicago Commission on Human Relations (Chicago: CHR, n.d.), p. 7; Community Relations Service, "Housing and Race Relations in Chicago," p. 37.

73 CHR, "Memorandum on Fernwood Park Homes," pp. 19–20.

74 CHR, *The People of Chicago*, pp. 10–11.

75 Ibid., p. 13; CHR to Mayor Martin H. Kennelly, October 28, 1948, Daniel M. Cantwell papers, CHS.

76 CHR, *The People of Chicago*, p. 11; CHR, *Fourth Chicago Conference on Civic Unity: Abridged Report of Proceedings* (Chicago: CHR, 1952), p. 39; Philip A. Johnson, *Call Me Neighbor, Call Me Friend* (New York: Doubleday, 1965), p. 34.
77 CHR, *The People of Chicago*, p. 20.
78 Ibid., p. 21; Joseph D. Lohman, *The Police and Minority Groups* (Chicago: n.p., n.d.), was the text used.
79 CHR, *The Trumbull Park Homes Disturbances*.
80 *Chicago Defender*, May 8, 15, 1954; November 12, 1955.
81 Elizabeth Wood to Members of the CHA Advisory Committee on Race Relations, April 27, 1954, and Wood to CHR, n.d., both in the BPI Papers.
82 Report on the Community Forum's Meeting on Trumbull Park, May 23, 1954, Irene McCoy Gaines Papers, CHS.
83 *Chicago Sun-Times*, December 14, 1954; Council Against Discrimination, Minutes of the Trumbull Park Homes Committee, May 6, 1954, CUL Papers.
84 CHR, *The Trumbull Park Homes Disturbances*, p. 35.
85 Operative L. G., Confidential Report, April 23, May 7, June 24, July 22, 1954, ACLU Papers.
86 CHR, *The Trumbull Park Homes Disturbances*, p. 50; Operative L. G., Confidential Report, July 17, 1954, ACLU Papers.
87 *Chicago Sun-Times*, July 31, 1957.

4. The loop versus the slums

1 Ferd Kramer to James L. Palmer, March 5, 1945; Dorothy Rubel to All Members of the Redevelopment Committee, January 6, 1954, both in the Metropolitan Housing and Planning Council Papers (hereafter cited as MHPC Papers), Manuscript Collection, The Library, University of Illinois at Chicago (UIC).
2 Metropolitan Housing and Planning Council to Planning Committee, City Council, October 1, 1951, MHPC Papers.
3 "Family Record for the Archives of the Chicago Historical Society [CHS]," in the guide to the Holman D. Pettibone Papers, CHS; *Chicago Sun-Times*, December 14, 1958; *Chicago Tribune*, March 15, 1952.
4 Martin Meyerson and Edward C. Banfield, *Politics, Planning, and the Public Interest: The Case of Public Housing in Chicago* (New York: Free Press, 1955), pp. 145–7.
5 Ibid.; Metropolitan Housing [and Planning] Council, Minutes of the Board of Governors Meeting, September 11, 1944; July 2, October 9, 1946; March 5, 1951, all in the MHPC Papers; Dorothy Rubel to Frances H. Morton, July 6, 1948, MHPC Papers. The MHPC board of governors included some academics like Louis Wirth, some housing reformers and public housing advocates, and even community organizer Saul Alinsky. Such members were in the minority, however, and

the council prided itself on its ability to work quietly and avoid confrontation.

6 Holman D. Pettibone, "Outline of a Long Range Program for the Redevelopment of Blighted Areas in the City of Chicago," September 12, 1947, speech delivered before the Businessmen's Conference on Urban Problems in Washington, D.C.; [Milton C. Mumford], "Memorandum for Discussion with the Urban Redevelopment Committee," Metropolitan Housing Council (mimeographed, n.d.), both in the Holman D. Pettibone Papers, CHS; Philip Klutznick to Milton Mumford, September 19, 1946, MHPC Papers.

7 Metropolitan Housing [and Planning] Council, Minutes of the Board Meeting, June 15, 1942; March 7, 1944; Metropolitan Housing [and Planning] Council, Minutes of a Special Meeting of the Executive Committee, July 14, 1944, all in the MHPC Papers.

8 Metropolitan Housing [and Planning] Council, Minutes of Meeting, July 6, 1943; Metropolitan Housing [and Planning] Council, Minutes of the Regular Meeting of the Board of Governors, April 4, 1944; Metropolitan Housing [and Planning] Council, "Financial Analysis of West Side Redevelopment Project" (mimeographed, February 11, 1947); Metropolitan Housing [and Planning] Council, "Medical Center Area Redevelopment Plan, Metropolitan Housing Council, 1945" (mimeographed, n.d.), all in the MHPC Papers.

9 [Mumford], "Memorandum for Discussion with the Urban Redevelopment Committee."

10 Ibid.; Metropolitan Housing and Planning Council, Minutes of the Meeting of the Redevelopment Committee, August 9, 1950; Metropolitan Housing [and Planning] Council, Biennial Report, 1946–1947 (Chicago: Metropolitan Housing [and Planning] Council, 1947), n.p., both in the MHPC Papers.

11 Metropolitan Housing [and Planning] Council, Stand and Fight (Chicago: Metropolitan Housing [and Planning] Council, n.d.); Minutes of the Meeting of the Redevelopment Committee, August 9, 1950, MHPC Papers.

12 Metropolitan Housing [and Planning] Council, Minutes of the Meeting of the New Executive Committee, Wednesday, April 7, 1943, MHPC Papers.

13 Metropolitan Housing and Planning Council, Minutes of the Meeting of the Redevelopment Committee, August 9, 1950; [Mumford] "Memorandum for Discussion with the Urban Redevelopment Committee"; L. D. McKendry to Milton C. Mumford, September 24, 1946; Milton C. Mumford to Holman D. Pettibone, May 12, 1952, all in the Pettibone Papers; Dorothy Rubel to Frances H. Morton, July 6, 1948.

14 Holman D. Pettibone to L. D. McKendry, April 3, 1945, Pettibone Papers.

15 James C. Downs, Jr., to L. D. McKendry, May 24, 1946; Milton C. Mumford to L. D. McKendry, October 10, 31, 1946; L. D. McKendry to

Milton C. Mumford, October 22, 1946; Miles Colean, "A Proposal to Construct Two Redevelopment Projects in Chicago" (mimeographed, June 26, 1947); Milt [Mumford] to Holman [Pettibone], July 18, 1947; Holman D. Pettibone to L. D. McKendry, February 4, 1946, all in the Pettibone Papers.

16 [Holman D. Pettibone], Memorandum for Conversation, Wednesday, March 6, 1946, Pettibone Papers.

17 Holman D. Pettibone to Hughston McBain, July 11, 1946; Holman D. Pettibone to Governor Green, July 9, 1946; [Mumford], "Memorandum for Discussion with the Urban Redevelopment Committee," p. 8, all in the Pettibone Papers.

18 David A. Wallace, "Residential Concentration of Negroes in Chicago" (Ph.D. dissertation, Harvard University, 1953), p. 319; "Basic Facts and Assumptions on Which These Bills are Based" (mimeographed, April 17, 1947), and "Three Decades of Redevelopment," March 24, 1954, both in the Pettibone Papers.

19 *Chicago Bee*, February 9, April 20, 1947; Newton C. Farr to Leverett Lyon, April 11, 1947, Pettibone Papers.

20 [Holman D. Pettibone], Notes on the Conference with Governor Green at Springfield, April 24, 1947; Holman D. Pettibone to Martin H. Kennelly, April 25, 1947, Pettibone Papers; Interview with Ira J. Bach, July 24, 1980.

21 Chicago Committee for Housing Action, Minutes of the Organization Meeting, April 25, 1947, Pettibone Papers; Dorothy Rubel to Frances H. Morton, July 6, 1948.

22 [Holman D. Pettibone], Memorandum on Conversation with Elmer Gertz in My Office on Wednesday, May 7, 1947 and Holman D. Pettibone to Martin H. Kennelly, May 2, 1947 and September 18, 1952, all in the Pettibone Papers.

23 [Holman D. Pettibone], Conversation with Mayor Kennelly at His Office, Thursday, May 6, 1947, Pettibone Papers.

24 See the List of Persons Present at Meeting of Senate Policy Committee – Governor's Mansion, Tuesday, May 6, 1947, Pettibone Papers.

25 "Slum Clearance and Redevelopment – Basic Facts and Assumptions" (mimeographed, May 5, 1947), Pettibone Papers; Chicago Committee on Housing Action – Second Report, May 8, 1947, MHPC Papers.

26 Holman D. Pettibone to Hughston McBain, July 11, 1947, Pettibone Papers.

27 Holman D. Pettibone to Martin H. Kennelly, September 18, 1952.

28 [Holman D. Pettibone], Notes on Conversation with Mayor Kennelly, May 6, 1947, Pettibone Papers; "Slum Clearance and Redevelopment – Basic Facts and Assumptions," May 5, 1947; Interview with Ferd Kramer, August 4, 1980.

29 Metropolitan Housing [and Planning] Council, *Stand and Fight*, passim; Milton C. Mumford to Hughston McBain, May 16, 1947.

30 Holman D. Pettibone to Martin H. Kennelly, September 18, 1952; Milton Mumford to Hughston McBain, May 16, 1947.

31 [Pettibone], Notes on Conversation with Mayor Kennelly at His Office, May 6, 1947.

32 Milton Mumford to Hughston McBain, May 16, 1947; Holman Pettibone to Martin H. Kennelly, September 18, 1952; Robert E. Merriam, "Are We Saving our Neighborhoods?" an address given before the City Club of Chicago, October 26, 1953, Leon Despres Papers, CHS.

33 Milton Mumford to Hughston McBain, May 16, 1947.

34 Bach interview.

35 Despite his trepidation, Mumford felt that "if I had to do it over again I would do it exactly as we have. It is my feeling that these risks are inherent in attempting to get anything done of a size which necessitates working at fairly high political levels, involving opposing administrations and political parties, and in an area in which nothing is ever reduced to writing and everybody is free to run out on everybody else." Milton C. Mumford to Hughston McBain, May 16, 1947. See also Holman D. Pettibone to George Dovenmuehle, December 17, 1956, Pettibone Papers, and *Chicago Defender*, May 10, 1947.

36 Pettibone believed, as did Mumford, that any explicit legislative provision "having to do with occupancy along racial lines...would be fatal to investment of private capital." Milton C. Mumford to Hughston McBain, May 16, 1947; [Pettibone], Notes on Conversation with Mayor Kennelly, May 6, 1947; [Pettibone], Memorandum on Conversation with Elmer Gertz, May 7, 1947.

37 J. F. Grossman to Martin H. Kennelly, May 29, 1947; Questions Concerning Pending Changes in Legislative Program, June 1947; Points Agreed at Conference of June 2, 1947, all in the Pettibone Papers.

38 See note 37.

39 Holman D. Pettibone to Dwight H. Green, June 24, 1947, Pettibone Papers.

40 Metropolitan Housing [and Planning] Council, *Biennial Report, 1946–1947*.

41 Holman D. Pettibone to Dwight H. Green, June 24, 1947; Dwight H. Green to Holman D. Pettibone, July 10, 1947, Pettibone Papers; Milton C. Mumford to Hughston McBain, May 16, 1947.

42 A slum or blighted area was defined as "any area not less...than two (2) acres located within the territorial limits of a municipality where buildings or improvements, by reason of dilapidation, obsolescence, overcrowding, faulty arrangement or design, lack of ventilation, light and sanitary facilities, excessive land coverage, deleterious land use or layout or any combination of these factors are detrimental to the public safety, health, morals, or welfare." See Housing and Redevelopment Coordinator, *Illinois Housing and Redevelopment Legislation, 1947–1949* (Chicago: n.p., n.d.).

43 [Pettibone], Memorandum of Conversation with Elmer Gertz, May 7, 1947; Clement E. Vose, *Caucasians Only: The Supreme Court, the NAACP,*

and the Restrictive Covenant Cases (Berkeley: University of California Press, 1959).

44 "Proposed Program" (mimeographed, May 5, 1947), Pettibone Papers; Points Agreed at Conference of June 2, 1947; Chicago Committee for Housing Action, "A Housing and Redevelopment Program for Chicago" (mimeographed, July 11, 1947), p. 1, MHPC Papers.

45 "Analysis of Governor's Redevelopment Bills," n.d., Business and Professional People for the Public Interest Papers (hereafter cited as BPI Papers), CHS.

46 Housing and Redevelopment Coordinator, *Illinois Housing and Redevelopment Legislation*, passim.

47 "Proposed Program," May 5, 1947.

48 Chicago Committee for Housing Action, "A Housing and Redevelopment Program for Chicago" (mimeographed, n.d.), p. 3 and passim; "The Chicago Dwellings Association" (mimeographed, n.d.), both in the MHPC Papers; Tom Buck to Don Maxwell, October 19, 1954 (?), Fort Dearborn Papers, Manuscript Collection, The Library, UIC; Wallace, "Residential Concentration of Negroes," pp. 290–1; Frank J. Gillespie, Jr., to James B. Hibben, June 5, 1957, MHPC Papers; *Chicago Defender*, January 1, 1955.

49 [Holman D. Pettibone], Memorandum for Discussion with Mayor, Wednesday, August 13, 1947, Pettibone Papers.

50 Ibid.; Address of Mayor Martin H. Kennelly at the Chicago Association of Commerce Luncheon, September 25, 1947, MHPC Papers; Chicago Committee for Housing Action, Minutes of the Meeting of September 18, 1947, Pettibone Papers.

51 *Chicago Tribune*, November 9, 1958; *Chicago Daily News*, April 10, 1958; Wallace, "Residential Concentration of Negroes," p. 292; Statement of MHPC on proposed ordinance for approval of IIT redevelopment project in the vicinity of 32nd and State streets, November 17, 1955, MHPC Papers; Carl Condit, *Chicago: 1930–1970* (Chicago: University of Chicago Press, 1974), p. 205; Harold M. Mayer and Richard C. Wade, *Chicago: Growth of a Metropolis* (Chicago: University of Chicago Press, 1969), pp. 380–2.

52 Michael Reese Hospital, *A Progress Report, 1952* (Chicago: Michael Reese Hospital, n.d.), pp. 59–64; idem, *A Proposed Housing Program* (Chicago: Michael Reese Hospital, n.d.), pp. 6–7; Condit, *Chicago*, pp. 205–6; Mayer and Wade, *Chicago: Growth of a Metropolis*, pp. 380–2.

53 Mumford and Pettibone were clearly aware of the hospital's activities, and most observers were encouraged by the CHA's use of eminent domain on behalf of private enterprise. It should be noted, however, that Mumford and Pettibone had approached both the mayor and the governor with their plans months earlier and that the MHPC West Side study was completed just as the hospital's planning staff was created. The pragmatic search for solutions on the part of powerful interests simply led, in several instances, to the harnessing of expanded

public powers. Michael Reese Hospital, *A Progress Report*, pp. 60–1; Reginald R. Isaacs to Grant Pick et al., May 18, 1949; Notes of telephone conversation with Holman Pettibone, n.d.; Newton Farr to Milford Mumford, October 31, 1946; James C. Downs, Jr., Statement, November 6, 1946, all in the MHPC Papers.

54 "Role of Institutions," n.d.; South Side Planning Board, Minutes of the Meeting of the Subcommittee on Planning Coordination, March 13, 1947, both in the MHPC Papers.

55 Illinois Institute of Technology (IIT) et al., *An Opportunity for Private and Public Investment in Rebuilding Chicago* (Chicago: n.p., 1947).

56 The report called for the reconstruction of a 3-square-mile area bordered by 22nd Street (Cermak Road), 39th Street, the Pennsylvania Railroad, and Lake Michigan. See *An Opportunity*, pp. 4–5; John L. Van Zant to Reginald Isaacs, June 24, 1947, MHPC Papers.

57 Kramer also claimed that he, personally, "had some influence" in getting the NYLIC to come to the South Side. See Ferd Kramer, "Accomplishments of the South Side Planning Board" (mimeographed, n.d.), p. 1; Remarks by Ferd Kramer Before the Housing Committee of the City Council on February 1, 1949; Dorothy Rubel, handwritten note, n.d., all in the MHPC Papers; see also [Holman D. Pettibone], Notes on the Meeting with Metropolitan Life Insurance Company on Housing, October 24, 1947, Pettibone Papers; Colean, "A Proposal to Construct Two Redevelopment Projects in Chicago," p. 30; Kramer interview.

58 Milt [Mumford] to Holman [Pettibone], July 18, August 1, 1947; [Holman D. Pettibone], Notes on Lunch Meeting at the Offices of Metropolitan Life Insurance Company, July 2, 1947; [Holman D. Pettibone], Notes on Meeting with Metropolitan Life Insurance Company on Housing, October 8, 23, 24, 1947; H. D. Pettibone to Mr. McKendry, June 21, 1948; Holman D. Pettibone to Howard Wood, October 16, 1950, all in the Pettibone Papers.

59 Otto Nelson said later that the NYLIC invested in the project as a result of calls by Pettibone and Mumford in which they "outlined the very forward looking legislation which had been adopted by the State and City." H. A. Moore to Holman D. Pettibone, November 13, 1950; O. L. Nelson to Holman Pettibone, April 20, 1948; [Holman D. Pettibone], Notes on Conversations in New York, May 5-6, 1948, all in the Pettibone Papers.

60 Commission on Human Relations (CHR), "Monthly Report of the Executive Director, August 1948" (mimeographed, n.d.), Exhibit A, Chicago Urban League Papers (hereafter cited as CUL Papers), Manuscript Collection, The Library, UIC; Milton Mumford to Martin H. Kennelly, September 3, 1948, in the Graham Aldis Papers, Manuscript Collection, The Library, UIC.

61 Milton Mumford to Martin H. Kennelly, September 3, 1948.

62 [Pettibone], Notes on Conversations in New York, May 5-6, 1948.

63 H. D. Pettibone to Mr. McKendry, May 17, 1948; *Chicago Defender*, July 24, 1948.

64 The delays in closing Cottage Grove Avenue, which did eventually become a "major issue," resulted when the Chicago Plan Commission, responding to local pressures placed on it by aldermen, failed to support the CLCC. See Metropolitan Housing and Planning Council, Resume of Meeting of the Redevelopment Committee, October 11, 1950, MHPC Papers; Bach interview.

65 Ira J. Bach, Memorandum to the Commissioners, July 9, 1954; O. L. Nelson to Holman Pettibone, May 17, 1950; Milton Mumford to Holman Pettibone, July 18, 1950; O. L. Nelson to Martin H. Kennelly, May 12, 1950; Chicago Land Clearance Commission (CLCC), Staff Report, May 29, 1950; Ira Bach to Martin Kennelly, June 1, 1950, all in the Pettibone Papers; Bach interview; Kramer interview.

66 Address of Mayor Martin H. Kennelly before the Chicago Association of Commerce Luncheon, Sherman Hotel, Thursday, September 25, 1947; Metropolitan Housing [and Planning] Council, Minutes of the Board of Governors, June 4, 1947, both in the MHPC Papers; Statement of Mr. Taylor in Re Relocation Sites, June 23, 1948, BPI Papers.

67 Philip M. Klutznick to City Council Committee on Housing, March 31, 1949, MHPC Papers.

68 David Wallace found that the CLCC had a reputation for being "brutal" in its relocation efforts and Nicholas von Hoffman, working in Chicago throughout this period, believed that the city's "track record" on relocation was "conspicuously poor." See Wallace, "Residential Concentration of Negroes," p. 261, and Nicholas von Hoffman to Rev. Martin Farrell, February 24, 1958, in the Saul Alinsky Papers, Manuscript Collection, The Library, UIC.

69 IIT et al., *An Opportunity*, pp. 1, 49; Notes on Relocation, March 21, 1947, MHPC Papers.

70 The final report omitted the offensive reference to "nooks and crannies" but retained its statistical reliance on their anticipated appearance. See Notes on Relocation, March 21, 1947; Oscar C. Brown to Reginald R. Isaacs, June 2, 1947, MHPC Papers.

71 IIT et al., *An Opportunity*, p. 49; Notes on Relocation, March 21, 1947; Oscar C. Brown to Reginald R. Isaacs, June 2, 1947. Michael Reese Hospital, in its *Proposed Housing Program*, handled the issue in much the same way. Avoiding responsibility for the problem and placing it squarely on the shoulders of the "CHA, Negro and housing organizations," it stoically noted that its neighbors would have to endure "a measure of temporary hardship." See Michael Reese Hospital, *Proposed Housing Program*, p. 9.

72 N. S. Keith to Ira J. Bach, October 26, November 28, 1950, January 6, 1951; N. S. Keith to John McKinlay, January 5, 1951; Ira J. Bach to Raymond M. Foley, July 29, 1949; Metropolitan Housing and Planning Council, Minutes of the Redevelopment Committee, January 18, 1952,

all in the MHPC Papers; O. L. Nelson to Thomas Buck, February 20, 1951, Pettibone Papers.

73 N. S. Keith to Ira J. Bach, January 6, 1951.

74 Chicago Urban League, *Urban Renewal and the Negro in Chicago* (Chicago: n.p., 1968), pp. 4–6, passim.

75 Also, none of the "single person families" were aided by authorities. Between 800 and 1,000 individuals were thrown on the rooming-house market. Many from the Lake Meadows site went to Woodlawn, Oakland, and North Kenwood and contributed greatly to the processes of "conversion" and overcrowding in those areas. Wallace, "Residential Concentration of Negroes," pp. 268–78; Interview with Julian Levi, July 29, 1980.

76 It should be kept in mind that the Lake Meadows project forced the relocation of only a fraction of all those uprooted by new urban construction in the 1940s and 1950s. The official figures on relocation are undoubtedly low as they represent only those living on a project site at the time of an official survey; many left such areas, however, before the surveys were conducted. Still, using official records to indicate minimal displacement, about 3,500 families and nearly 1,000 individuals were uprooted from the Lake Meadows site. Between 1948 and 1963, the city estimated that almost 50,000 families (averaging 3.3 persons each) and 18,000 individuals were relocated because of government programs. Urban renewal, expressway construction, and the building of public housing accounted for nearly 80% of those displaced. Of the total relocation load for the fifteen-year period, 55.2% were black, 29.2% were white, and 15.6% were not identified by race. It should be noted, however, that the greater portion of white relocatees were displaced by highway construction, which necessarily traversed the entire city; 67.3% of the 13,585 families uprooted by highways were white. In contrast, 79.6% of the 13,043 families relocated because of urban renewal and 74.2% of the 12,035 families dispossessed by the construction of public housing were black. See Metropolitan Housing and Planning Council, Minutes of the Meeting of the Redevelopment Committee, January 8, 1951, MHPC Papers; Chicago Urban League, *Urban Renewal and the Negro in Chicago*, passim; Community Renewal Program, "Relocation in Chicago" (mimeographed, April 1964), p. 1, Tables 1, 2 and passim, The Library, UIC.

77 Elizabeth Wood to Joseph L. Moss, March 20, 1950, Raymond M. Hilliard Papers, CHS; Ferd Kramer, "The Role of Private Enterprise in Urban Redevelopment," an address before the American Society of Planning Officials, National Planning Conference, August 15, 1950, Lea Taylor Papers, CHS.

78 *Chicago Tribune*, October 30, 1947; George R. Carr to Martin H. Kennelly, October 2, 1947, Citizens' Association of Chicago Papers, CHS; Elizabeth Wood to Joseph L. Moss, March 20, 1950; Address of Mayor

Martin H. Kennelly before the Chicago Association of Commerce, September 25, 1947.

79 This was not unusual. The selection of slum sites for public housing under the Housing Act of 1949 forced the CHA to become, along with renewal and highway construction, one of the three major causes of relocation in Chicago. See note 72.

80 Forty off-site families were persuaded to enter public housing for this purpose; in one case it was necessary to move two families into public housing to free a single unit for one ineligible site family. These activities, and the continual modification of income limits, made it clear that the function of the CHA was to house not only the poor but also the relatively poor who occupied a desired piece of property. With the passage of the Housing Act of 1949 and the subsequent selection of slum sites, it was contemplated that a raise of $250 to $300 in income limitations would "add 600 families" to those site residents already eligible for public housing. See Paul S. Freedman to the Commissioners, April 23, 1951, BPI Papers; Eri Hulbert, "Memorandum on Relocation: The Chicago Housing Authority Experience" (mimeographed, n.d.), pp. 36–8, Robert E. Merriam Papers, the Department of Special Collections, University of Chicago (UC) Library.

81 Hulbert, "Memorandum on Relocation," p. 25; Albert W. Logan, "The First Quarter Century of the Chicago Housing Authority, 1937–1962" (M.A. thesis, Roosevelt University, n.d.); Elizabeth Wood to Joseph L. Moss, April 7, 1948; Mary A. Young to Stephen Green, March 15, 1948, both in the Hilliard Papers.

82 John M. Kahlert to John W. Ballow, February 6, 1950, Hilliard Papers; Hulbert, "Memorandum on Relocation," p. 19.

83 Chicago Urban League, Report on the Benjamin Family, n.d., CUL Papers; Memorandum of Conversation with Father Farrell, February 20, 1951(?), Merriam Papers.

84 Metropolitan Housing and Planning Council, Minutes of the Meeting of the Redevelopment Committee, January 8, 1951.

85 Metropolitan Housing and Planning Council, Minutes of the Meeting of the Executive Committee, March 31, 1958, and Summary of MHPC Committee Report on Modernizing the City's Organization, November 28, 1956, both in the MHPC Papers. Later attempts to kill the public housing program in the General Assembly of Illinois met the fiercest opposition from large businesses and institutional interests as well as "do-gooders." The periodic introduction of the Larson bills, which called for a referendum in the neighborhoods surrounding proposed projects before they could be built, during the early 1950s, aroused the South Side Planning Board, the MHPC, Mayor Kennelly, and others who realized that public housing "served private enterprise." The Larson bills were passed twice and twice vetoed by the governor: once by Democrat Adlai Stevenson and once by Republican

William Stratton. See Holman D. Pettibone to Martin H. Kennelly, September 18, 1952; *SSPB News*, March 1953, in the Daniel M. Cantwell Papers, CHS; Statement of Father Daniel M. Cantwell, president of the Housing Conference of Chicago, urging the defeat of Senate Bill No. 150, made at Springfield, Ill., March 17, 1953; Statement by Mayor Kennelly in Reference to Senate Bill No. 159 – 68th General Assembly, both in the Cantwell Papers; Metropolitan Housing and Planning Council, February 9, March 6, 1953; Dorothy Rubel to All Members of the Board of Governors, April 20, 1953; all in the MHPC Papers; *Chicago Daily News*, March 20, 1953.

86 Notes on the Annual Dinner of the Chicago Council of Negro Organizations, June 26, 1950, Irene McCoy Gaines Papers, CHS.

87 Handbill in CUL Papers; CHR, Minutes of the Housing Committee Meeting, May 12, 1948, Taylor Papers. Mumford's position was a pragmatic one based on his and Pettibone's intention to accord blacks separate but equal treatment. "If the program can be used to further integration," he told the CHR, "well and good." "Thus far, however, there is no certainty that . . . capital will be available. If it should come about that redevelopment projects could be built only on an all-white or all-Negro basis, the Housing Coordinator will have no choice but to get them built. But, as an absolute minimum it can be counted on that a substantial proportion of such projects will be occupied by Negroes."

88 See the Contract Between the Chicago Land Clearance Commission and the New York Life Insurance Company for the Redevelopment of an Area on the South Side of the City of Chicago, not paginated, Pettibone Papers; Memo from J. Cassels to File, October 23, 1952, American Friends Service Committee Papers (hereafter cited as AFSC Papers), Manuscript Collection, The Library, UIC; Michael Reese Hospital, *Proposed Housing Program*, p. 9.

89 Louis Wirth and Reginald Isaacs to Michael Reese Hospital Board Committee on Mandel Clinic, June 4, 1948, Louis Wirth Papers, UC Archives; Memorandum from SSPB to Redevelopment Committee, November 22, 1946, MHPC Papers; Otto Nelson, Jr., to Chicago Land Clearance Commission, November 18, 1948; Ira J. Bach to Raymond M. Foley, August 18, 1949, Pettibone Papers.

90 Milton Mumford, Handwritten note on Otto Nelson to Chicago Land Clearance Commission, November 18, 1948; Ira J. Bach to the Commissioners, July 9, 1954, Pettibone Papers; Ed Holmgren to George and Eunice Greer, October 16, 1956, AFSC Papers.

91 Archibald J. Carey to Martin Meyerson, April 28, 1954, and Archibald J. Carey to Floyd Mulkey, March 28, 1949, both in the Archibald J. Carey, Jr., Papers, CHS.

92 Milton C. Mumford to Hughston McBain, May 16, 1947; Milton C. Mumford to Martin H. Kennelly, January 21, 1949, MHPC Papers; [Holman D. Pettibone], Memorandum on Meeting on Saturday, February 26, 1949 with President Devereaux Josephs of the NYLIC, Vice-

President Dickey of J. P. Morgan and Company, and Otto Nelson of NYLIC, Pettibone Papers.

93 Byron S. Miller, Memorandum Re Proposed Non-Discrimination Ordinance for Publicly Aided Housing, n.d.; Remarks by Ferd Kramer Before the Housing Committee of the City Council on February 1, 1949; Metropolitan Housing and Planning Council, Statement on the Carey Ordinance, all in the MHPC Papers; Wallace, "Residential Concentration of Negroes," pp. 278, 278n; Citizens' Association of Chicago, "Special Report Concerning the So-Called 'Carey Ordinance' " (mimeographed, n.d.), Carey Papers; Lillian Egerton, Statement at Public Hearings on February 28, 1949, For the Citizens' Association on the Carey Housing Ordinance, Carey Papers; Harriet E. Vittum to Harold Eckhart, March 16, 1949, Citizens' Association of Chicago Papers; *Chicago Daily News*, September 17, 1948; *Chicago Tribune*, February 13, 1949; *Chicago Sun-Times*, February 28, 1949.

94 Archibald J. Carey to Harold Eckhard, n.d., Carey Papers.

95 [CAD] to Martin H. Kennelly, February 18, 1949, Carey Papers; *Pittsburgh Courier*, January 15, 1949.

96 Meeting of the Delegation from the [CAD] and Alderman Robert E. Merriam, January 26, 1949, Carey Papers; *Chicago Defender*, February 5, 12, 1949; Robert E. Merriam to Robert E. Keohane, February 9, 1949, Cantwell Papers; Archibald J. Carey to Benjamin M. Becker, February 8, 1949, Carey Papers.

97 David Wallace contends that Ferd Kramer "deliberately misquoted" facts as they pertained to New York. See also Chester R. Davis to Thomas E. Keane, February 25, 1949, Pettibone Papers.

98 Milton C. Mumford to Martin H. Kennelly, January 21, 1949; Archibald J. Carey to Milton Mumford, January 24, 1949, Carey Papers.

99 Statement of Mayor Martin H. Kennelly on the Carey Ordinance, March 2, 1949, MHPC Papers; David J. Malarcher to the Editor, *Chicago Tribune*, March 16, 1949, Carey Papers; Holman D. Pettibone to Martin H. Kennelly, March 3, 1949, Pettibone Papers; Waitstill H. Sharp, "Annual Report Essentials for the Year 1949" (mimeographed, n.d.), p. 1, CUL Papers; *Chicago Tribune*, March 3, 1949; Archibald J. Carey to Val J. Washington, April 27, 1949, Carey Papers.

100 Milton Rakove, *Don't Make No Waves – Don't Back No Losers: An Insider's Analysis of the Daley Machine* (Bloomington: Indiana University Press, 1975), pp. 258–62, 274–5; James Q. Wilson, *Negro Politics: The Search for Leadership* (New York: Free Press, 1960), pp. 25, 34–6, 78–82; Harold F. Gosnell, *Negro Politicians: The Rise of Negro Politics in Chicago* (Chicago: University of Chicago Press, 1935; reprint ed., 1967), pp. 79, 181, 190, and idem, *Machine Politics: Chicago Model* (Chicago: University of Chicago Press, 1937; reprint ed., 1968), pp. 234–5.

101 Wilson, *Negro Politics*, pp. 78–82, 178; Gosnell, *Machine Politics*, pp. 234–5.

102 Bach interview; Mike Royko, *Boss: Richard J. Daley of Chicago* (New

York: New American Library, 1971), pp. 61–3; Len O'Connor, *Clout: Mayor Daley and His City* (Chicago: Regnery, 1975), pp. 86–8.

103   Director MHPC to Randall Cooper, December 5, 1951, MHPC Papers.

104   Cornelius Teninga, Statement Made November 14, 1950, Before the Housing Committee Against the New York Life Project, Citizens' Association of Chicago Papers; Cornelius Teninga, Statement Made Before the Chicago Plan Commission, September 13, 1950, MHPC Papers.

105   List of Those Opposed to Closing of Cottage Grove AV [sic], MHPC Papers.

106   Statement on behalf of Holman D. Pettibone at Hearing of Housing Committee, November 13, 1950, Pettibone Papers; Statement by Randall H. Cooper, November 13, 1950, and Dorothy Rubel to Frank Hecht, October 18, 1950, both in the MHPC Papers.

107   Holman D. Pettibone to Otto Nelson, September 29, 1950, Pettibone Papers.

108   Metropolitan Housing and Planning Council, Minutes of the Meeting of December 3, 1951, On the Closing of Cottage Grove Ave., MHPC Papers; *Chicago Defender*, December 22, 1951; Bach interview.

109   The last vestiges of outraged opposition manifested themselves in the gunfire of snipers who harassed the wreckers as they worked. *Chicago Tribune*, May 1, 1952.

110   Holman D. Pettibone to Ira Bach, March 19, 1952, Pettibone Papers.

111   Ira Bach to Holman D. Pettibone, March 24, 1952; Holman D. Pettibone to Ira Bach, March 24, 1952, Pettibone Papers.

112   For a description of the "business creed" as it operated in the first ghetto, see Thomas L. Philpott, *The Slum and the Ghetto: Neighborhood Deterioration and Middle-Class Reform, Chicago, 1880–1930* (New York: Oxford University Press, 1978), pp. 204–5 and passim. Roy Lubove noted Pittsburgh's "dramatic expansion of public enterprise and investment to serve corporate needs" immediately following World War II and called it a "reverse welfare state." Chicagoans were well aware of the "Pittsburgh Renaissance" but, as L. D. McKendry informed Holman Pettibone, the "Pittsburgh Plan" did not include acquiring, clearing, and selling valuable inner-city property to private developers at "written-down" values. See Roy Lubove, *Twentieth Century Pittsburgh: Government, Business, and Environmental Change* (New York: Wiley, 1969), p. 106; L. D. McKendry to Mr. H. D. Pettibone, April 1, 1952, Pettibone Papers.

113   When asked to comment on this chapter, Milton C. Mumford replied: "I have no quarrel with anything you write – I don't think those of us who worked at it were as prescient or quite as Machiavellian as it appears to seem – the program just looked like something that ought to be done in the interest of a lot of people, including self-interest of course. Most things that get done, do." He also quoted Winston Churchill: "The only guide to a man is his conscience; the only shield to his memory is the rectitude and sincerity of his actions. It is very impru-

dent to walk through life without this shield, because we are so often mocked by the failure of our hopes and the upsetting of our calculations; but with this shield, however the fates may play, we march always in the ranks of honor." Milton C. Mumford to the author, July 21, 1981.

5. A neighborhood on a hill

1 Jim [Downs] to Holman Pettibone, May 1952, Holman D. Pettibone Papers, Chicago Historical Society (CHS).

2 Julia Abrahamson, *A Neighborhood Finds Itself* (New York: Harper & Row, 1959); and Peter H. Rossi and Robert A. Dentler, *The Politics of Urban Renewal* (New York: Free Press, 1961).

3 Evelyn M. Kitagawa and Karl E. Taeuber, eds., *Local Community Fact Book: Chicago Metropolitan Area, 1960* (Chicago: Chicago Community Inventory, 1963), pp. 97, 117.

4 Abrahamson, *A Neighborhood Finds Itself*, p. 11; University of Chicago Round Table, "Are Slum Neighborhoods Beyond Control?" in the Lawrence A. Kimpton Papers, University of Chicago (UC) Archives; Kitagawa and Taeuber, *Local Community Fact Book*, p. 97; Rossi and Dentler, *The Politics of Urban Renewal*, p. 21.

5 Abrahamson, *A Neighborhood Finds Itself*, p. 15.

6 *Hyde Park Herald*, March 20, 1950; Rachel Marshall Goetz, "Miracle on Fifty-Seventh Street: Hyde Park-Kenwood Tries the Bootstrap Hoist" (mimeographed, n.d.), p. 5, in the South East Chicago Commission Papers (hereafter cited as SECC Papers), the Department of Special Collections, UC Library.

7 Hyde Park-Kenwood Community Conference, Minutes of General Meeting – Hyde Park Community Group, November 8, 1949, and Minutes of Meeting of the Steering Committee – Hyde Park Community Group, November 22, 1949, both in the Hyde Park-Kenwood Community Conference Papers (hereafter cited as HPKCC Papers), the Department of Special Collections, UC Library; Abrahamson, *A Neighborhood Finds Itself*, pp. 11–20.

8 Hyde Park-Kenwood Community Conference, Report to the Executive Committee, September 18, October 23, 1950, HPKCC Papers; *Hyde Park Herald*, November 1, 1950.

9 Abrahamson, *A Neighborhood Finds Itself*, passim; Roy F. Grahn to Julia Abrahamson, February 10, 1953, in the Leon Despres Papers, CHS; [Julia Abrahamson], Report of the Executive Director to the Board of Directors, January 20, February 17, April 21, 1953, all in the HPKCC Papers.

10 Julia Abrahamson received "groundless complaints whenever a Negro family moved into a block" as it was "taken for granted that the new residents intended to break the law." This led to many "fruitless inspections." If the "idea of mob action was shocking" to middle-class

Hyde Parkers, it was also apparent that they were hardly free of racial fears. Abrahamson, *A Neighborhood Finds Itself*, p. 31; Hyde Park-Kenwood Community Conference, Minutes of a Meeting of the Steering Committee, March 20, June 12, April 17, 1950; November 22, 1949, HPKCC Papers.

11 Rossi and Dentler, *The Politics of Urban Renewal*, pp. 130–2.

12 [Julia Abrahamson], Report of the Executive Director to the Board of Directors, March 17, 1953, HPKCC Papers.

13 Abrahamson, *A Neighborhood Finds Itself*, pp. 45–9, 120–2; Rossi and Dentler, *The Politics of Urban Renewal*, pp. 111–12.

14 Abrahamson, *A Neighborhood Finds Itself*, pp. 36–8; [Julia Abrahamson], Report of the Executive Director to the Board of Directors, April 15, December 16, 1952; January 20, February 17, April 21, December 15, 1953; December 14, 1954; October 18, 1955; [James Cunningham], Monthly Report of the Executive Director, October 16, 1956; Hyde Park-Kenwood Community Conference, Minutes of the Board of Directors, January 15, May 20, 1952; May 18, 1954; June 19, September 18, 1956; all in the HPKCC Papers.

15 Hyde Park-Kenwood Community Conference, "Statement of the Policy and Objectives of the Planning Committee (mimeographed, March 18, 1953), HPKCC Papers.

16 Leslie T. Pennington to Robert E. Merriam, January 18, 1952; Hyde Park-Kenwood Community Conference, Draft of Report by the Committee on Maintaining an Interracial Community in Hyde Park-Kenwood, January 19, 1954; Hyde Park-Kenwood Community Conference, Minutes of the Board of Directors, October 18, 1955, all in the HPKCC Papers.

17 Chicago Commission on Human Relations (CHR), "Memorandum on the Airport Homes" (mimeographed, n.d.), p. 39, Chicago Urban League Papers (hereafter cited as CUL Papers), Manuscript Collection, The Library, University of Illinois at Chicago (UIC).

18 Hyde Park-Kenwood Community Conference, Minutes of the HPKCC, February 15, 1955; Minutes of the Meeting of the Board of Directors, May 18, 1954; [Julia Abrahamson], Report of the Executive Director to the Board of Directors, May 18, September 21, 1954, all in the HPKCC Papers.

19 Hyde Park-Kenwood Community Conference, Joint Statement of the Committee to Maintain an Interracial Community and the Real Estate Committee, September 18, 1956, HPKCC Papers.

20 Ibid.; Abrahamson, *A Neighborhood Finds Itself*, pp. 294–9; "The Challenge of an Interracial Community" (mimeographed, n.d.), pp. 30–4, HPKCC Papers; "Recommended Policy Concerning Urban Renewal in Chicago: Suggestions from Leslie T. Pennington on Tenant Referral and Education for Living in an Interracial Community," passim, HPKCC Papers; *Hyde Park Herald*, September 12, 1956; March 6, 1957.

21 *Chicago Defender*, May 12, 1951.

22 [Julia Abrahamson], Report of the Executive Director to the Board of
    Directors, December 12, 1952; Hyde Park-Kenwood Community Con-
    ference, Minutes of the Meeting of the Board of Directors, January 15,
    1952, both in the HPKCC Papers.

23 Abrahamson *A Neighborhood Finds Itself*, p. 187.

24 Ibid., p. 188.

25 Rossi and Dentler, *The Politics of Urban Renewal*, p. 72; Abrahamson, *A
    Neighborhood Finds Itself*, pp. 189–92; Ozzie Badal, "The Factual Back-
    ground of the 'Hyde Park-Kenwood Story': A Progress Report,
    1949–1963" (mimeographed, n.d.), HPKCC Papers.

26 One longtime Hyde Park resident felt the crime situation was "better
    now than it was fifteen or twenty years ago, both on 55th Street and
    63rd Street." Other such residents agreed. The HPKCC went to the
    police for the "facts" and learned that the crime rate in the area be-
    tween 47th Street and the Midway *decreased* in 1951. Between August
    and late September of 1951 there was "no serious criminal activity
    between 47th and the Midway." See the Notes on a Meeting Held May
    23, 1951, and HPKCC to Block Leaders, September 28, 1951, both in
    the Louis Wirth Papers, UC Archives.

27 University of Chicago Chancellor Lawrence Kimpton saw the need to
    organize the community as there were already six agencies (including
    the HPKCC) working in the area. These groups ranged from one set of
    property owners seeking a substitute for restrictive covenants to an-
    other, Kimpton noted in a derisive aside aimed at the HPKCC, which
    threw "welcoming parties for new minority families." Moreover, there
    was little coordination among the groups as they all "cordially hate[d]
    one another." See Lawrence A. Kimpton, "Responsibilities of a Uni-
    versity to Its Community," a speech delivered before the Union League
    Club, April 16, 1953, Kimpton Papers; "Summary of Background on
    Conference, Commission, & University Relationships – 11/49 to 6/56,"
    HPKCC Papers.

28 Minute Book of the Hyde Park Community Council, Minutes of the
    Meeting February 25, March 27, 1952, SECC Papers; "Proposed By-
    Laws of the South East Chicago Commission" (mimeographed, n.d.),
    University Public Relations Papers on Urban Renewal, UC Archives;
    Hyde Park-Kenwood Community Conference, Report of the Board of
    Directors, April 15, 1952; "Summary of Background on Conference,
    Commission & University Relationships," both in HPKCC Papers; *Hyde
    Park Herald*, April 2, May 14, 21, 1952; Kimpton, "Responsibilities of a
    University"; SECC Newsletter No. IV, September 17, 1953; Handbill in
    Despres Papers; South East Chicago Commission, Minutes of the Board
    of Directors, May 12, 1952, SECC Papers.

29 "Statement on Community Interests," August 16, 1944; W. C. Munnecke
    to H. C. Daines, December 7, 1944; W. C. Munnecke to Lyndon H.
    Lesch, December 7, 1944; Lyndon H. Lesch to Wilbur C. Munnecke,
    September 15, 1944; Donald W. Murphey to Leo DeTray, December 3,

1947, all in the Presidents' Papers, 1940–6, UC Archives; Community Interests Office, Financial Report – July 1, 1945, through June 30, 1946; Detailed Report of Expenditures – 7/1/46 through 6/30/47, both in the Presidents' Papers, 1945–50, UC Archives. For a record of payments throughout 1946–7, see Donald W. Murphey to Leo DeTray, November 7, 1946; January 18, February 5, March 7, April 3, July 9, August 6, October 13, 1947, all in the Presidents' Papers, 1945–50.

30 *Chicago Defender*, November 6, 1937; Horace R. Cayton, "Negroes Live in Chicago," n.d., in the Claude Barnett Papers, CHS; Mr. Fairweather to President Hutchins, November 17, 1937, and L. R. Steere to Miss Allee, December 21, 1937, both in the Presidents' Papers, 1925–45, UC Archives; *Pulse* 3 (November 1939): 3; *Daily Maroon*, December 1, 1937.

31 Mr. Hutchins to Mr. Colwell, August 14, 1943; E. C. Colwell to Robert M. Hutchins, August 21, 1943; Lyndon H. Lesch to Mr. Munnecke, July 31, 1944; Committee of Racial Equality, "Discrimination at the University of Chicago" (mimeographed, n.d.), all in the President's Papers, 1925–45. Although it still supported restrictive covenants, the university was more embarrassed about it in 1944 than in 1937. When the university's role was again exposed, Lyndon Lesch of the Treasurer's Office wrote to the business manager: "We took all precautions to prevent this thing happening by issuing my personal check to a friend who was an officer of the Association, with instructions that he should deposit my check and draw his personal check to be given to the Association as an anonymous contribution. Our instructions, unfortunately were not followed." L. H. Lesch to Mr. Munnecke, July 31, 1944, Presidents' Papers, 1925–45.

32 The policies considered were not restricted to blacks. "Are we prepared," one administrator asked, "to have Jewish students make up 80% of the medical school student body?" See E. C. Colwell to Robert M. Hutchins, August 18, 1944, President's Papers, 1925–45.

33 Bob to Willie, August 26, 1944, Presidents' Papers, 1925–45, Box 60, Folder 1.

34 Ibid.; W. C. Munnecke to Mr. R. M. Hutchins, August 21, 1944, Presidents' Papers, 1925–45.

35 "Statement on Community Interests," p. 8; Donald W. Murphey to J. A. Cunningham, December 31, 1948, Presidents' Papers, 1945–50.

36 Lyndon H. Lesch to Herbert P. Zimmerman, October 1944; H. P. Zimmerman to Mr. Chairman, November 11, 1944, both in the Presidents' Papers, 1945–50.

37 "The Central Administration," n.d., Presidents' Papers, 1925–45, Box 38, Folder 9.

38 L[awrence] A. K[impton], Notes of the Board Meeting, May 13, 1954, and Statement to Alumni, February 25 or 26, 1955, both in the Kimpton Papers.

39 Deteriorating conditions, though undesirable in themselves, were thus deemed especially threatening *because* they preceded and permitted the entry of blacks; controlling "blight" was a way to control black

immigration. In the 1950s, the removal or prevention of such conditions was also used for that same end. It was more difficult, however, to face the race question openly in that era and so the rhetoric on "slum conditions" and "deterioration" dominated most public discussions and the race issue, rather than being seen as central to the community's problems, was doomed to be an "aspect" or "factor" within the larger problem of urban renewal. Robert B. Mitchell to Ferd Kramer, February 1, 1945, Metropolitan Housing and Planning Council Papers (hereafter cited as MHPC Papers), Manuscript Collection, The Library, UIC; E. Hector Coates, Preliminary Report – Woodlawn Rehabilitation, October 10, 1944; Frank J. O'Brien to Graham Aldis, March 30, 1939, both in the Presidents' Papers, 1940–6; Chicago Plan Commission, *Woodlawn Plan* (Chicago: Chicago Plan Commission, 1946).

40 Lyndon H. Lesch to Mr. Cunningham, November 23, 1948; Donald W. Murphey to J. A. Cunningham, November 24, 1948; August 8, 1949; May 25, 1950, all in the Presidents' Papers, 1945–50.

41 Donald W. Murphey to J. A. Cunningham, June 28, 1949; Ira J. Bach to James Cunningham, March 14, 1949; Howard H. Moore to J. A. Cunningham, December 16, 1948; J. A. Cunningham to Robert J. Havighurst, December 21, 1949; Rexford G. Tugwell to J. A. Cunningham, November 29, 1948, all in the Presidents' Papers, 1945–50.

42 "Statement Concerning University Community Conservation," April 27, 1949, Presidents' Papers, 1945–50.

43 Robert E. Merriam, "Can Our Neighborhoods Be Saved?" a speech delivered before the City Club of Chicago, October 29, 1951; "Are We Saving Our Neighborhoods?" a speech delivered before the City Club of Chicago, October 26, 1953; "The Merriam Record on Neighborhood Conservation" (mimeographed, n.d.), all in the Robert E. Merriam Papers, the Department of Special Collections, UC Library; Robert E. Merriam to Sir, May 7, 1953, CUL Papers; [Julia Abrahamson], Report of the Executive Director, Board Meeting, March 18, 1952, HPKCC Papers; Chicago City Council, *Journal of the Proceedings*, July 2, 1952, pp. 3511–16; Rossi and Dentler, *The Politics of Urban Renewal*, p. 77; *Chicago Defender*, November 22, 1952.

44 Interview with Julian Levi, July 29, 1980; Rossi and Dentler, *The Politics of Urban Renewal*, pp. 77–8.

45 Rossi and Dentler, *The Politics of Urban Renewal*, pp. 77–8; [Julia Abrahamson], Report of the Executive Director, Board Meeting, March 18, 1952, HPKCC Papers; South East Chicago Commission, Minutes of the Executive Committee Meeting, June 19, July 29, 1952, SECC Papers; *Hyde Park Herald*, January 3, 1951; *Chicago Tribune*, October 23, 1952; Metropolitan Housing and Planning Council, Minutes of the Board of Governors' Meeting, March 5, 1951, MHPC Papers; MHPC, *Conservation*, 3 vols. (Chicago: MHPC, 1953).

46 A conservation area was defined as "an area of not less than 160 acres in which the structures of 50% or more of the area are residential,

having an average age of thirty-five years or more. Such an area is not yet a slum or blighted area." See "The Urban Community Conservation Act – Its Background, Purposes, and Utilization" (mimeographed, 1953), p. 9, MHPC Papers; MHPC, *Conservation*, 3:223.

47 Memorandum by Nicholas von Hoffman, January 31, 1953, Saul Alinsky Papers, Manuscript Collection, The Library, UIC; Reginald R. Isaacs to Robert Merriam, October 30, 1951, SECC Papers.

48 "The Urban Community Conservation Act," passim; Jack M. Siegel, "Slum Prevention – A Public Purpose," n.d., MHPC Papers; Earl Kribben to Walker Butler, June 30, 1952, in the Walker Butler Papers, Manuscript Collection, The Library, UIC; Metropolitan Housing and Planning Council, Minutes of the Board of Governors' Meeting, June 5, 1953; Earl Kribben to Bernice T. Van der Vries, May 18, 1953; Earl Kribben to Warren Wood, June 25, 1953, all in the MHPC Papers. See also Remick McDowell to Earl Kribben, March 9, 1953; Earl Kribben to Governor Stratton, May 12, 1953; Earl Kribben, "A Brief Explanation of the Urban Community Conservation Act and Related Legislation" (mimeographed, n.d.), all in the MHPC Papers.

49 Metropolitan Housing and Planning Council, Minutes of the Executive Committee, October 29, 1953; Sydney Stein, Jr., to Edward Eagle Brown, April 27, 1953; Metropolitan Housing and Planning Council, Minutes of the Board of Governors' Meeting, April 3, 1953, all in the MHPC Papers.

50 Lawrence A. Kimpton to Walker Butler, July 1, 1953, Butler Papers; Handwritten notes, n.d., MHPC Papers.

51 Rossi and Dentler, *The Politics of Urban Renewal*, p. 85n.

52 When the 1941 act was first passed, blacks feared displacement under its provisions and the *Defender* referred to it as the "Land-Grab Bill." See David A. Wallace, "Residential Concentration of Negroes in Chicago" (Ph.D. dissertation, Harvard University, 1953), pp. 257, 257n, 258n; *Chicago Defender*, May 3, 1941; July 5, 1947; Al F. Gorman to Martin H. Kennelly, June 24, 1953, Pettibone Papers.

53 In 1947 both Reginald Isaacs and the MHPC questioned the wisdom of granting such sweeping powers to a private corporation. See Elmer Gertz to Holman D. Pettibone, June 11, 1947, Pettibone Papers; MHPC, *Conservation*, 3:223–5; Rossi and Dentler, *The Politics of Urban Renewal*, p. 158n; Levi interview.

54 *Hyde Park Herald*, May 29, 1956; Abrahamson, *A Neighborhood Finds Itself*, p. 241.

55 Rossi and Dentler, *The Politics of Urban Renewal*, pp. 88–90.

56 William B. Harrell, University of Chicago vice-president, Howard Goodman, University of Chicago trustee, Harold Moore, University of Chicago trustee, and Albert Svoboda were among the South West Hyde Park Neighborhood Redevelopment Corporation's officers. Rossi and Dentler, *The Politics of Urban Renewal*, p. 157.

57 Abrahamson, *A Neighborhood Finds Itself*, p. 206; Rossi and Dentler, *The Politics of Urban Renewal*, pp. 90, 158–9.

58 Even though far more realistic than Abrahamson's portrayal, Rossi and Dentler still overestimate the conference's impact on the planning process. Abrahamson, *A Neighborhood Finds Itself*, pp. 226–7; Rossi and Dentler, *The Politics of Urban Renewal*, pp. 191–219.

59 "I admire the successful effort of Henry Heald and the Illinois Institute [of Technology] in this connection," Kimpton also wrote; "we must go and do likewise." See Lawrence A. Kimpton, After-Dinner Speech at Inauguration Banquet, October 18, 1951, and the Outline for Board of Trustees Meeting, January 14, 1954, both in the Kimpton Papers.

60 Lawrence A. Kimpton, Address delivered at a public forum of the forty-third grand chapter of Kappa Alpha Psi fraternity, December 27, 1953, Kimpton Papers; Statement of Lawrence A. Kimpton, Chancellor of the University of Chicago, in Support of the Hyde Park-Kenwood Urban Renewal Plan, September 22, 1958, MHPC Papers; *Hyde Park Herald*, December 30, 1953; Minutes of the Committee of 6 Meeting, May 2, June 6, July 11, December 12, 1956; January 9, February 6, 1957, all in the HPKCC Papers; William M. Spencer to Lawrence A. Kimpton, May 3, 1955, University Public Relations Papers on Urban Renewal; St. Clair Drake to Leon Despres, November 27, 1956, Despres Papers, CHS.

61 Rossi and Dentler, *The Politics of Urban Renewal*, p. 75.

62 Julian Levi, "Institutional Expansion and the Urban Setting," pp. 4–5, a speech delivered at the Massachusetts Institute of Technology, July 10, 1959, University Public Relations Papers on Urban Renewal, Box 2, Folder 1.

63 Julian Levi, "Crucial Issues – Urban Renewal," a speech delivered before the National Conference in Government, September 16, 1958, University Public Relations Papers on Urban Renewal. Levi saw the HPKCC as a "bunch of do-gooders trying to talk their way out of a difficult situation." Abrahamson, *A Neighborhood Finds Itself*, p. 218.

64 Abrahamson, *A Neighborhood Finds Itself*, p. 218. See also Metropolitan Housing and Planning Council, Minutes of the Board of Governors' Meeting, November 2, 1956, MHPC Papers; Levi interview.

65 Abrahamson, *A Neighborhood Finds Itself*, pp. 215, 217–18.

66 Martin Millspaugh and Gurney Breckenfeld, *The Human Side of Urban Renewal* (New York: Washburn, 1958), pp. 96–8; Rossi and Dentler, *The Politics of Urban Renewal*, pp. 80–3; *Hyde Park Herald*, October 8, 1953; Hyde Park-Kenwood Community Conference, Minutes of the Meeting of the Board of Directors, February 17, 1953; Minutes of the Committee of 6 Meeting, September 12, 1956, both in the HPKCC Papers.

67 Hyde Park-Kenwood Community Conference, Minutes of the Board of Directors' Meeting, September 21, 1954; [Julia Abrahamson], Report of the Executive Director to the Board of Directors, September 21,

1954; Hyde Park-Kenwood Community Conference, Minutes of the HPKCC, February 21, 1955, all in the HPKCC Papers.

68 Hyde Park-Kenwood Community Conference, Minutes of the Board of Directors' Meeting, November 20, 1956; Hyde Park-Kenwood Community Conference, Minutes of the Planning Committee Meeting, August 8, 1954; Hyde Park-Kenwood Community Conference, Minutes of the Committee of 6 Meeting, April 25, 1955, all in the HPKCC Papers.

69 Abrahamson, *A Neighborhood Finds Itself*, pp. 222–3; Rossi and Dentler, *The Politics of Urban Renewal*, pp. 95–6; Hyde Park-Kenwood Community Conference, Minutes of the Special Meeting of the Executive Committee of Board of Directors and Planning Committee, July 30, 1954; [Julia Abrahamson], Report of the Executive Director to the Board of Directors, August 17, 1954; Hyde Park-Kenwood Community Conference, Minutes of the Meeting of the Board of Directors, August 17, 1954; Hyde Park-Kenwood Community Conference, Minutes of the Planning Committee, August 4, 1954, all in the HPKCC Papers.

70 Abrahamson, *A Neighborhood Finds Itself*, p. 226; Rossi and Dentler, *The Politics of Urban Renewal*, pp. 129–30.

71 Rossi and Dentler, *The Politics of Urban Renewal*, p. 144.

72 Minutes of the Committee of 6 Meeting, January 25, 1956; [James V. Cunningham], Report of the Executive Director to the Board of Directors, December 20, 1956, both in the HPKCC Papers.

73 Hyde Park-Kenwood Community Conference, Minutes of the HPKCC, January 17, 1956, HPKCC Papers.

74 [Julia Abrahamson], Report of the Executive Director to the Board of Directors, June 15, 1954; Hyde Park-Kenwood Community Conference, "Final Report of the Special Housing Committee," approved by the Board of Directors, September 17, 1957, and October 15, 1957, HPKCC Papers; Rossi and Dentler, *The Politics of Urban Renewal*, p. 151.

75 Hyde Park-Kenwood Community Conference, Minutes of the Planning Committee Meeting, August 10, 1954, HPKCC Papers.

76 Rossi and Dentler, *The Politics of Urban Renewal*, pp. 132–3.

77 Notes of Confidential discussion with Dick Aylward, August 25, 1955; Minutes of the Committee of 6 Meeting, September 26, 1956, both in the HPKCC Papers.

78 Abrahamson, *A Neighborhood Finds Itself*, p. 207; Levi interview.

79 Abrahamson, *A Neighborhood Finds Itself*, pp. 199–200; Rossi and Dentler, *The Politics of Urban Renewal*, pp. 90–1.

80 Abrahamson, *A Neighborhood Finds Itself*, p. 231; Rossi and Dentler, *The Politics of Urban Renewal*, pp. 92–5. One 55th Street businessman complained: "No one *ever* tried to talk with the business men about the planning, to get their ideas or cooperation. All we were ever asked...was how much money we'd sink into it." The same man also believed that the "university is running the whole damn show for its own interests." See Confidential discussion with Dick Aylward.

81 [Julia Abrahamson], Report of the Executive Director to the Board of Directors, May 17, 1955; Minutes of the Committee of 6 Meeting, October 10, 1956, January 9, 1957, all in the HPKCC Papers.

82 See the Minutes of the Committee of 6 Meeting, January 25, June 27, 1956, HPKCC Papers; Rossi and Dentler, *The Politics of Urban Renewal*, p. 159; Abrahamson, *A Neighborhood Finds Itself*, p. 236, ignores race.

83 "Statement Concerning University Community Conservation," p. 3; Lyndon H. Lesch to Mr. Munnecke, May 7, 1945, Presidents' Papers, 1940–6; Abrahamson, *A Neighborhood Finds Itself*, p. 206; Rossi and Dentler, *The Politics of Urban Renewal*, p. 173; "Neighborhood Redevelopment Commission Hearing," n.d., p. 2, and Handwritten notes, n.d., both in the Despres Papers.

84 *Hyde Park Herald*, November 7, 1956; Abrahamson, *A Neighborhood Finds Itself*, pp. 237–8; Rossi and Dentler, *The Politics of Urban Renewal*, p. 174; Handwritten notes, n.d., Despres Papers. See also "Statement on University Community Conservation," p. 3.

85 Rossi and Dentler, *The Politics of Urban Renewal*, p. 175; *Hyde Park Herald*, November 7, 1956.

86 Rossi and Dentler, *The Politics of Urban Renewal*, pp. 156–90.

87 *Hyde Park Herald*, April 25, May 29, 1956.

88 Minutes of the Committee of 6 Meeting, January 25, February 7, June 27, August 22, September 26, 1956, all in the HPKCC Papers; Handwritten notes, n.d., Despres Papers; *Hyde Park Herald*, November 14, 1956; Rossi and Dentler, *The Politics of Urban Renewal*, pp. 173–4; South East Chicago Commission, Minutes of the Executive Committee Meeting, July 2, 1956, Despres Papers; WVN to DEO, November 27, 1956, University Public Relations Papers on Urban Renewal.

89 Federal monies for the project became available under the Housing Act of 1954. The Housing and Home Finance Agency reserved $25,835,000 for use in Hyde Park. Abrahamson, *A Neighborhood Finds Itself*, p. 209.

90 Ibid., p. 210.

91 Rossi and Dentler, *The Politics of Urban Renewal*, pp. 191–219.

92 Mrs. Thomas Farr et al. to Leon Despres, June 17, 1958; Milton M. Cohen to Leon M. Despres, n.d.; Mrs. Ben Friedlander to Leon M. Despres, June 14, 1958; Spencer K. Binyon to Neighbor, December 2, 1958, all in the Despres Papers.

93 Hyde Park-Kenwood Community Conference, "Final Report of the Special Housing Committee"; Hyde Park-Kenwood Community Conference, Recommendations to the Community Conservation Board, May 15, 1958; Hyde Park-Kenwood Community Conference, Minutes of the Planning Committee Meeting, February 8, 1955; May 14, 1957; Hyde Park-Kenwood Community Conference, "Purposes and Background of the Special Housing Committee," n.d.; Hyde Park-Kenwood Community Conference, Recommendations of the Planning Committee to the Board of Directors, n.d.; Hyde Park-Kenwood Community Conference, Recommendations of the Committee to the Board of Di-

rectors, n.d.; Hyde Park-Kenwood Community Conference, Recommendations of the Committee to Maintain an Interracial Community, n.d., all in the HPKCC Papers; Abrahamson, *A Neighborhood Finds Itself*, pp. 202, 256, 261; Rossi and Dentler, *The Politics of Urban Renewal*, p. 142.

94 Minutes of the Committee of 6 Meeting, February 6, November 6, 1957, both in the HPKCC Papers.

95 After his reelection, Despres noted that his relationship with the university "left a great deal to be desired." See Leon M. Despres, Answers to Questions by E. T. Brigham, n.d., and an untitled typewritten essay, both in the Despres Papers.

96 Wanda to Len, n.d., Despres Papers.

97 Alice W. Schlessinger to Leon M. Despres, September 29, 1958; Edwin Silverman to Leon M. Despres, September 30, 1958; Elly White to Leon M. Despres, September 26, 1958, all in the Despres Papers.

98 Rossi and Dentler, *The Politics of Urban Renewal*, p. 142.

99 "Final Report of the Special Housing Committee," p. 5.

100 Hyde Park-Kenwood Community Conference, Draft – Public Housing Conference Actions Recommended, May 1, 1968, HPKCC Papers.

101 Rossi and Dentler believe that the virtual exclusion of public housing from the Final Plan was the result of making the program "bland enough" to attract widespread and powerful support. This implies that had the community been more united in its demands for public housing, it would have altered basic features of their proposal to gain public acceptance. There is no evidence to suggest that the university or the SECC would have changed their fundamental policy in response to such pressures. Indeed, on much less significant issues they had successfully deflected community demands, making slight concessions, seeming concessions, or no concessions at all. See Rossi and Dentler, *The Politics of Urban Renewal*, p. 64.

102 Statements given at the public hearings on the plan may be found in the Despres Papers.

103 Leon M. Despres to Robert E. Merriam, March 17, 1958, Despres Papers.

104 Robert E. Merriam to Leon M. Despres, April 7, 1958, Despres Papers.

105 *New World*, April 18, May 2, 9, 23, June 13, July 18, 25, August 1, 15, September 5, 1958.

106 See the Text of Speech by the Very Rev. Msgr. John J. Egan, Executive Director of the Cardinal's Conservation Committee, Before the Annual Convention of the Association of Community Councils of Chicago, May 21, 1958, Alinsky Papers; Statement of the Catholic Archdiocese of Chicago, n.d., MHPC Papers; Rossi and Dentler, *The Politics of Urban Renewal*, pp. 225–39.

107 Minutes of the Committee of 6 Meeting, December 5, 1960, HPKCC Papers; Daniel M. Cantwell to R. Sargent Shriver, June 12, 1958; Ben W. Heineman to R. Sargent Shriver, June 6, 1958, both in the Daniel M. Cantwell Papers, CHS; Levi interview.

108 Hyde Park-Kenwood Community Conference, Minutes of the Meeting of the Steering Committee, December 4, 1950, HPKCC Papers.

109 *The Field Foundation, Inc., A Review of Its Activities for the Year Ended September 30, 1954* (Chicago: Field Foundation, 1954), in the Catholic Interracial Council Papers (hereafter cited as CIC Papers), CHS.

110 *Hyde Park Herald*, February 6, 1957; Hyde Park-Kenwood Community Conference, Minutes of the Planning Committee, January 8, 1957; Minutes of the Committee of 6 Meeting, October 10, 1956, both in the HPKCC Papers. "If urban renewal could not work [in Hyde Park] – in an area with assets few other communities could boast – it would not work anywhere," Julia Abrahamson wrote. Yet by her own reasoning, even if it did work in Hyde Park, its value as an example for others was severely limited. It was Hyde Park's "unique assets" that permitted it to undergo renewal and set itself apart from other communities in the first place. Also, the exceptional assumption of public responsibilities by private parties because of the embryonic nature of urban renewal agencies in Chicago would not be possible in the future. Abrahamson, *A Neighborhood Finds Itself*, pp. 308–10.

111 *Hyde Park Herald*, May 14, 1958.

112 Metropolitan Housing and Planning Council, Minutes of the Board of Governors' Meeting, January 8, 1953; February 2, 1955, MHPC Papers; MHPC to Richard J. Daley, October 17, 1957, MHPC Papers. The initial operation of the Community Conservation Board under the 1953 legislation paralleled that of the Chicago Land Clearance Commission under the Blighted Areas Redevelopment Act of 1947. Both laws were written by particular interests for specific purposes and once the agencies envisaged by the laws were set up, they were monopolized by those interests for those purposes. Planning, the executive director of the CLCC wrote in 1951, "has been a difficult task, due to the fact that the Commission was drawn into direct operations almost immediately after its organization. Most of our energy and time has been expended in carrying out the operations of the New York Life Insurance Company's project." See Ira Bach, "Present Status and Recommendations on the Commission's Program," May 1, 1951, MHPC Papers.

113 Minutes of the Committee of 6 Meeting, December 19, 1956, HPKCC Papers; Committee on the Center for Neighborhood Renewal, Minutes of Meeting, February 27, 1958, Alinsky Papers.

114 Leon M. Despres to Robert E. Merriam, March 17, 1958; Memorandum submitted by Levi et al. to Mayor, July 1955, Despres Papers; Notes of Meeting of Lawrence A. Kimpton and Mayor, July 15, 1955, Kimpton Papers.

115 Report on Meeting with Mayor Daley, August 20, 1955, HPKCC Papers.

116 Lawrence A. Kimpton to Richard J. Daley, November 11, 1958, University Public Relations Papers on Urban Renewal.

117 Kimpton, "After-Dinner Speech"; Statement in Support of the Hyde Park-Kenwood Urban Renewal Plan.
118 As Leon Despres concluded, the central administration's motives were "to build a community in which the University could remain." Leon M. Despres to Don Sharon, April 1, 1965, Despres Papers.
119 Julian Levi to Carl W. Larsen, December 1, 1958, University Public Relations Papers on Urban Renewal.
120 Rossi and Dentler, *The Politics of Urban Renewal*, p. 183.
121 "Statement of the Catholic Archdiocese of Chicago," p. 7.
122 Abrahamson, *A Neighborhood Finds Itself*, p. 203; "Project Eligibility and Relocation," n.d., Despres Papers.
123 Comments on the attached findings about the relocation from Hyde Park A and B, January 1958, in the HPKCC Papers.
124 Hyde Park-Kenwood Community Conference, Minutes of the Meeting of the Planning Committee, September 10, 1956; Minutes of the Committee of 6 Meeting, October 3, 1956, both in the HPKCC Papers.
125 St. Clair Drake to Leon M. Despres, November 27, 1956.
126 Handwritten notes, n.d., Despres Papers.
127 Kimpton, "Address delivered...[before the] Kappa Alpha Psi fraternity," p. 3.

6. Divided we stand

1 [?] to Wilfred Sykes, August 23, 1953, in the Files of the Chicago Housing Authority (CHA); *Chicago Daily News*, March 7, 1956.
2 *South Deering Bulletin*, February 7, 1957.
3 It should be remembered that the Hyde Park-Kenwood Community Conference was being formed even as whites were rioting in Englewood. The contrast drawn between the rioters and the organizers was both sharp and explicit.
4 Julia Abrahamson, Report to the Executive Committee, October 23, 1950; Report to the Steering Committee, September 18, 1950, both in the Hyde Park-Kenwood Community Conference Papers (hereafter cited as the HPKCC Papers), the Department of Special Collections, University of Chicago (UC) Library; "The Challenge of an Interracial Community," (mimeographed, n.d.), in the South East Chicago Commission Papers (hereafter cited as the SECC Papers), the Department of Special Collections, UC Library; Interview with Julian Levi, July 29, 1980.
5 Michael Novak, *The Rise of the Unmeltable Ethnics* (New York: Macmillan, 1973), p. 166.
6 Richard Polenberg, *War and Society: The United States, 1941–1945* (Philadelphia: Lippincott, 1972), pp. 99–130; John Morton Blum, *V. Was for Victory: Politics and American Culture During World War II* (New York: Harcourt Brace Jovanovich, 1976), pp. 182–220; Richard Dalfiume, "The

'Forgotten Years' of the Negro Revolution," *Journal of American History* 55 (June 1968): 90–106.

7 George Frederickson, *The Black Image in the White Mind: The Debate on Afro-American Character and Destiny, 1817–1914* (New York: Harper & Row, 1972), pp. 330–1; Gunnar Myrdal, *An American Dilemma*, 2 vols. (New York: Harper & Row, 1962), 2:1003–4; Thomas F. Gossett, *Race: The History of an Idea in America* (New York: Schocken Books, 1965), pp. 409–59.

8 Carl Degler, "The Negro in America – Where Myrdal Went Wrong," *New York Times Magazine*, December 7, 1969, pp. 64ff.

9 Myrdal, *American Dilemma*, 2:1004, 1009–11, 1022.

10 President's Committee on Civil Rights, *To Secure These Rights* (Washington, D.C.: Government Printing Office, 1947), pp. 151–73 and passim; *Chicago Defender*, November 22, 1947.

11 Louis Wirth to A. L. Foster, June 11, 1943; Untitled speech by Mr. Wirth delivered at the Post War World Council Institute, July 8, 1943, both in the Louis Wirth Papers, UC Archives.

12 Bernard J. Sheil, Untitled Address delivered before the Sierra Club, October 26, 1945; "Restrictive Covenants vs. Brotherhood," an address delivered for the [CAD], May 11, 1946; "Delinquency and Racial Minority groups," an address delivered before the Annual Conference of Catholic Charities, September 27, 1942; "Racism," n.d.; Untitled Address delivered before the graduating class of DuSable High School, Chicago, June 24, 1943; "Our Unfinished Business," an address delivered at Xavier University, Cincinnati, April 8, 1943, all in the Bernard J. Sheil Papers, Chicago Historical Society (CHS); the Most Rev. Bernard J. Sheil, "Problems Facing the Church Today," lecture delivered October 18, 1942, in the Friendship House Papers, CHS.

13 August Meier and Elliott Rudwick, *CORE: A Study in the Civil Rights Movement* (Urbana: University of Illinois Press, 1975), pp. 4–39.

14 The CAD's slogan was "Nothing can stand in the way of an idea whose time has come."

15 Catholic Interracial Council, Report of the Organizational Committee, June 7, 1945, Catholic Interracial Council Papers (hereafter cited as CIC Papers), CHS.

16 Arvarh E. Strickland, *History of the Chicago Urban League* (Urbana: University of Illinois Press, 1966), pp. 107, 119, 122, 128, 130, 132; St. Clair Drake and Horace R. Cayton, *Black Metropolis: A Study of Negro Life in a Northern City*, 2 vols. (New York: Harcourt, Brace, 1945; reprint ed., New York: Harper & Row, Harper Torchbooks, 1962), 1:90, 106, 108, 184, 190; 2:554, 741–54.

17 Chicago Commission on Human Relations (CHR), *The People of Chicago: Five Year Report, 1947–1951* (Chicago: CHR, n.d.), p. 3.

18 CHR, *Human Relations in Chicago: Inventory in Human Relations, 1945–1948* (Chicago: CHR, 1949); CHR, *Human Relations in Chicago: Report for the Year 1946* (Chicago: CHR, n.d.), pp. 78, 78n.

19   Mayor's Committee on Race Relations, *Race Relations in Chicago* (Chicago: Committee on Race Relations, 1944); Edwin R. Embree, *Summary of Mayor's Conference on Race Relations* (Chicago: n.p., 1944); *City Planning in Race Relations: Proceedings of the Mayor's Conference on Race Relations – February, 1944* (Chicago: n.p., 1944); *Human Relations in Chicago: Report of Commissions and Charter of Human Relations* (Chicago: n.p., 1945); CHR, *Fourth Chicago Conference on Civic Unity: Abridged Report of Proceedings* (Chicago: CHR, 1952); CHR, *The People of Chicago*, p. 4 and passim; "Monthly Report of the Executive Director, November-December 1947" (mimeographed, n.d.), Exhibit B, Chicago Commons Papers, CHS.

20   *Chicago Defender*, September 25, 1943; MCHR, *Human Relations in Chicago: Report for the Year 1946*, pp. 23–4; CHR, "Monthly Report of the Executive Director, February 1947" (mimeographed, n. d.), p. 2; CHR, "Monthly Report of the Executive Director, November-December 1947" (mimeographed, n.d.), Exhibit B; CAD, *Newsletter*, May 1953, p. 5; December 1953, p. 7, all in the Chicago Urban League Papers (hereafter cited as CUL Papers), Manuscript Collection, The Library, University of Illinois at Chicago (UIC).

21   *Chicago Defender*, November 20, 1943; May 17, 1946; March 22, September 13, 1947; May 3, 1952; *Monthly Summary of Events and Trends in Race Relations* 3 (June 1946): 342; CHR, "Monthly Report of the Executive Director, July 1947" (mimeographed, n.d.), p. 14, The Library, University of Illinois at Urbana-Champaign; CHR, "Second Documentary Memorandum on the White Circle League" (mimeographed, n.d.), passim, Municipal Reference Library (MRL), City Hall, Chicago.

22   Homer Jack, "Should Restrictive Covenants be Prohibited by Law?" (mimeographed, n.d.) in the [CAD] folder, CHS; *Chicago Bee*, November 19, 1944; June 10, 1945; *Chicago Sun*, March 6, 1945; Robert C. Weaver to Robert R. Taylor, February 14, 1945; Daniel M. Cantwell to Robert R. Taylor, March 20, 1945; Robert R. Taylor to Daniel M. Cantwell, April 6, 1945, all in the Daniel M. Cantwell Papers, CHS.

23   *Chicago Bee*, June 17, July 1, November 4, 1945; May 26, 1946; *Chicago Defender*, March 16, 1946; Clement E. Vose, *Caucasians Only: The Supreme Court, the NAACP, and the Restrictive Covenant Cases* (Berkeley: University of California Press, 1959), pp. 58, 72–3.

24   Metropolitan Housing [and Planning] Council, Minutes of the Meeting of the Board of Governors, June 19, 1944; Minutes – Board of Governors Regular Monthly Meeting – November 1, 1944, both in the Metropolitan Housing and Planning Council Papers (herefter cited as the MHPC Papers), Manuscript Collection, The Library, UIC; *Chicago Defender*, April 21, 1945; *Chicago Bee*, November 3, 1946.

25   Minimizing the impact of these war-related changes was the fact that 1,500 of the black units were contained in the Altgeld Gardens, a far South Side development located on an industrial site; other black apartments were situated next to a middle-class black residential area. De-

spite this, the black occupation of the Altgeld Gardens was protested, and where the CHA housed blacks in previously white areas, such as the Cabrini Homes on the North Side, friction *was* encountered.

26 Robert C. Weaver, *The Negro Ghetto* (New York: Harper & Row, 1948), pp. 193–4; Martin Meyerson and Edward C. Banfield, *Politics, Planning, and the Public Interest* (New York: Free Press, 1955), p. 121.

27 Meyerson and Banfield, *Politics, Planning, and the Public Interest,* pp. 121–8.

28 Ibid., pp. 132–3; CHR, "Policy of the Commission on Human Relations Relative to Living Space" (mimeographed, n.d.), Cantwell Papers; *Chicago Defender,* August 26, 1950.

29 See Chapter 4, this volume.

30 Ibid.

31 See Chapter 5, this volume.

32 Ibid.

33 *Hyde Park Herald,* December 30, 1953; Lawrence A. Kimpton, Address delivered at a public forum of the forty-third grand chapter of Kappa Alpha Psi fraternity, December 27, 1953, in the Lawrence A. Kimpton Papers, University of Chicago (UC) Archives.

34 Kimpton, Address.

35 Ibid. It should be noted that the speech from which these lines are drawn was a collaborative effort. Black attorney William R. Ming provided the base for the speech, and Julian Levi and Kimpton revised it. Levi, understandably, told Kimpton that "there is a good deal to be gained by your making this statement." See Julian to Larry, December 7, 1953, Kimpton Papers.

36 For Hauser's views, see U.S. Commission on Civil Rights, *Hearings: Housing* (Washington, D.C.: Government Printing Office, 1959), pp. 633–42.

37 See Chapter 5, this volume; "Statement Concerning University Community Conservation," April 27, 1949, in the Presidents' Papers, 1945–50, UC Archives.

38 Minutes of the Committee of 6, June 27, October 3, December 12, 1956; January 9, February 6, 1957, all in the HPKCC Papers.

39 U.S. Commission on Civil Rights, *Hearings,* pp. 843–4.

40 [St. Clair] Drake to Leon Despres, November 27, 1956, Leon Despres Papers, CHS.

41 Otis Duncan and Beverly Duncan, *The Negro Population of Chicago* (Chicago: University of Chicago Press, 1957), pp. 38, 40, 42, 131–2; Frank T. Cherry, "Southern In-Migrant Negroes in North Lawndale, Chicago, 1949–1959; A Study of Internal Migration and Adjustment" (Ph.D. dissertation, University of Chicago, 1965), p. 25; "Summary of N.O.R.C. Survey" (mimeographed, n.d.), HPKCC Papers.

42 See Chapter 5, this volume.

43 *South Deering Bulletin,* August 5, 26, September 10, 1955; Daniel M. Cantwell to John H. Johnson, February 1, 1947, Cantwell Papers; Memorandum Re Clergy Discussion Group, August 8, 1956, CIC Papers.

44 Elizabeth Wood to CHR, n.d., Business and Professional People for the Public Interest Papers (hereafter cited as BPI Papers), CHS.
45 William Kornblum, *Blue Collar Community* (Chicago: University of Chicago Press, 1974), pp. 17, 30, 41, 66–7, 73, 118, 140, 159, 192, 196–8, 202–3, 212–13; *South Deering Bulletin*, August 5, September 24, October 29, 1955; April 28, 1958; Operative L. G., Confidential Report, May 15, 20, June 10, 1954; all in the American Civil Liberties Union–Illinois Division Papers (hereafter cited as ACLU Papers), the Department of Special Collections, UC Library.
46 The quotation is taken from an untitled and undated typewritten report found in the CIC Papers.
47 The overwhelming consciousness of "racial" interests can be followed in the daily surveillance reports filed by the ACLU's undercover operative in the South Deering community. These reports, which cover the period between April 13 and October 6, 1954, are located in Folder 9, Box 11, and Folder 1, Box 12, ACLU Papers.
48 William Dunbaugh to Elizabeth Wood, December 9, 1946, CHA Files; *Calumet Index*, June 23, August 13, 22, 1947; *South End Reporter*, August 20, 1947; all are clippings found in the CUL Papers.
49 John Higham, *Send These to Me* (New York: Atheneum, 1975), p. 12.
50 Rudolph J. Vecoli stressed the coexistence of the Italian immigrant's desire to own his own home in Chicago and the persistence of Old World cultural traits and values. Humbert Nelli, however, even as he was arguing for the rapid assimilation of Chicago's Italians, also noted that the "purchase of property formed a principal objective" of the group and that it constituted a "major emphasis for their putting all family members to work." See Vecoli, "Chicago's Italians Prior to World War I: A Study of Their Social and Economic Adjustment" (Ph.D. dissertation, University of Wisconsin, 1963), pp. 216, 232–4; Nelli, *The Italians in Chicago, 1880–1930: A Study in Ethnic Mobility* (New York: Oxford University Press, 1970), pp. 34, 37. Chicago's Czechs are treated in Alex Gottfried, *Boss Cermak of Chicago: A Study of Political Leadership* (Seattle: University of Washington Press, 1962), pp. 25–47. See also Edward R. Kantowicz, "Polish Chicago: Survival Through Solidarity," in Melvin G. Holli and Peter d'A. Jones, eds., *The Ethnic Frontier: Essays in the History of Group Survival in Chicago and the Midwest* (Grand Rapids, Mich.: Eerdmans, 1977), pp. 179–209; Victor Greene, *For God and Country: The Rise of Polish and Lithuanian Ethnic Consciousness in America, 1860–1910* (Madison, Wis.: State Historical Society of Wisconsin, 1975), pp. 14–27; Stephan Thernstrom, *Poverty and Progress: Social Mobility in a Nineteenth Century City* (Cambridge, Mass.: Harvard University Press, 1964), pp. 115–37, 154–7, 161–2; Josef Barton, *Peasants and Strangers: Italians, Rumanians, and Slovaks in an American City* (Cambridge, Mass.: Harvard University Press, 1975), pp. 101–4; 122–3.
51 The position of the Lithuanian press, as well as that of other immigrant groups, can be followed in the translations contained in the

WPA's Foreign Language Press Survey (hereafter cited as FLPS). See *Lietuva*, December 11, 1908; August 20, September 3, 10, 1909; January 7, 1910; June 27, 1913; March 14, 1914, all in FLPS.

52 Breckinridge is quoted in Nelli, *The Italians in Chicago*, p. 34; McDowell is quoted in Thomas L. Philpott, *The Slum and the Ghetto: Neighborhood Deterioration and Middle-Class Reform, Chicago, 1880–1930* (New York: Oxford University Press, 1978), p. 233; see also Barton, *Peasants and Strangers*, pp. 123, 208, note 5; Jane Addams, *Twenty Years at Hull House* (New York: Macmillan, 1930), p. 232; idem, "The Housing Problem in Chicago," *The Annals* 20 (July-December 1902): 99–107.

53 Although finding considerable urban movement, Howard Chudacoff noted in his quantitative analysis of Omaha that he "focused on the fact of residential mobility, while avoiding the motivation for the movement." Howard Chudacoff, "A New Look at Ethnic Neighborhoods: Residential Dispersion and the Concept of Visibility in a Medium-Sized City," *Journal of American History* 60 (June 1973): 91; see also Thomas Kessner, *The Golden Door: Italian and Jewish Immigrant Mobility in New York City, 1880–1915* (New York: Oxford University Press, 1977), p. 147; Nelli, *The Italians in Chicago*, pp. 29, 34, 36, 46; Vecoli, "Chicago's Italians," pp. 189–209; Kathleen Neils Conzen, "Immigrants, Immigrant Neighborhoods, and Ethnic Identity: Historical Issues," *Journal of American History* 66 (December 1979): 603–15.

54 Nelli, *The Italians in Chicago*, pp. 204, 206, 243; Vecoli, "Chicago's Italians," pp. 210–19.

55 Edith Abbott, *The Tenements of Chicago, 1908–1935* (Chicago: University of Chicago Press, 1936), pp. 81–4; *Interpreter*, June 1936, and Vladimir Geringer to J. Monaghan, September 13, 1937, both in FLPS.

56 In studying Jews and Italians in New York, Kessner found persistence rates for the immigrants rising even as the settlement of new uptown areas caused many to "disperse from the city core"; the opening of these districts had the concomitant effect of keeping more newcomers in the city. "Flexibility," he concluded, "added to rather than detracted from stability." Kessner, *The Golden Door*, pp. 148, 160. It should also be noted here that both Kessner and Nelli have effectively criticized Paul Frederick Cressey's earlier model of population succession. But Nelli, at least, implicitly accepts Cressey's link between outward movement and assimilation – his main point of dispute seems to be simply that Cressey underestimated the amount of Italian movement. It should be clear that the mere fact of movement does not necessarily prove assimilation. See Paul Frederick Cressey, "Population Succession in Chicago, 1898–1930," *American Journal of Sociology* 44 (July 1938): 59–69; idem, "The Succession of Cultural Groups in Chicago" (Ph.D. dissertation, University of Chicago, 1930); Richard G. Ford, "Population Succession in Chicago," *American Journal of Sociology* 56 (September 1950): 156–60; Kessner, *The Golden Door*, pp. 156–60; Nelli, *The Italians in Chicago*, pp. 43–53, 204–6, 243.

57 *Report of the U.S. Immigration Commission*, 42 vols. (Washington, D.C.: Government Printing Office, 1911), 26:329. See also Gerald D. Suttles, *The Social Order of the Slum: Ethnicity and Territory in the Inner City* (Chicago: University of Chicago Press, 1968); William Kornblum, *Blue Collar Community*; Herbert Gans, *The Urban Villagers* (New York: Free Press, 1962).

58 For the propensity of the second generation to purchase homes more frequently than other native-born Americans, see Stanley Lieberson, "Comparative Segregation and Assimilation of Ethnic Groups" (Ph.D. dissertation, University of Chicago, 1960), pp. 138–40. Lieberson also makes it clear that there is something more than economic competence at work here. He found that high ownership groups had lower median home values and lower median rents than groups with smaller proportions of homeowners.

59 The community area data must be used with caution, even though the ethnic composition of the area is known, because we do not know which individuals owned homes. Despite this difficulty, however, the community area data does appear to be consistent with the other evidence. With this in mind, the ethnic composition of the selected areas should be noted. Interestingly, North Lawndale had the highest percentage of foreign-born (59.3%). More than half (53.5%) of North Lawndale's foreign-born, however, were Russians, and the next largest groups were the Poles (15.7%) and Germans (12.5%), indicating the sources of the area's heavily Jewish population. Englewood, with a much higher rate of homeownership, had only 19.4% of its residents born outside the United States. As a predominantly Irish and German neighborhood, however, it still displayed relatively high rates of homeownership and persistence despite the fact that most of its inhabitants were born in the United States by the mid-twentieth century. As expected, Hyde Park had but 12.4% of its population foreign-born (29.1% of those were German and 25.1% were Russian, again indicating the sources of its strong Jewish contingent), whereas West Lawn, Roseland, and South Deering had 25%, 34.6%, and 44.4% of their populations born outside the United States. Most significant here, Roseland had 20.3% of its foreign-born of Scandinavian origin and another 26.2% listed as "Other" (probably reflecting its Dutch founders who did not have their own category). The largest specified group in South Deering was the Italian contingent (19%), but 41.7% of its foreign-born population was also listed as "Other" and certainly reflects the area's Slavic population. The largest foreign-born groups in West Lawn were the Germans (32%), Italians (13.6%), and the Lithuanians (11.8%). All of this data is drawn from Chicago Plan Commission, *Residential Chicago* (Chicago: Chicago Plan Commission, 1943).

60 *Chicago Defender*, October 20, 1958; CHR, "Monthly Report of the Executive Director, November–December 1947," Exhibit B, pp. 2–3; Kath-

erine Brueher, "A Study of Negro-White Relations in Chicago," Summer 1948, both in the Chicago Commons Papers, CHS.

61 The pattern of response in North Lawndale is clearly revealed by innumerable documents in the Greater Lawndale Conservation Commission Papers (hereafter cited as GLCC Papers), CHS. Jews, British immigrants, and native Americans offered the least resistance to racial succession in Cleveland during the 1920s as well. See Kenneth L. Kusmer, *A Ghetto Takes Shape: Black Cleveland, 1870–1930* (Urbana: University of Illinois Press, 1976), p. 170.

62 Daniel M. Cantwell, "Postscript on the Cicero Riot," *The Commonweal* 54 (September 14, 1951): 544.

63 Homer A. Jack, "Cicero Nightmare," *The Nation* 173 (July 28, 1951): 64–5; William Gremley, "Social Control in Cicero," *British Journal of Sociology* 3 (1952): 326.

64 It was not simply ownership but also the proper maintenance of property that was elevated to the status of a "moral concept." See Gremley, "Social Control in Cicero," p. 331; Mary Yedinak, "Cicero – Why It Rioted" (B.A. thesis, University of Illinois at Urbana-Champaign, 1967), pp. 39–41, 48, 57, 61, 72.

65 *South Deering Bulletin*, May 21, 1955.

66 Howard Chudacoff believes that the "visibility" of particular groups in specific places results in the labeling of "ethnic" neighborhoods. Unless, however, one also implies that a strong measure of *control* accompanies "visibility," the concept is incomplete. Kantowicz has correctly criticized Chudacoff and Nelli for their failure to take into account the "social and cultural aspects of the ghetto." See Chudacoff, "A New Look at Ethnic Neighborhoods," pp. 77, 89; Kantowicz, "Polish Chicago," p. 393, note 10; Suttles, *The Social Order of the Slum*, pp. 41–60, 99–118 and passim. Perhaps this lasting sense of ethnic proprietorship resembles nothing so much as it does the establishment of one of John Higham's "charter groups" on a neighborhood scale. In the mid-twentieth century, however, such urban communities were faced not with the prospect of assimilating newcomers but with that of being overwhelmed. In this sense, such local "founding fathers," could, perhaps, be compared with New England intellectuals in the last decade of the nineteenth century. See Higham, *Send These to Me*, p. 6.

67 Even through the 1930s, the Cicero-Berwyn area was viewed as a place not where "assimilated" Czechs could "melt" into the larger American society but as a locale where "the younger and more ambitious generation has taken another leap ahead." Although modern Chicagoans may question the characterization of these areas as "beauty spots," the significant fact was that the "wholly detached" or "two-family type" dwellings were viewed not as status symbols in an abstract sense but as a mark of achievement for the Czech community. *Interpreter*, June 1936, and Vladimir Geringer to J. Monaghan, Septem-

ber 13, 1937, both in FLPS; Gremley, "Social Control in Cicero," p. 330.

68 *Dziennik Chicagoski*, October 10, 1891, FLPS; Untitled essay, July 10, 1937, Stephen S. Bubacz Papers, Manuscript Collection, The Library, UIC.

69 Visitation Parish, *Diamond Jubilee* (Chicago: Visitation Parish, n.d.), pp. 23, 25, 28, 29, 30.

70 Zorita Wise Mikva, "The Neighborhood Improvement Association: A Counter-force to the Expansion of Chicago's Negro Population" (M.A. thesis, University of Chicago, 1951), pp. 23, 23n; Stanley Buder, *Pullman: An Experiment in Industrial Order and Community Planning* (New York: Oxford University Press, 1967), pp. 80, 122. See also the *Calumet Index*, June 20, 1949 celebrating the 100th anniversary of the founding of the Roseland settlement.

71 Judy Miller, Report from Trumbull Park, October 10, March 14, 1957, both in the American Friends Service Committee Papers (hereafter cited as AFSC Papers), Manuscript Collection, The Library, UIC; Operative L. G., Confidential Report, May 7-9, June 10, 17, 21, July 27, 30, September 3, 1954, all in the ACLU Papers.

72 A survey by Bruno Bettelheim and Morris Janowitz revealed that the level of hostility toward intermarriage "was most similar to that displayed against close residence with Negroes." They also found that the difference between the number of those who objected to Negroes moving in next door and of those who thought "intermarriage . . . should be prevented [was] below statistical significance." Bruno Bettelheim and Morris Janowitz, *Social Change and Prejudice Including Dynamics of Prejudice* (Glencoe, Ill.: Free Press, 1964), pp. 134, 134n. Alvin Winder found that even those whites who stayed as blacks moved into their neighborhood planned to leave when their young children reached adolescence; they feared the social ties they would make as they reached dating age. See Alvin Winder, "White Attitudes Towards Negro-White Inter-Action in an Area of Changing Racial Composition," *Journal of Social Psychology* 41 (February 1955): 92. See also Operative L. G., Confidential Report, May 17, 18, 30, 1954, ACLU Papers.

73 *Calumet Index*, June 23, 1947, clipping in the CUL Papers; Kornblum, *Blue Collar Community*, p. 213.

74 Joseph Beauharnais to Chicago Urban League, October 26, 1951, CUL Papers; Cicero Civic Commission, *This Is Cicero* (n.p., n.d.); *Chicago Daily News*, November 1, 1956; *Daily Calumet*, August 15, 1953; *Calumet Index*, June 19, 23, August 25, 1947, all clippings in the CUL Papers; Philip Johnson, *Call Me Neighbor, Call Me Friend* (New York: Doubleday, 1965), p. 27; Winder, "White Attitudes," pp. 94–5; *Chicago Defender*, January 4, 1947; Joseph R. Thomas, "Race Relations in Chicago," n.d., Holman D. Pettibone Papers, CHS.

75 Metropolitan Housing [and Planning] Council, Minutes of the Board

Meeting, June 15, 1942, MHPC Papers; U.S. Commission on Civil Rights, *Hearings*, pp. 770–1.

76 *South Deering Bulletin*, September 10, 1955.

77 For the sense of travail among traditionalists who saw "Americanism" entering their "homes through doors and windows," see *Dziennik Zwiazkowy*, December 5, 1911, FLPS.

78 "Goodbye Dixie – Chicago Here We Come" (mimeographed, n.d.), ACLU Papers.

79 *South Deering Bulletin*, May 7, 1955, copy found in the CIC Papers; ibid., July 31, 1958; quotation taken from "A New Approach to Residential Segregation – The East Side Civic League," n.d., AFSC Papers; Operative L. G., Confidential Report, May 7, 18, June 5, 7, 17, 18, 20, 21, July 27, 1954, all in the ACLU Papers.

80 William E. Geidt and John E. Cullerton to H. T. Kearney, September 10, 1953; K. Koster to CUL, January 19, 1954; Memorandum from Board of CUL to the Community Fund's Special Committee, August 3, 1954; H. B. Law to Linn Brandenburg, September 15, 1954; Sidney Williams to Carey McWilliams, May 20, 1954, all in the CUL Papers; Sidney Williams to CIC, October 15, 1953, CIC Papers; Strickland, *History of the Chicago Urban League*, pp. 182–3.

81 Rose Helper, *Racial Policies and Practices of Real Estate Brokers* (Minneapolis: University of Minnesota Press, 1969), pp. 172–3, 255–6, and passim.

82 Yedinak, "Cicero," pp. 26–7; Speech by Senator Paul Douglas in Illinois on the Cicero Riots and Their Aftermath, n.d.; Herbert Monte Levy to Joseph Rauh, Jr., Esq., September 20, 1951; Edward H. Meyerding to Sen. Paul Douglas, October 31, 1951; "Indictments Returned by the Cook County Grand Jury Investigating the Cicero Riot" (mimeographed, September 18, 1951), all in the ACLU Papers; Confidential Memorandum to File from D. McNamara, November 26, 1951; David McNamara to Will Katz, October 29, 1951, both in the CIC Papers; Gremley, "Social Control in Cicero," pp. 327, 337.

83 It was in the wake of this riot that the White Circle League was created. Displaying a mixture of antiblack and antisubversive themes, the league, from its inception, wanted to "oust the Reds from America" as well as to "preserve white neighborhoods." See CHR, "Documentary Report of the Anti-Racial Demonstrations and Violence Against the Home and Persons of Mr. and Mrs. Roscoe Johnson, 7153 St. Lawrence Avenue, July 25, 1949" (mimeographed, n.d.), pp. 14, 21, 23, 24, 28, Appendix D, CUL Papers; the goals of the White Circle League were emblazoned on its stationery. See, for example, Joseph Beauharnais to CUL, October 26, 1951, CUL Papers.

84 Joseph H. McGarry, "Trials of Defendants in Peoria Street Disturbances" (mimeographed, 1950), pp. 4–5 and passim, CUL Papers.

85 See Hyde Park-Kenwood Community Conference, Minutes of a Meeting of the Steering Committee, March 20, 1950, HPKCC Papers; CHR,

"Peoria Street Incident" (mimeographed, n.d.), passim, MRL; CHR, Meeting of the Mayor's Commission on Human Relations, Friday, November 18, 1949, Chicago Commons Papers; Edgar Bernhard to Mayor Martin Kennelly, November 21, 1949; "Vultures on Peoria Street" (mimeographed, n.d.); American Civil Liberties Union, Minutes of the Executive Committee, November 17, 1949; Ed to Edgar Bernhard, November 19, 1949, all in the ACLU Papers; David McNamara to Raymond A. Cowell, February 19, 1952, CIC Papers; *Chicago Sun-Times*, November 30, 1949; *Pittsburgh Courier*, April 1, 1950; W. H. Sharp to Editor, *Chicago Daily News*, August 16, 1950, CUL Papers.

86   CHR, "Record of Events Prior to Move-In Day at Fernwood Park Homes" (mimeographed, n.d.), passim, CUL Papers; Community Relations Service, "Housing and Race Relations in Chicago" (mimeographed, September 22, 1948), Archibald J. Carey, Jr., Papers, CHS.

87   *Calumet Index*, August 18, September 8, 1947; *South End Reporter*, August 20, 1947, all clippings found in the CUL Papers; see also Homer Jack, "Documented Memorandum XIII: The Mayor's Commission on Human Relations" (mimeographed, n.d.), passim, Friendship House Papers.

88   The *South Deering Bulletin* claimed that the CHA was filled with "Comrades and some red travelers" [sic] who wanted to "mix" the "colored people and the foreign-born." See the *South Deering Bulletin*, June 10, 1955; *Calumet Index*, June 16, 1947, clipping in the CUL Papers; Lloyd Davis to Francis W. McPeek, September 24, 1954; *Daily Calumet*, January 4, 1955, both in the CIC Papers; *Southeast Economist*, March 22, 1956, clipping in the AFSC Papers; *Daily Calumet*, October 14, 1953, and *South End Reporter*, October 21, 1953, both quoted in CHR, *The Trumbull Park Homes Disturbances: A Chronological Report August 4, 1953 to June 30, 1955* (Chicago: CHR, n.d.), pp. 24–5.

89   Cornelius Teninga, Statement Made November 14, 1950, Before the Housing Committee Against New York Life Project, Citizens' Association of Chicago Papers, CHS; Cornelius Teninga, Statement Made Before the Chicago Plan Commission, September 13, 1950, Pettibone Papers.

90   Notes on Alderman DuBois's statement on the Carey Ordinance at the March 2, 1949, Council Meeting, Carey Papers.

91   "Family Guide for the Archives of the Chicago Historical Society," in the guide to the Holman D. Pettibone Papers, CHS; *Chicago Tribune*, March 15, 1952; Gottfried, *Boss Cermak*, p. 91; Lloyd Wendt and Herman Kogan, *Big Bill of Chicago* (Indianapolis: Bobbs-Merrill, 1953), p. 151; Devereux Bowly, *The Poorhouse: Subsidized Housing in Chicago, 1895–1976* (Carbondale: Southern Illinois University Press, 1978), p. 49; Meyerson and Banfield, *Politics, Planning, and the Public Interest*, pp. 45–55; Operative R. B., Report on Carl Buck, August 9, 1954; Operative L. G., Confidential Report, June 15, 1954; Edward H. Meyerding to Francis McPeek, October 27, 1954, all in the ACLU Papers; Homer

Jack, "Trumbull Park: A National Symptom of the Shame and Glory of the Churches" (mimeographed, n.d.), MHPC Papers.

92 Memorandum of interview with Reginald Isaacs – July 3, 1951, Robert E. Merriam Papers, the Department of Special Collections, UC Library.

93 Typed report by von Hoffman, Mackelman [sic] – Housing Coordinator's Office, July 12, 1957, Saul Alinsky Papers, Manuscript Collection, The Library, UIC; Levi interview.

94 Levi interview.

95 Ibid.

96 Cornelius Teninga, Statement Made Before the Chicago Plan Commission, September 13, 1950; *South Deering Bulletin*, February 7, 1957.

97 *Chicago Defender*, July 3, 1943; Waitstill H. Sharp, "Annual Report Essentials for the Year 1949" (mimeographed, n.d.), CUL Papers; B. E. Schaar, "Discrimination, Fear, and FEPC," February 1953, CUL Papers.

98 Jack, "Cicero Nightmare," pp. 64–5; CHR, "Record of Events Prior to Move-In at Fernwood Park," p. 3; *Chicago Sun-Times*, July 14, 1951; Chicago Division, ACLU to Editor, *Chicago Daily News*, December 9, 1946, ACLU Papers; John L. Yancey to Hon. Martin H. Kennelly, August 13, 1953, CIC Papers; *Chicago Defender*, November 19, 1949; *New York Times*, July 15, 24, 1951.

99 Memorandum from George Houser and Bayard Rustin to Cicero Committee of the [CAD], n.d., AFSC Papers; P. P. Pullen to Kenneth E. Rice, March 29, 1945, Pettibone Papers; Ruth Sable to Sidney Williams, n.d., CUL Papers; Report from Judy Miller, September 19, 1957; Diane to Ed Holmgren, October 18, 1956, both in AFSC Papers.

100 Address delivered by Robert Sargent Shriver, Jr., president of the Catholic Interracial Council of Chicago, December 9, 1957, CIC Papers.

101 Report to the Field Foundation, November 30, 1951; Memo to Housing Opportunities Program Committee from Ed Holmgren Re Trumbull Park Program Proposals, January 19, 1956, both in AFSC Papers; Daniel M. Cantwell to Will, August 25, 1951, Cantwell Papers; Bayard Rustin, Memorandum to Joint Committee of the American Friends Service Committee and the Catholic Interracial Council, September 11, 1951, CIC Papers. For the proposal to infiltrate South Deering, see the Memo to Barbara Moffett from Ed Holmgren Re Housing Sessions – CRP Round-Up, January 16, 1956, AFSC Papers.

102 Community Relations Service, "Housing and Race Relations in Chicago," p. 53.

103 *Chicago Maroon*, April 3, 1956; *South Deering Bulletin*, March 8, 1956.

104 U.S. Commission on Civil Rights, *Hearings*, pp. 769–77, 910–11.

105 Ibid.; Memo from Judy Miller, August 25, 1959, AFSC Papers.

106 Newton Farr, "Errors in the New York Life Project," n.d., Pettibone Papers.

107 *South Deering Bulletin*, October 1, 1955; *Chicago Tribune*, January 31, 1952.

108 Catholics, especially urban Catholics, have been identified as strong supporters of McCarthyism. Although no final judgments can be made on the basis of the analysis here, it does suggest that domestic issues and some deep social changes provided a receptive audience for the Wisconsin senator's charges of subversion. At any rate, it is clear that there was considerable concern about "Reds" in government well before McCarthy became nationally prominent (although his popularization of the issue undoubtedly gave it both additional credence and respectability).

109 Memorandum Re problems confronting CIC in its dealings with the clergy, n.d., CIC Papers.

7. Making the second ghetto

1 Earl Kribben to Governor William Stratton, May 12, 1953, and June 30, 1953, both in Metropolitan Housing and Planning Council Papers (hereafter cited as the MHPC Papers), Manuscript Collection, The Library, University of Illinois at Chicago (UIC); "The Loop and the Slums" (mimeographed, November 3, 1953), MHPC Papers.

2 Statement of William Schmidt, n.d.; Metropolitan Housing and Planning Council, Minutes of the Board of Governors' Meeting, November 14, 1952, both in the MHPC Papers; Memorandum by Nicholas von Hoffman, January 31, 1953, Saul Alinsky Papers, Manuscript Collection, The Library, UIC.

3 For vigilantism, see Richard Maxwell Brown, *Strain of Violence: Historical Studies of American Violence and Vigilantism* (New York: Oxford University Press, 1977); idem, "Historical Patterns of Violence in America" and "The American Vigilante Tradition," both in Hugh Davis Graham and Ted Robert Gurr, eds., *Violence in America: Historical and Comparative Perspectives* (New York: New American Library, 1969), pp. 45–84, 154–217; see also Eric J. Hobsbawm, *Primitive Rebels: Studies in Archaic Forms of Social Movement in the 19th and 20th Centuries* (New York: Norton, 1965), pp. 108–25; Charles Tilly, "Collective Violence in European Perspective," in Graham and Gurr, *Violence in America*, p. 10; idem, "The Changing Place of Collective Violence," in Melvin Richter, ed., *Essays in Theory and History* (Cambridge, Mass.: Harvard University Press, 1970), pp. 139–64.

4 *Chicago Defender*, October 30, December 11, 1948; August 27, 1953.

5 Interview with Fred Henderson, June 29, 1951[?], Robert E. Merriam Papers, the Department of Special Collections, University of Chicago (UC) Library; Memorandum from J. Cassels to File re visit with Fred Henderson, September 11, 1952; Memorandum from J. Cassels to File re visit with Cameron Urquhart, July 28, 1952, both in the American Friends Service Committee Papers (hereafter cited as AFSC Papers), Manuscript Collection, The Library, UIC; *Chicago Defender*, May 1,

1954; Memorandum to Alinsky from Nicholas von Hoffman, November 30, 1959, Alinsky Papers.

6   Chicago Commission on Race Relations (CCRR), *The Negro in Chicago* (Chicago: University of Chicago Press, 1922), p. 115.

7   *Chicago Defender*, September 14, 1946; CHR, "Monthly Report of the Executive Director, February 1947" (mimeographed, n.d.), p. 11; CHR, "Monthly Report of the Executive Director, August 1948" (mimeographed, n.d.), pp. 13–15, both in the Chicago Urban League Papers (hereafter cited as CUL Papers), Manuscript Collection, The Library, UIC; see also Chapter 2, this volume, for the frequency of post–World War II violence in Bridgeport.

8   CHR, "Report on 3309 South Lowe Avenue" (mimeographed, n.d.), passim, Municipal Reference Library (MRL), City Hall, Chicago; Mike Royko, *Boss: Richard J. Daley of Chicago* (New York: New American Library, 1971), p. 134.

9   *Chicago Defender*, May 8, 1948; Jane Jacobs, *The Death and Life of Great American Cities* (New York: Vintage Books, 1961), pp. 297–9; *The New World*, April 25, 1958; Martin Millspaugh and Gurney Breckenfeld, *The Human Side of Urban Renewal* (New York: Washburn, 1953), chap. 4.

10 An obvious exception to this generalization is the Cicero disorder where a large disturbance *was* successful in maintaining the area's racial homogeneity and was not symptomatic of a breakdown in community solidarity. Cicero did not, however, border the Chicago ghetto and was not subjected to the persistent pressure endured by Park Manor, Englewood, and Bridgeport.

11 Elizabeth Wood to Raymond A. Voight, October 28, 1940; Elizabeth Wood to May Lumsden, May 23, 1938; Elizabeth Wood to Mr. Abraham Freedman, March 17, 1942; Emil G. Hirsch to Priscilla Gray, February 16, 1943; Elizabeth Wood to Catherine Henck, September 10, 1942; Elizabeth Wood to the Commissioners, August 2, 1943, all in the Business and Professional People for the Public Interest Papers (hereafter cited as BPI Papers), Chicago Historical Society (CHS); A. L. Foster to Lea Taylor, November 24, 1937, and January 28, 1938, both in the Lea Taylor Papers, CHS; Minutes of the CHA, January 17, 1938, Chicago Housing Authority (CHA). The neighborhood composition rule was adopted from the Department of the Interior; devised by Harold Ickes, it was accepted by blacks and "public housers" alike in the 1930s. See Martin Meyerson and Edward C. Banfield, *Politics, Planning, and the Public Interest* (New York: Free Press, 1955), pp. 121–2. See also David A. Wallace, "Residential Concentration of Negroes in Chicago" (Ph.D. dissertation, Harvard University, 1953), pp. 225, 227n.

12 Elizabeth Wood to Catherine Henck, September 10, 1942; H. A. White to Elizabeth Wood, February 3, 1944; Elizabeth Wood to the Commissioners, August 2, 1943, all in the BPI Papers; Meyerson and Banfield, *Politics, Planning, and the Public Interest*, pp. 121–3. The 80/20 policy for

the Cabrini Homes represented a desire to adhere to the neighborhood composition rule and also a new goal of producing integrated projects. Selecting a "mixed" area, the CHA envisaged a "mixed" development. The Brooks Homes, another wartime project, similarly had a projected 80/20 tenant split, but with a black majority. As at Cabrini, it was impossible to secure sufficient white tenants and the project became all black. See Devereux Bowly, Jr., *The Poorhouse: Subsidized Housing in Chicago, 1895–1976* (Carbondale: Southern Illinois University Press, 1978), pp. 40–2.

13 Meyerson and Banfield, *Politics, Planning and the Public Interest*, pp. 123–6; Chapter 6, this volume.

14 Interestingly, ex-CHA Commissioner Robert R. Taylor felt that the CHA could "have avoided racial trouble" if it had placed all the temporary veterans' projects on the North or Northwest sides. This, of course, is problematical, but it is likely that Taylor was implicitly referring to what should have been the anticipated reactions of the city's heavily ethnic and working-class South Side. Memorandum from J. Cassels to File re Visit with Robert Taylor, June 12, 1952, AFSC Papers.

15 CHR, "Memorandum on the Airport Homes" (mimeographed, n.d.), p. 9, CUL Papers; [CAD], "Documented Memorandum VIII: The Racial Factor in the Airport Housing Dispute" (mimeographed, n.d.), p.1, Welfare Council of Chicago Papers, CHS; Daniel M. Cantwell to Edward J. Kelly, December 3, 1946, Daniel M. Cantwell Papers, CHS; Edward J. Kelly to Rev. Daniel M. Cantwell, December 21, 1946, Cantwell Papers; for Kelly's "protection" of the CHA, see Meyerson and Banfield, *Politics, Planning, and the Public Interest*, p. 128.

16 CHR, "Memorandum on the Fernwood Park Homes" (mimeographed, n.d.), p. 31, CUL Papers; Archibald J. Carey to Dorothy C. Patton, August 18, 1947, in the Archibald J. Carey, Jr., Papers, CHS; Chicago City Council, *Journal of the Proceedings*, October 15, 1947, p. 1032; Paul Michael Green, "Irish Chicago: The Multiethnic Road to Machine Success," in Melvin G. Holli and Peter d'A. Jones, eds., *Ethnic Chicago* (Grand Rapids, Mich.: Eerdmans, 1981), pp. 212–59.

17 Chicago City Council, *Journal of the Proceedings*, October 15, 1947, p. 1032; *Chicago Defender*, December 6, 1947; Minutes of the Board of Governors' Meeting, November 5, 1947, MHPC Papers; Statement of Robert R. Taylor, Chairman of the Authority to the City Council Subcommittee on the Housing Authority Hearings, November 20, 1947, Citizens' Association of Chicago Papers, CHS; Daniel M. Cantwell to Martin H. Kennelly, November 5, 1947, Cantwell Papers; Typed Agenda for the CHA Meeting, November 5, 1947; "The Authority Welcomes an Investigation," n.d.; Milton Shufro to Archibald J. Carey, October 16, 1947, all in the Carey Papers.

18 Zorita Wise Mikva, "The Neighborhood Improvement Association: A Counter-force to the Expansion of Chicago's Negro Population" (M.A. thesis, University of Chicago, 1951), pp. 29–38 and passim; Fannie R.

Karant to Elizabeth Wood, October 2, 1947; CHA Inter-Office Memorandum from Edward J. Fruchtman to Elizabeth Wood, November 4, 1947, both in the Carey Papers.

19 Handwritten notes by Holman D. Pettibone, n.d.; Holman D. Pettibone to Martin Kennelly, January 2, 1952, both in the Holman D. Pettibone Papers, CHS; Statement of Ferd Kramer to the Senate Committee on Efficiency and Economy – Springfield, Ill., March 17, 1953, Cantwell Papers; Statement of Mr. Taylor in Re Relocation Sites, June 23, 1948, BPI Papers; Metropolitan Housing [and Planning] Council, Minutes of the Board of Governors, June 4, 1947; Statement by Winholtz, Executive Director, South Side Planning Board to City Council, February 27, 1950, both in the MHPC Papers; see also Chapter 4, this volume.

20 *Chicago Tribune*, October 16, 1947; *Chicago Times*, October 15, 1947.

21 Wayne McMillen, Statement to the Joint Committee on Housing, November 7, 1947; CHA, Untitled typewritten statement, October 27, 1947; "Report on the Chicago Housing Authority," n.d., all in the MHPC Papers; "A Digest of Hearings Held for the Study of the Chicago Housing Authority, November 20–21, 24, 1947," p. 3, Chicago Commons Papers, CHS.

22 Helen A. Shanahan to Gentlemen, October 20, 1947, Citizens' Association of Chicago Papers; *Southtown Economist*, October 19, 22, 1947; Hyde Park Community Planning Association, *Newsletter*, October 28, 1947; Leverett Lyon to Holman D. Pettibone, October 28, 1947, all in the Pettibone Papers.

23 *Chicago Tribune*, October 30, 1947.

24 George R. Carr to Honorable Martin H. Kennelly, October 2, 1947; Citizens' Association of Chicago, Staff Recommendations on Housing Bond Referendum, September 25, 1947; "A Report Concerning Housing Bond Issues Submitted to Referendum November 4" (mimeographed, n.d.), all in the Citizens' Association of Chicago Papers.

25 Chicago City Council, *Journal of the Proceedings*, March 15, 1948, p. 2046.

26 Ibid., p. 2049; "Report on the Chicago Housing Authority," n.d., Carey Papers; "A Digest of Hearings," passim. Members of the "technical advisory committee," who worked closely with the aldermen and were largely responsible for the subcommittee's report, were James C. Downs, Jr., George Dovenmuehle of Dovenmuehle, Inc., Graham Aldis of Aldis and Company, and Philip Klutznick, president of American Community Builders, Inc.

27 Chicago City Council, *Journal of the Proceedings*, March 15, 1948, p. 2040.

28 Meyerson and Banfield, *Politics, Planning, and the Public Interest*, pp. 36–7, 86–7; Memorandum of Record of an Interview with Robert R. Taylor, June 26, 1956, BPI Papers; Leon Despres to Richard H. Newhouse, Jr., April 19, 1971, Leon Despres Papers, CHS.

29 Elizabeth Wood to the Commissioners, July 28, 1947, BPI Papers; Minutes of the Meeting of the Executive Committee, July 12, 1948, MHPC

Papers; CHR, Minutes of the Housing Committee, March 16, 1948, Taylor Papers; CHR, "Monthly Report of the Executive Director, August 1948," pp. 3–4; Chicago Urban League, Minutes of the Special Joint Meeting of the Board of Directors and Housing Committee, July 14, 1948, CUL Papers.

30 Meyerson and Banfield, *Politics, Planning, and the Public Interest*, pp. 129–31; Memorandum to Members of the Executive Committee, June 25, 1948, MHPC Papers. The sites were actually selected at a closed meeting held in Mayor Kennelly's office, which, according to critics, "made a mockery of the public hearing subsequently held." See Helen Van de Woestyne to Martin Kennelly, March 8, 1950, BPI Papers.

31 Affidavit of Claude A. Benjamin, n.d., BPI Papers; Unidentified clipping, n.d.; "An Analysis of the Nine Proposed Relocation Housing Sites," n.d., both in Cantwell Papers; Chicago City Council, *Journal of the Proceedings*, August 27, 1948, pp. 2730, 2732–5; Meyerson and Banfield, *Politics, Planning, and the Public Interest*, p. 131; [CAD], "Documented Memorandum XVI: Site Selection for Chicago's Relocation Housing" (mimeographed, n.d.), and Part 2, [CAD] Folder, CHS.

32 Meyerson and Banfield, *Politics, Planning, and the Public Interest*, pp. 130–1; Public Housing Association, *Newsletter*, August 15, 1948; *Chicago Defender*, August 21, 1948; Statement of the Metropolitan Housing and Planning Council, August 23, 1948, MHPC Papers; Unidentified clipping, n.d., Cantwell Papers; *Chicago Sun-Times*, August 18, 1948.

33 Meyerson and Banfield, *Politics, Planning, and the Public Interest*, pp. 148–50.

34 Ibid., pp. 153–87; Metropolitan Housing and Planning Council, Minutes of the Meeting of the Board of Governors, March 1, 1950, MHPC Papers.

35 One of the aldermen thus "punished" for his support of the CHA was called a "nigger-lover" by his colleagues in the city council. See the Notes Respecting a Meeting with Mr. Claude Benjamin, April 9, 1968, BPI Papers.

36 Archibald Carey, Jr., "Minority Report," n.d., BPI Papers; Meyerson and Banfield, *Politics, Planning, and the Public Interest*, pp. 189–98; *Chicago Defender*, April 15, 1950. David Wallace contends that the CHA missed its chance with its modified proposal and that "the issue could have been forced over the Mayor's protest with relative ease." He also concludes that this failure and subsequent delay was a "major turning point" and that public opinion, which had previously supported the CHA because of its popular veterans' housing program, began to ebb. Wallace, however, offers little evidence to support these contentions, and it is clear that the pressure of public opinion – manifested by the reaction *against* the veterans' program – was responsible for both the council's power over the housing authority and its reluctance to work with it. Meyerson and Banfield also conclude that, although some thought the new package would be accepted by the council,

there were "no very good grounds for thinking so." See Wallace,
"Residential Concentration of Negroes," p. 242; Meyerson and Banfield,
Politics, Planning, and the Public Interest, p. 195.

37 Meyerson and Banfield, *Politics, Planning, and the Public Interest*, pp.
195–200.

38 Robert C. Weaver to Wayne McMillen, December 12, 1950, in the
Louis Wirth Papers, UC Archives; Chicago Urban League, "League's
Position on Proposed Compromise Housing Sites," n.d., CUL Papers;
Chicago Defender, April 29, May 6, 1950.

39 [CAD], Minutes of the Regular Monthly Meeting of the Executive
Board, June 13, 1950, CUL Papers; Ferd Kramer to CHA, May 1, 1950,
MHPC Papers.

40 Meyerson and Banfield, *Politics, Planning, and the Public Interest*, pp.
206–8.

41 Ibid., pp. 208–22.

42 Ibid., pp. 225–39. In lending their assent to the council's proposal and
Burke's "solution," the CHA embraced policies laid out a generation
before by the governor's 1919 riot commission. The "dual solution"
never died. Indeed, faced with the problem of relocating blacks from
the Ida B. Wells Homes site in 1935 (it was the last of the city's PWA
projects), Holman Pettibone received a memorandum outlining alternatives that echoed Governor Lowden's charge to improve the "colored belt" and presaged Burke's phased construction program. The
only practical solution, the memorandum advised Pettibone, was to
"stagger" the demolition of old buildings, tearing down only those
whose tenants could be accommodated in existing ghetto housing. As
project units became available, more demolition could follow. Burke's
discovery of the "interstices" of slum sites in 1950 merely embellished
with engineer's jargon what was by then a traditional approach. See P.
P. Pullen, "Problems Encountered in Connection With the PWA Negro
Housing Project" (mimeographed, April 30, 1936), Pettibone Papers.

43 Meyerson and Banfield, *Politics, Planning, and the Public Interest*, pp.
242–6.

44 Wallace, "Residential Concentration of Negroes," pp. 232–3; "Address
by Elizabeth Wood, Executive Secretary of the Chicago Housing Authority at 'A Tribute to Good Government Dinner Given in Her Honor
by Chicago Citizens at the Red Lacquer Room of the Palmer House,'"
October 9, 1952, CUL Papers; *Chicago Defender*, October 18, 1952.

45 Meyerson and Banfield, *Politics, Planning, and the Public Interest*, pp.
84–6, 131–2.

46 Public Housing Association, *Newsletter*, February 15, 1949; *Pittsburgh
Courier*, January 15, 1949.

47 Griffenhagen and Associates, "Report on Certain Policies and Procedures of the Chicago Housing Authority" (mimeographed, August 13,
1953); Notes on Meeting with Ed Holmgren, March 14, 1968, BPI Papers; "Facts Concerning CHA's Tenant Selection," n.d., AFSC Papers.

48 Elizabeth Wood to Commissioner Wayne McMillen, October 17, 1950; Elizabeth Wood to Mr. Sykes, March 30, 1953; Ed Holmgren to Elizabeth Wood, March 27, 1953; April 8, 9, 1953, all in the files of the CHA; Rhea Osten to Albert G. Rosenberg, October 30, 1952; Elizabeth Wood to the Commissioners, August 23, 1954, BPI Papers.

49 Confidential Memorandum from J. Cassels to File, April 23, 1953; Memorandum from J. Cassels to File re Visit with Housing Committee of CAD, August 7, 1952, both in AFSC Papers; Joseph P. Antonow and Samuel D. Friefeld to Wayne McMillen, August 8, 1952, Cantwell Papers.

50 Memorandum from J. Cassels to File re Visit with Housing Committee of CAD, August 7, 1952; Memorandum from J. Cassels to File re Meeting of Housing Committee of Council Against Discrimination with Commissioners of the Chicago Housing Authority, September 2, 1952, both in the AFSC Papers; Joseph P. Antonow and Samuel D. Friefeld to Wayne McMillen, August 8, 1952; Wayne McMillen to Waitstill H. Sharp, August 11, 1952; Samuel D. Friefeld and Waitstill H. Sharp to Wayne McMillen, August 15, 1952; Thomas E. Colgan, Confidential Memorandum to Willoughby Abner, June 22, 1953; Samuel D. Friefeld, Memorandum to Julian Keiser and Members of CAD Housing Committee, June 5, 1953, all in the Cantwell Papers; CAD, *Newsletter*, June 1953, CUL Papers; *Chicago Defender* May 2, 9, 16, July 9, 1953; *Chicago Daily News*, April 27, 1953; CAD, Minutes of the Monthly Board Meeting, May 19, 1953; CAD, Executive Committee Meeting, August 4, 1953, all in the Barratt O'Hara Papers, Manuscript Collection, The Library, UIC.

51 For the violence at Trumbull Park, see Arnold R. Hirsch, "Making the Second Ghetto: Race and Housing in Chicago: 1940–1960" (Ph.D. dissertation, University of Illinois at Chicago Circle, 1978), chap. 3.

52 Operative L. G., Confidential Report, June 12, 18, July 3, 8, 9, 13, 15, 1954, in the American Civil Liberties Union–Illinois Division Papers (hereafter cited as ACLU Papers), the Department of Special Collections, UC Library.

53 Willoughby Abner to Francis McPeek, December 1, 1953; Elizabeth Wood to the Commissioners, October 6, December 16, 1953; Paul S. Freedman to Francis W. McPeek, November 6, 1953, all in the files of the CHA; see also Hirsch, "Making the Second Ghetto," pp. 111, 115–18.

54 AFSC, "Trumbull Park: A Progress Report" (mimeographed, March 1957), pp. 5–6; Chicago Branch, NAACP, Policy Statement with Respect to the Chicago Housing Authority drafted by the Housing Committee, n.d.; American Friends Service Committee, Minutes of the Housing Opportunities Program Meeting, February 27, 1958, all in the AFSC Papers; Elizabeth Wood to the Commissioners, March 31, 1954, in the files of the CHA.

55 Elizabeth Wood to John R. Fugard, February 2, 1954, in the files of the

CHA; Operative L. G., Confidential Report, July 27, August 5, 7, 8, 1954, ACLU Papers.

56 Operative L. G., Confidential Report, August 9, 11, 13, 1954; Kale Williams to Alvin E. Rose, January 13, 1959, both in the ACLU Papers; Lloyd Davis to David F. Freeman, September 2, 1954, Catholic Interracial Council Papers (hereafter cited as CIC Papers), CHS; CHR, *The Trumbull Park Homes Disturbances: A Chronological Report August 4, 1953 to June 30, 1955* (Chicago: CHR, n.d.), p. 50; Judy Miller to Harriet White, October 27, 1958, ACLU Papers; Affidavit of Edward H. Palmer, June 7, 1968, BPI Papers. The lack of white applicants and the quota on blacks combined to produce an average occupancy rate of 92% at Trumbull Park Homes, with "10 to 20 units empty at a time." If a white family left the project, a vacancy report was sent directly to the Central Referral Office (CRO); if a black family left, the CRO would be notified by telephone first that it was a "Negro vacancy." The CRO never referred blacks to the Trumbull Park Homes unless it had "Negro vacancies." If black families applied directly to the Trumbull Park Homes rental office, they were told that they had to go through the CRO. When whites applied at the Trumbull Park office, they were accepted "subject only to income verification" by the CRO. Palmer stated that the purpose of these procedures was to "ameliorate community resistance to Negro occupancy" and that it was "an appropriate policy for the conditions existing at Trumbull Park." Its only fault, he believed, was that "the level of the quota was not revised to keep pace with the changing times."

57 *Chicago Daily News*, October 16, 1953; *Chicago Tribune*, October 17, 1953; James A. Thomas to Marjorie G. Kelly, October 24, 1953, Merriam Papers.

58 Meyerson and Banfield, *Politics, Planning, and the Public Interest*, p. 267n; Daniel M. Cantwell to Robert George, September 2, 1954; James C. Downs, Jr., to Daniel M. Cantwell, September 8, 1954, both in the Cantwell Papers; *Work*, n.d., clipping found in the MHPC Papers; *Chicago Sun-Times*, April 15, 17, July 22, December 15, 1953; *Chicago Daily News*, n.d., and other unidentified clippings, all found in the Cantwell Papers; Albert N. Logan, Jr., "The First Quarter-Century of the Chicago Housing Authority, 1937–1962" (M.A. thesis, Roosevelt University, n.d.), p. 14.

59 Robert Gruenberg, "Trumbull Park: Act II," *Nation* 179 (September 18, 1954): 230–2; *Chicago Sun-Times*, August 26, 1954.

60 Chicago Urban League, Press release, August 30, 1954, CUL Papers.

61 Ibid.; CHA, Press release, August 31, 1954, MHPC Papers. CHA Chairman John Fugard called Wood's allegations "simply malicious."

62 Cora M. Patton to Mayor Kennelly, September 20, 1954, ACLU Papers; James C. Downs, Jr., to John R. Fugard, April 12, 1954, in the files of the CHA; Homer A. Jack to Archibald J. Carey, September 8, 1954, Carey Papers.

63 Operative L. G., Confidential Report, August 4, 7, 29, 1954, ACLU Papers; *Chicago Defender*, October 2, 1954; Homer A. Jack to Archibald J. Carey, September 8, 1954. There is some question as to whether Wood was objecting to the principle of the quota or merely its size. During the debate on the relocation projects, she made known her feelings that the 10% quota imposed was "improper." But she did prove willing to "gamble" that the quota might "have a reassuring effect" on white communities. Later, in October 1953, she expressed a willingness to accept a 10% to 15% quota on blacks at Trumbull Park – the same quota previously imposed in other white areas. This would mean the acceptance of forty-five to seventy black families in South Deering, not twenty-five. See Meyerson and Banfield, *Politics, Planning, and the Public Interest*, p. 134; Memorandum from James Cassels to File Re Trumbull Park Homes, October 1, 1953, AFSC Papers.

64 It was also clear that those who orchestrated her removal wanted to minimize public reaction to it. Fugard initially urged her to remain with the housing authority (thus weakening the contention that Wood was fired because she was difficult to work with and not because of her policies) and, later, it was alleged that James Downs suggested that CHA staff members urge Wood to accept two years' severance pay "in lieu of issuing any statement." See Homer A. Jack to Archibald J. Carey, September 8, 1954.

65 Gruenberg, "Trumbull Park"; *Chicago Defender*, September 4, 18, 1954; Metropolitan Housing and Planning Council, Minutes of the Board of Governors' Meeting, September 10, 1954, MHPC Papers; Lea Taylor to Mr. Fugard, August 30, 1954, Chicago Commons Papers; Secretary to Mr. Carey to Claude A. Barnette [sic], September 13, 1954, Carey Papers; Illinois Division, ACLU, Executive Committee Minutes, September 2, 9, November 18, 1954; Operative L. G., Confidential Report, August 24–31, 1954, ACLU Papers.

66 [Welfare Council of Metropolitan Chicago], Minutes of Meeting of Advisory Committee to the CHA, October 7, 1953, Taylor Papers.

67 Affidavit of Tamaara Tabb, n.d., BPI Papers.

68 Report of Inter-Group Agencies Conference with Alvin Rose, June 16, 1959, p. 2; George Weber to Harry J. Schneider, October 2, 1959; Draft of Affidavit of Edward Holmgren, n.d., BPI Papers.

69 "Data from Chicago Housing Authority Records Showing Negro and White Occupancy, By Number of Families of Specified Projects," n.d.; Excerpts from Deposition of Alvin E. Rose, n.d., p. 15; Affidavit of Kale W. Williams, Jr., n.d., all in BPI Papers; CHR, "Monthly Report of the Executive Director, January 1955" (mimeographed, n.d.), pp. 2, 5–6, CUL Papers; Memorandum from Jane Weston to file, February 26, 1950, AFSC Papers.

70 Memorandum from Kale Williams to File, February 4, 1959; Report of Inter-Group Agencies Conference with Alvin E. Rose, June 16, 1959; Excerpts from Deposition of Alvin E. Rose, n.d., p. 15; Affidavit of

Kale W. Williams, Jr., n.d., all in BPI Papers; Memorandum from Judy Miller and Kale Williams to Bill Berry et al. Re Meeting with Alvin Rose, June 16, 1959; Kale Williams to Ken Douty, June 26, 1959, both in ACLU Papers.

71 W. B. Kean, Memorandum to the Commissioners, May 23, 1955, BPI Papers; *South Deering Bulletin*, October 1, 1955; Lloyd Davis to David F. Freeman, March 1, 1955, CIC Papers.

72 Welfare Council of Metropolitan Chicago, Advisory Committee to the Chicago Housing Authority, "Report on Site Selection in Public Housing in Chicago," December 1956, p. 3, Alinsky Papers; Ferd Kramer to James C. Downs, Jr., February 26, 1956; Metropolitan Housing and Planning Council, Minutes of the Meeting of the Executive Committee, February 20, 1956; "Chicago Housing Authority Sites Proposed 1956–1958 Program," June 18, 1958, all in the MHPC Papers; Alexander Polikoff to John W. Hunt, July 13, 1967, BPI Papers. For the success of local communities in rejecting proposed sites, see the *Daily Calumet*, February 3, 5, 1955, and Metropolitan Housing and Planning Council, Minutes of the Meeting of the Public Housing and Relocation Committee, Tuesday, February 24, 1959, MHPC Papers.

73 Deposition of Emil G. Hirsch, March 8, 1968, BPI Papers.

74 Deposition of Louis Kreinberg, June 9, 1967; Notes on Meeting with Ed Holmgren, March 14, 1968; Excerpts from Deposition of Alvin Rose, n.d.; Notes on address by Alvin E. Rose before the meeting of the Planning and Housing Committee of the City Club of Chicago, January 17, 1958; Excerpts from Humphrey Affidavit and Deposition, n.d., all in BPI Papers.

75 Affidavit of Harold M. Baron, n.d., pp. 3–5, BPI Papers.

76 Reply Brief of Plaintiffs in Support of Motion for Summary Judgment in Their Favor, n.d., BPI Papers.

77 *Chicago Tribune*, December 24, 1958; Typed statement of John W. Baird, chairman of the Committee on Housing of the MHPC, re CHA sites, July 6, 1966, MHPC Papers.

78 Alvin E. Rose to William E. Bergeron, October 23, 1963; Joseph Burstein to Marie C. McGuire, December 11, 1963; Roger P. Pascal to Alexander Polikoff, November 10, 1967; [Chicago Housing Authority], Minutes of the Managers' Meeting, July 17, August 21, 1963, all in BPI Papers.

79 U.S. Commission on Civil Rights, *Hearings: Housing* (Washington, D.C.: Government Printing Office, 1959), pp. 723, 726–7.

80 Elizabeth Wood to the Commissioners, March 31, 1954, in the files of the CHA.

81 James Q. Wilson, *Negro Politics: The Search for Leadership* (New York: Free Press, 1960), pp. 88–9; Unidentified clipping, October 20, 1965, Ely Aaron Papers, Manuscript Collection, The Library, UIC.

82 Arvarh E. Strickland, *History of the Chicago Urban League* (Urbana: University of Illinois Press, 1966), pp. 172–4; Sidney Williams to Martin

Kennelly, November 29, 1949, CIC Papers; Curtis D. MacDougall to Louis Wirth, January 14, February 14, 1950; Wirth to MacDougall, January 17, February 8, 1950; all in the Wirth Papers; "Meeting of the Conference to End Mob Violence," January 7, 1950, CUL Papers.

83 *Pittsburgh Courier*, December 17, 31, 1949; Minutes of the [CAD] Board of Directors, January 10, 1950, CUL Papers. Wilson, *Negro Politics*, p. 218; Sidney Williams to Homer Jack, December 19, 1949, Carey Papers.

84 Wilson, *Negro Politics*, pp. 160–1.

85 Strickland, *History of the Chicago Urban League*, pp. 155–214; Wilson, *Negro Politics*, pp. 111, 140–3, and for the weakened condition of the Chicago Chapter of the NAACP, pp. 162, 288.

86 Wilson, *Negro Politics*, pp. 63–4, 162, 283.

87 See the handbills in the "Champions" folder of the CUL Papers.

88 Handwritten Snowdenville Community Council Occasional Bulletin #1, February 1948, CUL Papers; CHR, Minutes of the Housing Committee Meeting, March 16, 1948, Taylor Papers.

89 *Chicago Defender*, March 27, April 3, 1948.

90 CHR, Minutes of the Housing Committee Meeting, May 12, 1948, Taylor Papers; William E. Hill to D. E. Mackelmann, May 28, 1948; Memorandum to Community Relations Committee, South Side Planning Board (SSPB), from William E. Hill, Re: An Effective Community Relations Program for the South Side Planning Board, March 4, 1948, both in the MHPC Papers; SSPB, Minutes of the Meeting of the Executive Committee, July 30, 1948, Wirth Papers; *Chicago Defender*, January 9, 1948; January 8, 22, 1949; August 12, December 2, 1950; Wilford G. Winholz to Arch, March 28, 1949, Carey Papers.

91 Wilson, *Negro Politics*, pp. 117–22; Frayser T. Lane speaking at the meeting of the Champions, March 25, 1949, Carey Papers.

92 Wilson, *Negro Politics*, p. 73; Miles Colean, *Renewing Our Cities* (New York: Twentieth Century Fund, 1953), pp. 80–1, 93; H[olman] D. P[ettibone] to L. D. McKendry, February 8, 1951, Pettibone Papers; Interview with Ira J. Bach, July 24, 1980.

93 Peter Rossi and Robert Dentler, *The Politics of Urban Renewal* (New York: Free Press, 1961), p. 180.

94 Wilson, *Negro Politics*, pp. 86–7, 182–3, 202–4, 253–4; Rossi and Dentler, *The Politics of Urban Renewal*, p. 181.

95 Wilson, *Negro Politics*, p. 185.

96 Ibid., pp. 181–2.

97 Ibid., pp. 187–8.

98 *Chicago Defender*, July 19, August 2, 1947; March 13, 27, April 3, 1948; May 7, 1949; December 11, 1954; Handwritten Snowdenville Community Council Occasional Bulletin #1, February 1948; CHR, Minutes of the Housing Committee Meeting, March 16, 1948, Taylor Papers; *The Crusader*, March 1, 1958, Despres Papers.

99 *Chicago Defender*, August 23, 1952; February 13, 1954; April 18, 1957; A. L. Foster to Reginald DuBois, March 11, 1954, Carey Papers.

100   George B. Nesbitt, "Approaches and Objectives Useful to Inter-group
      Relations Officials in Connection with Local Slum Clearance and Re-
      development Programs," n.d., CUL Papers; Wallace, "Residential Con-
      centration of Negroes," p. 301.
101   Robert H. Murphy to Harry Schneider, October 28, 1963, BPI Papers;
      Statement of James C. Downs, Jr., at the Meeting of the Housing
      Committee of the City Council, March 16, 1954, Carey Papers.
102   Carl Condit, *Chicago, 1930–1970* (Chicago: University of Chicago Press,
      1974), p. 152; Logan, "The First Quarter-Century of the Chicago Hous-
      ing Authority," pp. 54, 56.
103   *Southeast Economist*, May 26, 1949, clipping in the Cantwell Papers.
104   Metropolitan Housing and Planning Council, Memorandum of con-
      clusions of special Board Meeting on Public Housing in Chicago, De-
      cember 31[?], MHPC Papers.
105   Deposition of Leon M. Despres, May 24, 1967, BPI Papers.

Epilogue

1   Glen E. Holt and Dominic A. Pacyga, *Chicago: A Historical Guide to the
    Neighborhoods; The Loop and the South Side* (Chicago: Chicago Historical
    Society, 1979), pp. 54–5; Remarks by Ferd Kramer – Washington Con-
    ference, Young Men's Activities Committee – Mortgage Bankers' Asso-
    ciation, January 16, 1953, p. 5, in the Metropolitan Housing and Planning
    Council Papers (hereafter cited as MHPC Papers), Manuscript Collec-
    tion, The Library, University of Illinois at Chicago (UIC).
2   Holt and Pacyga, *Chicago*, pp. 80–4.
3   Remarks by Ferd Kramer to the Potomac Chapter of the National
    Association of Housing and Redevelopment Officials, November 18,
    1960, MHPC Papers; Interview with Ferd Kramer, August 4, 1980.
4   Ferd Kramer, Speech Before Mortgage Bankers' Association of America
    and ACTION, Inc., February 21, 1962, MHPC Papers; Kramer interview.
5   Interview with Julian Levi, July 29, 1980; Evelyn M. Kitagawa and Karl
    E. Taeuber, eds., *Local Community Fact Book: Chicago Metropolitan Area,
    1960* (Chicago: Chicago Community Inventory, 1963), p. 97; U.S., De-
    partment of Commerce, Bureau of the Census, *1970 Census of Popula-
    tion and Housing: Census Tracts, Chicago, Ill. Standard Metropolitan Statistical
    Area, Part I* (Washington, D.C.: Government Printing Office, 1972),
    pp. 44–5.
6   Thomas L. Philpott, *The Slum and the Ghetto: Neighborhood Deterioration
    and Middle-Class Reform, Chicago, 1880–1930* (New York: Oxford Uni-
    versity Press, 1978), pp. 209–27; Devereux Bowly, Jr., *The Poorhouse:
    Subsidized Housing in Chicago, 1895–1976* (Carbondale: Southern Illinois
    University Press, 1978), pp. 124–9.
7   Bowly, *The Poorhouse*, pp. 8–16; Philpott, *The Slum and the Ghetto*, pp.
    244–69; Remarks by Ferd Kramer–Washington Conference, pp. 1–2.
8   Chicago's redevelopment experience, Ferd Kramer believed, "grew

out of a process of evolution which began in the late twenties." He praised Marshall Field and Julius Rosenwald for plunging "into the unknown arena of redevelopment" even while noting their shortcomings. Kramer also recognized "governmental sorties into slum clearance" in the 1930s, including the use of eminent domain and New York's use of a tax freeze to entice the Metropolitan Life Insurance Company into building Stuyvesant Town. Chicago's business community learned from these approaches, Kramer claimed, and – because the Constitution of the state of Illinois prohibited New York-style tax subsidies – experimented with some new techniques. See Remarks by Ferd Kramer – Washington Conference, pp. 2–3.

9   Philpott, *The Slum and the Ghetto*, pp. 204–5.
10 Mike Royko, *Boss: Richard J. Daley of Chicago* (New York: New American Library, 1971), pp. 155–8.
11 Bowly, *The Poorhouse*, pp. 189–94; the *Gautreaux* case can be followed in the Business and Professional People for the Public Interest Papers (hereafter cited as BPI Papers), Chicago Historical Society (CHS).
12 Royko, *Boss*, p. 158; Bowly, *The Poorhouse*, pp. 188–9; Len O'Connor, *Clout: Mayor Daley and His City* (Chicago: Regnery, 1975), p. 194.
13 *Chicago Tribune*, June 18, 21, 1981.
14 Ibid., January 18, June 21, 1981.
15 Ibid., June 21, October 31, 1981.
16 Illinois and New York were the first states to pass laws intended to encourage the revitalization of deteriorated areas in 1941. The Illinois law, which provided for the creation of neighborhood redevelopment corporations, remained unused, however, until amended by Julian Levi and the SECC on behalf of the University of Chicago in 1953. It then served as the basis for the second phase of Hyde Park's urban renewal. The pioneering elements of the 1947 and 1953 Illinois legislation will be discussed later. See Miles Colean, *Renewing Our Cities* (New York: Twentieth Century Fund, 1953), p. 28, and Chapter 5, this volume.
17 The difficulties of the federal effort are cataloged in Herbert Gans, "The Failure of Urban Renewal: A Critique and Some Proposals," *Commentary* (April 1965): 29–37.
18 For the local character of urban renewal, see Robert P. Groberg, "Urban Renewal Realistically Appraised," in James Q. Wilson, ed., *Urban Renewal: The Record and the Controversy* (Cambridge, Mass.: MIT Press, 1966), pp. 510–11, 530; Wallace Smith, "The Federal Bulldozer: A Review," in ibid., p. 532; Scott Greer, *Urban Renewal and American Cities* (Indianapolis: Bobbs-Merrill, 1965), pp. 96–7, 119–22. See also Martin Anderson, *The Federal Bulldozer: A Critical Analysis of Urban Renewal, 1949–1962* (Cambridge, Mass.: MIT Press, 1964); idem, "Fiasco of Urban Renewal," *Harvard Business Review* 43 (January-February 1965): 6–21; Mark I. Gelfand, *A Nation of Cities: The Federal Government and Urban America, 1933–1965* (New York: Oxford University Press, 1975), p. 109;

Richard O. Davies, *Housing Reform During the Truman Administration* (Columbia: University of Missouri Press, 1966). This is not to say, of course, that Chicago lacked its own "reformers" or "planners" who pushed vigorously for redevelopment and, later, renewal. Chicago had plenty of both. The Metropolitan Housing and Planning Council, for example, as a "reform" group, was of considerable significance. It is simply that such elements, alone, lacked the power to realize their goals. Their efforts, consequently, were complementary but subordinate to those "interests" with the ability to move the city's and the state's political structures. Their presence also provided a veneer of "reform" for the local program.

19 For the origins of federal housing legislation, see Ashley A. Foard and Hilbert Fefferman, "Federal Urban Renewal Legislation," *Law and Contemporary Politics* 23 (Autumn 1960): 635–84; Gelfand, *A Nation of Cities*, pp. 105–56; Colean, *Renewing Our Cities*, p. 29.

20 Public Versus Private Housing, April 12, 1945, in the Holman D. Pettibone Papers, CHS.

21 Kramer interview.

22 National Commission on Urban Problems, *Building the American City* (Washington, D.C.: Government Printing Office, 1968), p. 156; Foard and Fefferman, "Federal Urban Renewal Legislation," pp. 635–41; Gelfand, *A Nation of Cities*, p. 137.

23 The President's Advisory Committee on Government Housing Policies and Programs, *A Report to the President of the United States* (Washington, D.C.: Government Printing Office, 1953); see also the separately bound Appendix to that *Report*, Jack M. Siegel and C. William Brooks, *Slum Prevention Through Conservation and Rehabilitation* (Washington, D.C.: Government Printing Office, 1953), pp. 52–70, 122–32; Colean, *Renewing Our Cities*, p. 137; Jack M. Siegel, "Slum Prevention – A Public Purpose," n.d., MHPC Papers; Muriel Beadle, *The Hyde Park-Kenwood Urban Renewal Years* (Chicago, n. p., 1964), p. 16.

24 Anderson, *The Federal Bulldozer*, passim; Charles Abrams, *The City Is the Frontier* (New York: Harper & Row, 1965), p. 74 and passim.

25 Abrams, *The City Is the Frontier*, pp. 75, 82–5; Gelfand, *A Nation of Cities*, p. 213; National Commission on Urban Problems, *Building the American City*, p. 153. Abrams's conclusion that the program was "perverted" is weakened by his comment that the formula was "faulty from the beginning." He did not, however, consider the intentions of those who designed the "faulty" mechanism in the first place. This situation was a virtual replay of the reactions provoked by the passage of the Illinois Redevelopment Act of 1947 on the part of those who took its statement of legislative intent as the real rationale for its enactment.

26 The National Commission on Urban Problems disagreed with this contention, but it looked back only to the drafting of the federal legislation itself in seeking the program's "original intent." It did not look

at the cities themselves in the years before federal activity. *Building the American City*, p. 157.

27 Robert C. Weaver, *Dilemmas of Urban America* (New York: Atheneum, 1969), p. 48; National Commission on Urban Problems, *Building the American City*, p. 156; Abrams, *The City Is the Frontier*, pp. 80–91, 186–7; Gelfand, *A Nation of Cities*, p. 170.

28 Abrams, *The City Is the Frontier*, pp. 150, 179, 237; Gelfand, *A Nation of Cities*, pp. 205–16; Gans, "The Failure of Urban Renewal," pp. 29–37; National Commission on Urban Problems, *Building the American City*, p. 158; Greer, *Urban Renewal and American Cities*, p. 151.

29 The MHPC was the most prominent "reform" group in developing and supporting the Urban Community Conservation Act. Racial considerations were *not*, apparently, uppermost in the council's thinking, although the fact that "slums" were being created faster than they were being destroyed (an idea filled with racial implications) was. The MHPC *was* aware, however, of some "unpleasant insinuations" that contended that the "main purpose" of their proposal was to exclude the expanding black population from conservation areas and that they were receiving some support for the "wrong reasons." As the institution that directed the renewal of Hyde Park under that legislation, though, it was the intentions of the University of Chicago, not those of the MHPC, that were of material importance. See "The Loop and Slums," November 1953, p. 11, MHPC Papers. See also Michael J. White, *Urban Renewal and the Changing Residential Structure of the City* (Chicago: University of Chicago Press, 1980), p. 203.

30 Robert Caro, *The Power Broker: Robert Moses and the Fall of New York* (New York: Vintage Books, 1975), pp. 777, 962–9, 974, 976.

31 Harold Kaplan, "Urban Renewal in Newark," in Wilson, ed., *Urban Renewal*, pp. 233–58.

Index

349

362   **Index**